*Everyman, I will go with thee,*
*and be thy guide*

THE EVERYMAN
LIBRARY

*The Everyman Library was founded by J. M. Dent
in 1906. He chose the name Everyman because he wanted
to make available the best books ever written in every
field to the greatest number of people at the cheapest possible
price. He began with Boswell's 'Life of Johnson';
his one-thousandth title was Aristotle's 'Metaphysics',
by which time sales exceeded forty million.*

*Today Everyman paperbacks remain true to
J. M. Dent's aims and high standards, with a wide range
of titles at affordable prices in editions which address
the needs of today's readers. Each new text is reset to give
a clear, elegant page and to incorporate the latest thinking
and scholarship. Each book carries the pilgrim logo,
the character in 'Everyman', a medieval morality play,
a proud link between Everyman
past and present.*

George Gissing

# THE WHIRLPOOL

*Edited by*
**WILLIAM GREENSLADE**
*University of the West of England, Bristol*

**EVERYMAN**
J. M. DENT · LONDON
CHARLES E. TUTTLE
VERMONT

Introduction and other critical material © J. M. Dent 1997

This edition first published in Everyman Paperbacks in 1997

All rights reserved

J. M. Dent
Orion Publishing Group
Orion House, 5 Upper St Martin's Lane,
London WC2H 9EA
and
Charles E. Tuttle Co., Inc.
28 South Main Street,
Rutland, Vermont 05701, USA

Printed in Great Britain by
The Guernsey Press Co. Ltd, Guernsey, C. I.

This book if bound as a paperback is subject to the
condition that it may not be issued on loan or otherwise
except in its original binding.

British Library Cataloguing-in-Publication Data
is available upon request.

ISBN 0 460 87781 X

# CONTENTS

*Note on the Author and Editor*   vi
*Chronology of Gissing's Life and Times*   viii
*Introduction*   xvii
*Note on the Text*   xxxi

THE WHIRLPOOL   1

Part the First   3
Part the Second   123
Part the Third   299

*Notes*   421
*Gissing and his Critics*   436
*Suggestions for Further Reading*   452
*Text Summary*   454
*Acknowledgements*   459

# NOTE ON THE AUTHOR AND EDITOR

GEORGE GISSING was born in Wakefield in 1857, the oldest of five children. His father, a pharmacist, died when he was thirteen. In 1872 Gissing won a scholarship to Owens College, Manchester. He was a brilliant student, but his prospects were blasted when in 1876 he was caught stealing from the college cloakroom. He had hoped to use the money to reclaim a young prostitute, Nell Harrison, with whom he had fallen in love. After serving one month's imprisonment, he left for America, where he stayed for a year and began to publish short stories. Back in England in 1877, he lived with Nell, whom he married in 1879. The marriage was unhappy, the couple separated and Nell died in 1888. During these years Gissing survived on the proceeds of private tuition and some journalism. His first novel, *Workers in the Dawn* (1880), initiated a series of books that dealt powerfully with the poverty and degradation of the London poor: *The Unclassed* (1884), *Demos* (1886), *Thyrza* (1887) and *The Nether World* (1889). After this series he travelled on the Continent and his fiction expanded in other directions, more often adopting a middle-class setting, though never abandoning the subject of poverty. *The Emancipated* (1890) was followed by the novels that made his reputation: *New Grub Street* (1891), *Born in Exile* (1892), *The Odd Women* (1893), *In the Year of Jubilee* (1894) and *The Whirlpool* (1897). In the 1890s he also published many short stories. In 1891 he married Edith Underwood, who bore him two sons, Walter and Alfred. This second marriage proved as disastrous as the first and Gissing left Edith in 1897. Though he now had a considerable reputation as a novelist, he never achieved financial security. He did, however, enjoy the friendship of such writers as H. G. Wells, and from 1899 till his death in 1903 he lived (mostly in France) with Gabrielle Fleury, an admirer who had offered to translate his work. Among his notable later books were his critical study of Dickens (1898), his travel book *By the*

*Ionian Sea* (1901) and the partly autobiographical *Private Papers of Henry Ryecroft* (1903). Gissing died – of lung disease – at the age of forty-six. He had written twenty-two novels.

WILLIAM GREENSLADE is a Lecturer in English at the University of the West of England, Bristol. He is the author of *Degeneration, Culture and The Novel 1880–1940* (1994), and a number of articles on late-nineteenth-century British literature and culture.

# CHRONOLOGY OF GISSING'S LIFE

| Year | Age | Life |
|---|---|---|
| 1857 | | 22 November; born in Wakefield, Yorks, eldest child of Thomas Waller and Margaret Bedford Gissing |
| 1859 | 1 | 15 September: William Gissing (brother) born |
| 1860 | 3 | 25 November: Algernon Gissing (brother) born |
| 1863–70 | 5–12 | Attends local schools in Wakefield. 27 October: Margaret Emily Gissing (sister) born |
| 1867 | 9 | 4 April: Ellen Sophia Gissing (sister) born |
| 1870 | 13 | 28 December: his father dies |

# CHRONOLOGY OF HIS TIMES

| Year | Literary Context | Historical Events |
|---|---|---|
| 1857 | Flaubert, *Madame Bovary* <br> Dickens, *Little Dorrit* | Indian Mutiny <br> Matrimonial Causes Act |
| 1859 | Darwin, *The Origin of Species* <br> George Eliot, *Adam Bede* <br> Wagner, *Tristan und Isolde* | War of Italian liberation <br> Palmerston's second Cabinet |
| 1860 | George Eliot, *The Mill on the Floss* <br> Collins, *The Woman in White* | *Essays and Reviews*: rational attack on religious orthodoxy |
| 1861 | Dickens, *Great Expectations* <br> Meredith, *Evan Harrington* | US Civil War begins <br> Death of Prince Albert <br> Pasteur's germ theory of disease |
| 1862 | George Eliot, *Romola* <br> Hugo, *Les Misérables* | Bismarck becomes Prussian Chancellor <br> Married Woman's Property Act |
| 1863 | Gaskell, *Sylvia's Lovers* <br> Death of Thackeray <br> Manet, *Luncheon on the Grass* | |
| 1864 | Dickens, *Our Mutual Friend* | Geneva Convention (Red Cross) |
| 1865 | Death of Elizabeth Gaskell | Russell's second Cabinet <br> Assassination of Lincoln; end of American Civil War |
| 1866 | Gaskell, *Wives and Daughters* | Field's transatlantic cable <br> Derby's third Cabinet |
| 1867 | | Second Reform Act |
| 1868 | | February: Disraeli's first Cabinet <br> December: Gladstone's first Cabinet |
| 1869 | Lecky, *History of European Morals* | |
| 1870 | Death of Dickens <br> Wagner, *Die Walküre* | Forster's Education Act <br> Franco-Prussian War <br> Opening of Suez Canal |

| Year | Age | Life |
|------|-----|------|
| 1871 | 13 | George and his brothers sent to Lindow Grove School, Alderley Edge, Cheshire |
| 1872 | 14 | Enters Owens College, Manchester, and becomes one of its brightest students |
| 1875 | 18 | Winter: meets Marianne Helen Harrison (b. 1858), a young prostitute, known as Nell, whom he attempts to redeem |
| 1876 | 18 | 31 May: caught stealing money in the cloakroom of Owens College. 6 June: convicted and sentenced to one month's imprisonment. 7 June: expelled from College. September: sails to America |
| 1877 | 19 | Teaches for two months. March–July: writes and publishes short stories in Chicago. September–October: returns to England. Settles in London, where Nell joins him. |
| 1878 | 20 | Completes his first novel, which a publisher rejects. Gives private lessons until 1888. |
| 1879 | 21 | January: meets Eduard Bertz, a German socialist refugee. April: receives a small inheritance. 27 October: marries Nell |
| 1880 | 22 | Publishes *Workers in the Dawn* at his own expense, shortly after his brother William's death. Through Frederic Harrison, the Positivist leader, is in touch with Turgenev, who asks him to write articles for *Vestnik Evropy* (*The Messenger of Europe*) |
| 1882 | 24 | Separates from Nell. Completes 'Mrs Grundy's Enemies' (never published) |
| 1884 | 26 | June: *The Unclassed* |

| Year | Literary Context | Historical Events |
|------|------------------|-------------------|
| 1871 | George Eliot, *Middlemarch* <br> Hardy, *Desperate Remedies* | Paris Commune |
| 1872 | W. W. Reade, *The Martyrdom of Man* <br> Butler, *Erewhon* | Secret Ballot Act |
| 1874 | Hardy, *Far from the Madding Crowd* <br> Monet, *Impression: Sunrise* | Disraeli's second Cabinet |
| 1876 | George Eliot, *Daniel Deronda* <br> Meredith, *Beauchamp's Career* | Victoria becomes Empress of India <br> Invention of telephone <br> Bulgarian atrocities |
| 1877 | Ibsen, *Pillars of Society* <br> Zola, *L'Assommoir* | Russo-Turkish War, 1877–8 <br> Edison's phonograph |
| 1878 | Hardy, *The Return of the Native* | Earliest use of electricity <br> Congress of Berlin |
| 1879 | Ibsen, *A Doll's House* <br> James, *Daisy Miller* | London telephone exchange |
| 1880 | Disraeli, *Endymion* <br> Death of George Eliot and Flaubert <br> Dvořák, *First Symphony* | Gladstone's second Cabinet <br> Invention of bicycle <br> Transvaal declares itself a republic |
| 1881 | Ibsen, *Ghosts* <br> James, *The Portrait of a Lady* | |
| 1882 | Besant, *All Sorts and Conditions of Men* <br> Gilbert and Sullivan, *Iolanthe* | Phoenix Park murders <br> F. Forest invents the combusion engine <br> Married Women's Property Act |
| 1883 | Nietzsche, *Thus Spake Zarathustra* | |
| 1884 | Moore, *A Mummer's Wife* <br> Burne-Jones, *King Cophetua and the Beggar Maid* | Third Reform Act <br> Fabian Society founded |

| Year | Age | Life |
|------|-----|------|
| 1886 | 28 | March: *Demos*. First journey to France. June: *Isabel Clarendon*. Meets Thomas Hardy |
| 1887 | 29 | April: *Thyrza*. 23 June: meets Edward Clodd |
| 1888 | 30–1 | 28 February: Nell dies. September–March 1889: stays in Paris, then Italy. November: *A Life's Morning* |
| 1889 | 31–2 | April: *The Nether World*. November–February 1890: travels to Greece and southern Italy |
| 1890 | 32 | March: *The Emancipated*. September: meets Edith Underwood |
| 1891 | 33–4 | January: moves to Exeter. 25 February: marries Edith Underwood. April: *New Grub Street*. 10 December: Walter Gissing (son) born |
| 1892 | 34 | February: *Denzil Quarrier*. May: *Born in Exile* |
| 1893 | 35 | April: *The Odd Women*. June: moves to Brixton. Begins to write short stories regularly for periodicals |
| 1894 | 36–7 | September: moves to Epsom. December: *In the Year of Jubilee* |
| 1895 | 37–8 | April: *Eve's Ransom*. December: *Sleeping Fires* |
| 1896 | 38 | January: *The Paying Guest*. 20 January: Alfred Gissing (son) born. 20 November: meets H. G. Wells |
| 1897 | 39 | February: leaves Edith. April: *The Whirlpool*. September: separates from Edith and travels to Italy. November: *Human Odds and Ends* |

| Year | Literary Context | Historical Events |
|------|------------------|-------------------|
| 1885 | Meredith, *Diana of the Crossways* <br> Gilbert and Sullivan, *The Mikado* | Fall of Khartoum <br> Salisbury's first Cabinet |
| 1886 | James, *The Bostonians* <br> Stevenson, *Dr Jekyll and Mr Hyde* | Liberals split on Home Rule <br> February: Gladstone's third Cabinet <br> August: Salisbury's second Cabinet |
| 1887 | Hardy, *The Woodlanders* <br> Strindberg, *The Father* | Victoria's Golden Jubilee |
| 1888 | Kipling, *Plain Tales from the Hills* <br> Mrs H. Ward, *Robert Elsmere* | |
| 1889 | Stevenson, *The Master of Ballantrae* <br> Gilbert and Sullivan, *The Gondoliers* | London Dock Strike |
| 1890 | 'Mark Rutherford', *Miriam's Schooling* | Parnell scandal <br> First 'tube' railway |
| 1891 | Hardy, *Tess of the D'Urbervilles* <br> Morris, *News from Nowhere* <br> Tchaikovsky, *Nutcracker* | Free elementary education |
| 1892 | Kipling, *Barrack-Room Ballads* | Gladstone's fourth Cabinet <br> Panama scandal |
| 1893 | Crackenthorpe, *Wreckage* | Foundation of Independent Labour Party |
| 1894 | Moore, *Esther Waters* <br> Hardy, *Life's Little Ironies* | Collapse of the three-decker novel <br> Lord Rosebery's Cabinet |
| 1895 | Hardy, *Jude the Obscure* <br> Conrad, *Almayer's Folly* | Trial of Oscar Wilde <br> Jameson raid <br> Salisbury's third Cabinet |
| 1896 | Wells, *The Wheels of Chance* | |
| 1897 | Conrad, *The Nigger of the 'Narcissus'* <br> Tate Gallery opens | Victoria's Diamond Jubilee <br> First aeroplane flight |

| Year | Age | Life |
|------|-----|------|
| 1898 | 40 | February: *Charles Dickens: A Critical Study.* April–May: returns from Italy via Germany and settles in Dorking. 6 July: meets Gabrielle Fleury. August: *The Town Traveller* |
| 1899 | 41 | May–June: joins Gabrielle in France. They settle in Paris. October: *The Crown of Life* |
| 1900 | 42 | April: spends the whole month in England. Late May–mid-November: stays at St Honoré-les-Bains |
| 1901 | 43–4 | May: *Our Mutual Friend the Charlatan.* June: *By the Ionian Sea.* Late June: Enters the East Anglian Sanatorium, Nayland, Suffolk, where he remains until early August. December: moves from Paris to Arcachon. |
| 1902 | 44 | January: Edith sent to an asylum. July: moves to Ciboure, near St Jean-de-Luz |
| 1903 | 45–6 | January: *The Private Papers of Henry Ryecroft.* July: moves to Ispoure, near St Jean-Pied-de-Port. 28 December: dies at 1.15 p.m. 31 December: is buried at St Jean-de-Luz |
| 1904 | | September: *Veranilda* |
| 1905 | | June: *Will Warburton* |
| 1906 | | May: *The House of Cobwebs* |

| Year | Literary Context | Historical Events |
|------|------------------|-------------------|
| 1898 | Shaw, *Plays Pleasant and Unpleasant*<br>Rodin, *The Kiss* | Fashoda incident<br>Discovery of radium |
| 1899 | Wilde, *The Important of Being Earnest*<br>Elgar, *Enigma Variations* | Boer War starts |
| 1900 | Conrad, *Lord Jim*<br>Wells, *Love and Mr Lewisham* | Relief of Ladysmith and Mafeking |
| 1901 | Kipling, *Kim* | Death of Victoria<br>Accession of Edward VII |
| 1902 | James, *The Wings of the Dove*<br>Conrad, *Youth*<br>Butler, *The Way of All Flesh* | End of Boer War<br>Balfour's Cabinet |
| 1903 | Shaw, *Man and Superman*<br>Conrad, *Typhoon* | |
| 1904 | Conrad, *Nostromo* | Anglo-French Agreement<br>Rutherford: discovery of radioactivity |
| 1905 | James, *The Golden Bowl* | Campbell-Bannerman Prime Minister |
| 1906 | Galsworthy, *The Man of Property* | Sweeping Liberal victory at General Election |

# INTRODUCTION

George Gissing's readers must have been surprised by *The Whirlpool*. The books they knew him by – *The Nether World*, *New Grub Street*, *Born in Exile*, *The Odd Women* and *In the Year of Jubilee* – were peopled by all those marginal figures who made up his distinctive fictional world: the 'unclassed' poor, displaced intellectuals, unintegrated 'odd' women, the aspiring lower-middle class. Now they read about a moneyed, *rentier* society, more usually associated with the novels of George Meredith or Henry James.

London, with its zones and spaces defined by work and class, had shaped the contours of Gissing's work, in ways which were quite distinctive in late nineteenth-century fiction. But *The Whirlpool* marks a shift in emphasis. Now the meaning of London is to be found not only in specific landscapes, but in a condition of contemporary life, shaped by forces which drove forward nation and empire. *The Way We Live Now* was Trollope's title for his novel of 1875, charting the rise and fall of a politician and financier: Gissing's novel tackles this theme for the *fin de siècle*.

Published in the year of Queen Victoria's Diamond Jubilee, *The Whirlpool* was advertised in the *Bookseller* alongside titles such as *National Progress During the Queen's Reign* and *The Queen's Diamond Jubilee Bible*.[1] Here was the second great state occasion on which the official version of the imperial nation was displayed to the world as spectacle (Gissing had closely worked the 1887 event into *In the Year of Jubilee*). But beneath the show of pageantry lay other forces: 'the passionate feeling for trade', 'an enormous selfish advertisement' – this is what it amounted to for Henry James.[2]

Gissing, too, saw that English society in the 1890s was in the grip of energies which were barely understood, in an increasingly specialised, complex culture. And like James he wanted to use the novel form to represent the play of these forces which, he felt, were deforming contemporary life.

Those days of June 1897 were symptomatic, in retrospect, of the high summer of the British Empire; the point at which it might still be claimed that imperial Britain would continue to expand, and so progress, almost as a fact of nature. Yet the reality of empire, for writers from Kipling and Conrad to J. A. Hobson and Olive Schreiner, was a more contested and sordid affair. In one portion of it Cecil Rhodes and the British South Africa Company had recently been involved in an undignified strategy to wrest newly discovered gold mines from the Boer Republics; the ignominy of the December 1895 Jameson Raid had followed and Gissing privately noted the complicity of the establishment: here was a case of 'capitalist greed': no peace was to be had 'so long as these men of the money-market are permitted to control public life – as they practically do'.[3]

From the mid-1880s gambling in stocks and profit-taking were rife as never before. Large-scale foreign speculation in securities had markedly increased as over-valued shares were acquired by legions of new trust companies. In 1890 Baring Brothers, a leading merchant bank, narrowly avoided collapse. Then, as now, financial scandal was never long out of the headlines.[4]

In the opening chapters of *The Whirlpool* Gissing allows full rein to the career of speculative finance. The novel openly flaunts the spectacle of uncertainty and instability which accompanies it; its consequences spill out across moral and legal boundaries as money threatens to assume a life of its own. In the drawing-rooms of the West End, the smoking-rooms of the gentleman's club, and in conversations in hansoms which thread their way between these locations, Gissing gives us a world founded upon, but tripped up by, so-called 'securities'. This pervasive sense of instability is created through significant detail: a carriage-horse slips at a crossing, a shadowy stockbroker (spoken of, but never encountered) is named Tripcony, recalling that older risk-taker, the Elizabethan conycatcher. Through such touches Gissing allows us to sense the slippery, hazardous texture of life at the heart of the imperial state.

Worlds usually kept separate, collide. The stock market, which makes or breaks those who live by rentier capital invested in Bennet Frothingham's emblematically named 'Britannia Loan, Assurance, Investment, and Banking Company Limited', is usually kept at arm's length from the comfortable salon culture which Harvey Rolfe enjoys at the Frothingham's Hampstead home. But in *The Whirlpool* Gissing enacts the separation by which the reality of capitalist relations is habitually maintained and obscured. Anxiety, fuelled by rumour, flows into the musical soirée as worried investors look for the absent banker. Harvey registers the unease and begins to analyse it: 'A man such as Bennet Frothingham ... must himself be responsible for a good deal of folly ... what monstrous cruelties and mendacities might underlie the surface of this gay and melodious existence!' (p. 38).

Each character feels the consequences of the bank crash, but in different ways. Frothingham's suicide results in considerable loss of income for Mrs Frothingham, but also for the Carnabys, Sibyl Carnaby's mother and the Abbotts. Edgar Abbott dies of an overdose and his widow is left both poor and chastened. The Carnabys emigrate. And Alma Frothingham suffers shame and loss of social status because of her father's fraud. The crash has changed lives irrevocably and all the subsequent events and plot lines of the novel can be traced directly back to it.

In *The Whirlpool*, just as the world of finance penetrates the salon world founded upon it, so the sanctities of private life become increasingly mortgaged to a new fierceness in conduct which would be taken to new depths of moral duplicity in another turn-of-the-century novel of imperial London: Henry James's *The Wings of a Dove* (1902). Gissing finds an appropriate form in which to translate these tendencies of modernity into consciousness, and to explore its operation in personal life. The novel is deliberately structured to intensify a persistent sense of insecurity. The quest for domestic peace is ironically undercut by repeated shifts from place to place: for Alma and Harvey the West End of London gives way to North Wales, then to the West End again, and to the London suburbs of Pinner and Gunnersbury; the Carnabys take in Australia and the Far East before returning to London, with sorties to industrial Coventry by Hugh in the quest for income. And there is the ubiquity of the millionaire Cyrus Redgrave, gliding between soirée, concert-hall, his continental houses and his Wimbledon bungalow.

Social restlessness, and, from time to time, their opposites, are embodied in a range of modes: sociological anatomy, domestic realism, the melodrama of intrigue and mystery, and, very strikingly, styles of insinuating, coded speech, where little is said and much is understood. And, whatever James might have thought, the dramatic realism of his dialogue is one of Gissing's great formal achievements: we think of Harvey's proposal to Alma, the tension between Alma and Harvey before her recital, the brilliant horror of Mrs Strangeways's blackmail, or the confrontation between Alma and the Carnabys after Hugh's release from prison.

But as Gissing's critics noted at the time, it is the Zolaesque choice of title (substituted midway through the composition of the novel for the less suggestive 'Benedict's Household') which is this novel's most original and productive stroke. The effectiveness of the 'whirlpool' turns on Gissing's discovery of its metaphoric potential. It is an image which, as Rachel Bowlby has noted, combines the 'endless (ceaseless and pointless) "whirl of fashionable life" and the equally circular and groundless circulation of money'.[5] Speculation and risk apply to human relationships as well as money. The whirlpool, which eventually engulfs almost every character in the novel is, above all, a condition of modernity: it offers Gissing both a way of writing about contemporary civilisation and a diagnosis of it.

Gissing was influenced by other contemporary, frequently apocalyptic, diagnoses of the *fin de siècle* present. He certainly took account of Max Nordau's *Degeneration* (1895), which reported urgently on the 'vertigo and whirl of our frenzied life'.[6] In the same year there appeared an article, 'Nervous Diseases and Modern Life' in which 'modern life' was equated to a condition of more or less permanent nervous over-stimulation. Its author, the eminent pathologist Clifford Allbutt, pointed to 'hysteria, to neurasthenia, to the fretfulness, the melancholy, the unrest due to living at high pressure, to the whirl of the railway, the pelting of telegrams, the strife of business, the hunger for riches, the lust of vulgar minds for coarse and instant pleasures'.[7] Many of these perceived symptoms are recognisably displayed in *The Whirlpool*; indeed Allbutt's title could easily stand as the novel's subtitle.

Harvey mistakenly thinks himself insulated from the whirlpool way of life. Unlike the Carnabys and the Abbotts, he is not financially damaged by the Frothingham crash (his wisely invested inheritance brings him a steady £900 per year). But, as if to find some point to his rather pointless condition of existence, he generalises his situation into an unease with the over-complexity of modernity, couched in a rhetoric of blinkered certainty: 'Some of us are so over-civilised that it makes a reaction of wholesome barbarism in the rest,' he tells Carnaby at the outset: 'we're rotting at home – some of us sunk in barbarism, some coddling themselves in over-refinement' (p. 16). The ethic of 'wholesome barbarism', which rebukes the decadence and indolence of *rentier* culture, is a topical concern of the 1890s, and it is broached here, appropriately, in the bluff language of the opinionated clubman: 'let us be healthy, and have breathing space . . . What's the use of preaching peace and civilisation, when we know that England's just beginning her big fight . . . we have to lead the world . . . and we must do it by breaking heads' (p. 16). Harvey's eventual conversion from this outlook to something more worthy of the subtlety with which he anatomises the social whirlpool of high society, will be central to the novel.

His rhetorical projection of his own frustration is flesh and blood in his friend Hugh Carnaby, Gissing's brilliant portrait of the confused and repressed man of action. We find the type also in other novels of this period, by Meredith, Buchan and Conrad,[8] and later by Forster and Lawrence. Carnaby's manly nature makes him unfit for modern decadence, and so for the complexities of a London society which, by contrast, brings out the tenacious survival capacity of his wife, Sibyl. Even when the Carnabys find a more primitive life abroad, the sybaritic Sybil can't be tempted into the outback.

Back home Hugh enjoys the company of the practical types, celebrated by Kipling – here, Coventry engineers and craftsmen – but he is all too vulnerable to the stifling, hothouse life of the London *rentier*. The imperialist impulse, according to the economist Joseph Schumpeter, was 'atavistic in character';[9] however Hugh is less a degenerate throwback like Conan Doyle's maimed colonial, Dr Roylott,[10] than an innocent whose unfitness is his manly simplicity: ironically it is Hugh's touching faith in Sibyl's purity which leads him to murder the man he believes is her seducer.

Cyrus Redgrave, the object of Alma's unresolved and complex desire, is an example of a self-interested and morally questionable figure. Redgrave covers himself in a rather tired aestheticism; his Paterian ethic of living in the imagination, his 'sympathy with infinite forms of life' (p. 247), is an instance of the ambivalence of modernity which Gissing sees straight through.

And the decadence cult, in its embracing of moral relativism and the affirmation of self, does have much in common with the ethic of social-Darwinian fierceness which it ostensibly opposes:[11] Redgrave's beguiling cult of the self is, after all, a cover for his predatory designs on women. As the narrator remarks, 'he had so often come and seen and conquered' (p. 87).

## II

During the early stages of composing *The Whirlpool* Gissing had announced to his friend Eduard Bertz that the theme of his novel (at this stage with the title 'Benedict's Household') was 'the decay of domestic life amongst certain classes of people, & much stress is laid upon the question of *children*'.[12] Why was this topic of such consuming interest? Part of the reason lies in Gissing's own recent marital difficulties with his second wife, Edith Underwood, whom he had married in 1891. From Gissing's point of view, Edith showed little sympathy with his vocation as a writer, and little talent as a mother or domestic manager: she clearly brought out the more authoritarian side of Gissing's fastidious temperament. Their relationship deteriorated markedly through 1895, and an effort to get back on to an even keel with a family holiday, that August, ended in disaster, amid upsets over recalcitrant domestic servants. There were also angry scenes which centred on their young son or on Edith's increasingly erratic behaviour. Gissing removed the four-year-old Walter from their home in Epsom to his sisters' home in Wakefield in April 1896, another son, Alfred, having been born that January. After Gissing finished *The Whirlpool*, he left home for Devon (partly on medical advice) for a period of three months. The final separation was not long in coming.

It is against this background that the importance of Gissing's visit to North Wales, in the days immediately after he had deposited Walter at Wakefield, can be measured. In experiencing a short period of release from his own domestic bondage, Gissing could sense both the distance from the whirlpool, but also the impossibility of moving beyond it. The sheer acculumation of domestic difficulties Gissing had lived through prevents him from seeing a realistic alternative, but none the less allows him to pinpoint, with characteristic sociological insight, a condition of life.

Gissing's imagination always works best with situations of impasse. The extent to which the 'decay of domestic life' is a presence in *The Whirlpool* can be gauged from numerous instances of failed relationships, incompetent and untrustworthy servants and repeated references to the advantages of reducing their number, or doing away with them altogether. Ironically, it is in joint revolt against what they take to be domestic bondage that Alma and Harvey can unite in the short-lived practical idealism of their choice of domestic life.

A choice of life was a highly modern idea in the 1890s. It fused with the 'marriage question' which, so persistently debated in the nineties, challenged the grip of conventional, patriarchal relationships: it also looks to other styles of living, where men and women might conduct themselves more openly, and equally. That Gissing does not allow Alma and Harvey to redraw a workable map of marriage is significant, in this context, because it shows us what kind of novelist Gissing could not be, and so what he was. Although he was well up with the fiction of the 'New Woman' (he read George Egerton, M. M. Dowie and Hardy) he could not realise in fiction anything like the radical comradeship of a truly experimental relationship such as we find in *Jude the Obscure* (1895). Harvey and Alma show little of that self-conscious and articulate inspection of the terms of nature and ideology which engage Jude Fawley and Sue Bridehead, the most interesting couple in *fin de siècle* literature. Yet Gissing characteristically turns limitation to artistic advantage by doing what he is best at: showing us the impress on relationships of what is inescapable: the pressures of the shared condition of living – of modernity located in the modern metropolis – and enacting the drama of the individual's subjection to it. Alma and Harvey's marriage experiment, then, is not so much an experiment as a 'proof' of the over-determining effects of the environment, and its psychological and physiological consequences.

It is no accident that the most compelling episode in the North Wales phase of the novel (Book Two, chapters 1–4) is one which was shaped by Gissing's encounter with the mountains overlooking the Lleyn Peninsula in April 1896.[13] The Carn Bodvean scene is important in a number of respects, recalling not only Flaubert's *Madame Bovary*, but aspects of Ibsen's *Hedda Gabler* (which Gissing read in 1891).[14] Alma, like Ibsen's tragic heroine, is intensely jealous of another intelligent, bookish woman, and yet grateful for any interlude which might dispel the *ennui* which two years of marriage in remotest Wales has produced. Like Thea and Eilert Loveborg, Mary Abbott and Harvey can converse as responsible, purposeful adults in a way that wife and husband cannot.

The spatial composition of the episode is significant; as Patrick Parrinder puts it: 'with Harvey and Mrs Abbott on the mountain-side, airily discussing the education of children and the "whirlpool way of life", while Alma's physical revolt against pregnancy takes place down in the valley'.[15] The scene suggests a symbolic ejection of Alma from that discursive territory: her only eloquence is a physical one, as she channels her jealousy of the pair into assertion of a physical kind (Hedda's assertion ends her life and her pregnancy). Alma rashly takes out a horse and trap, of which she has no previous experience, and her bodily revolt finds expression in a miscarriage brought on in the wake of an hysterical attack. Hysteria was a common enough condition to nervous women of the *fin de siècle*: it expressed the 'insoluble conflict' between women's desire to 'act as individuals and the internalized obligations to submit to the needs of the family and to conform to the model of self-sacrificing "womanly" behaviour'.[16]

It is, then, through the subjection of Alma's 'nature', including her body, that the pressures of modernity are most acutely felt. Harvey, of course, suffers no such comparable damage. Yet Gissing's obvious partiality should not altogether surprise us, since it is always difficult to talk of the psychology of Gissing's characters removed from the condition of life to which they are subject. To put the point another way, Gissing allows his women to think beyond the domestic space to which they were too often consigned, yet requires them to suffer the consequences of venturing into what was still, for the period, the hazardous space – socially and morally – between private and public life. To become visible, in this novel, is to risk all.

At the opposite pole, Basil Morton's home at Greystone to which Harvey periodically retreats could not be more risk-free. Here is a projection of a desire for order, removed from a world of perpetual conflict which makes such order impossible, and from which Alma must be excluded. But when he tries to bring life to these scenes, Gissing fails; the writing of these unconvincing encounters at Greystone is, all too often, cloying and sentimental. This is Mrs Morton: 'Four children she had borne ... into her pure and healthy mind had never entered a thought at conflict with motherhood. Her breasts were the fountain of life; her babies clung to them, and grew large of limb' (pp. 302–3). Gissing gives us here the literary equivalent of the popular genre of 'motherhood' paintings which flourished at the turn of the century.[17]

This paragon of motherhood and fertility has generally attracted critical disbelief,[18] but what needs more attention is Gissing's perfectly serious treatment of an idea, growing in popularity among the more enlightened middle-classes, of a self-sufficient, servant-free and capable motherhood, answering, with varying degrees of self-consciousness, the eugenic call for a fitter, imperial race. Here is an idea which Gissing shares with other writers and acquaintances such as H. G. Wells and Grant Allen, but it simply doesn't engage him imaginatively, and he is too good a writer to be didactic about it, as Allen tends to be. Motherhood, for the narrator of *The Woman Who Did* (1895) is the 'full realization of woman's faculties, the natural outlet for woman's wealth of emotion'.[19] But in *The Whirlpool* Mrs Morton represents not a norm but a sadly impossible ideal which he does not dwell on for long. Instead Gissing, the disenchanted realist, anatomises Alma, the bored and inefficient mother who shows little interest in Hughie, suffers an induced miscarriage, and, despite her devotion, is prevented by part-inherited tendencies from sustaining her second child beyond two weeks of its life.

## III

Yet *The Whirlpool* does not engage our attention simply through its sociological exactness or its naturalistic documentation. Gissing creates and sustains throughout the novel a truthful psychological drama of tragic proportions. Despite good intentions on both sides, Alma and Harvey are manifestly wrong for each other. Alma, her father's daughter, must live through risk-taking; Harvey's commitment to passive withdrawal offers an inappropriate counterweight. Their efforts to compromise and to achieve the emotional honesty necessary to preserve a rational relationship, simply come too late. Alma is on a downward spiral, in the grip of feelings which she cannot rationally control. Even when Alma and Harvey have apparently secured a new *modus vivendi* after her recital, she continues to be haunted by the shadow of her father's disgrace, by the fear that she will be compromised by what the Carnabys know about her, by the fear that her good name will be for ever affected in Harvey's eyes, and that she is vulnerable to blackmail from Mrs Strangeways. Believing that Harvey would not understand, were the truth to come out, she is unable to share any of her fears with him: such an accumulation of fear and guilt takes her nearer and nearer the fatal draught of morphine.

Earlier she has grown more and more resentful of Harvey's lack of interest in her musical ambition, so that his very liberality about her movements and her affairs is proof to her of his lack of concern (in this she is surely half right). 'Alma was at heart dissatisfied with the liberty ... which ... [he] seemed so willing to allow her.' Harvey's 'incuriousness' (which recalls his own interpretation of the marriage experiment in Wales) appears to be enabling were it not for the fact that he wishes 'to be left alone, not to be worried with her dependence upon him' (p. 235). This is only one instance of Harvey's 'benign' neglect of Alma, on a large scale. With the narrator's prompting – 'So, once more, did he oust common-sense with what he imagined a riper wisdom' (p. 209) – Harvey's inadequacy becomes more and more apparent.

Part of Harvey's trouble is his vanity. He does not want to seem an unattractive, ageing pedagogue: 'Face to face with a woman in the prime of her beauty, he heard a voice warning him against the pedantic spirit of middle age ...' (p. 209). Alma might reasonably expect to enjoy the fruits of Harvey's greater experience, yet when she makes her first re-entry into society for three years, she does so alone: she is accompanied to Mrs Strangeways's soirée, not by Harvey, but by Sibyl. And Alma's delusions about her ability to survive as a professional violinist on a modest talent require a more convincing opposition from Harvey than she receives. While Harvey does point out to her that it would be inadvisable to come 'before the public' before receiving the endorsement of a musician of Wilenski's high standing, Alma's inability to take the message might have persuaded him to redouble his efforts on her behalf, rather than be guided by his fear of alienating her. In one all-too typical

interview with her he begins with 'unwonted decision' on
buckle before 'that peculiar force of Alma's personality whic
had long ago subdued him' (p. 209).

So, without his knowing, Harvey's conscious liberality trans-
mutes into neglect of Alma and her needs. As she busies herself
with plans for the forthcoming concert, the reiteration of their
project of non-interference now appears to be the merest convenience: 'We are neither of us to stand in the other's way – isn't
that the agreement?' (p. 226) Alma says. She shares in their talk
of freedom in marriage, but now Gissing allows us to catch the
nuanced tone of her resentment: his handling of speech, here, is
masterly. Alma's new-found resistance to Harvey is a resistance
to the rhetoric; her use of it, now, is unmistakeably sarcastic.

## IV

Harvey's development is, of course, a major theme of the novel,
but it is a development quite at a tangent to his relationship
with Alma. As Gissing explained in his famous rebuke to Wells,
it was 'the change wrought in his views & sentiments by the fact
of his becoming a father'.[20] The question of children – how they
are spoken of in this culture, how they are valued – is addressed
memorably in Henry James's *What Maisie Knew*, but Gissing's
treatment of this subject in *The Whirlpool* has its own profund-
ity. While at the start Harvey claims he can't give a damn about
children (a sentiment which is undermined almost at once by his
prompt and humane handling of the problem of the Wager
children), this unthinking machismo gives way to a more mature
and feminine understanding. Cynical generalisation is replaced
by patient observation and inquiry. As Gissing, himself, wrote
'he is ripe in that experience which kills the cruder egoism.'[21]
Gissing's treatment of this theme, which draws on topical
debates about the ethics of rearing the imperial child,[22] is
singular in the literature of the 1890s.

'What sort of world will it be for Hugh?' Harvey asks
(p. 143). How should he educate him for the future? Should he
cultivate 'his sympathetic emotions', or should he agree with
Basil Morton that 'our little crabs must grow their hard shell or
they've got no chance' (p. 319)? But this end-of-the-century
brooding on the prospect for the young is a particular case of
that fascination with what's to come, so characteristic of the

novel as a whole. And the question of the future – to what is the whirlpool leading – becomes, inevitably in 1897, merged with the future of the nation. In the fictional 1886, Harvey sees England 'just beginning her big fight – the fight that will put all history into the shade! (p. 16). We shall, he says, 'fight like blazes in the twentieth century' (p. 19). After reading Kipling's *Barrack-Room Ballads* at the end of the novel, ten years on, he sees 'millions of men, natural men, revolting against the softness and sweetness of civilisation; men all over the world; hardly knowing what they want and what they don't want' (p. 415). He ventriloquises for the 'average Englander': 'By God! We are the British Empire, and we'll just show 'em what *that* means' (p. 416).

What *that* means he predicts with the kind of spirited pessimism and heavy irony which are Harvey's trademark: 'We may reasonably hope, old man, to see our boys blown into small bits by the explosive that hasn't got its name yet' (p. 416). Twenty years later Gissing's elder son Walter, the model for Hughie Rolfe, was killed by a shell at the Somme, in the slaughter of July 1916, aged twenty-four. In the event nothing could prepare the little crabs of the *fin de siècle* for the mass slaughter of trench warfare. The First World War was the outcome of a world spinning out of control, a Europe in the grip of forces which Gissing had grasped imaginatively. *The Whirlpool*, uniquely among realist novels of the *fin de siècle*, permits us now, what was denied to Gissing and his readers, a sense of the sad logic by which the irrational, circulating energies of the whirlpool of modernity sustained the cold rationality of the war machine.

WILLIAM GREENSLADE

## References

1. *Bookseller*, April 1897, p. 290.
2. Henry James, 'London Notes' in M. Shapira (ed.), *Henry James: Selected Literary Criticism*, Harmondsworth: Penguin, 1963, pp. 208–12 (p. 209, p. 210).
3. Gissing to Eduard Bertz, 9 May 1896, in P. Mattheisen, A. C. Young and P. Coustillas (eds), *The Collected Letters of George*

*Gissing*, Athens, Ohio: Ohio University Press, 1990–7, VI, 100–1 and editors' note to 100–1; E. H. H. Green, *The Crisis of Conservatism: The Politics, Economics and Ideology of the British Conservative Party 1880–1914*, London: Routledge, 1995, pp. 70, 73.

4. See W. T. C. King, *History of the London Discount Market*, London: Frank Cass, 1936; 1972, pp. 306–7; David Kynaston, *The City of London Vol 1: A World of Its Own 1850–1890*, London: Chatto and Windus, 1994, ch. 21, and my note to p. 8.

5. See Rachel Bowlby, review of *The Whirlpool*, ed. Patrick Parrinder, *Gissing Newsletter*, 21 (April 1985): 22–9 (p. 23).

6. Max Nordau, *Degeneration*, London: William Heinemann, 1985; 1913, p. 42.

7. T. C. Allbutt, 'Nervous Diseases and Modern Life', *Contemporary Review*, 67 (1895): 210–31 (p. 214).

8. William Greenslade, 'Fitness and the Fin de Siècle', in John Stokes (ed.) *Fin de Siècle/Fin du Globe*, Basingstoke: Macmillan, 1992, 37–51 (pp. 46–7).

9. J. A. Schumpeter, *Imperialism and Social Classes*, Oxford: Basil Blackwell, 1951, p. 84.

10. Arthur Conan Doyle, 'The Adventures of the Speckled Band' (1892), in *The Complete Stories of Sherlock Holmes*, Harmondsworth: Penguin, 1981, pp. 257–73.

11. See John Goode, *George Gissing: Ideology and Fiction*, London: Vision, 1978, pp. 190–1; John Sloan, *George Gissing: The Cultural Challenge*, Basingstoke: Macmillan, 1989, p. 143.

12. Gissing to Bertz, 9 May 1896, in Mattheisen et al. (eds), *Collected Letters of George Gissing*, VI, 123.

13. See note to p. 14.

14. Pierre Coustillas (ed.), *London and the Life of Literature in Late-Victorian England: The Diary Of George Gissing*, Brighton: Harvester, 1978, p. 273 (entry for 17 March 1892).

15. Patrick Parrinder, Introduction to *The Whirlpool*, xvii.

16. Elaine Showalter, *The Female Malady: Women, Madness and English Culture*, London: Virago, 1987, p. 144.

17. For example, *Maternity* by Thomas B. Kennington (1856–1916), *Hush a Bye* by George Neale (1863–1940) or *The First Born* by Fred Elwell (1870–1958).

18. See Adrian Poole, *Gissing in Context*, Basingstoke: Macmillan, 1975, p. 203; Katherine B. Linehan, '*The Odd Women*: Gissing's

Imaginative Approach to Feminism', *Modern Language Quarterly*, 40 (4) (1979): 358–75 (p. 363).

19. Grant Allen, *The Woman Who Did*, 1895; Oxford: Oxford University Press, 1996, p. 94.

20. Gissing to H. G. Wells, 9 August 1897, in *Collected Letters*, VI, 320; see p. 442 in Gissing and his Critics.

21. Gissing to Wells, ibid, p. 320; see p. 442 in Gissing and his Critics.

22. See note to pp. 318–19.

23. Pierre Coustillas, 'Walter Leonard Gissing (1891–1916): An Anniversary', *Gissing Journal*, 32 (3) (July 1996): 13–23 (pp. 20–2).

# NOTE ON THE TEXT

Gissing began serious planning of *The Whirlpool* in February 1896, and delivered the completed manuscript to his publisher, Lawrence and Bullen, on 21 December 1896 (*Diary*, p. 430). Having made what he believed to be a final correction of the proofs the following January, he received from his editor, Arthur Bullen, in early February 1897, another proof marked with additional suggestions for excisions – totalling about ten pages. After some initial surprise, Gissing accepted that most of these amounted to 'surplusage' and was happy to concur.

Study of the 180-page manuscript (the printer's copy, held by the Huntington Library, California) confirms that the exercise of deletion was largely in the interests of concision: with one or two exceptions little of significance was lost in the pruning. None the less Gissing did feel obliged to restore about fifty lines 'here & there – points of character or bits of colour I could not bring myself to give up' (Gissing to Bullen, 8 February 1897, *CL*, VI, 230). Because this proof does not survive, it is impossible to determine which of the deleted passages Gissing successfully reinstated.

The novel was published in a one-volume edition of 2000 copies by Lawrence and Bullen in April 1897; a second impression of 2000 copies appeared in May, and a third later that year. George Bell and Son published the novel in their 'Indian and Colonial Library' in 1897. There were other impressions in 1901 (A. H. Bullen), and in 1911 and 1915 (Sidgwick and Jackson). More recently, there have been editions from Watergate Classics (with an introduction by Myfanwy Evans, 1948), from Harvester Press (edited by Patrick Parrinder, 1977; 1985) and from Hogarth Press (with an introduction by Gillian Tindall, 1984). The first American edition was published by Frederick A. Stokes Co. in 1898 and a further three impressions followed that year. There was a further reprint by AMS Press in 1969.

This edition of *The Whirlpool* is based on the first edition of the novel (London: Lawrence and Bullen, 1897). Obvious errors have been silently corrected and there is some slight modernisation (for instance, the full point is omitted after certain common abbreviations such as Mr, Dr, St; and where the original text uses double quotation marks, this text uses single ones, and vice versa).

# THE WHIRLPOOL

PART THE FIRST

# CHAPTER I

Harvey Rolfe was old enough to dine with deliberation, young and healthy enough to sauce with appetite the dishes he thoughtfully selected. You perceived in him the imperfect epicure. His club had no culinary fame; the dinner was merely tolerable; but Rolfe's unfinished palate flattered the second-rate cook. He knew nothing of vintages; it sufficed him to distinguish between Bordeaux and Burgundy; yet one saw him raise his glass and peer at the liquor with eye of connoisseur. All unaffectedly; for he was conscious of his shortcoming in the art of delicate living, and never vaunted his satisfactions. He had known the pasture of poverty, and the table as it is set by London landladies; to look back on these things was to congratulate himself that nowadays he dined.

Beyond the achievement of a vague personal distinction at the Metropolitan Club, he had done nothing to make himself a man of note, and it was doubtful whether more than two or three of the members really liked him or regarded him with genuine interest. His introduction to this circle he owed to an old friend, Hugh Carnaby, whose social position was much more clearly defined: Hugh Carnaby, the rambler, the sportsman, and now for a twelvemonth the son-in-law of Mrs Ascott Larkfield. Through Carnaby people learnt as much of his friend's history as it concerned anyone to know: that Harvey Rolfe had begun with the study of medicine, had given it up in disgust, subsequently was 'in business', and withdrew from it on inheriting a competency. They were natives of the same county, and learnt their Latin together at the Grammar School of Greystone, the midland town which was missed by the steam highroad, and so preserves much of the beauty and tranquillity of days gone by. Rolfe seldom spoke of his own affairs, but in talking of travel he had been heard to mention that his father had engineered certain lines of foreign railway. It seemed that Harvey had no purpose in life, save that of enjoying himself. Obviously he read a good deal, and Carnaby credited him with profound historical knowledge; but he neither wrote nor threatened to do so. Something of cynicism appeared in his talk of public matters; politics amused him, and his social views lacked consistency, tending, however, to an indolent conservatism. Despite his convivial qualities, he had traits of the reserved, even of the unsociable, man: a slight awkwardness in bearing, a mute shyness with strangers, a hesitancy in ordinary talk, and occasional bluntness of assertion or contradiction, suggesting a contempt which possibly he did not intend. Hugh Carnaby declared that the true Rolfe only showed himself after a bottle of wine; maintained, moreover, that Harvey had vastly improved since he entered upon a substantial income. When Rolfe was five and twenty, Hugh being two years younger, they met after a long separation, and found each other intolerable; a decade later their meeting led to hearty friendship. Rolfe had become independent, and was tasting his freedom in a twelve-month's travel. The men came face to face one day on the deck of a steamer at Port Said. Physically, Rolfe had changed so much that the other had a difficulty in recognising him; morally, the change was not less marked, as Carnaby very soon became aware. At thirty-seven this process of development was by no means arrested, but its slow and subtle working escaped observation – unless it were that of Harvey Rolfe himself.

His guest this evening, in a quiet corner of the dining-room where he generally sat, was a man, ten years his junior, named Morphew: slim, narrow-shouldered, with sandy hair, and pale, delicate features of more sensibility than intelligence; restless, vivacious, talking incessantly in a low, rapid voice, with frequent nervous laughs which threw back his drooping head. A difference of costume – Rolfe wore morning dress, Morphew the suit of ceremony* – accentuated the younger man's advantage in natural and acquired graces; otherwise, they presented the contrast of character and insignificance. Rolfe had a shaven chin, a weathered complexion, thick brown hair; the penumbra of middle-age had touched his countenance, softening here and there a line which told of temperament in excess. At this moment his manner inclined to a bluff jocularity, due in some measure to the bottle of wine before him, as also was the tinge of colour upon his cheek; he spoke briefly, but listened with smiling interest to his guest's continuous talk. This ran on the subject of the money-market, with which the young man boasted some practical acquaintance.

'You don't speculate at all?' Morphew asked.

'Shouldn't know how to go about it,' replied the other in his deeper note.

'It seems to me to be the simplest thing in the world if one is content with moderate profits. I'm going in for it seriously – cautiously – as a matter of business. I've studied the thing – got it up as I used to work at something for an exam. And here, you see, I've made five pounds at a stroke – five pounds! Suppose I make that every now and then, it's worth the trouble, you know – it mounts up. And I shall never stand to lose much. You see, it's Tripcony's interest that I should make profits.'

'I'm not quite sure of that.'

'Oh, but it *is*! Let me explain – '

These two had come to know each other under peculiar circumstances a year ago. Rolfe was at Brussels, staying – his custom when abroad – at a hotel unfrequented by English folk. One evening on his return from the theatre, he learnt that a young man of his own nationality lay seriously ill in a room at the top of the house. Harvey, moved by compassion, visited the unfortunate Englishman, listened to his ravings, and played the part of Good Samaritan. On recovery, the stranger made full disclosure of his position. Being at Brussels on a holiday, he had got into the company of gamblers, and, after winning a large sum (ten thousand francs, he declared), had lost not only that, but all else that he possessed, including his jewellery. He had gambled deliberately; he wanted money, money, and saw no other way of obtaining it. In the expansive mood of convalescence, Cecil Morphew left no detail of his story unrevealed. He was of gentle birth, and had a private income of three hundred pounds, charged upon the estate of a distant relative; his profession (the bar) could not be remunerative for years, and other prospects he had none. The misery of his situation lay in the fact that he was desperately in love with the daughter of people who looked upon him as little better than a pauper. The girl had pledged herself to him, but would not marry without her parents' consent, of which there was no hope till he had at least trebled his means. His choice of a profession was absurd, dictated merely by social opinion; he should have been working hard in a commercial office, or at some open-air pursuit.

Naturally he turned again to the thought of gambling, this time the great legalised game of hazard, wherein he was as little likely to prosper as among the blacklegs* of Brussels. Rolfe liked him for his ingenuousness, and for the vein of poetry in his nature. The love affair still went on, but Morphew seldom alluded to it, and his seasoned friend thought of it as a youthful ailment which would pass and be forgotten.

'I'm convinced,' said the young man presently, 'that any one who really gives his mind to it can speculate with moderate success. Look at the big men – the brokers and the company promoters, and so on; I've met some of them, and there's nothing in them – nothing! Now, there's Bennet Frothingham.* You know him, I think?'

Rolfe nodded.

'Well, what do you think of him? Isn't he a very ordinary fellow? How has he got such a position? I'm told he began just in a small way – by chance. No doubt *he* found it so easy to make money he was surprised at his success. Tripcony has told me a lot about him. Why, the "Britannia" brings him fifteen thousand a year; and he must be in a score of other things.'

'I know nothing about the figures,' said Rolfe, 'and I shouldn't put much faith in Tripcony; but Frothingham, you may be sure, isn't quite an ordinary man.'

'Ah, well, of course there's a certain knack – and then, experience –'

Morphew emptied his glass, and refilled it. Nearly all the tables in the room were now occupied, and the general hum of talk gave security to intimate dialogue. Flushed and bright-eyed, the young man presently leaned forward.

'If I could count upon five hundred, she would take the step.'

'Indeed?'

'Yes, that's settled. What do you think? Plenty of people live very well on less.'

'You want my serious opinion?'

'If you *can* be serious.'

'Then I think that the educated man who marries on less than a thousand is either mad or a criminal.'

'Bosh! We won't talk about it.'

They rose, and walked towards the smoking-room, Rolfe giving a nod here and there as he passed acquaintances. In the hall someone addressed him.

'How does Carnaby take this affair?'

'What affair?'

'Don't you know? Their house has been robbed – strip̦ It's in the evening papers.'

Rolfe went on into the smoking-room, and read the report ͻf his friend's misfortune. The Carnabys occupied a house in Hamilton Terrace.* During their absence from home last night, there had been a clean sweep of all such things of value as could easily be removed. The disappearance of their housekeeper, and the fact that this woman had contrived the absence of the servants from nine o'clock till midnight, left no mystery in the matter. The clubmen talked of it with amusement. Hard lines, to be sure, for Carnaby, and yet harder for his wife, who had lost no end of jewellery; but the thing was so neatly and completely done, one must needs laugh. One or two husbands who enjoyed the luxury of a housekeeper betrayed their uneasiness. A discussion arose on the characteristics of housekeepers in general, and spread over the vast subject of domestic management,* not often debated at the Metropolitan Club. In general talk of this kind Rolfe never took part; smoking his pipe, he listened and laughed, and was at moments thoughtful. Cecil Morphew, rapidly consuming cigarettes as he lay back in a soft chair, pointed the moral of the story in favour of humble domesticity.

In half an hour, his guest having taken leave, Rolfe put on his overcoat, and stepped out into the cold, clammy November night. He was overtaken by a fellow Metropolitan – a grizzled, scraggy-throated, hollow-eyed man, who laid a tremulous hand upon his arm.

'Excuse me, Mr Rolfe, have you seen Frothingham recently?'

'Not for a month.'

'Ah! I thought perhaps – I was wondering what he thought about the Colebrook smash.* To tell you the truth, I've heard unpleasant rumours. Do you – should you think the Colebrook affair would affect the "Britannia"in any way?'

It was not the first time that this man had confided his doubts and timidities to Harvey Rolfe; he had a small, but to him important, interest in Bennet Frothingham's wide-reaching affairs, and seemed to spend most of his time in eliciting opinion on the financier's stability.

'Wouldn't you be much more comfortable,' said Rolfe, rather bluntly, 'if you had your money in some other kind of security?'

'Ah, but, my dear sir, twelve and a half per cent – twelve and a half! I hold preference shares of the original issue.'

'Then I'm afraid you must take your chance.'

'But,' piped the other in alarm, 'you don't mean that—'

'I mean nothing, and know nothing. I'm the last man to consult about such things.'

And Rolfe, with an abrupt 'Goodnight,' beckoned to a passing hansom. The address he gave was Hugh Carnaby's, in Hamilton Terrace.

Twice already the horse had slipped at slimy crossings, when, near the top of Regent Street, it fell full length, and the abrupt stoppage caused a collision of wheels with another hansom which was just passing at full speed in the same direction. Rolfe managed to alight in the ordinary way, and at once heard himself greeted by a familiar voice from the other cab. His acquaintance showed a pallid, drawn, all but cadaverous visage, with eyes which concealed pain or weariness under their friendly smile. Abbott was the man's name. Formerly a lecturer at a provincial college, he had resigned his post on marrying, and taken to journalism.

'I want to speak to you, Rolfe,' he said hurriedly, 'but I haven't a moment to spare. Going to Euston – could you come along for a few minutes?'

The vehicles were not damaged; Abbott's driver got quickly out of the crowd, and the two men continued their conversation.

'Do you know anything of Wager?' inquired the journalist, with a troubled look.

'He came to see me a few evenings ago – late.'

'Ha, he did! To borrow money, wasn't it?'

'Well, yes.'

'I thought so. He came to me for the same. Said he'd got a berth at Southampton. Lie, of course. The fellow has disappeared, and left his children – left them in a lodging-house at Hammersmith. How's that for cool brutality? The landlady found my wife's address, and came to see her. Address left out on purpose, I dare say. There was nothing for it but to take care of the poor little brats. – Oh, damn!'

'What's the matter?'

'Neuralgia – driving me mad. Teeth, I think. I'll have every one wrenched out of my head if this goes on. Never mind. What do you think of Wager?'

'I remember, when we were at Guy's,* he used to advocate the nationalisation of offspring. Probably he had some personal interest in the matter, even then.'

'Hound! I don't know whether to set the police after him or not. It wouldn't benefit the children. I suppose it's no use hunting for his family?'

'Not much, I should say.'

'Well, lucky we have no children of our own. Worst of it is, I don't like the poor little wretches, and my wife doesn't either. We must find a home for them.'

'I say, Abbott, you must let me go halves at that.'

'Hang it, no! Why should you support Wager's children? They're relatives of ours, unfortunately. But I wanted to tell you that I'm going down to Waterbury.' He looked at his watch. 'Thirteen minutes – shall I do it? There's a good local paper, the *Free Press*, and I have the offer of part-ownership. I shall buy, if possible, and live in the country for a year or two, to pick up my health. Can't say I love London. Might get into country journalism for good. Curse this torment!'

In Tottenham Court Road, Rolfe bade his friend goodbye, and the cab rushed on.

## CHAPTER 2

It was half past ten when Rolfe knocked at the door in Hamilton Terrace. He learnt from the servant that Mr Carnaby was at home, and had company. In the room known as the library, four men sat smoking; their voices pealed into the hall as the door opened, and a boisterous welcome greeted the newcomer's appearance.

'Come to condole?' cried Hugh, striding forward with his man-of-the-wide-world air, and holding out his big hand. 'No doubt they're having a high old time at the club. Does it please them? Does it tickle them?'

'Why, naturally. There's the compensation, my boy – you contribute to the gaiety of your friends.'

Carnaby was a fair example of the well-bred, well-fed English-man – tall, brawny, limber, not uncomely, with a red neck, a powerful jaw, and a keen eye. Something more of repose, of self-possession, and a slightly more intellectual brow, would have made him the best type of conquering, civilising Briton. He came of good family, but had small inheritance; his tongue told of age-long domination; his physique and carriage showed the horseman, the game-stalker, the nomad. Hugh had never bent over books since the day when he declined the university and got leave to join Colonel Bosworth's* exploring party in the Caucasus. After a boyhood of straitened circumstances, he profited by a skilful stewardship which allowed him to hope for some seven hundred a year; his elder brother, Miles, a fine fellow, who went into the army, pinching himself to benefit Hugh and their sister Ruth. Miles was now Major Carnaby, active on the North-West Frontier. Ruth was wife of a mission-ary in some land of swamps; doomed by climate, but of spirit indomitable. It seemed strange that Hugh, at five and thirty, had done nothing particular. Perhaps his income explained it – too small for traditional purposes, just large enough to foster indolence. For Hugh had not even followed up his promise of becoming an explorer; he had merely rambled, mostly in pursuit of fowl or quadruped. When he married, all hope for him was at an end. The beautiful and brilliant daughter of a fashionable widow, her income a trifle more than Carnaby's own; devoted to the life of cities, wherein she shone; an enchantress whose spell would not easily be broken, before whom her husband bowed in delighted subservience – such a woman might flatter Hugh's pride, but could scarce be expected to draw out his latent energies and capabilities. This year, for the first time, he had visited no wild country; his journeying led only to Paris, to Vienna. In due season he shot his fifty brace on somebody's grouse-moor, but the sport did not exhilarate him.

An odd and improbable alliance, that between Hugh Carnaby and Harvey Rolfe. Yet in several ways they suited each other. Old-time memories had a little, not much, to do with it; more of the essence of the matter was their feeling of likeness in difference. Ten years ago Carnaby felt inclined to call his old school-fellow a 'cad'; Harvey saw nothing in Hugh but robust snobbishness. Nowadays they had the pleasant sense of under-standing each other on most points, and the result was a good deal of honest mutual admiration. The one's physical vigour and adroitness, the other's active mind, liberal thoughts, studious habits, proved reciprocally attractive. Though in unlike ways, both were impressively modern. Of late it had seemed as if the man of open air, checked in his natural courses, thrown back upon his meditations, turned to the student, with hope of guidance in new paths, of counsel amid unfamiliar obstacles. To the observant Rolfe, his friend's position abounded in speculative interest. With the course of years, each had lost many a harsher characteristic, whilst the inner man matured. That their former relations were gradually being reversed, neither perhaps had consciously noted; but even in the jests which passed between them on Harvey's arrival this evening, it appeared plainly enough that Hugh Carnaby no longer felt the slightest inclination to regard his friend as an inferior.

The room, called library, contained one small case of books, which dealt with travel and sport. Furniture of the ordinary kind, still new, told of easy circumstances and domestic comfort. Round about the walls hung a few paintings and photographs, intermingled with the stuffed heads of animals slain in the chase, notably that of a great ibex with magnificent horns.

'Come, now, tell me all about it,' said Rolfe, as he mixed himself a glass of whisky and water. 'I don't see that anything has gone from this room.'

'Don't you?' cried his host, with a scornful laugh. 'Where are my silver-mounted pistols? Where's the ibex-hoof made into a paperweight? And' – he raised his voice to a shout of comical despair – 'where's my cheque-book?'

'I see.'

'I wish *I* did. It must break the record for a neat house-robbery, don't you think? And they'll never be caught – I'll bet you anything you like they won't. The job was planned weeks ago; that woman came into the house with no other purpose.'

'But didn't your wife know anything about her?'

'What can one know about such people? There were references, I believe – as valuable as references usually are. She must be an old hand. But I'm sick of the subject; let's drop it. – You were interrupted, Hollings. What about that bustard?'

A very tall, spare man, who seemed to rouse himself from a nap, resumed his story of bustard-stalking in Spain* last spring. Carnaby, who knew the country well, listened with lively interest, and followed with reminiscences of his own. He told of a certain boar, shot in the Sierras, which weighed something like four hundred pounds. He talked, too, of flamingoes on the 'marismas' of the Guadalquivir; of punting day after day across the tawny expanse of water; of cooking his meals on sandy islets at a fire made of tamarisk and thistle; of lying wakeful in the damp, chilly nights, listening to frogs and bitterns. Then again of his ibex-hunting on the Cordilleras of Castile, when he brought down that fine fellow whose head adorned his room, the horns just thirty-eight inches long. And in the joy of these recollections there seemed to sound a regretful note, as if he spoke of things gone by and irrecoverable, no longer for him.

One of the men present had recently been in Cyprus, and mentioned it with disgust. Rolfe also had visited the island, and remembered it much more agreeably, his impressions seeming to be chiefly gastronomic; he recalled the exquisite flavour of Cyprian hares, the fat francolin,* the delicious beccaficoes* in commanderia wine; with merry banter from Carnaby, professing to despise a man who knew nothing of game but its taste. The conversation reverted to technicalities of sport, full of terms and phrases unintelligible to Harvey; recounting feats with 'Empress' and 'Paradox',* the deadly results of a 'treble A', or of 'treble-nesting slugs', and boasting of a 'right and left with No. 6'. Hugh appeared to forget all about his domestic calamity; only when his guests rose did he recur to it, and with an air of constemptuous impatience. But he made a sign to Rolfe, requesting him to stay, and at midnight the two friends sat alone together.

'Sibyl has gone to her mother's,' began Hugh in a changed voice. 'The poor girl takes it pluckily. It's a damnable thing, you know, for a woman to lose her rings and bracelets and so on – even such a woman as Sibyl. She tried to laugh it off, but I could see – we must buy them again, that's all. And that reminds me – what's your real opinion of Frothingham?'

Harvey laughed.

'When such a lot of people go about asking that question, it would make *me* rather uneasy if I had anything at stake.'

'They do? So it struck me. The fact is, we have a good deal at stake. The dowager swears by Frothingham. I believe every penny she has is in the "Britannia", one way or another.'

'It's a wide net,' said Rolfe musingly. 'The Britannia Loan,

Assurance, Investment, and Banking Company, Limited. Very good name, I've often thought.'

'Yes; but, look here, you don't seriously doubt—'

'My opinion is worthless. I know no more of finance than of the Cabala.* Frothingham personally I rather like, and that's all I can say.'

'The fact is, I have been thinking of putting some of my own – yet I don't think I shall. We're going away for the winter. Sibyl wants to give up the house, and I think she's right. For people like us, it's mere foolery to worry with a house and a lot of servants. We're neither of us cut out for that kind of thing. Sibyl hates housekeeping. Well, you can't expect a woman like her to manage a pack of thieving, lying, lazy servants. The housekeeper idea hasn't been a conspicuous success, you see, and there's nothing for it but hotel or boarding-house.'

'If you remember,' said Rolfe, 'I hinted something of the kind a year ago.'

'Yes; but – well, you know, when people marry they generally look for a certain natural consequence. If we have no children, it'll be all right.'

Rolfe meditated for a moment.

'You remember that fellow Wager – the man you met at Abbott's? His wife died a year ago, and now he has bolted, leaving his two children in a lodging-house.'

'What a damned scoundrel!' cried Hugh, with a note of honest indignation.

'Well, yes; but there's something to be said for him. It's a natural revolt against domestic bondage. Of course, as things are, someone else has to bear the bother and expense; but that's only our state of barbarism. A widower with two young children and no income – imagine the position. Of course, he ought to be able to get rid of them in some legitimate way – state institution – anything you like that answers to reason.'

'I don't know whether it would work.'

'Some day it will. People talk such sentimental rubbish about children. I would have the parents know nothing about them till they're ten or twelve years old. They're a burden, a hindrance, a perpetual source of worry and misery. Most wives are sacrificed to the next generation – an outrageous absurdity. People snivel over the deaths of babies; I see nothing to grieve about. If a child dies, why, the probabilities are it *ought* to die; if it lives, it lives, and you get survival of the fittest.* We don't want to choke the world with people, most of them rickety and wheezing; let us be healthy, and have breathing space.'

'I believe in *that*,' said Carnaby.

'You're going away, then. Where to?'

'That's the point,' replied Hugh, moving uneasily. 'You see, with Sibyl – . I have suggested Davos.* Some people she knows are there – girls who go in for tobogganing, and have a good time. But Sibyl's afraid of the cold. I can't convince her that it's nothing to what we endure here in the beastliness of a London winter. She hates the thought of ice and snow and mountains. A great pity; it would do her no end of good. I suppose we must go to the Riviera.'

He shrugged his shoulders, and for a moment there was silence.

'By-the-bye,' he resumed, 'I have a letter from Miles, and you'd like to see it.'

From a pile of letters on the table he selected one written on two sheets of thin paper, and handed it to Rolfe. The writing was bold, the style vigorous, the matter fresh and interesting. Major Carnaby had no graces of expression; but all the more engrossing was his brief narrative of mountain warfare, declaring its truthfulness in every stroke of the pen.

'Fine fellow!' exclaimed Rolfe, when he had read to the end. 'Splendid fellow!'

'Isn't he! And he's seeing life.'

'That's where you ought to be, my boy,' remarked Rolfe, between puffs of tobacco.

'I dare say. No use thinking about it. Too late.'

'If I had a son,' pursued Harvey, smiling at the hypothesis, 'I think I'd make a fighting man of him, or try to. At all events, he should go out somewhere, and beat the big British drum, one way or another. I believe it's our only hope. We're rotting at home – some of us sunk in barbarism, some coddling themselves in over-refinement. What's the use of preaching peace and civilisation, when we know that England's just beginning her big fight* – the fight that will put all history into the shade! We have to lead the world; it's our destiny; and we must do it by breaking heads. That's the nature of the human animal, and will be for ages to come.'

Carnaby nodded assent.

'If we were all like your brother,' Rolfe went on. 'I'm glad he's fighting in India, and not in Africa. I can't love the buccaneering shopkeeper,* the whisky-distiller with a rifle – ugh!'

'I hate that kind of thing. The gold grubbers and diamond bagmen! But it's part of the march onward. We must have money, you know.'

The speaker's forehead wrinkled, and again he moved uneasily. Rolfe regarded him with a reflective air.

'That man you saw here tonight,' Carnaby went on, 'the short, thick fellow – his name is Dando – he's just come back from Queensland. I don't quite know what he's been doing, but he evidently knows a good deal about mines. He says he has invented a new process for getting gold out of ore – I don't know anything about it. In the early days of mining, he says, no end of valuable stuff was abandoned, because they couldn't smelt it. Something about pyrites* – I have a vague recollection of old chemistry lessons. Dando wants to start smelting works for his new process, somewhere in North Queensland.'

'And wants money, I dare say,' remarked the listener, with a twinkle of the eye.

'I suppose so. It was Carton that brought him here for the first time, a week ago. *Might* be worth thinking about, you know.'

'I have no opinion. My profound ignorance of everything keeps me in a state of perpetual scepticism. It has its advantages, I dare say.'

'You're very conservative, Rolfe, in your finance.'

'Very.'

'Quite right, no doubt. Could you join us at Nice or some such place?'

'Why, I rather thought of sticking to my books. But if the fogs are very bad—'

'And you would seriously advise us to give up the house?'

'My dear fellow, how can you hesitate? Your wife is quite right; there's not one good word to be said for the ordinary life of an English household. Flee from it! Live anywhere and anyhow, but don't keep house in England. Wherever I go, it's the same cry: domestic life is played out. There isn't a servant to be had – unless you're a Duke and breed them on your own estate. All ordinary housekeepers are at the mercy of the filth and insolence of a draggle-tailed, novelette-reading feminine democracy. Before very long we shall train an army of men-servants, and send the women to the devil.'

'Queer thing, Rolfe,' put in his friend, with a laugh; 'I've noticed it of late, you're getting to be a regular woman-hater.'

'Not a bit of it. I hate a dirty, lying, incapable creature, that's all, whether man or woman. No doubt they're more common in petticoats.'

'Been to the Frothinghams' lately?'

'No.'

'I used to think you were there rather often.'

Rolfe gave a sort of grunt, and kept silence.

'To my mind,' pursued the other, 'the best thing about Alma is that she appreciates my wife. She has really a great admiration for Sibyl; no sham about it, I'm sure. I don't pretend to know much about women, but I fancy that kind of thing isn't common – real friendship and admiration between them. People always say so, at all events.'

'I take refuge once more,' said Rolfe, 'in my fathomless ignorance.'

He rose from his chair, and sat down again on a corner of the table. Carnaby stood up, threw his arms above his head, and yawned with animal vehemence, the expression of an intolerable ennui.

'There's something damnably wrong with us all – that's the one thing certain.'

'Idleness, for one thing,' said Rolfe.

'Yes. And I'm too old to do anything. Why didn't I follow Miles into the army? I think I was more cut out for that than for anything else. I often feel I should like to go to South Africa and get up a little war of my own.'

Rolfe shouted with laughter.

'Not half a bad idea, and the easiest thing in the world, no doubt.'

'Nigger-hunting; a superior big game.'

'There's more than that to do in South Africa,' said Harvey. 'I was looking at a map in Stanford's* window the other day, and it amused me. Who believes for a moment that England will remain satisfied with bits here and there? We have to swallow the whole, of course. We shall go on fighting and annexing, until – until the decline and fall of the British Empire. That

hasn't begun yet. Some of us are so over-civilised that it makes
a reaction of wholesome barbarism in the rest. We shall fight
like blazes in the twentieth century. It's the only thing that keeps
Englishmen sound; commercialism is their curse. Happily, no
sooner do they get fat than they kick, and somebody's shin
suffers; then they fight off the excessive flesh. War is England's
Banting.'*

'You'd better not talk like that to Sibyl.'

'Why, frankly, old man, I think that's your mistake. But you'll
tell me, and rightly enough, to mind my own business.'

'Nonsense. What do you mean exactly? You think I ought
to—'

Hugh hesitated, with an air of uneasiness.

'Well,' pursued his friend cautiously, 'do you think it's right
to suppress your natural instincts? Mightn't it give her a new
interest in life if she came round a little to your point of view?'

'Queer thing, how unlike we are, isn't it?' said Carnaby, with
a sudden drop of his tone to amiable ingenuousness. 'But, you
know; we get along together very well.'

'To be sure. Yet you are going to rust in the Riviera when you
want to be on the Himalayas. Wouldn't it do your wife good to
give up her books and her music for a while and taste fresh air?'

'I doubt if she's strong enough for it.'

'It would make her stronger. And here's a good opportunity.
If you give up housekeeping (and housekeepers), why not reform
your life altogether? Go and have a look at Australia.'

'Sibyl hates the sea.'

'She'd soon get over that. Seriously, you ought to think of it.'

Carnaby set his lips and for a moment hung his head.

'You're quite right. But—'

'A little pluck, old fellow.'

'I'll see what can be done. Have another whisky?'

They went out into the hall, where a dim light through
coloured glass illumined a statue in terracotta, some huge
engravings, the massive antlers of an elk, and furniture in carved
oak.

'Queer feeling of emptiness,' said Carnaby, subduing his
voice. 'I feel as if they'd carried off everything, and left bare
walls. Sibyl couldn't stay in the place. Shall I whistle for a cab?
By Jove! that reminds me, the whistle has gone; it happened to
be silver. A wedding present from that fool Benson, who broke

his neck in a steeplechase three weeks after.' Harvey laughed, and stepped out into the watery fog.

## CHAPTER 3

A cab crawling at the upper end of the terrace took him quickly home. He entered with his latch-key as a church clock tolled one.

It was a large house, within a few minutes' walk of Royal Oak Station.* Having struck a match, and lit a candle which stood upon the hall table (indicating that he was the last who would enter tonight), Harvey put up the door-chain and turned the great key, then went quietly upstairs. His rooms were on the first floor. A tenancy of five years, with long absences, enabled him to regard this niche in a characterless suburb as in some sort his home; a familiar smell of books and tobacco welcomed him as he opened the door; remnants of a good fire kept the air warm, and dispersed a pleasant glow. On shelves which almost concealed the walls, stood a respectable collection of volumes, the lowest tier consisting largely of what secondhand booksellers, when invited to purchase, are wont to call 'tomb-stones' – that is to say, old folios, of no great market value, though good brains and infinite labour went to the making of them. A great table, at one end of which was a tray with glasses and a water-bottle, occupied the middle of the floor; nearer the fireplace was a small writing-desk. For pictures little space could be found; but over the mantelpiece hung a fine water-colour, the flood of Tigris and the roofs of Bagdad burning in golden sunset. Harvey had bought it at the gallery in Pall Mall* not long ago; the work of a man of whom he knew nothing; it represented the farthest point of his own travels, and touched profoundly his vague historico-poetic sensibilities.

Three letters lay on the desk. As soon as he had lit his lamp, and exchanged his boots for slippers, he looked at the envelopes, and chose one addressed in a woman's hand. The writer was Mrs Bennet Frothingham.

'We have only just heard, from Mrs Carnaby, that you are back in town. *Could* you spare us tomorrow evening? It would be so nice of you. The quartet will give Beethoven's F minor,* and Alma says it will be well done – the conceit of the child! We hope to have some interesting people. What a shocking affair of poor Mrs Carnaby's! I never knew anything *quite* so bad. – Our united kind regards.'

Harvey thrust out his lips, in an ambiguous expression, as he threw the sheet aside. He mused before opening the next letter. This proved to be of startling contents: a few lines scribbled informally, undated, without signature. A glance at the post-mark discovered 'Liverpool'.

'The children are at my last address – you know it. I can do no more for them. If the shabby Abbotts refuse – as I dare say they will – it wouldn't hurt you to keep them from the workhouse. But it's a devilish hard world, and they must take their chance.'

After a stare and a frown, Harvey woke the echoes with boisterous laughter. It was long since any passage in writing had so irresistibly tickled his sense of humour. Well, he must let Abbott know of this. It might be as well, perhaps, if he called on Mrs Abbott tomorrow, to remove any doubt that might remain in her mind. The fellow Wager being an old acquaintance of his, he could not get rid of a sense of far-off responsibility in this matter; though, happily, Wager's meeting with Mrs Abbott's cousin, which led to marriage and misery, came about quite independently of him.

The last letter he opened without curiosity, but with quiet interest and pleasure. It was dated from Greystone;* the writer, Basil Morton, had a place in his earliest memories, for, as neighbours' children, they had played together long before the grammar-school days which allied him with Hugh Carnaby.

'For aught I know,' began Morton, 'you may at this moment be drifting on the Euphrates, or pondering on the site of Alexandreia Eschate.* It is you who owe me an account of yourself; nevertheless, I am prompted to write, if only to tell you that I have just got the complete set of the Byzantine Historians.* A catalogue tempted me, and I did buy.'

And so on in the same strain, until, in speaking of nearer matters, his style grew simpler.

'Our elder boy begins to put me in a difficulty. As I told you, he has been brought up on the most orthodox lines of Anglicanism; his mother – best of mothers and best of wives, but in this respect atavistic – has had a free hand, and I don't see how it could have been otherwise. But now the lad begins to ask awkward questions, and to put me in a corner; the young rascal is a vigorous dialectician and rationalist – odd result of such training. It becomes a serious question how I am to behave. I cannot bear to distress his mother, yet how can I tell him that I literally believe those quaint old fables? *Solvetur vivendo*,* of course, like everything else, but just now it worries me a little. Generally I can see a pretty clear line of duty; here the duty is divided, with a vengeance. Have you any counsel?'

Harvey Rolfe mumbled impatiently; all domestic matters were a trial to his nerves. It seemed to him an act of unaccountable folly to marry a woman from whom one differed diametrically on subjects that lay at the root of life; and of children he could hardly bring himself to think at all, so exasperating the complication they introduced into social problems which defied common-sense. He disliked children; fled the sight and the sound of them in most cases, and, when this was not possible, regarded them with apprehension, anxiety, weariness, anything but interest. In the perplexity that had come upon him, Basil Morton seemed to have nothing more than his deserts. 'Best of mothers and of wives', forsooth! An excellent housekeeper, no doubt, but what shadow of qualification for wifehood and motherhood in this year 1886? The whole question was disgusting to a rational man – especially to that vigorous example of the class, by name Harvey Rolfe.

Late as it was, he did not care to go to bed. This morning he had brought home a batch of books from the London Library,* and he began to turn them over, with the pleasure of anticipation. Not seldom of late had Harvey flattered himself on the growth of intellectual gusto which proceeded in him together with a perceptible decline of baser appetites, so long his torment and his hindrance. His age was now seven and thirty; at forty he might hope to have utterly trodden under foot the instincts at war with mental calm. He saw before him long years of congenial fellowship, of bracing travel, of well-directed studiousness. Let problems of sex and society go hang! He had found a better way.

On looking back over his life, how improbable it seemed, this happy issue out of crudity, turbulence, lack of purpose, weakness, insincerity, ignorance. First and foremost he had to thank good old Dr Harvey, of Greystone; then, his sister, sleeping in her grave under the old chimes she loved; then, surely himself, that seed of good within him which had survived all adverse influences – watched, surely, by his unconscious self, guarded long, and now deliberately nurtured. Might he not think well of himself.

His library, though for the most part the purchase of late years, contained books which reminded him of every period of his life. Up yonder, on the top shelf, were two score volumes which had belonged to his father, the share that fell to him when he and his sister made the ordained division: scientific treatises out of date, an old magazine, old books of travel. Strange that, in his times of folly, he had not sold these as burdensome rubbish; he was very glad now, when love and reverence for things gone by began to take hold upon him. There, at the same height, stood a rank of school-books preserved for him by his sister till she died; beside them, medical works, relics of his abortive study when he was neither boy nor man. Descending, the eye fell upon yellow and green covers, dozens of French novels, acquired at any time from the year of his majority up to the other day; in the mass, they reminded him of a frothy season, when he boasted a cheap Gallicism, and sneered at all things English. A sprinkling of miscellaneous literature accounted for ten years or more when he cared little to collect books, when the senses raged in him, and only by miracle failed to hurl him down many a steep place. Last came the serious acquisitions, the bulk of his library: solid and expensive works – historians, archæologists, travellers, with noble volumes of engravings, and unwieldy tomes of antique lore. Little enough of all this had Rolfe digested, but more and more he loved to have erudition within his reach. He began to lack room for comely storage; already a large bookcase had intruded into his bedroom. If he continued to purchase, he must needs house himself more amply; yet he dreaded the thought of a removal.

He knew enough and to spare of life in lodgings. His experience began when he came up as a lad to Guy's Hospital, when all lodgings in London shone with the glorious light of liberty. It took a wider scope when, having grasped his little patrimony, he threw physic to the dogs,* and lived as a gentleman at large. In those days he grew familiar with many kinds of 'apartments' and their nomadic denizens. Having wasted his substance, he found refuge in the office of an emigration agent,* where, by slow degrees, he proved himself worth a couple of hundred pounds per annum. This was the 'business' to which Hugh Carnaby vaguely referred when people questioned him concerning his friend's history.

Had he possessed the commercial spirit, Harvey might have made his position in this office much more lucrative. Entering nominally as a clerk, he undertook from the first a variety of duties which could only be discharged by a man of special abilities; for instance, the literary revision of seductive pamphlets and broadsheets issued by his employer to the public contemplating emigration. These advertisements he presently composed, and, from the point of view of effectiveness, did it remarkably well. How far such work might be worthy of an honest man, was another question, which for several years scarcely troubled his conscience. Before long a use was found for his slender medical attainments; it became one of his functions to answer persons who visited the office for information as to the climatic features of this or that new country, and their physical fitness for going out as colonists. Of course, there was demanded of him a radical unscrupulousness, and often enough he proved equal to the occasion; but as time went on, bringing slow development of brain and character, he found these personal interviews anything but agreeable. He had constantly before him the spectacle of human misery and defeat, now and then in such dread forms that his heart sank and his tongue refused to lie. When disgust made him contemplate the possibility of finding more honourable employment, the manifest difficulties deterred him.

He held the place for nearly ten years, living in the end so soberly and frugally that his two hundred pounds seemed a considerable income; it enabled him to spend his annual month of holiday in continental travel, which now had a significance very different from that of his truancies in France or Belgium before he began to earn a livelihood. Two deaths, a year's interval between them, released him from his office. Upon these events and their issue he had not counted; independence came to him as a great surprise, and on the path of self-knowledge he had far to travel before the significance of that and many another turning-point grew clear to his backward gaze.

Seeking for a comfortable abode, he discovered these rooms

in Bayswater. They were to let furnished, the house being occupied by a widow not quite of the ordinary type of landlady, who entertained only bachelors, and was fairly conscientious in the discharge of her obligations. Six months later, during Harvey's absence abroad, this woman died, and on his return the house had already been stripped of furniture. For a moment he inclined to take a house of his own, but from this perilous experiment he was saved by an intimation that, if he were willing to supply himself with furniture and service, an incoming tenant would let him occupy his old quarters. Harvey grasped at the offer. His landlord was a man named Buncombe, a truss manufacturer, who had two children, and seemingly no wife. The topmost storey Buncombe assigned to relatives of his own – a middle-aged woman, Mrs Handover, with a sickly grown-up son, who took some part in the truss business. For a few weeks Rolfe was waited upon by a charwoman, whom he paid extravagantly for a maximum of dirt and discomfort; then the unsatisfactory person fell ill, and, whilst cursing his difficulties, Harvey was surprised by a visit from Mrs Handover, who made an unexpected suggestion – would Mr Rolfe accept her services in lieu of the charwoman's, paying her whatever he had been accustomed to give? The proposal startled him. Mrs Handover seemed to belong pretty much to his own rank of life; he was appalled at the thought of bidding her scrub floors and wash plates; and indeed it had begun to dawn upon him that, for a man with more than nine hundred a year, he was living in a needlessly uncomfortable way. On his reply that he thought of removing, Mrs Handover fell into profound depression, and began to disclose her history. Very early in life she had married a man much beneath her in station, with the natural result. After some years of quarrelling, which culminated in personal violence on her husband's part, she obtained a judicial separation. For a long time the man had ceased to send her money, and indeed he was become a vagabond pauper, from whom nothing could be obtained; she depended upon her son, and on the kindness of Buncombe, who asked no rent. If she could earn a little money by work, she would be much happier, and with tremulous hope she had taken this step of appealing to her neighbour in the house.

Harvey could not resist these representations. When the new arrangement had been in operation for a week or so, Harvey began to reflect upon Mrs Handover's personal narrative, and in some respects to modify his first impulsive judgment thereon. It seemed to him not impossible that Mr Handover's present condition of vagabond pauper might be traceable to his marriage with a woman who had never learnt the elements of domestic duty. Thoroughly well-meaning, Mrs Handover was the most incompetent of housewives. Yet such was Harvey Rolfe's delicacy, and so intense his moral cowardice, that year after year he bore with Mrs Handover's defects, and paid her with a smile the wages of two first-rate servants. Dust lay thick about him; he had grown accustomed to it, as to many another form of sluttishness. After all, he possessed a quiet retreat for studious hours, and a tolerable sleeping-place, with the advantage of having his correspondence forwarded to him when he chose to wander. To be sure, it was not final; one would not wish to grow old and die amid such surroundings; sooner or later, circumstance would prompt the desirable change. Circumstance, at this stage of his career, was Harvey's god; he waited upon its direction with an air of wisdom, of mature philosophy.

Of his landlord, Buncombe, he gradually learnt all that he cared to know. The moment came when Buncombe grew confidential, and he, too, had a matrimonial history to disclose. Poverty played no part in it; his business flourished, and Mrs Buncombe, throughout a cohabitation of five years, made no complaint of her lot. All at once – so asserted Buncombe – the lady began to talk of dullness; for a few months she moped, then of a sudden left home, and in a day or two announced by letter that she had taken a place as barmaid at a music-hall. There followed an interview between husband and wife, with the result, said Buncombe, that they parted the best of friends, but with an understanding that Mrs Buncombe should be free to follow her own walk in life, with a moderate allowance to supplement what she could earn. That was five years ago. Mrs Buncombe now sang at second-rate halls, and enjoyed a certain popularity, which seemed to her an ample justification of the independence she had claimed. She was just thirty, tolerably good-looking, and full of the enjoyment of life. Her children, originally left in the care of her mother, whom Buncombe supported, were now looked after by the two servants of the house, and Buncombe seemed to have no conscientious troubles on that score; to Harvey Rolfe's eye it was plain that the brother and sister were growing up as vicious little savages, but he permitted himself no remark on the subject.

After a few conversations, he gained an inkling of Buncombe's motive in taking a house so much larger than he needed. This magnificence was meant as an attraction to the roaming wife, whom, it was clear, Buncombe both wished and hoped to welcome back before very long. She did occasionally visit the house, though only for an hour or two; just to show, said Buncombe, that there was no ill-feeling. On his part, evidently, there was none whatever. An easy-going, simple-minded fellow, aged about forty, with a boyish good temper and no will to speak of, he seemed never to entertain a doubt of his wife's honesty, and in any case would probably have agreed, on the least persuasion, to let bygones be bygones. He spoke rather proudly than otherwise of Mrs Buncombe's artistic success.

'It isn't every woman could have done it, you know, Mr Rolfe.'

'It is not,' Harvey assented.

Only those rooms were furnished which the little family used, five or six in all; two or three stood vacant, and served as playgrounds for the children in bad weather. Of his relatives at the top, Buncombe never spoke; he either did not know, or viewed with indifference, the fact that Mrs Handover served his lodger in a menial capacity. About once a month he invited three or four male friends to a set dinner, and hilarity could be heard until long after midnight. Altogether it was a strange household, and, as he walked about the streets of the neighbourhood, Harvey often wondered what abnormalities even more striking might be concealed behind the meaningless uniformity of these heavily respectable housefronts. As a lodger he was content to dwell here; but sometimes by a freak of imagination he pictured himself a married man, imprisoned with wife and children amid these leagues of dreary, inhospitable brickwork, and a great horror fell upon him.

No. In his time he had run through follies innumerable, but from the supreme folly of hampering himself by marriage, a merciful fate had guarded him. It was probably the most remarkable fact of his life; it heightened his self-esteem, and appeared to warrant him in the assurance that a destiny so protective would round the close of his days with tranquillity and content.

Upon this thought he lay down to rest. For half an hour Basil Morton's letter had occupied his mind: he had tried to think out the problem it set forth, not to leave his friend quite unanswered; but weariness prevailed, and with it the old mood of self-congratulation.

Next morning the weather was fine; that is to say, one could read without artificial light, and no rain fell, and far above the house-tops appeared a bluish glimmer, shot now and then with pale yellowness. Harvey decided to carry out his intention of calling upon Mrs Abbott. She lived at Kilburn,* and thither he drove shortly before twelve o'clock. He was admitted to a very cosy room, where, amid books and pictures, and by a large fire, the lady of the house sat reading. Whatever the cause, it seemed to him that his welcome fell short of cordiality, and he hastened to excuse himself for intruding at so early an hour.

'I received a letter last night which I thought you had better know of without delay.'

'From that man – Mr Wager?' said Mrs Abbott quickly and hopefully, her face brightening.

'Yes. But there's nothing satisfactory in it. He writes from Liverpool, and merely says that the children are at his lodgings, and he can do no more for them.'

Mrs Abbott set her lips in an expression almost of sullenness. Rolfe had never seen her look thus, but it confirmed a suspicion which he had harboured concerning her. Why, he hardly knew – for she always presented a face of amiability, and talked in gentle, womanly tones – a doubt as to Abbott's domestic felicity haunted his mind. Perhaps he now saw her, for the first time, as she commonly appeared to her husband – slightly peevish, unwilling to be disturbed, impatient when things did not run smoothly.

'You saw my husband yesterday?' was her next remark, not very graciously uttered.

'We met in the street last night – before I got Wager's letter. He was suffering horribly from neuralgia.'

Harvey could not forbear to add this detail, but he softened his voice and smiled.

'I don't wonder at it,' returned the lady; 'he takes no care of himself.'

Harvey glanced about the room. Its furnishing might be called luxurious, and the same standard of comfort prevailed through the house. Considering that Edgar Abbott, as Rolfe knew, married on small means, and that he had toiled unremittingly to support a home in which he could seldom enjoy an hour's leisure, there seemed no difficulty in explaining this neglect of his own health. It struck the visitor that Mrs Abbott might have taken such considerations into account, and have spoken of the good fellow more sympathetically. In truth, Harvey did not quite like Mrs Abbott. Her age was about seven and twenty. She came of poor folk, and had been a high-school teacher; very clever and successful, it was said, and Harvey could believe it. Her features were regular, and did not lack sweetness; yet, unless an observer were mistaken, the last year or two had emphasised a certain air of conscious superiority, perchance originating in the schoolroom. She had had one child; it struggled through a few months of sickly life, and died of convulsions during its mother's absence at a garden-party. To all appearances, her grief at the loss betokened tenderest feeling. When, in half a year's time, she again came forth into the world, a change was noted; her character seemed to have developed a new energy, she exhibited wider interests, and stepped from the background to become a leader in the little circle of her acquaintances.

'Have you read this?' asked his hostess abruptly, holding up to him a French volume, Ribot's *L'Hérédité Psychologique*.*

'No. That kind of thing doesn't interest me much.'

'Indeed! I find it *intensely* interesting.'

Harvey rose; he was in no mood for this kind of small-talk. But no sooner had he quitted his chair, than Mrs Abbott threw her book aside, and spoke in another tone, seriously, though still with a perceptible accent of annoyance.

'Of course that man's children are here, and I suppose it is our duty to provide for them till some other arrangement is made. But I think we ought to put the matter in the hands of the police. Don't you, Mr Rolfe?'

'I'm afraid there's small chance of making their father support them. He is certainly out of England by now, and won't easily be caught.'

'The worst of it is, they are anything but *nice* children. What could one expect with such a father? Since their poor mother died, they have been in the hands of horrible people – low-class landladies, no doubt; their talk shocks me. The last amusement they had, was to be taken by somebody to Tussaud's,* and now they can talk of nothing but "the hunted murderer" – one sees it on the walls, you know; and they play at being murderer and policeman, one trying to escape the other. Pretty play for children of five and seven, isn't it?'

Rolfe made a gesture of disgust.

'I know the poor things can't help it,' pursued Mrs Abbott, with softer feeling, 'but it turns me against them. From seeing so little of their father, they have even come to talk with a vulgar pronunciation, like children out of the streets – almost. It's dreadful! When I think of my cousin – such a sweet, good girl, and *these* her children – oh, it's horrible!'

'They are very young,' said Harvey, in a low voice, perturbed in spite of himself. 'With good training—'

'Yes, of course we must put them in good hands somewhere.'

Plainly it had never occurred to Mrs Abbott that such a task as this might, even temporarily, be undertaken by herself; her one desire was to get rid of the luckless brats, that their vulgarity might not pain her, and the care of them encumber her polite leisure.

After again excusing himself for this call, and hearing his apology this time more graciously received, Harvey withdrew from the cosy study, and left Mrs, Abbott to her *Hérédité Psychologique*. On his way to lunch in town, he thought of the overworn journalist groaning with neuralgia, and wondered how Mrs Abbott would relish a removal to the town of Waterbury.

## CHAPTER 4

Uncertain to the last moment, Harvey did at length hurry into his dress clothes, and start for Fitzjohn Avenue.* He had little mind for the semi-fashionable crowd and the amateur music, but he could not answer Mrs Bennet Frothingham with any valid excuse, and, after all, she meant kindly towards him. Why he enjoyed so much of this lady's favour it was not easy to understand; intellectual sympathy there could be none between them, and as for personal liking, on his side it did not go beyond that naturally excited by a good-natured, feather-brained, rather pretty woman, whose sprightliness never passed the limits of decorum, and who seemed to have better qualities than found scope in her butterfly existence. Perhaps he amused her, being so unlike the kind of man she was accustomed to see. His acquaintance with the family dated from their social palingenesis,* when, after obscure prosperity in a southern suburb, they fluttered to the northern heights, and were observed of the paragraphists. Long before that, Bennet Frothingham had been known in the money-market; it was the 'Britannia' – Loan, Assurance, Investment, and Banking Company, Limited – that made him nationally prominent, and gave an opportunity to his wife (in second marriage) and his daughter (by the first). Three years ago, when Carnaby (already lured by the charms of Sibyl Larkfield) presented his friend Rolfe as 'the man who had been to Bagdad', Alma Frothingham, not quite twenty-one, was studying at the Royal Academy of Music, and, according to her friends, promised to excel alike on the piano and the violin, having at the same time a 'really remarkable' contralto voice. Of late the young lady had abandoned singing, rarely used the pianoforte, and seemed satisfied to achieve distinction as a violinist. She had founded an Amateur Quartet Society, whose performances were frequently to be heard at the house in Fitzjohn Avenue.

Last winter Harvey had chanced to meet Alma and her stepmother at Leipzig, at a Gewandhaus* concert. He was invited to go with them to hear the boys' motet at the Thomaskirche;* and with this intercourse began the change in their relations from mere acquaintance to something like friendship. Through the following spring Rolfe was a familiar figure at the Frothinghams'; but this form of pleasure soon wearied him, and he was glad to escape from London in June. He knew the shadowy and intermittent temptation which beckoned him to that house; music had power over him, and he grew conscious of watching Alma Frothingham, her white little chin on the brown fiddle, with too exclusive an interest. When 'that fellow' Cyrus Redgrave, a millionaire, or something of the sort, began to attend these gatherings with a like assiduity, and to win more than his share of Miss Frothingham's conversation, Harvey felt a disquietude which happily took the form of disgust, and it was easy enough to pack his portmanteau.

Through the babble of many voices in many keys, talk
mingling with laughter more or less melodiously subdued, he
made his way up the great staircase. As he neared the landing,
there sounded the shrill squeak of a violin and a 'cello's deep
harmonic growl. His hostess, small, slender, fair, and not yet
forty, a jewel-flash upon her throat and in the tiara above her
smooth low forehead, took a step forward to greet him.

'Really? How delightful! I shot at a venture, and it was a hit
after all!'

'They are just beginning?'

'The quartet – yes. Herr Wilenski has promised to play
afterwards.'

He moved on, crossed a small drawing-room, entered the
larger room sacred to music, and reached a seat in the nick of
time. Miss Frothingham, the violin against her shoulder, was
casting a final glance at the assembly, the glance which could
convey a noble severity when it did not forthwith impose silence.
A moment's perfect stillness, and the quartet began. There were
two ladies, two men. Miss Frothingham played the first violin,
Mr Æneas Piper the second; the 'cello was in the hands of Herr
Gassner, and the viola yielded its tones to Miss Dora Leach.
Harvey knew them all, but had eyes only for one; in truth, only
one rewarded observation. Miss Leach was a meagre blonde,
whose form, face, and attitude enhanced by contrast the graces
of the First Violin. Alma's countenance shone – possibly with
the joy of the artist, perhaps only with gratified vanity. As she
grew warm, the rosy blood mantled in her cheeks and flushed
her neck. Every muscle and nerve tense as the strings from which
she struck music, she presently swayed forward on the points of
her feet, and seemed to gain in stature, to become a more
commanding type. Her features suggested neither force of
intellect or originality of character: but they had beauty, and
something more. She stood a fascination, an allurement, to the
masculine sense. Harvey Rolfe had never so responded to this
quality in the girl; the smile died from his face as he regarded
her. Of her skill as a musician, he could form no judgment; but
it seemed to him that she played very well, and he had heard her
praised by people who understood the matter; for instance, Herr
Wilenski, the virtuoso, from whom – in itself a great compliment
– Alma was having lessons.

He averted his eyes, and began to seek for known faces among

the audience. His host he could not discover; Mr Frothingh.
must be away from home this evening; it was seldom he failed
to attend Alma's concerts. But near the front sat Mrs Ascott
Larkfield, a dazzling figure, and, at some distance, her daughter
Mrs Carnaby, no shadow of gloom upon her handsome features.
Hugh was not in sight; probably he felt in no mood for parties.
Next to Mrs Carnaby sat 'that fellow', Cyrus Redgrave, smiling
as always, and surveying the people near him from under
drooping brows, his head slightly bent. Mr Redgrave had thin
hair, but a robust moustache and a short peaked beard; his
complexion was a rifle sallow; he lolled upon the chair, so that,
at moments, his head all but brushed Mrs Carnaby's shoulder.

Long before the close of the piece, Rolfe had ceased to listen,
his thoughts drifting hither and thither on a turbid flood of
emotion. During the last passage – *allegro molto leggieramente*
– he felt a movement round about him as a general relief, and
when, on the last note, there broke forth (familiar ambiguity)
sounds of pleasure and of applause, he at once stood up. But he
had no intention of pressing into the throng that rapidly
surrounded the musicians. Seeing that Mr Redgrave had vacated
his place, whilst Mrs Carnaby remained seated, he stepped
forward to speak with his friend's wife. She smiled up at him,
and lifted a gloved finger.

'No! Please don't!'

'Not sit down by you?'

'Oh, certainly. But I saw condolence in your face, and I'm
tired of it. Besides, it would be mere hypocrisy in you.'

Harvey gave a silent laugh. He had tried to understand Sibyl
Carnaby, and at different times had come to very different
conclusions regarding her. All women puzzled, and often discon-
certed, him; with Sibyl he could never talk freely, knowing not
whether to dislike or to admire her. He was not made on the
pattern of Cyrus Redgrave, who probably viewed womankind
with instinctive contempt, yet pleased all with the flattery of his
homage.

'Well, then, we won't talk of it,' he said, noticing, in the same
moment, that her person did not lack the adornment of jewels.
Perhaps she had happened to be wearing these things on the
evening of the robbery; but Rolfe felt a conviction that, under
any circumstances, Sibyl would not be without rings and
bracelets.

'They certainly improve,' she remarked, indicating the quartet with the tip of her fan.

Her opinions were uttered with calm assurance, whatever the subject. An infinite self-esteem, so placid that it never suggested the vulgarity of conceit, shone in her large eyes and dwelt upon the beautiful curve of her lips. No face could be of purer outline, of less sensual suggestiveness; it wore at times an air of cold abstraction which was all but austerity. Rolfe imagined her the most selfish of women, thought her incapable of sentiment; yet how was her marriage to be accounted for, save by supposing that she fell in love with Hugh Carnaby? Such a woman might surely have sold herself to great advantage; and yet – odd incongruity – she did not impress one as socially ambitious. Her mother, the ever-youthful widow, sped from assembly to assembly, unable to live save in the whirl of fashion; not so Sibyl. Was she too proud, too self-centred? And what ambition did she nourish?

Or was it all an illusion of the senses? Suppose her a mere graven image, hollow, void. Call her merely a handsome woman, with the face of some remarkable ancestress, with just enough of warmth to be subdued by the vigorous passion of such a fine fellow as Carnaby. On the whole, Rolfe preferred this hypothesis. He had never heard her say anything really bright, or witty, or significant. But Hugh spoke of her fiine qualities of head and heart; Alma Frothingham made her an exemplar, and would not one woman see through the vacuous pretentiousness of another?

Involuntarily, he was gazing at her, trying to read her face.

'So you think we ought to go to Australia,' said Sibyl quietly, returning his look.

Hugh had repeated the conversation of last night; indiscreet, but natural. One could not suppose that Hugh kept many secrets from his wife.

'I?' He was confused. 'Oh, we were talking about the miseries of housekeeping—'

'I hate the name of those new countries.'

It was said smilingly, but with what expression in the word 'hate'!

'Vigorous cuttings from the old tree,' said Rolfe. 'There is England's future.'

'Perhaps so. At present they are barbarous, and I have a decided preference for civilisation. So have you, I am quite sure.'

Rolfe murmured his assent; whereupon Sibyl rose, just bent her head to him, and moved with graceful indolence away.

'Now she hates *me*,' Harvey said in his mind; 'and much I care!'

As a matter of courtesy, he thought it well to move in Miss Frothingham's direction. The crowd was thinning; without difficulty he approached to within a few yards of her, and there exchanged a word or two with the player of the viola, Miss Leach – a good, ingenuous creature, he had always thought; dangerous to no man's peace, but rather sentimental, and on that account to be avoided. Whilst talking, he heard a man's voice behind him, pretentious, coarse, laying down the law in a musical discussion.

'No, no; Beethoven is not *Klaviermäszig*.* His thoughts are symphonic – they need the orchestra ... A string quartet is to a symphony what a delicate water-colour is to an oil-painting ... Oh, I don't care for his playing at all! he has not – what shall I call it? – *Sehnsucht*.'*

Rolfe turned at length to look. A glance showed him a tall, bony young man, with a great deal of disorderly hair, and shaven face; harsh-featured, sensual, utterly lacking refinement. He inquired of Miss Leach who this might be, and learnt that the man's name was Felix Dymes.

'Isn't he a humbug?'

The young lady was pained and shocked.

'Oh, he is very clever,' she whispered. 'He has composed a most beautiful song – don't you know it? – "Margot". It's very likely that Topham may sing it at one of the Ballad Concerts.'

'Now I've offended *her*,' said Rolfe to himself. 'No matter.'

Seeing his opportunity, he took a few steps, and stood before Alma Frothingham. She received him very graciously, looking him straight in the face, with that amused smile which he could never interpret. Did it mean that she thought him 'good fun'? Had she discussed him with Sibyl Carnaby, and heard things of him that moved her mirth? Or was it pure good nature, the overflowing spirits of a vivacious girl?

'So good of you to come, Mr Rolfe. And what did you think of us?'

This was characteristic. Alma delighted in praise, and never hesitated to ask for it. She hung eagerly upon his unready words.

'I only show my ignorance when I talk of music. Of course, I liked it.'

'Ah! then you didn't think it very good. I see—'

'But I *did*! Only my opinion is worthless.'

Alma looked at him, seemed to hesitate, laughed; and Harvey felt the conviction that, by absurd sincerity, he had damaged himself in the girl's eyes. What did it matter?

'I've been practising five hours a day,' said Alma, in rapid, ardent tones. Her voice was as pleasant to the ear as her face to look upon; richly feminine, a call to the emotions. 'That isn't bad, is it?'

'Tremendous energy!'

'Oh, music is my religion, you know. I often feel sorry I haven't to get my living by it; it's rather wretched to be only an amateur, don't you think?'

'Religion shouldn't be marketable,' joked Harvey.

'Oh, but you know what I mean. You are *so* critical, Mr Rolfe. I've a good mind to ask Father to turn me out of house and home, with just half-a-crown. Then I might really do something. It would be splendid! – Oh, what do you think of that shameful affair in Hamilton Terrace? Mrs Carnaby takes it like an angel. They're going to give up housekeeping. Very sensible, I say. Everybody will do it before long. Why should we be plagued with private houses?'

'There are difficulties—'

'Of course there are, and men seem to enjoy pointing them out. They think it a crime if women hate the bother and misery of housekeeping.

'I am not so conservative.'

He tried to meet her eyes, which were gleaming fixedly upon him; but his look fell, and turned as quickly from the wonderful white shoulders, the throbbing throat, the neck that showed its colour against swan's-down. To his profound annoyance, someone intervened – a lady bringing someone else to be introduced. Rolfe turned on his heel, and was face to face with Cyrus Redgrave. Nothing could be suaver or more civil than Mr Redgrave's accost; he spoke like a polished gentleman, and, for aught Harvey knew, did not misrepresent himself. But Rolfe had a prejudice; he said as little as possible, and moved on.

In the smaller drawing-room he presently conversed with his hostess. Mrs Frothingham's sanguine and buoyant temper seemed proof against fatigue; at home or as a guest she wore the same look of enjoyment; vexations, rivalries, responsibilities, left no trace upon her beaming countenance. Her affections were numberless; her ignorance, as an observer easily discovered, was vast and profound; but the desire to please, the tact of a gentlewoman, and thorough goodness of heart, appeared in all her sayings and doings; she was never offensive, never wholly ridiculous. Small-talk flowed from her with astonishing volubility, tone and subject dictated by the characteristics of the person with whom she gossiped; yet her preference was for talk on homely topics, reminiscences of a time when she knew not luxury. 'You may not believe it,' she said to him in a moment of confidence, 'but I assure you I am a very good cook.' Rolfe did not quite credit the assurance, but he felt it not improbable that Mrs Frothingham would accept a reverse of fortune with much practical philosophy; he could imagine her brightening a small house with the sweetness of her disposition, and falling to humble duties with sprightly goodwill. In this point she was a noteworthy exception among the prosperous women of his acquaintance.

'And what have you been doing?' she asked, not as a mere phrase of civility, but in a voice and which a look of genuine interest.

'Wasting my time, for the most part.'

'So you always say; but it can't be true. I know the kind of man who wastes his time, and you're not a bit like him. Nothing would gratify my curiosity more than to be able to watch you through a whole day. What did you think of the quartet?'

'Capital!'

'I'm sure they would make wonderful progress, and Alma does work so hard! I'm only afraid she may injure her health.'

'I see no sign of it yet.'

'She's certainly looking very well,' said Mrs Frothingham, with manifest pride and affection. Of Alma she always spoke thus; nothing of the step-mother was ever observable.

'Mr Frothingham is not here this evening!'

'I really don't know why,' replied the hostess, casting her eyes round the room. 'I quite expected him. But he has been dreadfully busy the last few weeks. And people do worry him so. Somebody called whilst we were at dinner, and refused to believe that Mr Frothingham was not at home, and made quite a disturbance at the door – so they told me afterwards. I'm really quite nervous sometimes; crazy people are always wanting to see him – people who really ought not to be at large. No doubt they have had their troubles, poor things; and everybody thinks my husband can make them rich if only he chooses.'

A stout, important-looking man paused before Mrs Frothingham, and spoke familiarly.

'I'm looking for B. F. Hasn't he put in an appearance yet?'

'I really hope he's enjoying himself somewhere else,' replied the hostess, rising, with a laugh. 'You leave him no peace.'

The stout man did not smile, but looked gravely for a moment at Rolfe, a stranger to him, and turned away.

Herr Wilenski, the virtuoso, was about to play something; the guests moved to seat themselves. Rolfe, however, preferred to remain in this room, where he could hear the music sufficiently well. He had not quite recovered from his chagrin at the interruption of his talk with Alma – a foolishness which made him impatient with himself. At the same time, he kept thinking of the 'crazy people' of whom Mrs Frothinham spoke so lightly. A man such as Bennet Frothingham must become familiar with many forms of 'craziness', must himself be responsible for a good deal of folly such as leads to downright aberration. Recalling Mrs Frothingham's innocent curiosity concerning his own life, Harvey wished, in turn, that it were possible for him to watch and comprehend the business of a great finance-gambler through one whole day. What monstrous cruelties and mendacities might underlie the surface of this gay and melodious existence! Why was the stout man looking for 'B. F.'? Why did he turn away with such a set countenance? Why was that old bore at the club in such a fidget about the 'Britannia'?

Ha! There indeed sounded the violin! It needed no technical intelligence to distinguish between the playing of Wilenski and that of Alma Frothingham. Her religion, forsooth! Herr Wilenski, one might be sure, talked little enough about his 'religion'. What did Alma think as she listened? Was she overcome by the despair of the artist-soul struggling in its immaturity? Or did she smile, as ever, and congratulate herself on the five hours a day, and tell herself how soon she would reach perfection if there were real necessity for it? Hopeless to comprehend a woman.

The senses warred upon the wit; seized by calenture,* one saw through radiant mists.

He did not like the name 'Alma'. It had a theatrical sound, a suggestion of unreality.

The *maestro* knew his audience; he played but for a quarter of an hour, and the babble of tongues began again. Rolfe, sauntering before the admirable pictures which hung here as a mere symbol of wealth, heard a voice at his shoulder.

'I'm very thirsty. Will you take me down?'

His heart leapt with pleasure; Alma must have seen it in his eyes as he turned.

'What did Wilenski play?' he asked confusedly, as they moved towards the staircase.

'Something of Grieg's Mr Wilbraham is going to sing "Wie bist du, meine Königinn"* – Brahms, you know. But you don't really care for music.'

'What an astounding accusation!'

'You don't really care for it. I've known that since we were at Leipzig.'

'I have never pretended to appreciate music as you do. That needs education, and something more. Some music wearies me, there's no denying it.'

'You like the Melody in F?'*

'Yes, I do.'

Alma laughed, with superiority, but not ill-naturedly.

'And I think it detestable – but of course that doesn't matter. When I talk about books you think me a nincompoop. – That word used to amuse me so when I was a child. I remember laughing wildly whenever I saw or heard it. It *is* a funny word, isn't it?'

'The last I should apply to you,' said Rolfe in an absent undertone, as he caught a glimpse of the white teeth between her laughing lips.

They entered the supper-room, where as yet only a few people were refreshing themselves. Provisions for a regiment spread before the gaze; delicacies innumerable invited the palate: this house was famed for its hospitable abundance. Alma, having asked her companion to get her some lemonade, talked awhile with two ladies who had begun to eat and drink in a serious spirit; waiting for her, Rolfe swallowed two glasses of wine to counteract a certain dullness and literalness which were wont to possess him in such company.

'I won't sit down,' she said. 'No, thanks, nothing to eat. I wonder where Papa is? Now, *he* enjoys music, though he is no musician. I think Papa a wonderful man. For years he has never had more than six hours sleep; and the work he does! He *can't* take a holiday; idleness makes him ill. We were down in Hampshire in July with some relatives of Mamma's – the quietest, sleepiest village – and Papa tried to spend a few days with us, but he had to take to flight; he would have perished of ennui.'

'Life at high pressure,'* remarked Rolfe, as the least offensive comment he could make.

'Yes; and isn't it better than life at low?' exclaimed the girl, with animation. 'Most people go through existence without once exerting all the powers that are in them. I should hate to die with the thought that I hadn't really lived myself *out*. A year ago Papa took me into the City to see the offices of *Stock and Share*, just after the paper started. It didn't interest me very much; but I pretended it did, because Papa always takes an interest in *my* affairs. But I found there was something else. After we had seen the printing machinery, and so on, he took me up to the top of the building into a small room, where there was just a table and a chair and a bookshelf; and he told me it was his first office, the room in which he had begun business thirty years ago. He has always kept it for his own, and just as it was – a fancy of his. There's no harm in my telling you; he's very proud of it, and so am I. That's energy!'

'Very interesting indeed.'

'I must go up again,' she added quickly. 'Oh, there's miss Beaufoy; do let me introduce you to Miss Beaufoy.'

She did so, unaware of Rolfe's groaning reluctance, and at once disappeared.

The supper-room began to fill. As soon as he could escape from Miss Beaufoy, who had a cavalier of her own, Harvey ascended the stairs again, and found a quiet corner, where he sat for a quarter of an hour undisturbed. Couples and groups paused to talk near him, and whenever he caught a sentence it was the merest chatter, meaningless repetition of commonplaces which, but for habit, must have been an unutterable weariness to the least intelligent of mortals. He was resolved never to come here again; never again to upset his peace of mind and sully his self-respect by grimacing amid such a crowd. He enjoyed human fellowship, timely merry-making; but to throng one's house with people for whom, with one or two exceptions, one cared not a snap of the fingers, what was this but sheer vulgarism? As for Alma Frothingham, long ago he had made up his mind about her. Naturally, inevitably, she absorbed the vulgarity of her atmosphere. All she did was for effect: it was her cue to pose as the artist; she would keep it up through life, and breathe her last, amid perfumes, declaring that she had 'lived herself out'.

In his peevishness he noticed that women came up from supper with flushed cheeks and eyes unnaturally lustrous. What a grossly sensual life was masked by their airs and graces! He had half a mind to start tomorrow for the Syrian deserts.

'Do let us see you again soon,' said his hostess, as he took leave of her. 'Come in at five o'clock on Wednesday, that's our quiet day; only a few of our *real* friends. We shall be in town till Christmas, for certain.'

On the stairs he passed Mr Felix Dymes, the composer of 'Margot'.

'Oh, it's the easiest thing in the world,' Mr Dymes was saying, 'to compose a song that will be popular. I'll give you the recipe, and charge nothing. You must have a sudden change to the minor, and a waltz refrain – that's all. Oh yes, there's money in it. I know a man who—'

Rolfe had never left the house in such a bad temper.

## CHAPTER 5

When he awoke next morning, the weather was so gloomy that he seriously resumed his thought of getting away from London. Why, indeed, did he make London his home, when it would be easy to live in places vastly more interesting, and under a pure sky? He was a citizen of no city at all, and had less desire than ever to bind himself to a permanent habitation. All very well so long as he kept among his male friends, at the club and elsewhere; but this 'society' played the deuce with him, and he had not the common-sense, the force of resolve, to keep out of it altogether.

Well, he must go to his bank this morning, to draw cash.

It was about twelve o'clock when he stood at the counter, waiting with his cheque. The man before him talked with the teller.

'Do you know that the "Britannia" has shut up?'

'The bank? No!'

'But it has. I passed just now, and there were a lot of people standing about. Closed at half-past eleven, they say.'

Harvey had a singular sensation, a tremor at his heart, a flutter of the pulses, a turning cold and hot; then he was quite calm again, and said to himself, 'Of course.' For a minute or two the quiet routine of the bank was suspended; the news passed from mouth to mouth; newcomers swelled a gossiping group in front of the counter, and Harvey listened. The general tone was cynical; there sounded scarcely a note of indignation; no one present seemed to be personally affected by the disaster. The name of Bennet Frothingham was frequently pronounced, with unflattering comments.

'Somebody'll get it hot,' remarked one of the speakers; and the others laughed.

Rolfe, having transacted his business, walked away. It struck him that he would go and look at the closed bank, but he did not remember the address; a policeman directed him, and he walked on, the distance not being very great. At the end of the street in which the building stood, signs of the unusual became observable – the outskirts of a crowd, hanging loose in animated talk, as after some exciting occurrence; and before the bank itself was gathered a throng of men, respectability's silk hats mingling with the felts and caps of lower strata. Here and there a voice could be heard raised in anger, but the prevailing emotion seemed to be mere curiosity. The people who would suffer most from the collapse of this high-sounding enterprise could not reach the scene of calamity at half an hour's notice; they were dwellers in many parts of the British Isles, strangers most of them to London city, with but a vague mental picture of the local habitation of the Britannia Loan, Assurance, Investment, and Banking Company, Limited.

His arm was seized, and a voice said hoarsely in his ear –

'By God! too late.'

Hugh Carnaby had tumbled out of a cab, and saw his friend in the same moment that he got near enough to perceive that the doors of the bank were shut.

'The thieves have lost no time,' he added, pale with fury.

'You had warning of it?'

Hugh pulled him a few yards away, and whispered –

'Bennet Frothingham shot himself last night.'

Again Harvey experienced that disagreeable heart-shock, with the alternation of hot and cold.

'Where? At home?'

'At the office of *Stock and Share*. Come farther away. It'll be in the evening papers directly, but I don't want those black-guards to hear me. I got up late this morning, and as I was having breakfast, Sibyl rushed in. She brought the news; had it from some friend of her mother's, a man connected somehow with *Stock and Share*. I thought they would shut up shop, and came to try and save Sibyl's balance – a couple of hundred, that's all – but they've swallowed it with the rest.'

'With the rest?'

Hugh laughed mockingly.

'Of hers. Devilish bad luck Sibyl has. It was just a toss-up that a good deal of my own wasn't in, one way or another.'

'Do you know any more about Frothingham?'

'No. Only the fact. Don't know when it was, or when it got known. We shall have it from the papers presently. I think every penny Mrs Larkfield had was in.'

'But it may not mean absolute ruin,' urged Harvey.

'I know what to think when B. F. commits suicide. We shall hear that some of the others have bolted. It'll be as clean a sweep as our housekeeper's little job.'

'I've had queer presentiments,' Harvey murmured.

'Why, damn it, so have I! So had lots of people. But nobody ever does anything till it's too late. I must get home again with my agreeable news. You'll be going to the club, I dare say? They'll have plenty to talk about for the next month or two.'

'Try to come round tonight to my place.'

'Perhaps. It depends on fifty chances. There's only one thing I know for certain – that I shall get out of this cursed country as soon as possible.'

They parted, and Harvey walked westward. He had no reason for hurry; as usual, the tumult of the world's business passed him by; he was merely a looker-on. It occurred to him that it might be a refreshing and a salutary change if for once he found himself involved in the anxieties to which other men were subject; this long exemption and security fostered a too exclusive regard of self, an inaptitude for sympathetic emotion, which he recognised as the defect of his character. This morning's events had startled him, and given a shock to his imagination; but already he viewed them and their consequences with a self-possession which differed little from unconcern. Bennet Frothingham, no doubt, had played a rascally game, foreseeing all along the issues of defeat. As to his wife and daughter, it would be strange if they were not provided for; suffer who might, they would probably live on in material comfort, and nowadays that was the first consideration. He was surprised that their calamity left him so unmoved; it showed conclusively how artificial were his relations with these persons; in no sense did he belong to their world; for all his foolish flutterings, Alma Frothingham remained a stranger to him, alien from every point of view, personal, intellectual, social. And how many of the people who crowded to her concert last night would hear the news this morning with genuine distress on her account? Gratified envy would be the prevailing mood, with rancorous hostility in the minds of those who were losers by Bennet Frothingham's knavery or ill-fortune. Hugh Carnaby's position called for no lament; he had a sufficient income of his own, and would now easily overcome his wife's pernicious influence; with or without her, he would break away from a life of corrupting indolence, and somewhere beyond seas 'beat the British drum' – use his superabundant vitality as nature prompted.

After all, it promised to clear the air. These explosions were periodic, inevitable, wholesome. The Britannia Loan, &c, &c, &c, had run its pestilent course; exciting avarice, perturbing quiet industry with the passion of the gamester, inflating vulgar ambition, now at length scattering wreck and ruin. This is how mankind progresses. Harvey Rolfe felt glad that no theological or scientific dogma constrained him to a justification of the laws of life.*

At lunchtime, newspaper boys began to yell. The earliest placards roared in immense typography. In the Metropolitan Club, sheets moist from the press suddenly descended like a fall of snow. Rolfe stood by a window and read quietly. This first report told him little that he had not already learnt, but there were a few details of the suicide. Frothingham, it appeared, always visited the office of *Stock and Share* on the day before publication. Yesterday, as usual, he had looked in for half an hour at three o'clock; but unexpectedly he came again at seven in the evening, and for a third time at about eleven, when the printing of the paper was in full swing. 'It was supposed by the persons whom he then saw that Mr Frothingham finally quitted the office; whether he actually left the building or not seems to remain uncertain. If so, he re-entered without being observed, which does not seem likely. Between two and three o'clock this morning, when *Stock and Share* was practically ready for distribution, a man employed on the premises is said, for some unexplained reason, to have ascended to the top floor of the building, and to have entered a room ordinarily unused. A gas-jet was burning, and the man was horrified to discover the dead body of Mr Frothingham, at full length on the floor, in his hand a pistol. On the alarm being given, medical aid was at once summoned, and it became evident that death had taken place more than an hour previously. That no one heard the report of a pistol can be easily explained by the noise of the machinery below. The dead man's face was placid. Very little blood had issued from the wound, and the shot must have been fired with a remarkably steady hand.'

'A room on the top floor of the building, ordinarily unused – ' What story was it that Alma Frothingham told last night, of her visit to the office of *Stock and Share*? Rolfe had not paid much attention to it at the time; now he recalled the anecdote, and was more impressed by its significance. That room, his first place of business, the scene of poor beginnings, Bennet Frothingham had chosen for his place of death. Perhaps he had long foreseen this possibility, had mused upon the dramatic fitness of such an end; for there was a strain of melancholy in the man, legible on his countenance, perceptible in his private conversation. Just about the time when Alma laughingly told the story, her father must have been sitting in that upper room, thinking his last thoughts; or it might be that he lay already dead.

Later issues contained much fuller reports. The man who found the body had explained his behaviour in going up to the unused room, and it relieved the dark affair with a touch of comedy. Before coming to work, he had quarrelled with his wife, and, rather than go home in the early hours of the morning, he hit upon the idea of finding a sleeping-place here on the premises, to which he could slink unnoticed. 'It's little enough sleep I get in my own house,' was his remark to the reporter who won his confidence. Clubmen were hilarious over this incident, speculating as to the result of its publication on the indiscreet man's domestic troubles.

It was not unremarked that a long time elapsed between the discovery of the suicide and its being heard of by anyone who had an interest in making it generally known. With the exception of two persons, all who were engaged upon the production of the newspaper went home in complete ignorance of what had happened, so cautiously and successfully was the situation dealt with by the sub-editor and his informant. When, after an examination by the doctor, who had been summoned in all secrecy, it became necessary to communicate with the police, the employees had all gone away, and the printed sheets had been conveyed to the distributing agents. Naturally, the sub-editor of *Stock and Share* preserved a certain reticence in the matter; but one could hardly be mistaken in assuming that the directors of the Britannia Company – two or three of them, at all events – had an opportunity of surveying their position long before the hour when this momentous news got abroad

With regard to the company's affairs, only conjecture could be as yet indulged in. In view of the immediate stoppage of business, it was pretty safe to surmise that alarming disclosures awaited the public. No one, of course, would be justified in prejudging the case against the unhappy man who, amid seemingly brilliant circumstances, had been driven to so desperate an act.

And so on, and so on, in one journal after another, in edition upon edition. Harvey Rolfe read them till he was weary, listened to the gossip of the club till he was nauseated. He went home at length with a headache, and, having carefully avoided contact with Buncombe or Mrs Handover, made an effort to absorb himself in a volume of Gregorovius,* which was at present his study. The attempt was futile. Talk still seemed to buzz about him; his temples throbbed; his thoughts wandered far and wide. Driven to bed long before his accustomed hour, he heard raucous voices rending the night, bellowing in hideous antiphony from this side of the street and the other, as the vendors

of a halfpenny paper made the most of what Providence had
sent them.

The first thing after breakfast next morning, he posted a line
to Hugh Carnaby. 'Is there any way in which I can be of use to
you? If you think not, I shall be off tomorrow to Greystone for
a few days. I feel as if we were all being swept into a ghastly
whirlpool which roars over the bottomless pit.* Of course, I
will stay if I can do anything, no matter what. Otherwise,
address for a week to Basil Morton's.'

This he dropped into the nearest pillar-box, and, as the sun
was endeavouring to shine, he walked the length of the street, a
pretence of exercise. On his way back he was preceded by a
telegraph boy, who stopped at Buncombe's front door, and
awoke the echoes with a twofold double knock. Before the
servant could open, Harvey was on the steps.

'What name?'

'Rolfe.'

'For me, then.'

He tore open the envelope.

'Could you come at once? Something has happened. –
Abbott.'

The boy wished to know if there would be a reply. Harvey
shook his head, and stepped into the hall, where he stood
reflecting. What could have happened that Edgar Abbott should
summon him? Had his wife run away? – Ah, to be sure, it must
have something to do with Wager's children – an accident, a
death. But why send for *him*?

He made a little change in his dress, and drove forthwith to
Kilburn. As his cab stopped, he saw that all the blinds in the
front of the Abbotts' house were drawn down. Death, then,
obviously. It was with a painful shaking of the nerves that he
knocked for admission.

'Mr Abbott – ?'

The servant girl, who had a long-drawn face, said nothing,
but left him where he stood, returning in a moment with a
mumbled 'Will you please to come in, sir?' He followed her to
the room in which he had talked with Mrs Abbott two days
ago; and she it was who again received him. Her back to the
light, she stood motionless.

'Your husband has telegraphed for me—'

A voice that struggled with a sob made thick reply –

'No – I – he is dead!'

The accent of that last monosyllable was heart-piercing. It seemed to Harvey as though the word were new-minted, so full it sounded of dreadful meaning.

'Dead?'

Mrs Abbott moved, and he could see her face better. She must have wept for hours.

'He has been taking morphia – he couldn't sleep well – and then his neuralgia. The girl found him this morning, at seven o'clock – there.'

She pointed to the couch.

'You mean that he had taken an overdose – by accident – '

'It *must* have been so. He had to work late – and then he must have lain down to sleep.'

'Why here?'

'A flood of anguish whelmed her. She uttered a long moan, all the more terrible for its subdual to a sound that could not pass beyond the room. Her struggle for self-command made her suffering only the more impressive, the more grievous to behold.

'Mr Rolfe, I sent for you because you are his old friend. I meant to tell you all the truth, as I know it. I *can't* tell it before strangers – in public! I *can't* let them know – the shame – the shame!'

Harvey's sympathy gave way to astonishment and strange surmise. Hurriedly he besought her not to reveal anything in her present distress; to wait till she could reflect calmly, see things in truer proportion. His embarrassment was heightened by an inability to identify this woman with the Mrs Abbott he had known; the change in her self-presentment seemed as great and sudden as that in her circumstances. Face and voice, though scarce recognisable, had changed less than the soul of her – as Harvey imaged it. This entreaty she replied to with a steadiness, a resolve, which left him no choice but to listen.

'I cannot, dare not, think that he did this knowingly. No! He was too brave for that. He would never have left me in that way – to my despair. But it was my fault that made him angry – no, not angry; he was never that with me, or never showed it. But I had behaved with such utter selfishness—'

Her misery refused to word itself. She sank down upon a chair and sobbed and moaned.

'Your grief exaggerates every little fault,' said Harvey.

'No – you must hear it all – then perhaps I can hide my shame from strangers. What use would it be if they knew? It alters nothing – it's only in my own heart. I have no right to pain you like this. I will tell you quietly. You know that he went to Waterbury, on business. Did he tell you? – it was to buy a share in a local newspaper. I, in my blindness and selfishness, disliked that. I wanted to live here; the thought of going to live in the country seemed unbearable. That Edgar was overworked and ill, seemed to me a trifle. Don't you remember how I spoke of it when you came here the other morning? – I can't understand myself. How could I think so, speak so!'

The listener said nothing.

'He did what he purposed – made a bargain, and came back to conclude the purchase by correspondence. But his money – the small capital he counted upon – was in "Britannia" shares; and you know what happened yesterday – yesterday, the very day when he went to sell the shares, thinking to do so without the least difficulty.'

Harvey gave a grim nod.

'He came home, and I showed that I was glad—'

'No! You accuse yourself unreasonably.'

'I tell you the truth, as my miserable conscience knows it. I was crazy with selfishness and conceit. Rightly, he left me to my cowardly temper, and went out again, and was away for a long time. He came back to dinner, and then the suffering in his face all but taught me what I was doing. I wanted to ask him to forgive me – to comfort him for his loss; but pride kept me from it. I couldn't speak – I couldn't! After dinner he said he had a lot of work to do, and came into this room. At ten o'clock I sent him coffee. I wished to take it myself – O God! if only I had done so! I *wished* to take it, and speak to him, but still I couldn't. And I knew he was in torture; I saw at dinner that pain was racking him. But I kept away, and went to my own bed, and slept – whilst he was lying here.'

A rush of tears relieved her. Harvey felt his own eyes grow moist.

'It was only that he felt so worn out,' she pursued. 'I know how it was. The pain grew intolerable, and he went upstairs for his draught, and then – not having finished his work – he thought he would lie down on the sofa for a little; and so sleep overcame him. He never meant *this*. If I thought it, I couldn't live!'

'Undoubtedly you are right,' said Harvey, summoning an accent of conviction. 'I knew him very well, and he was not the man to do that.'

'No? You are sure of it? You feel it impossible, Mr Rolfe?'

'Quite impossible. There are men – oh, you may assure yourself that it was pure accident. Unfortunately, it happens so often.'

She hung on his words, leaning towards him, her eyes wide and lips parted.

'So often! I have seen so many cases, in the papers. And he was absent-minded. But what right have I to seek comfort for myself? Was I any less the cause of his death? But must I tell all this in public? Do you think I ought to?'

With comfortable sincerity Rolfe was able to maintain the needlessness of divulging anything beyond the state of Abbott's health and his pecuniary troubles.

'It isn't as if we had lived on ill terms with each other,' said the widow, with a sigh of gratitude. 'Anything but that. Until of late we never knew a difference, and the change that came was wholly my fault. I hadn't the honesty to speak out and say what was in my mind. I never openly opposed his wish to leave London. I pretended to agree to everything, pretended. He showed me all his reasons, put everything simply and plainly and kindly before me, and if I had said what I thought, I feel sure he would have given it up at once. It was in my own hands to decide one way or the other.'

'Why should you reproach yourself so with mere thoughts, of which he never became aware?'

'Oh, it was yesterday, when he came back from the City. He knew then that I was glad he couldn't carry out his purpose. He looked at me as he never had done before – a look of surprise and estrangement. I shall always see that look on his face.'

Harvey talked in the strain of solace, feeling how extraordinary was his position, and that of all men he had least fitness for such an office. It relieved him when, without undue abruptness, he could pass to the practical urgencies of the case. Were Wager's children still in the house? Alas! they were, and Mrs Abbott knew not what to do about them.

'You can't think of anyone who would take them – for a day or two, even?'

Among her acquaintances there was not one of whom she could venture to ask such a service. 'People have such a dread of children.' Her sister was a governess in Ireland; other near relatives she had none. Edgar Abbott's mother, old and in feeble health, lived near Waterbury; how was the dreadful news to be conveyed to her?

Harvey bestirred himself. Here, at all events, was a call to active usefulness; he felt the privilege of money and leisure.

'Can you give me the name of any one at Waterbury who would be a fit person to break the news to Mrs Abbott?'

Two names were mentioned, and he noted them.

'I will send telegrams at once to both.'

'You will say it was an accident—'

'That shall be made clear. As for the children, I think I can have them taken away this morning. In the house where I live there is a decent woman who I dare say would be willing to look after them for the present. Will you leave this entirely in my hands?'

'I am ashamed – I don't know how to thank you.'

'No time shall be lost.' He rose. 'If Mrs Handover will help us, I will bring her here; then I shall see you again. In any case, of course, I will come back – there will be other business. But you ought to have some friend – some lady.'

'There's *no* one I can ask.'

'Oh, but of all the people you know in London – surely!'

'They are not friends in that sense. I understand it now – fifty acquaintances; no friend.'

'But let me think – let me think. What was the name of that lady I met here, whose children you used to teach?'

'Mrs Langland. She is very kind and friendly, but she lives at Gunnersbury* – so far – and I couldn't trouble her.'

Upon one meeting and a short conversation, with subsequent remarks from Edgar Abbott, Rolfe had grounded a very favourable opinion of Mrs Langland. She dwelt clearly in his mind as 'a woman with no nonsense about her', likely to be of much helpfulness at a crisis such as the present. With difficulty he persuaded Mrs Abbott to sit down and write a few lines, to be posted at once to Gunnersbury.

'I haven't dared to ask her to come. But I have said that I am alone.'

'Quite enough, I think, if she is at home.'

He took his leave, and drove back to Bayswater, posting the letter and despatching two telegrams on the way.

Of course, his visit to Greystone was given up.


## CHAPTER 6


Hugh Carnaby was gratified by the verdict of *felo de se*.\* He applauded the jury for their most unexpected honesty. One had taken for granted the foolish tag about temporary madness, which would have been an insult to everybody's common-sense.

'It's a pity they no longer bury at four cross-roads, with a stake in his inside. (Where's that from? I remember it some-how.)\* The example wouldn't be bad.'

'You're rather early-Victorian,' replied Sibyl, who by this term was wont to signify barbarism or crudity in art, letters, morality, or social feeling. 'Besides, there's no merit in the verdict. It only means that the City jury is in a rage. Yet every one of them would be dishonest on as great a scale if they dared, or had the chance.'

'Something in that, I dare say,' conceded Hugh.

He admired his wife more than ever. Calm when she lost her trinkets, Sibyl exhibited no less self-command now that she was suddenly deprived of her whole fortune, about eight hundred a year. She had once remarked on the pleasantness and fitness of a wife's possessing in her own name an income equal to that of her husband; yet she resigned it without fuss. Indeed, Sibyl never made a fuss about anything. She intimated her wishes, and, as they were always possible of gratification, obtained them as a matter of course. Naturally, since their marriage, she and Hugh had lived to the full extent of their means. Carnaby had reduced his capital by a couple of thousand pounds in preliminary expenses, and debt to the amount of two or three hundred was outstanding at the end of the first twelvemonth; but Sibyl manifested no alarm.

'We have been great fools,' she said, alluding to their faith in Bennet Frothingham.

'It's certain that *I* have,' replied her husband. 'I oughtn't to have let your mother have her way about that money. If there had been a proper settlement, you would have run no risk. Trustees couldn't have allowed such an investment.'

The same day Sibyl bought a fur for her neck which cost fifteen guineas. The weather was turning cold, and she had an account at the shop.

That afternoon, too, she went to see her mother, and on returning at six o'clock looked into the library, where Hugh sat by the fire, a book in his hand. Carnaby found the days very long just now. He shunned his clubs, the Metropolitan and the Ramblers', because of a fear that his connection with the 'Britannia' was generally known; to hear talk on the subject would make him savage. He was grievously perturbed in mind by his position and prospects; and want of exercise had begun to affect his health. As always, he greeted his wife's entrance with a smile, and rose to place a chair for her.

'Thanks, I won't sit down,' said Sibyl. 'You look comfortable.'

'Well?'

She looked at him reflectively, and said in balanced tones –

'I really think I can boast of having the most selfish mother in England.'

Hugh had his own opinion concerning Mrs Ascott Larkfield, but would not have ventured to phrase it.

'How's that?'

'I never knew anyone who succeeded so well in thinking steadily and exclusively of herself. It irritates me to see her since this affair; I shan't go again. I really didn't know what a detestable temper she has. Her talk is outrageous. She doesn't behave like a lady. Could you believe that she has written a violent letter to Mrs Frothingham – "speaking her mind", as she says? It's disgraceful!'

'I'm sorry she has done that. But it isn't every one that can bear injury as you do, Sibyl.'

'I supposed she could behave herself. She raises her voice, and uses outrageous words, and shows temper with the servants. I wouldn't spend a day in that house now on any account. And, after all, I find she hasn't lost much more than I have. She will be able to count on six hundred a year at least.'

Carnaby received the news with a brightened visage.

'Oh come! That's something.'

'She took very good care, you see, not to risk everything herself.'

'It's possible,' said Hugh, 'that she hadn't control of all her money.'

'Oh yes, she had. She let that fact escape in her fury – congratulated herself on being so far prudent. Really, I never knew a more hateful woman.'

It was said without vehemence, with none of that raising of the voice which so offended her: a deliberate judgment, in carefully chosen words. Hugh tried to smile, but could not quite command his features; they expressed an uneasy thoughtfulness.

'Do you go out this evening?' he asked, after a pause.

'No; I'm rather tired and out of sorts. Dinner is at seven. I shall go to bed early.'

The police had as yet failed to get upon the track of the felonious housekeeper, known as Mrs Maskell. Mrs Carnaby's other servants still kept their places, protesting innocence, and doubtless afraid to leave lest they should incur suspicion. Domestic management was now in the hands of the cook. Sibyl always declared that she could not eat a dinner she had had the trouble of ordering, and she seemed unaffectedly to shrink from persons of the menial class, as though with physical repulsion. Perforce she submitted to having her hair done by her maid, but she found the necessity disagreeable.

The dinner was simple, but well cooked. Sibyl never ate with hearty appetite, and declined everything not of excellent quality; unlike women in general, she was fastidious about wine, yet took of it sparingly; liqueurs, too, she enjoyed, and very strong coffee. To a cigarette in the mouth of a woman she utterly objected; it offended her sense of the becoming, her delicate perception of propriety. When dining alone or with Hugh, she dressed as carefully as for a ceremonious occasion. Any approach to personal disorder or neglect was inconceivable in Sibyl. Her husband had, by accident, heard her called 'the best-groomed woman in London'; he thought the praise well merited, and it flattered him.

At table they talked of things as remote as possible from their immediate concerns, and with the usual good humour. When he rose to open the door, Hugh said –

'Drawing-room or library?'

'Library. You would like to smoke.'

For ten minutes he sat with his arms on the table, his great well-shapen hands loosely clenched before him. He drank nothing. His gaze was fixed on a dish of fruit, and widened as if in a growing perplexity. Then he recovered himself, gave a snort, and went to join his wife.

Sibyl was reading a newspaper. Hugh lit his pipe in silence, and sat down opposite to her. Presently the newspaper dropped, and Sibyl's eyes were turned upon her husband with a smile.

'Well?'

'Well?'

They smiled at each other amiably.

'What do you suggest, Birdie?'

The fondling name was not very appropriate, and had not been used of late; Carnaby hit upon it in the honeymoon days, when he said that his wife was like some little lovely bird, which he, great coarse fellow, had captured and almost feared to touch lest he should hurt it. Hugh had not much originality of thought, and less of expression.

'There are places, you know, where one lives very comfortably on very little,' said Sibyl.

'Yes; but it leads to nothing.'

'What *would* lead to anything?'

'Well, you see, I have capital, and some use ought to be made of it. Everybody nowadays goes in for some kind of business.'

She listened with interest, smiling, meditative.

'And a great many people come out of it – wishing they had done so before.'

'True,' said Carnaby; 'there's the difficulty. I had a letter from Dando this morning. He has got somebody to believe in his new smelting process – somebody in the City; talks of going out to Queensland shortly. Really – if I could be on the spot – '

He hesitated, timidly indicating his thoughts. Sibyl mused, and slowly shook her head.

'No; wait for reports.'

'Yes; but it's those who are in it first, you see.'

Sibyl seemed to forget the immediate subject, and to let her thoughts wander in pleasant directions. She spoke as if on a happy impulse.

'There's one place I think I should like – though I dread the voyage.'

'Where's that?'

'Honolulu.'

'What has put that into your head?'

'Oh, I have read about it. The climate is absolute perfection, and the life exquisite. How do you get there?'

'Across America, and then from San Francisco. It's anything but a cheap place, I believe.'

'Still, for a time. The thing is to get away, don't you think?'

'No doubt of that. – Honolulu – by Jove! it's an idea. I should like to see those islands myself.'

'And it isn't commonplace,' remarked Sibyl. 'One would go off with a certain éclat. Very different from starting for the Continent in the humdrum way.'

The more Carnaby thought of it, the better he liked this suggestion. That Sibyl should voluntarily propose so long a journey surprised and delighted him. The tropics were not his favourite region, and those islands of the Pacific offered no scope for profitable energy; he did not want to climb volcanoes, still less to lounge beneath bananas and breadfruit-trees, however pleasant such an escape from civilisation might seem at the first glance. A year of marriage, of idleness amid amusements, luxuries, extravagances, for which he had no taste, was bearing its natural result in masculine restiveness. His robust physique and temper, essentially combative, demanded liberty under conditions of rude or violent life. He was not likely to find a satisfying range in any mode of existence that would be shared by Sibyl. But he clutched at any chance of extensive travel. It might be necessary – it certainly would be – to make further incision into his capital, and so diminish the annual return upon which he could count for the future; but when his income had already become ludicrously inadequate, what did that matter? The years of independence were past; somehow or other, he must make money. Everybody did it nowadays, and an 'opening' would of course present itself, something would of course 'turn up'.

He stretched his limbs in a sudden vast relief.

'Bravo! The idea is excellent. Shall we sell all this stuff?' waving a hand to indicate the furniture.

'Oh, I think not. Warehouse it.'

Hugh would have rejoiced to turn every chair and table into hard cash, not only for the money's sake, but for the sense of freedom that would follow; but he agreed, as always, to whatever his wife preferred. They talked with unwonted animation. A great atlas was opened, routes were fingered; half the earth's circumference vanished in a twinkling. Sibyl, hitherto mewed within the circle of European gaieties and relaxations, all at once let her fancy fly – tasted a new luxury in experiences from which she had shrunk.

'I'll order my outfit tomorrow. Very light things, I suppose? Who could advise me about that?'

Among a number of notes and letters which she wrote next day was one to Miss Frothingham. 'Dear Alma,' it began, and it ended with 'Yours affectionately' – just as usual.

'Could you possibly come here some day this week? I haven't written before, and haven't tried to see you, because I felt sure you would rather be left alone. At the same time I feel sure that what has happened, though for a time it will sadden us both, cannot affect our friendship. I want to see you, as we are going away very soon, first of all to *Honolulu*. Appoint your own time; I will be here.'

By return of post came the black-edged answer, which began with 'Dearest Sibyl,' and closed with 'Ever affectionately'.

'I cannot tell you how relieved I am to get your kind letter. These dreadful days have made me ill, and one thing that increased my misery was the fear that I should never hear from you again. I should not have dared to write. How noble you are! – but then I always knew that. I cannot come tomorrow – you know why – but the next day I will be with you at three o'clock, if you don't tell me that the hour is inconvenient.'

They met at the appointed time. Mrs Carnaby's fine sense of the becoming declared itself in dark array; her voice was tenderly subdued; the pressure of her hand, the softly lingering touch of her lips, conveyed a sympathy which perfect taste would not allow to become demonstrative. Alma could at first say nothing. The faint rose upon her cheek had vanished; her eyes were heavy, and lacked their vital gleam; her mouth, no longer mobile and provocative, trembled on the verge of sobs, pathetic, childlike. She hung her head, moved with a languid, diffident step, looked smaller and slighter, a fashionable garb of woe aiding the unhappy transformation.

'I oughtn't to have given you this trouble,' said Sibyl. 'But perhaps you would rather see me here – '

'Yes – oh yes – it was much better – '

'Sit down, dear. We won't talk of wretched things, will we? If I could have been of any use to you – '

'I was so afraid you would never—'

'Oh, you know me better than that,' broke in Mrs Carnaby, almost with cheerfulness, her countenance already throwing off the decorous shadow, like a cloak that had served its turn. 'I hope I am neither foolish nor worldly-minded.'

'Indeed, indeed not! You are goodness itself.'

'How is Mrs Frothingham?'

The question was asked with infinite delicacy, head and body bent forward, eyes floatingly averted.

'Really ill, I'm afraid. She has fainted several times – yesterday was unconscious for nearly half an hour.'

Sibyl flinched. Mention of physical suffering affected her most disagreeably; she always shunned the proximity of people in ill health, and a possibility of infection struck her with panic.

'Oh, I'm so sorry. But it will pass over.'

'I hope so. I have done what I could.'

'I'm sure you have.'

'But it's so hard – when every word of comfort sounds heartless – when it's kindest to say nothing – '

'We won't talk about it, dear. You yourself – I can see what you have gone through. You must get away as soon as possible; this gloomy weather makes everything worse.'

She paused, and with an air of discreet interest awaited Alma's reply.

'Yes, I hope to get away. I shall see if it's possible.'

The girl's look strayed with a tired uncertainty; her hands never ceased to move and fidget; only the habits of good breeding kept her body still.

'Of course, it is too soon for you to have made plans.'

'It's so difficult,' replied Alma, her features more naturally expressive, her eyes a little brighter. 'You see, I am utterly dependent upon Mamma. I had better tell you at once – Mamma will have enough to live upon, however things turn out. She has money of her own; but of course I have nothing – nothing whatever. I think, most likely, Mamma will go to live with her sister, in the country, for a time. She couldn't bear to go on living in London, and she doesn't like life abroad. If only I could do as I wish!'

'I guess what that would be,' said the other, smiling gently.

'To take up music as a profession – yes. But I'm not ready for it.'

'Oh, half a year of serious study; with your decided talent, I should think you couldn't hesitate. You are a born musician.'

The words acted as a cordial. Alma roused herself, lifted her drooping head and smiled.

'That's the praise of a friend.'

'And the serious opinion of one not quite unfit to judge,' rejoined Sibyl, with her air of tranquil self-assertion. 'Besides, we have agreed – haven't we? – that the impulse is everything. What you wish for, try for. Just now you have lost courage; you are not yourself. Wait till you recover your balance.'

'It isn't that I want to make a name, or anything of that sort,' said Alma, in a voice that was recovering its ordinary pitch and melody. 'I dare say I never should; I might just support myself, and that would be all. But I want to be free – I want to break away.'

'Of course!'

'I have been thinking that I shall beg Mamma to let me have just a small allowance, and go off by myself. I know people at Leipzig – the Gassners, you remember. I could live there on little enough, and work, and feel free. Of course, there's really no reason why I shouldn't. I have been feeling so bound and helpless; and now that nobody has any right to hinder me, you think it would be the wise thing?'

Alma had occasionally complained to her friend, as she did the other evening to Harvey Rolfe, that easy circumstances were not favourable to artistic ambition, but no very serious disquiet had ever declared itself in her ordinary talk. The phrases she now used, and the look that accompanied them, caused Sibyl some amusement. Only two years older than Alma, Mrs Carnaby enjoyed a more than proportionate superiority in knowledge of the world; her education had been more steadily directed to that end, and her natural aptitude for the study was more pronounced. That she really liked Alma seemed as certain as that she felt neither affection nor esteem for any other person of her own sex. Herself not much inclined to feminine friendship, Alma had from the first paid voluntary homage to Sibyl's intellectual claims, and thought it a privilege to be admitted to her intimacy; being persuaded, moreover, that in Sibyl, and in Sibyl alone, she found genuine appreciation of her musical talent. Sibyl's choice of a husband had secretly surprised and disappointed her, for Hugh Carnaby was not the type of man in whom she felt an interest, and he seemed to her totally unworthy of his good fortune; but this perplexity passed and was forgotten. She saw that Sibyl underwent no subjugation; nay, that the married woman did but perfect herself in those qualities of mind and mood whereby she had shone as a maiden. It was a combination of powers and virtues which appeared to Alma little short of the ideal in womanhood. The example influenced her developing character in ways she recognised, and in others of which she remained quite unconscious.

'I think you couldn't do better,' Mrs Carnaby replied to the last question; 'provided that – '

She paused intentionally, with an air of soft solicitude, of bland wisdom.

'That's just what I wanted,' said Alma eagerly. 'Advise me – tell me just what you think.'

'You want to live alone, and to have done with all the silly conventionalities and proprieties – our old friend Mrs Grundy,* in fact.'

'That's it! You understand me perfectly, as you always do.'

'If it had been possible, we would have lived together.'

'Ah! how delightful! Don't speak of what can't be.'

'I was going to say,' pursued Sibyl thoughtfully, 'that you will meet with all sorts of little troubles and worries, which you have never had any experience of. For one thing, you know' – she leaned back, smiling, at ease – 'people won't behave to you quite as you have been accustomed to expect. Money is very important even to a man; but to a woman it means more than you can imagine.'

'Oh, but I shan't be living among the kind of people—'

'No, no. Perhaps you don't quite understand me yet. It isn't the people you seek who matter, but the people that will seek *you*; and some of them will have very strange ideas – very strange indeed.'

Alma looked self-conscious, kept her eyes down, and at length nodded.

'Yes. I think I understand.'

'That's why I said "provided". You are not the ordinary girl, and you won't imagine that I feared for you; I know you too well. It's a question of being informed and on one's guard. I don't think there's anyone else who would talk to you like this. It doesn't offend you?'

'Sibyl!'

'Well, then, that's all right. Go into the world by all means, but go prepared – armed; the word isn't a bit too strong, as I know perfectly. Some day, perhaps – but there's no need to talk about such things now.'

Alma kept a short silence, breaking it at length with note of exultation.

'I'm quite decided now. I wanted just to hear what you would say. I shan't wait a day longer than I can help. The old life is over for me. If only it had come about in some other way, I should be singing with rapture. I'm going to begin to live!'

She quivered with intensity of feeling, or with that excitement of the nerves which simulates intense feeling in certain natures. A flush stole to her cheek; her eyes were once more full of light. Sibyl regarded her observantly and with admiration.

'You never thought of the stage, Alma?'

'The stage? Acting?'

'No; I see you never did. And it wouldn't do – of course it wouldn't do. Something in your look – it just crossed my mind – but of course you have much greater things before you. It means hard work, and I'm only afraid you'll work yourself all but to death.'

'I shouldn't wonder,' replied the girl, with a little laugh of pride in this possibility.

'Well, I too am going away, you know.'

Alma's countenance fell, shame again crept over it, and she murmured, 'O Sibyl – !'

'Don't distress yourself the least on my account. That's an understood thing; no mention, no allusion, ever between us. And the truth is that my position is just a little like yours: on the whole, I'm rather glad. Hugh wants desperately to get to the other end of the world, and I dare say it's the best thing I could do to go with him. No roughing it, of course; that isn't in my way.'

'I should think not, indeed!'

'Oh, I may rise to those heights, who knows! If the new

sensation ever seemed worth the trouble. – In a year or two, we shall meet and compare notes. Don't expect long descriptive letters; I don't care to do indifferently what other people have done well and put into print – it's a waste of energy. But you are sure to have far more interesting and original things to tell about; it will read so piquantly, I'm sure, at Honolulu.'

They drank tea together, and talked, in all, for a couple of hours. When she rose to leave, Alma, but for her sombre drapings, was totally changed from the limp, woebegone, shrinking girl who had at first presented herself.

'There's no one else,' she said, 'who would have behaved to me so kindly and so nobly.'

'Nonsense! But *that's* nonsense, too. Let us admire each other; it does us good, and is so very pleasant.'

'I shall say goodbye to no one but you. Let people think and say of me what they like; I don't care a snap of the fingers. Indeed, I *hate* people.'

'Both sexes impartially?'

It was a peculiarity of their intimate converse that they never talked of men, and a jest of this kind had novelty sufficient to affect Alma with a slight confusion.

'Impartially – quite,' she answered.

'Do make an exception in favour of Hugh's friend, Mr Rolfe. I abandon all the rest.'

Alma betrayed surprise.

'Strange! I really thought you didn't much like Mr Rolfe,' she said, without any show of embarrassment.

'I didn't when I first knew him; but he grows upon one. I think him interesting; he isn't quite easy to understand.'

'Indeed he isn't.'

They smiled with the confidence of women fancy-free, and said no more on the subject.

Carnaby came home to dinner brisk and cheerful; he felt better than for many a day. Brightly responsive, Sibyl welcomed his appearance in the drawing-room.

'Saw old Rolfe for a minute at the club. In a vile temper. I wonder whether he really has lost money, and won't confess? Yet I don't think so. Queer old stick.'

'By-the-bye, what *is* his age?' asked Alma unconcernedly.

'Thirty-seven or eight. But I always think of him as fifty.'

'I suppose he'll never marry?'

'Rolfe? Good heavens, no! Too much sense – hang it, you know what I mean! It would never suit *him*. Can't imagine such a thing. He gets more and more booky. Has his open-air moods, too, and amuses me with his Jingoism.* So different from his old ways of talking; but I didn't care much about him in those days. Well, now, look here, I've had a talk with a man I know, about Honolulu, and I've got all sorts of things to tell you. – Dinner? Very glad; I'm precious hungry.'

## CHAPTER 7

About the middle of December, Alma Frothingham left England, burning with a fever of impatience, resenting all inquiry and counsel, making pretence of settled plans, really indifferent to everything but the prospect of emancipation. The disaster that had befallen her life, the dishonour darkening upon her name, seemed for the moment merely a price paid for liberty. The shock of sorrow and dismay had broken innumerable bonds, overthrown all manner of obstacles to growth of character, of power. She gloried in a new, intoxicating sense of irresponsibility. She saw the ideal life in a release from all duty and obligation – save to herself.

Travellers on that winter day from Antwerp into Germany noticed the English girl, well dressed, and of attractive features, whose excited countenance and restless manner told of a journey in haste, with something most important, and assuredly not disagreeable, at the end of it. She was alone, and evidently quite able to take care of herself. Unlike the representative English *Fräulein*, she did not reject friendly overtures from strangers; her German was lame, but she spoke it with enjoyment, laughing at her stumbles and mistakes. With her in the railway carriage she kept a violin-case. A professional musician? 'Noch nicht' was her answer, with a laugh. She knew Leipzig? Oh dear, yes, and many other parts of Germany; had travelled a good deal; was an entirely free and independent person, quite without national prejudice, indeed without prejudice of any kind. And in the same breath she spoke slightingly, if not contemptuously, of England and everything English.

At Leipzig she stayed until the end of April, living with a family named Gassner, people whom she had known for some years. Only on condition that she would take up her abode with this household had Mrs Frothingham consented to make her an allowance and let her go abroad. Alma fretted at the restriction; she wished to have a room of her own in a lodging-house; but the family life improved her command of German – something gained. To music, meanwhile, she gave very little attention, putting off with one excuse after another the beginning of her serious studies. She seemed to have quite forgotten that music was her 'religion', and, for the matter of that, appeared to have no religion at all. 'Life' was her interest, her study. She made acquaintances, attended concerts and the theatre, read multitudes of French and German novels. But her habits were economical. All the pleasures she desired could be enjoyed at very small expense, and she found her stepmother's remittances more than sufficient.

In April she gained Mrs Frothingham's consent to her removal from Leipzig to Munich. A German girl with whom she had made friends was going to Munich to study art. For reasons, vague even to herself (so ran her letters to Mrs Frothingham), she could not 'settle' at Leipzig. The climate did not seem to suit her. She had suffered from bad colds, and, in short, was doing no good. At Munich lived an admirable violinist, a friend of Herr Wilenski's, who would be of great use to her. 'In short, dear Mamma, doesn't it seem to you rather humiliating that at the age of four-and-twenty I should be begging for permission to go here and there, do this or that? I know all your anxieties about me, and I am very grateful, and I feel ashamed to be living at your expense, but really I must go about making a career for myself in my own way.' Mrs Frothingham yielded, and Alma took lodgings in Munich together with her German friend.

English newspapers were now reporting the trial of the directors of the Britannia Company, for to this pass had things come. The revelations of the law-court satisfied public curiosity, and excited indignant clamour. Alma read, and tried to view the proceedings as one for whom they had no personal concern; but her sky darkened, her heart grew heavy. The name of Bennet Frothingham stood for criminal recklessness, for huge rascality; it would be so for years to come. She had no courage to take up her violin; the sound of music grew hateful to her, as if mocking at her ruined ambition.

Three months had passed since she received her one and only letter from Honolulu; two months since she had written to Sibyl. On a blue day of spring, when despondency lowered upon her, and all occupation, all amusements seemed a burden, she was driven to address her friend on the other side of the world, to send a cry of pain and hopelessness to the dream-island of the Pacific.

'What is the use of working at music? The simple truth is, that since I left England I have given it up. I am living here on false pretences; I shall never care to play the violin again. What sort of a reception could I expect from an English audience? If I took another name, of course it would get known who I was, and people would just come to stare at me – pleasant thought! And I have utterly lost confidence in myself. The difficulties are great, even where there is great talent, and I feel I have nothing of the kind. I might toil for years, and should do no good. I feel I am not an artist – I am beaten and disgraced. There's nothing left but to cry and be miserable, like any other girl who has lost her money, her hopes, everything. Why don't you write to me? If you wait till you get this, it will be six or seven weeks before I could possibly hear. And a letter from you would do me so much good.'

Some one knocked at her door. She called '*Herein*!' and there appeared a little boy, the child of her landlady, who sometimes ran errands for her. He said that a gentleman was asking to see her.

'*Ein Deutscher?*'

'*Nein. Ein Engländer, glaub'ich, und ein schnurriges Deutsch ist's, das er verbricht!*'*

Alma started up, shut her unfinished letter in the blotting-case, and looked anxiously about the room.

'What is his name? Ask him to give you his name.'

The youngster came back with a card, and Alma was astonished to read the name of 'Mr Felix Dymes'. Why, she had all but forgotten the man's existence. How came he here? What right had he to call? And yet she was glad – nay, delighted. Happily, she had the sitting-room (shared with her art-studying friend) to herself this morning.

'Bring him up here,' she said to the boy hurriedly, 'and ask him to wait a minute for me.'

And she escaped to make a rapid change of dress. For Alma was not like Sibyl Carnaby in perpetual regard for personal finish; she dressed carelessly, save when the occasion demanded pains; she liked the ease of gowns and slippers, of loose hair and free throat; and this taste had grown upon her during the past months. But she did not keep Mr Dymes waiting very long, and on her entrance he gazed at her with very frank admiration. Frank, too, was his greeting – that of a very old and intimate friend, rather than of a drawing-room acquaintance. He came straight from England, he said; a spring holiday, warranted by the success of his song 'Margot', which the tenor, Topham, had sung at St James's Hall.* A few days ago he had happened to see Miss Leach, who gave him Miss Frothingham's address, and he could not deny himself the pleasure of calling. Chatting thus, he made himself comfortable in a chair, and Alma sat over against him. The man was loud, conceited, vulgar; but, after all, he composed very sweet music, which promised to take the public ear; and he brought with him a waft from the happiness of old days; and how could one expect small proprieties of a bohemian, an artist? Alma began to talk eagerly, joyously.

'And what are you doing, Miss Frothingham?'

'Oh, fiddling a little. But I haven't been very well.'

'I can see that. Yet in another sense you look a better than ever.'

He began to hum an air, glancing round the room.

'You haven't a piano. Just listen to this; how do you think it will do?' He hummed through a complete melody. 'Came into my head last night. Wants rather sentimental words – the kind of thing that goes down with the British public. Rather a good air, don't you think?'

Felix Dymes had two manners of conversation. In a company at all ceremonious, and when it behoved him to make an impression, he talked as the artist and the expert in music, with many German phrases, which he pronounced badly, to fill up the gaps in his knowledge. His familiar stream of talk was very different: it discarded affectation, and had a directness, a vigour, which never left one in doubt as to his actual views of life. How melody of any kind could issue from a nature so manifestly ignoble might puzzle the idealist. Alma, who had known a good many musical people, was not troubled by this difficulty; in her present mood, she submitted to the arrogance of success, and felt a pleasure, an encouragement, in Dymes's bluff *camaraderie*.

'Let me try to catch it on the violin,' she said when, with nodding head and waving arm, he had hummed again through his composition.

She succeeded in doing so, and Dymes raised his humming to a sentimental roar, and was vastly pleased with himself.

'I like to see you in a place like this,' he said. 'Looks more business-like – as if you really meant to do something. Do you live here alone?'

'With a friend.'

Something peculiar in Dymes's glance caused her to add, 'A German girl, an art student.' Whereat the musician nodded and smiled.

'And what's your idea? Come now, let's talk about it. I wonder whether I could be of any use to you – awfully glad if I could.'

Alma was abashed, stammered her vague projects, and reddened under the man's observant eye.

'Look here,' he cried, with his charming informality, 'didn't you use to sing? Somebody told me you had a pretty good voice.'

'Oh, that was long ago.'

'I wish you'd let me hear you.'

'No, no! I don't sing at all.'

'Pity, if it's true. I want to write a serio-comic opera, a new sort of thing, and it struck me you were just cut out for that kind of singing. You have the face and the – you know – the refinement; sort of thing not easy to find. It's a poor chance, I'm afraid, coming out as a violinist.'

Half inclined to resent his impertinence, yet subdued by the practical tone and air of superior knowledge, Alma kept a grave face. Dymes, crossing his legs, went on with talk of projects he had in view, all intended to be lucrative. He had capital; nothing great, just a comfortable sum which he was bent on using to the best advantage. His songs would presently be bringing him in a few hundreds a year – so he declared – and his idea of life was to get as much enjoyment as possible without working over-hard for it. The conversation lasted for a couple of hours, Dymes growing even more genial and confidential, his eyes seldom moving from Alma's face.

'Well,' he said at length, rising, 'it's very jolly to see you again, after all this time. I shall be staying here for a few days. You'll let me call tomorrow?'

At once glad and sorry to see him go, Alma laughingly gave the desired permission. When, that evening, she looked at her unfinished letter, it seemed such a miserable whine that she tore it up in annoyance. Dymes's visit had done her good; she felt, if not a renewal of hope, at all events the courage which comes of revived spirits.

The next day she awaited his arrival with a pleasant expectation. He entered humming an air – another new composition – which again she caught from him and played on the violin.

'Good, don't you think? I'm in great vein just now – always am in the spring, and when the weather's fine. I say, you're looking much better today – decidedly more fit. What do you do here for exercise? Do you go to the Englische Garten? Come now, will you? Let's have a drive.'

With sudden coldness Alma excused herself. The musician scrutinised her rapidly, bit his lip, and looked round to the window; but in a moment he had recovered his loud good humour.

'You'll hardly believe it, but it's the plain truth, that I came all this way just to see you. I hadn't thought of coming to Germany till I met Miss Leach and heard about you. Now I'm so far, I might as well go on into Italy, and make a round of it. I wish you were coming too.'

Alma made no reply. He scrutinised her as before, and his features worked as if with some emotion. Then, abruptly, he put a blunt question.

'Do you think people who go in for music, art, and that kind of thing, ought to marry?'

'I never thought about it at all,' Alma replied, with a careless laugh, striking a finger across the strings of the violin which she held on her lap.

'We're generally told they shouldn't,' pursued Dymes, in a voice which had lost its noisy confidence, and was a little uncertain. 'But it all depends, you know. If people mean by marriage the ordinary kind of thing – of course, that's the deuce. But it needn't be. Lots of people marry nowadays and live in a rational way – no house, or bother of that kind; just going about as they like, and having a pleasant, reasonable life. It's easy enough with a little money. Sometimes they're a good deal of help to each other; I know people who manage to be.'

'Oh, I dare say,' said Alma when he paused. 'It all depends, as you say. You're going on to Italy at once?'

Her half-veiled eyes seemed to conceal amusement, and there was good-humoured disdain in the setting of her lips. With audacity so incredible that it all but made her laugh, Dymes, not heeding her inquiry, jerked out the personal application of his abstract remarks. Yes, it was a proposal of marriage – marriage on the new plan, without cares or encumbrance; a suggestion rather than a petition; off-hand, unsentimental, yet perfectly serious, as look and tone proclaimed.

'There's much to be said for your views,' Alma replied, with humorous gravity, 'but I haven't the least intention of marrying.'

'Well, I've mentioned it.' He waved his hand as if to overcome an unwonted embarrassment. 'You don't mind?'

'Not a bit.'

'I hope we shall meet again before long, and – some day, you know – you may see the thing in another light. You mustn't think I'm joking.'

'But it *is* rather a joke.'

'No; I never was more in earnest about anything, believe me. And I'm convinced it's a good idea. However, you know one thing – if I can be of use to you, I shall. I'll think it over – your chances and so on; something may suggest itself. You're not cut out for everyday things.'

'I try to hope not.'

'Ah, but you can take my word for it.'

With this comforting assurance, Felix Dymes departed. No melodrama; a hand-grip, a significant nod, a loud humming as he went downstairs.

Alma presently began a new letter to Sibyl Carnaby. It was written in a cheery humour, though touched by the shadow of distressful circumstance. She told the story of Mr Dymes's visit, and made merry over it. 'I am sure this is the very newest thing in "proposals". Though I live in such a dull, lonely way, it has made me feel that I am still in touch with civilisation. And really, if the worst come to the worst – but it's dangerous to joke about such things.' She touched lightly on the facts of her position. 'I'm afraid I have not been doing very much. Perhaps this is a fallow time with me; I may be gaining strength for great achievements. Unfortunately, I have a lazy companion. Miss Steinfeld (you know her from my last letter, if you got it) only pretends to work. I like her for her thorough goodness and her intelligence; but she is just a little *melancholisch*, and so not exactly the companion I need. Her idea just now is that we both need "change"and she wants me to go with her to Bregenz,* on the Bodensee. Perhaps I shall when the weather gets hot.'

It had surprised her to be told by Felix Dymes that he obtained her address at Munich from Miss Leach, for the only person in England to whom she had yet made known her departure from Leipzig was her step-mother. Speak of her how they might, her acquaintances in London still took trouble to inform themselves of her movements. Perhaps the very completeness of the catastrophe in which she was involved told in her favour; possibly she excited much more interest than could ever have attached to her whilst her name was respected. There was new life in the thought. She wrote briefly to Dora Leach, giving an account of herself, which, though essentially misleading, was not composed in a spirit of conscious falsehood. For all her vanity, Alma had never aimed at effect by practice of deliberate insincerities. Miss Leach was informed that her friend could not find much time for correspondence. 'I am living in the atmosphere of art, and striving patiently. Some day you shall hear of me.' And when the letter was posted, Alma mused long on the effect it would produce.

With the distinguished violinist, the friend of Herr Wilenski, spoken of to Mrs Frothingham, she had as yet held no communication, and through the days of early summer she continued to neglect her music. Indolence grew upon her; sometimes she spent the whole day in a dressing-gown, seated or reclining, with a book in her hand, or totally unoccupied. Sometimes the military bands in the public gardens tempted her to walk a little, or she strolled with Miss Steinfeld through the picture galleries; occasionally they made short excursions into the country. The art student had acquaintances in Munich, but did not see much of them, and they were not the kind of people with whom Alma cared to associate.

In July it was decided that they should go for a few weeks to Bregenz; their health called for the change, which, as Miss

Steinfeld knew of a homely *pension*, could be had at small expense. Before their departure the art student was away for a few days, and, to relieve the dreariness of an existence which was becoming burdensome, Alma went out alone one afternoon, purposing a trip by steam-tram to the gardens at Nymphenburg. She walked to the Stiglmeyerplatz, where the tram starts, and there stood waiting. A carriage drove past, with a sound of English voices, which drew her attention. She saw three children, a lady, and a gentleman. The last-mentioned looked at her, and she recognised Cyrus Redgrave. Whether he knew her face seemed uncertain. Hoping to escape unobserved, she turned quickly, and walked a few yards. Before she faced round again, a quick footstep approached her, and the next moment Mr Redgrave stood, hat in hand, courteously claiming her acquaintance.

'I thought I could not possibly be mistaken!'

The carriage, having stopped for him to alight, was driving away.

'That is my sister and her children,' said Redgrave, when he had warmly shaken hands and expressed his pleasure at the meeting. 'You never met her. Her husband is in India, and you see me in full domesticity. This morning I posted a note to you; of course, you haven't received it yet.'

Alma did her best to behave with dignity. In any case it would have been trying to encounter such a man as Redgrave – wealthy, elegant, a figure in society, who must necessarily regard her as banished from polite circles; and in her careless costume she felt more than abashed. For the first time a sense of degradation, of social inferiority, threatened to overwhelm her self-respect.

'How did you know my address?' she asked, with an involuntary imitation of hauteur, made pathetic by the flush on her face and the lingering half-smile.

'Mrs Frothingham kindly gave it me. – You were walking this way, I think? – My sister is living at Stuttgart, and I happened to come over just in time to act as her courier on a journey to Salzburg. We got here yesterday, and go on tomorrow, or the day after. I dropped you a note, asking if I might call.'

'Where have you seen Mamma lately?' asked Alma, barely attentive to the explanations he was giving her.

'In London, quite by chance. In fact, it was at Waterloo

Station. Mrs Frothingham was starting for the country, and I happened to be going to Wimbledon. I told her I might possibly see you on my way through Munich.'

Alma began to recover herself. That Cyrus Redgrave should still take an interest in her was decidedly more gratifying than the eccentric compliment of Felix Dymes. She strove to forget the humiliation of having been found standing in a public place, waiting for a tram-car. In Redgrave's manner no change was perceptible, unless, indeed, he spoke with more cordiality, which must be prompted by kind feeling. Their acquaintance covered only a year or two, and had scarcely amounted to what passes for friendship, but Redgrave seemed oblivious of late unpleasant events.

'I'm glad you didn't call unexpectedly,' she said, trying to strike a light note. 'I'm a student now – no longer an amateur – and live as a student must.'

'So much the better. I'm a natural bohemian myself, and like nothing so well as to disregard ceremony. And, by-the-bye, that's the very reason why I ran away from my sister to speak to you; I knew you would dislike formalities. I'm afraid I was rather glad than otherwise to escape. We have been taking the children for a drive – charming little rascals, but for the moment my domestic instincts are satisfied. Mrs Frothingham mentioned that you were living with a friend – an art student.'

'We go away for a holiday in a day or two,' said Alma, more at her ease. 'To Bregenz – do you know it?'

'By name only. You go in a day or two? I wish you would let me know your address there,' he added, with frank friendliness. 'I go on with my sister to Salzburg, and then turn off on my own account; I might be able to pass your way, and I should so much like to have a talk with you – a real talk, about music and all sorts of things. Did I ever tell you of my little place at Riva, head of Lake Garda? Cosy little nook, but I'm not there very often; I half thought of going for a week or two's quietness. Quite cool there by the lake. But I really must try to see you at Bregenz – do let me.'

He begged it as a favour, a privilege, and Alma without hesitation told him where she would be living.

'For a few weeks? Oh, then, I shall make a point of coming that way. You're not working too hard, I hope? I know you don't do things by halves. When I first heard you were going in seriously for music, I said to myself, "*Tant mieux*, another great violinist!"'

The listener reddened with delight; her step became elastic; she carried her head gallantly, and feared not the glances Redgrave cast at her.

'I have learnt not to talk about myself,' she said, bestowing a smile upon him. 'That's the first bad habit to be overcome by the amateur converted.'

'Capital! An axiom worth putting into print, for the benefit of all and sundry. Now I must say goodbye; that fellow yonder will take me back to the domesticities.' He hailed an empty carriage. 'We shall meet again among the mountains. *Auf Wiedersehn*!'

Alma continued to walk along the Nymphenburg road, unconscious of external things. The tram for which she had been waiting passed by; she no longer cared to go out into the country. It was enough to keep moving in the bright sunshine, and to think her thoughts.

No; people had by no means forgotten her. Whilst she was allowing herself to fall into gloom and indolence, her acquaintances, it was evident, made her a constant subject of talk, of speculation; just what she had desired, but had lost courage to believe. They expected great things of her; her personal popularity and her talents had prevailed against the most prejudicial circumstance; people did not think of her as the daughter of Bennet Frothingham, – unless to contrast the hopefulness of her future with the black calamity that lay behind.

She waxed philosophical. How everything in this world tends to good! At her father's death she had mourned bitterly; it had struck her to the heart; his imprudence (she could never use, even in thought, a harsher word) pained more than it shamed her, and not a day passed but she sorrowed over the dishonour that darkened his memory. Yet were not these woes and disasters the beginning of a new life for *her*! In prosperity, what would she ever have become? Nothing less than being thrown out into the world could have given her the impulse needed to realise a high ambition. '*Tant mieux*, another great violinist!' How sincerely, how inspiringly, it was said!

And Alma's feet had brought her home again before she paused to reflect that, for all purposes of ambition, the past half-year had been utterly wasted. Never mind; after her return from Bregenz!

On her table lay Redgrave's note; a very civil line or two, requesting permission to call. There was another letter, black-bordered, which came from her step-mother. Mrs Frothingham said that she had been about to write for several days, but all sorts of disagreeable business had hindered her; even now, she could only write hurriedly. In the last fortnight she had had to go twice to London. 'And really I think I shall be obliged to go and live there again, for a time; so many things have to be seen to. It might be best, perhaps, if I took a small flat. I was going to say, however, that the last time I went up, I met Mr Redgrave, and we had quite a long talk – about *you*. He was most sincerely interested in your future; indeed it quite surprised me, for I will confess that I had never had a very high opinion of him. I fancy he suffered *no loss*. His behaviour to me was that of a gentle-man, very different from that of some people I could name. But it was *you* he spoke of most. He said he was shortly going to Germany, and begged me to let him have your address, and really I saw no harm in it. He may call upon you. If so, let me hear all about it, for it will interest me very much.'

Alma had half a mind to reply at once, but on reflection decided to wait. After all, Mr Redgrave might not keep his promise of coming to see her at Bregenz, and in that event a very brief report of what had happened would suffice. But she felt sure that he meant to come.

And decidedly she hoped it; why, she was content to leave a rosy vagueness.

## CHAPTER 8

Alma and her German friend silently agreed in foreseeing that they would not live together much longer. Miss Steinfeld, eager at first to talk English, was relapsing into her native tongue, and as Alma lazily avoided German, they conversed in different languages, each with a sprinkling of foreign phrase. The English girl might have allied herself with a far worse companion; for, in spite of defects which resembled Alma's own, vagueness of purpose, infirmity of will, Miss Steinfeld had a fund of moral principle which made her talk wholesome and her aspirations an influence for good. She imagined herself in love with an artist whom she had seen only two or three times, and no strain could have been more exalted than that in which she confided her romance to the sympathetic Alma. Sympathetic, that is, within her limits; for Miss Frothingham had never been in love, and rarely indulged a mood of sentiment. Her characteristic emotions she of course did not reveal, save unconsciously, and Miss Steinfeld knew nothing of the tragic circumstances which explained her friend's solitude.

In the first days at Bregenz they felt a renewal of pleasure in each other's society; Alma's spirits were much improved; she enjoyed the scenery, and lived in the open air. There was climbing of mountains, the Pfänder with its reward of noble outlook, and the easier Gebhardsberg, with its hanging woods; there was boating on the lake, and rambling along its shores, with rest and refreshment at some Gartenwithschaft. Miss Steinfeld, whose reading and intelligence were superior to Alma's, liked to explore the Roman ruins and linger in the museum. Alma could not long keep up a pretence of interest in the relics of Brigantium; but she said one day, with a smile –

'I know someone who would enjoy this kind of thing – an Englishman – very learned – '

'Old?' inquired her friend significantly.

'Yes – no. Neither old nor young. A strange man; rather interesting. I've a good mind,' she added mischievously, 'to send him a photograph.'

'Of yourself?'

'Oh dear, no!' He wouldn't care for that. A view of the Alt-Stadt.'

And in her mood of frolic she acted upon the thought. She purchased two or three views, had them done up for post, and addressed them to Harvey Rolfe, Esq, at the Metropolitan Club; for his private address she could not remember, but the club remained in her mind from Sibyl's talk of it. when the packet was gone, of course she regretted having sent it. More likely than not, Mr Rolfe considered himself to have ended all acquaintance with the disgraced family, and, if he recognised her handwriting, would just throw the photographs aside. Let him; it mattered nothing, one way or the other.

When a week had passed, the novelty of things wore off; the friends began to wander apart; Miss Steinfeld made acquaintances in the *pension*, and Alma drifted into solitude. At the end of a fortnight she was tired of everything, wished to go away, thought longingly of England. It was plain that Mr Redgrave would not come; he had never seriously meant it; his *Auf Wiedersehen* was a mere civility to get rid of her in the street. Why had he troubled to inquire about her at all? Of course it didn't matter – nothing mattered – but if ever she met him again! Alma tried her features in expression of cold scornfulness.

On the next day, as she was returning from an idle walk with her friend along the Lindau road, Mr Redgrave met them. He was dressed as she had never seen him, in flannels, with a white necktie loosely knotted and a straw hat. Not till he had come near enough to salute did she recognise him; he looked ten years younger.

They talked as if the meeting were of daily occurrence. Redgrave addressed himself to Miss Steinfeld as often as to Alma, and showed a graceful command of decorous commonplace. He had arrived early this morning, had put up at the Oesterreichischer Hof, was already delighted with Brogenz. Did Miss Steinfeld devote herself to landscape? Had she done anything here? Had Miss Frothingham brought her violin? They strolled pleasantly to the Hafen promenade, and parted at length with assurances of meeting again, as if definite appointment were needless.

'That is my idea of the English gentleman,' said Miss Steinfeld afterwards. 'I think I should have taken him for a lord. No doubt he is very rich?'

'Oh, pretty well off,' Alma replied, with assumed indifference. 'Ten thousand pounds a year, I dare say.'

'Ten thousand! *Lieber Himmel*! And married?'

'No.'

'In Parliament, I suppose?'

'No.'

'Then, what does he do?'

'Oh, amuses himself.'

Each became occupied with her thoughts. Alma's were so agreeable, that Miss Steinfeld, observing her, naturally fell into romantic speculation.

Redgrave easily contrived that his next walk should be with

Miss Frothingham alone. He overtook her next morning, soon after she had left the house, and they rambled in the Gebhards-berg direction.

'Now let us have the promised talk,' he began at a favourable moment. 'I've been thinking about you all the time.'

'Did you go to your place on Lake Garda?'

'Yes; just to look at it, and get it put in order. I hope to be there again before long. You didn't doubt I should come?'

'You left it uncertain.'

'To be sure. Life is uncertain. But I should have been desperately disappointed if I hadn't found you here. There are so many things to be said about going in for music as a profession. You have the talent, you have the physical strength, I think.' His eye flattered her from head to foot. 'But, to be a great artist, one must have more than technical qualifications. It's the soul that must be developed.'

Alma laughed.

'I know it. And what is your receipt for developing the soul?'

Redgrave paused in his walk. Smiling, he gave a twist to his moustache, and appeared to meditate profoundly.

'The soul – well, it has a priggish sound. Let us say the character; and that is developed through experience of life.'

'I'm getting it.'

'Are you? In the company of Miss Steinfeld? I'm afraid that won't carry you very far. Experience means emotion; certainly, for a woman. Believe me, you haven't begun to live yet. You may practise on your violin day and night, and it won't profit you – until you have *lived*.'

Alma was growing serious. These phrases harmonised well enough with her own insubstantial thoughts and idly-gathered notions. When preparing to escape from England, she had used much the same language. But, after all, what did it mean? What, in particular, did Cyrus Redgrave mean, with his expressive eyes, and languid, earnest tone?

'You will say that a girl has few opportunities. True, thanks to her enslavement by society.'

'I care nothing for society,' Alma interposed.

'Good! I like the sound of that defiance; it has the right ring. A man hasn't often the pleasure of hearing that from a woman he can respect. It's easy, of course, to defy the laws of a world one doesn't belong to; but you, who are a queen in your circle, and may throne, at any moment, in a wider sphere – it means much when you refuse to bow down before the vulgar idols, to be fettered by superstitions.'

His aim was dark to her, but she tasted the compliment which ignored her social eclipse. Redgrave's conversation generally kept on the prosaic levels – studiously polite, or suavely cynical. It was a new experience to see him borne on a wave of rhetoric; yet not borne away, for he spoke with an ease, a self-command, which to older ears would have suggested skill rather than feeling. He had nothing of the ardour of youth; his poise and deliberation were quite in keeping with the two score years that subtly graved his visage; the passions in him were sportive, half-fantastical, as though, together with his brain, they had grown to a ripe worldliness. He inspired no distrust; his good nature seemed all-pervading; he had the air of one who lavishes disinterested counsel, and ever so little exalts himself with his facile exuberance of speech.

'I have seen much of artists; known them intimately, and studied their lives. One and all, they date their success from some passionate experience. From a cold and conventional existence can come nothing but cold and conventional art. You left England, broke away from the common routine, from the artificial and the respectable. That was an indispensable first step, and I have told you how I applauded it. But you cannot stop at this. I begin to fear for you. There is a convention of unconventionality: poor quarters, hard life, stinted pleasures – all that kind of thing. I fear its effect upon you.'

'What choice have I?' exclaimed Alma, moved to familiar frankness. 'If I *am* poor, I must live poorly.'

He smiled graciously upon her, and raised his hand almost as though he would touch her with reassuring kindness; but it was only to stroke his trimmed beard.

'Oh, you have a choice, believe me,' came his airy answer. 'There's no harm in poverty that doesn't last too long. You may have profited by it; it is an experience. But now – Don't let us walk so far as to tire you. Yes, we will turn. Variety of life, travel, all sorts of joys and satisfactions – these are the things you need.'

'And if they are not within my reach?' she asked, without looking at him.

'By-the-bye' – he disregarded her question – 'your friend, Mrs Carnaby, has taken a long flight.'

'Yes.'

The monosyllable was dropped. Alma walked with her eyes on the ground, trailing her sunshade.

'I didn't think she had much taste for travel. But you know her so much better than I do.'

'She is enjoying herself,' said Alma.

'No need for *you* to go so far. Down yonder' – he nodded southward – 'I was thinking, the other day, of the different kinds of pleasure one gets from scenery in different parts of the world. I have seen the tropics; they left me very much where I was, intellectually. It's the human associations of natural beauty that count. You have no desire to go to the islands of the Pacific?'

'I can't say that I have.'

'Of course not. The springs of art are in the old world. Among the vines and the olives one hears a voice. I must really try to give you some idea of my little place at Riva.'

He began a playful description – long, but never tedious; alluring, yet without enthusiasm – a dreamy suggestion of refined delights and luxuries.

'I have another place in the Pyrenees, to suit another mood; and not long ago I was sorely tempted by the offer of a house not far from Antioch,* in the valley of the Orontes – a house built by an Englishman. Charming place, and so entirely off the beaten track. Isn't there a fascination in the thought of living near Antioch? Well away from bores and philistines. No Mrs Grundy with her clinking tea-cups. I dare say the house is still to be had. – Oh, do tell me something about your friend, Fräulein Steinfeld. Is she in earnest? Will she do anything?'

His eloquence was at an end. Thenceforward he talked of common things in unemotional language; and when Alma parted from him, it was with a sense of being tired and disappointed.

On the following day she did not see him at all. He could not have left Bregenz, for, of course, he would have let her know. She thought of him incessantly, reviewing all his talk, turning over this and that ambiguous phrase, asking herself whether he meant much or little. It was natural that she should compare and contrast his behaviour with that of Felix Dymes. If his motive were not the same, why did he seek her society? And if it were? If at length he spoke out, summing his hints in the plain offer of all those opportunities she lacked?

A brilliant temptation. To leave the world as Alma Frothingham, and to return to it as Mrs Cyrus Redgrave!

But, in that event, what of her musical ambitions? He spoke of her art as the supreme concern, to which all else must be subordinate. And surely that was his meaning when he threw scorn upon 'bores and philistines'. Why should the fact of his wealth interfere with her progress as an artist? Possibly, on the other hand, he did not intend that she should follow a professional career. Cannot one be a great artist without standing on public platforms? Was it his lordly thought to foster her talents for his own delectation and that of the few privileged?

Her brain grew confused with interpreting and picturing. But once more she had made an advance in self-esteem. She could await the next meeting with a confidence and pride very unlike her sensations in the Stiglmeyerplatz at Munich.

It took place on the second day. This time Redgrave did not wait upon accident; he sent a note, begging that he might have the pleasure of another talk with her. He would call at a certain hour, and take his chance of finding her at home. When he presented himself, Alma was sitting in the common room of the *pension* with two German ladies; they in a few minutes withdrew, and familiar conversation became possible. As the windows stood open, and there were chairs upon the balcony, Redgrave shortly proposed a move in that direction. They sat together for half an hour.

When Redgrave took his leave, it was without shaking of hands – with no *Auf Wiedersehen*. He smiled, he murmured civilities; Alma neither smiled nor spoke. She was pale, and profoundly agitated.'

So this was his meaning? – made plain enough at last, though with the most graceful phrasing. Childish vanity and ignorance had forbidden her to dream of such an issue. She had not for a moment grasped the significance to a man of the world of the ruin and disgrace fallen upon her family. In theory she might call herself an exile from the polite world; none the less did she imagine herself still illumined by the social halo, guarded by the divinity which doth hedge a member of the upper-middle class.* Was she not a lady? And who had ever dared to offer a lady an

insult such as this?* Shop-girls, minor actresses, the inferior sort
of governess, must naturally be on their guard; their insecurity
was traditional; novel and drama represented their moral vicis-
situdes. But a lady, who had lived in a great house with many
servants, who had founded an Amateur Quartet Society, the
hem of whose garment had never been touched with irreverent
finger – could *she* stand in peril of such indignity?

Not till now had she called to mind the forewarnings of Sibyl
Carnaby, which, at the time of hearing them, she did not at all
understand. 'People,' said Sibyl, 'would approach her with
strange ideas.' This she might have applied to the grotesque
proposal (as it seemed to her) of Felix Dymes, or to the risk of
being tempted into premature publicity by a business offer from
some not very respectable impresario. What Sibyl meant was
now only too clear; but how little could Mrs Carnaby have
imagined that her warning would be justified by one of her own
friends – by a man of wealth and consideration.

She durst not leave the house for fear of encountering
Redgrave, who, if they crossed by chance, might fancy she
invited another meeting. She dreaded the observation of women,
especially of Miss Steinfeld. The only retreat was her bedroom,
and here she secluded herself till dinner-time. At this meal she
must needs face the company or incur remark. She tried to
return her friend's smile with the ordinary unconcern. After
dinner there was no avoiding Miss Steinfeld, whose air of
extreme discretion showed that she had an inkling of events,
and awaited confidences.

'Mr Redgrave has gone – he called to say goodbye.'

'*So?*'

Irritated by self-consciousness, revolting against a misinterpre-
tation which would injure her vanity, though it was not likely
to aim at her honour, Alma had recourse to fiction.

'I daresay you guess? – Yes, and I refused.'

Miss Steinfeld was puzzled. It did not astonish her that a girl
should reject ten thousand pounds per annum, for that she was
too high-minded; but she had thought it beyond doubt that
Alma's heart was engaged. Here, it had seemed to her, was the
explanation of a mystery attaching to this original young
Englishwoman; unhoped, the brilliant lover, the secretly
beloved, had sought her in her retirement. And after all, it was
a mistake.

'I don't care for him a bit,' Alma went on. 'It had to be got over and done with, that was all.'

She felt ashamed of herself. In childhood she had told falsehoods freely, but with the necessity for that kind of thing the habit had fallen away. Solace, however, was at hand, for the German girl looked at her with a new interest, a new sympathy, which Alma readily construed as wonder and admiration, if not gentle envy. To have refused an offer of marriage from a handsome man of great wealth might be counted for glory. And Alma's momentary shame yielded to a gratification which put her outwardly at ease.

The restless night brought torment of the mind and harassed spirits. Redgrave's proposal echoed in the vacant chambers of her life, sounding no longer an affront, but an allurement. Why, indeed, had she repelled it so unthinkingly? It did not necessarily mean scandal. He had not invited her to open defiance of the world. 'You can absolutely trust me; I am discretion itself. All resources are at my command.' Why had she rejected with scorn and horror what was, perhaps, her great opportunity, the one hope of her struggling and sinking ambition? She had lost faith in herself; in her power to overcome circumstances, not yet in her talent, in her artistic birthright. Redgrave would have made her path smooth. 'I promise you a great reputation in two or three years' time.' And without disgrace, without shadow of suspicion, it would all be managed, he declared, so very easily. For what alternative had she rebuffed him?

Redgrave's sagacity had guided him well up to a certain point, but it had lost sight of one thing essential to the success of his scheme. Perhaps because he was forty years of age, perhaps because he had so often come and seen and conquered, perhaps because he made too low an estimate of Bennet Frothingham's daughter, – he simply overlooked sentimental considerations. It was a great and a fatal oversight. He went far in his calculated appeal to Alma's vanity; had he but credited her with softer passions, and given himself the trouble to play upon them, he would not, at all events, have suffered so sudden a defeat. Men of Redgrave's stamp grow careless, and just at the time of life when, for various causes, the art which conceals art has become indispensable. He did not flatter himself that Alma was ready to fall in love with him; and here his calm maturity served him ill. To his own defect of ardour he was blinded by habit. After all, the affair had little consequence. It had only suggested itself after the meeting in Munich, and perhaps – he said to himself – all things considered, the event was just as well.

But Alma felt the double insult, to her worldly honour, to her womanhood. The man had not even made pretence of loving her; and this, whilst it embittered her disappointment, strengthened her to cast from her mind the baser temptation. Marriage she would have accepted, though doubtless with becoming hesitancy; the offer could not have been made without one word of tenderness (for Cyrus Redgrave was another than Felix Dymes), and she had not felt it impossible to wed this polished capitalist. Out of the tumult of her feelings, as another day went by, issued at length that one simple and avowable sense of disappointment. She had grasped the prize, and heated her imagination in regarding it; had overcome natural reluctances, objections personal and moral; was ready to sit down and write to Mrs Frothingham the splendid, startling announcement. And here she idled in her bedroom, desolate, hopeless, wishing she had courage to steal down at night to the waters of the Bodensee, and end it all.

On the third day she returned to Munich, having said farewell to her friend, who was quite prepared for the parting. From Munich she proceeded to Leipzig, and there entered again the family circle of the Gassners. She had no intention of staying for very long; the pretence of musical study could not be kept up; but her next step was quite uncertain.

A fortnight later, Mrs Frothingham wrote thus: –

'I am sending you on a letter which, if I am not mistaken, comes from Mr Rolfe. Do tell me if I am right. Odd that he should write to you, if it is he. You have not told me yet whether you saw Mr Redgrave again. But I see that you don't care much, and perhaps it is as well.'

The forwarded letter had been originally addressed to the care of Mrs Frothingham, and Alma, at a glance, recognised Harvey Rolfe's writing. He dated from London. Was he mistaken, he began, in thinking that certain photographs from Bregenz had come to him by Miss Frothingham's kindness? For his part, he had spent June in a ramble in South-west France, chiefly by the Dordogne, and through a strange, interesting bit of marsh-country, called La Double. 'I hardly know how I got there, and I shall not worry you by writing any account of the expedition.

But at a miserable village called La Roche Chalais,* where I had a most indigestible supper and a bed unworthy of the name, I managed to fall ill, and quite seriously thought, "Ah, here is the end!" It has to come somewhere, and why not on a *grabat** at La Roche Chalais? A mistake; I am here again, wasting life as strenuously as ever. Would you let me hear from you? I should think it a great addition to your kindness in sending the views.' And so, with every good wish, he remained, &c.

Having nothing better to do, Alma got out a map of France, and searched for La Roche Chalais; but the place was too insignificant to be marked. On the morrow, being still without occupation, she answered Rolfe's letter, and in quite a playful vein. She had no time to correspond with people who 'wasted their lives'. To her, life was a serious matter enough. But he knew nothing of the laborious side of a musician's existence, and probably doubted its reality. As an afterthought, she thanked him gravely for his letter, and hoped that some day, when she had really 'done something', they might meet and renew their friendship.

## CHAPTER 9

On an afternoon in September, Harvey Rolfe spent half an hour at a certain London bookseller's, turning over books that dealt with the theory and practice of elementary education. Two or three of them he selected, and ordered to be sent to a lady at Gunnersbury. On his way out he came upon an acquaintance making a purchase in another department of the shop. It was some months since he had seen Cecil Morphew, who looked in indifferent health, and in his dress came near to shabbiness. They passed out together, Morphew carrying an enwrapped volume, which he gave Rolfe to understand was a birthday present – for *her*. The elder man resisted his inclination to joke, and asked how things were going on.

'Much the same as usual, except that her father is in very bad health. It's brutal, but I wish he would die.'

'Naturally.'

'That's what one's driven to, you see. And anyone but you,

who know me, would set me down as a selfish, calculating beast. Can't help it. I had rather have her penniless. – Will you come in here with me? I want to buy some pyrogallic acid.'*

In the street again, Morphew mentioned that he had taken up photography.

'It gives me something to do, and it takes me out into the open air. This beastly town is the ruin of me, in every way. – Come to my rooms for an hour, will you? I'll show you some attempts; I've only just tried my hand at developing. And it's a long time since we had a talk.'

They made for a Chelsea omnibus and mounted.

'I thought you were never in town at this time,' Morphew resumed. 'I want to get away, but can't afford it; devilish low-water with me. I must have a bicycle. With that and the camera I may just manage to live; often there seems little enough to live for. – Tripcony? Oh, Tripcony's a damned swindler; I've given him up. Speculation isn't quite so simple as I imagined. I made a couple of hundred, though – yes, and lost nearly three.'

The young man's laugh was less pleasant to hear than formerly. Altogether, Rolfe observed in him a decline, a loss of refinement as well as of vitality.

'Why don't you go into the country?' he said. 'Take a cottage and grow cabbages; dig for three hours a day. It would do you no end of good.'

'Of course it would. I wish I had the courage.'

'I'm going to spend the winter in Wales,' said Harvey. 'An out-of-the-world place in Carnarvonshire – mountains and sea. Come along with me, and get the mephitis* blown out of you. You've got town disease, street-malaria, lodging-house fever.'

'By Jove, I'll think of it,' replied the other, with a strange look of eagerness. 'But I don't know whether I can. No, I can't be sure. But I'll try.'

'What holds you?'

'Well, I like to be near, you know, to *her*. And then – all sorts of difficulties –'

Morphew had his lodgings at present in a street near Chelsea Hospital, a poor-looking place, much inferior to those in which Rolfe had formerly seen him. His two rooms were at the top, and he had converted a garret into a dark chamber for his photographic amusement. Dirt and disorder made the sitting-room very uninviting; Rolfe looked about him, and wondered what principle of corruption was at work in the young man's life.

Morphew showed a new portrait of his betrothed, Henrietta Winter; a comely face, shadowed with pensiveness. 'Taken at Torquay; she sent it a day or two ago. – I've been thinking of giving her up. If I do, I shall do it brutally and savagely, to make it easy for her. I've spoilt her life, and I'm pretty sure I've ruined my own.'

He brought out a bottle of whisky and half filled two tumblers. His own measure he very slightly diluted, and drank it off at once.

'You're at a bad pass, my boy,' remarked Rolfe. 'What's wrong? Something more than usual, I know. Make a clean breast of it.'

Morphew continued to declare that he was only low-spirited from the longstanding causes, and, though Rolfe did not believe him, nothing more could at present be elicited. The talk turned to photography, but still had no life in it.

'I think you had better dine with me this evening,' said Harvey.

'Impossible. I wish I could. An engagement.'

The young man shuffled about, and after a struggle with embarrassment, aided by another tumbler of whisky, threw out something he wished to say.

'It's deuced hard to ask you, but – could you lend me some money?'

'Of course. How much? Why do you make such a sputter about it?'

'I've been making a fool of myself – got into difficulties. Will you let me have fifty pounds?'

'Yes, if you'll promise to clear at once out of this dust-bin, and in a month or so come into Wales.'

'You're an awfully good fellow, Rolfe, – and I'm a damned fool. I promise! I will! I'll get out of it, and then I'll think about breaking with that girl. Better for both of us – but you shall advise me. – I'll tell you everything some day. I can't now. I'm too ashamed of myself.'

When he got home, Harvey wrote a cheque for fifty pounds, and posted it at once.

Not many days after, there came to him a letter from Mrs Frothingham. With this lady he had held no communication since the catastrophe of last November; knowing not how to address her without giving more pain than his sympathy could counterbalance, he remained silent. She wrote from the neighbourhood of Swiss Cottage,* where she had taken a flat; it was her wish, if possible, to see him 'on a matter of business', and she requested that he would make an appointment. Much wondering in what business of Mrs Frothingham's he could be concerned, Harvey named his time, and went to pay the call. He ascended many stairs, and was conducted by a neat servant-maid into a pleasant little drawing-room, where Mrs Frothingham rose to receive him. She searched his face, as if to discern the feeling with which he regarded her, and her timid smile of reassurance did not lack its pathos.

'Mr Rolfe, it seems years since I saw you.'

She was aged a little, and her voice fell in broken notes, an unhappy contrast to the gay, confident chirping of less than twelve months ago.

'I have only been settled here for a week. I thought of leaving London altogether, but, after all, I had to come backwards and forwards so often, – it was better to have a home here, and this little flat will just suit me, I think.'

She seemed desirous of drawing attention to its modest proportions.

'I really don't need a house, and lodgings are so wretched. These flats are a great blessing – don't you think? I shall manage here with one servant, only one.'

Rolfe struggled with the difficulty of not knowing what to say. There was nothing for it but to discourse as innocently as might be on the advantages of flats, their increasing popularity, and the special charms of this particular situation. Mrs Frothingham eagerly agreed with everything, and did her best to allow no moment of silence.

'You have heard from Miss Frothingham, I think?' she presently let fall, with a return of anxiety.

'Not very long ago. From Leipzig.'

'Yes. Yes. – I don't know whether she will stay there. You know she is thinking of taking up music professionally? – Yes. Yes. – I do so hope she will find it possible, but of course that kind of career is so very uncertain. I'm not sure that I shouldn't be glad if she turned to something else.'

The widow was growing nervous and self-contradictory. With

a quick movement of her hands, she suddenly resumed in another tone.

'Mr Rolfe, I do so wish you would let me speak to you in confidence. I want to ask your help in a most delicate matter. Not, of course, about my step-daughter, though I shall have to mention her. It is something quite personal to myself. If I could hope that you wouldn't think it tiresome – I have a special reason for appealing to you.'

He would gladly, said Harvey, be of any use he could.

'I want to speak to you about painful things,' pursued his hostess, with an animation and emphasis which made her more like the lady of Fitzjohn Avenue. 'You know everything – except my own position, and that is what I wish to explain to you. I won't go into details. I will only say that a few years ago my husband made over to me a large sum of money – I had none of my own – and that it still belongs to me. I say belongs to me; but there is my trouble. I fear I have no right whatever to call it mine. And there are people who have suffered such dreadful losses. Some of them you know. There was a family named Abbott. I wanted to ask you about them. Poor Mr Abbott – I remember reading—'

She closed her eyes for an instant, and the look upon her face told that this was no affectation of an anguished memory.

'It was accident,' Rolfe hastened to say. 'The jury found it accidental death.'

'But there was the loss – I read it all. He had lost everything. Do tell me what became of his family. Someone told me they were friends of yours.'

'Happily they had no children. There was a small life-insurance. Mrs Abbott used to be a teacher, and she is going to take that up again.'

'Poor thing! Is she quite young?'

'Oh, about thirty, I should say.'

'Will she go into a school?'

'No. Private pupils at her own house. She has plenty of courage, and will do fairly well, I think.'

'Still, it is shocking that she should have lost all – her husband, too, just at that dreadful time. This is what I wanted to say, Mr Rolfe. Do you think it would be possible to ask her to accept something – ? I do so feel,' she hurried on, 'that I ought to make some sort of restitution – what I can – to those who lost everything. I am told that things are not quite hopeless; something may be recovered out of the wreck some day. But it will be such a long time, and meanwhile people are suffering so. And here am I left in comfort – more than comfort. It isn't right; I couldn't rest till I did something. I am glad to say that I have been able to help a little here and there, but only the kind of people whom it's easy to help. A case like Mrs Abbott's is far worse, yet there's such a difficulty in doing anything; one might only give offence. I'm sure my name must be hateful to her – as it is to so many.'

Rolfe listened with a secret surprise. He had never thought ill of Mrs Frothingham; but, on the other hand, had never attributed to her any save superficial qualities, a lightsome temper, pleasure in hospitality, an easy good nature towards all the people of her acquaintance. He would not have supposed her capable of substantial sacrifices; least of all, on behalf of strangers and inspired by a principle. She spoke with the simplest sincerity; it was impossible to suspect her motives. The careless liking with which he had always regarded her was now infused with respect; he became gravely attentive, and answered in a softer voice.

'She was embittered at first, but is overcoming it. To tell you the truth, I think she will benefit by this trial. I don't like the words that are so often used in cant; I don't believe that misery does any good to most people – indeed, I know very well that it generally does harm. But Mrs Abbott seems to be an exception; she has a good deal of character; and there were circumstances – well, I will only say that she faces the change in her life very bravely.'

'I do wish I knew her. But I daren't ask that. It's too much to expect that she could bear to see me and listen to what I have to say.'

'The less she's reminded of the past the better, I think.'

'But would it not be possible to do something? I am told that the sum was about fifteen hundred pounds. The whole of that I couldn't restore; but half of it – I could afford so much. Could I offer to do so – not directly, in my own name, but through you?'

Harvey reflected, his head and body bent forward, his hands folded together. In the flat beneath, someone was jingling operetta on a piano not quite in tune; the pertinacious vivacity of the airs interfered with Harvey's desire to view things seriously. He had begun to wonder how large a capital Mrs Frothingham had at her command. Was it not probable that she could as easily bestow fifteen hundred pounds as the half of that sum? But the question was unworthy. If in truth she had set herself to undo as much as possible of the wrong perpetrated by her husband, Mrs Frothingham might well limit her benefactions, be her fortune what it might.

'I will do whatever you desire,' he said, with deliberation. 'I cannot answer for Mrs Abbott, but, if you wish it, she shall know what you have in mind.'

'I do wish it,' replied the lady earnestly. 'I beg you to put this before her, and with all the persuasion you can use. I should be very, very glad if she would allow me to free my conscience from a little of this burden. Only that I dare not speak of it, I would try to convince you that I am doing what my dear husband himself would have wished. You can't believe it; no one will ever believe it; even Alma, I am afraid – and that is so cruel, so dreadful; but he did not mean to wrong people in this way. It wasn't in his nature. Who knew him better than I, or so well? I know – if he could come back to us—'

Her voice broke. The piano below jingled more vivaciously than ever, and a sound of shrill laughter pierced through the notes. Afraid to sit silent, lest he should seem unsympathetic and sceptical, Rolfe murmured a few harmless phrases, tending to nervous incoherence.

'I am thinking so much about Alma,' pursued the widow, recovering self-command. 'I am so uncertain about my duty to her. Of her own, she has nothing; but I know, of course, that her father wished her to share in what he gave me. It is strange, Mr Rolfe, that I should be talking to you as if you were a relative – as if I had a right to trouble you with these things. But if you knew how few people I dare speak to. Wasn't it so much better for her to lead a very quiet life? And so I gave her only a little money, only enough to live upon in the simplest way. I hoped she would get tired of being among strangers, and come back. And now I fear she thinks I have behaved meanly and selfishly. And we were always so kindly disposed to each other, such thorough friends; never a word that mightn't have passed between a mother and her own child.'

'I gathered from her letter,' interposed Harvey, 'that she was well contented and working hard at her music.'

'Do you think so? I began to doubt – she wrote in low spirits. Of course, one can't say whether she would succeed as a violinist. Oh, I don't like to think of it! I must tell you that I haven't said a word to her yet of what I am doing; I mean, about the money. I know I ought to consider *her* as much as other people. Poor girl, who has suffered more, and in so many ways? But I think of what I keep for myself as hers. I was not brought up in luxury, Mr Rolfe. It wouldn't seem to me hard to live on a very little. But in this, too, I must consider Alma. I daren't lose all my acquaintances. I must keep a home for Alma, and a home she wouldn't feel ashamed of. Here, you see, she could have her friends. I have thought of going to Leipzig; but I had so much rather she came to London – if only for us just to talk and understand each other.'

Harvey preserved the gravest demeanour. Of Alma he would not permit himself to speak, save in answer to a direct question; and that was not long in coming.

'I am sure you think I should be quite open with her?'

'That would seem to me the best.'

'Yes; she shall know all my thoughts. But with regard to Mrs Abbott, I know so well what she would say. I beg you to do me that kindness, Mr Rolfe.'

'I will write to Mrs Abbott at once.'

The interview was at an end; neither had anything more to say. They parted with looks of much mutual kindliness, Harvey having promised to make another call when Mrs Abbott's reply had reached him.

After exchanging letters with Mrs Abbott, Harvey went over to see her; for the sake of both persons concerned, he resolved to leave no possibility of misunderstanding. A few days passed in discussions and reflections, then, at the customary hour for paying calls, he again ascended the many stairs to Mrs Frothingham's flat. It had rained all day, and in this weather there seemed a certainty that the lady would be at home. But, as he approached the door, Harvey heard a sound from within which discomposed him. Who, save one person, was likely to be playing on the violin in these rooms? He paused, cast about him a glance of indecision, and finally pressed the electric bell.

Mrs Frothingham was not at home. She might return very shortly.

'Is – Miss Frothingham at home?'

The servant did not straightway admit him, but took his name. On his entering the drawing-room, three figures appeared before him. He saw Alma; he recognised Miss Leach; the third lady was named to him as Miss Leach's sister.

'You knew I was in London?' Alma remarked rather than inquired.

'I had no idea of it – until I heard your violin.'

'My violin, but not my playing. It was Miss Leach.'

From the first word – her 'Ah, how d'you do' as he entered – Alma's tone and manner appeared to him forced, odd, unlike anything he remembered of her. In correcting him, she gave a hard, short laugh, glancing at Dora Leach in a way verging upon the ill-bred. Her look had nothing amiable, though she continuously smiled, and when she invited the visitor to be seated, it was with off-hand familiarity very unflattering to his ear.

'You came to see Mamma, of course. I dare say she won't be long. She had to go through the rain on business with someone or other – perhaps you know. Have you been in London all the summer? Oh no, I remember you told me you had been somewhere in France; on the Loire, wasn't it?'

Rolfe dropped a careless affirmative. His temper prompted him to ask whether Miss Frothingham knew the difference between the Loire and the Garonne; but on the whole he was more puzzled than offended. What had come over this young woman? Outwardly she was not much altered – a little thinner in the face, perhaps; her eyes seeming a trifle darker and deeper set; but in the point of demeanour she had appreciably suffered. Her bearing and mode of speech were of that kind which, in a man, would be called devil-may-care. Was it a result of student-life? If her stinted allowance had already produced effects such as this, Mrs Frothingham was justified in uneasiness.

He turned to Miss Leach, and with her talked exclusively for some minutes. As soon as civility permitted, he would rise and make his escape. Alma, the while, chatted with the younger sister, whom she addressed as 'Gerda'. Then the door opened, and Mrs Frothingham came in, wearing her out-of-doors costume; she fixed her eyes on Rolfe with a peculiar intensity, and gave him cordial welcome, though in few and nervous words.

'I am no longer alone, you see.' She threw a swift side-glance at Alma. 'It is a great pleasure.'

'Does it rain still, Mamma?' asked Alma in a high voice.

'Not just now, my dear; but it's very disagreeable.'

'Then I'll walk with you to the station.' She addressed the sisters. 'Dora and Gerda can't stay; they have an appointment at five o'clock. They'll come again in a day or two.'

After the leave-takings, and when Alma, with a remark that she would not be long, had closed the door behind her, Mrs Frothingham seated herself and began to draw off her gloves. The bonnet and cloak she was wearing, though handsome and in the mode, made her look older than at Rolfe's last visit. She was now a middle-aged woman, with emphasis on the qualifying term; in home dress she still asserted her sex, grace of figure and freshness of complexion prevailing over years and sorrows. At this moment, moreover, weariness, and perhaps worry, appeared in her countenance.

'Thank you so much for coming,' she said quietly. 'You must have been surprised when you saw—'

'I was, indeed.'

'And my surprise was still greater, when, without any warning, Alma walked into the room two days ago. But I was so glad, so very glad.'

She breathed a little sigh, looking round.

'Hasn't Alma given her friends any tea? I must ring – Thank you. – Oh, the wretched, wretched day! I seem to notice the weather so much more than I used to. Does it affect you at all?'

Not till the tea-tray was brought in, and she had sipped from her cup, did Mrs Frothingham lay aside these commonplaces. With abrupt gravity, and in a subdued voice, she at length inquired the result of Rolfe's delicate mission.

'I think,' he replied, 'that I made known your wish as clearly and urgently as possible. I have seen Mrs Abbott, and written to her twice. It will be best, perhaps, if I ask you to read her final letter. I have her permission to show it to you.'

He drew the letter from its envelope, and with a nervous hand Mrs Frothingham took it for perusal. Whilst she was thus occupied, Rolfe averted his eyes; when he knew that she had read to the end, he looked at her. She had again sighed, and Harvey could not help imagining it an involuntary signal of relief.

'I am very glad to have read this, Mr Rolfe. If you had merely told me that Mrs Abbott refused, I should have felt nothing but pain. As it is, I understand that she *could* only refuse, and I am most grateful for all she says about me. I regret more than ever that I don't know her.'

As she handed the letter back, it shook like a blown leaf. She was pale, and spoke with effort. But in a few moments, when conversation was resumed, her tone took a lightness and free-dom which confirmed Rolfe's impression that she had escaped from a great embarrassment; and this surmise he inevitably connected with Alma's display of strange ill-humour.

Not another word passed on the subject. With frequent glances towards the door, Mrs Frothingham again talked com-monplace. Harvey, eager to get away, soon rose.

'Oh, you are not going? Alma will be back in a momont.'

And as her step-mother spoke, the young lady reappeared.

'Why didn't you give your friends tea, dear?'

'I forgot all about it. That comes of living alone. Dora has composed a gavotte, Mamma. She was playing it when Mr Rolfe came. It's capital! Is Mr Rolfe going?'

Harvey murmured his peremptory resolve. Mrs Frothingham, rising, said that she was almost always at home in the afternoon; that it would always give her so much pleasure—

'You remain in England?' asked Harvey, barely touching the hand which Alma cavalierly offered.

'I really don't know. Perhaps I ought to, just to look after Mamma.'

Mrs Frothingham uttered a little exclamation, and tried to laugh. On the instant, Harvey withdrew.

By the evening's post on the following day he was surprised to receive a letter addressed in Alma's unmistakable hand. The contents did not allay his wonder.

DEAR ME ROLFE,

I am sure you will not mind if I use the privilege of a fairly long acquaintance and speak plainly about something that I regard as important. I wish to say that I am quite old enough, and feel quite competent, to direct the course of my own life. It is very kind of you, indeed, to take an interest in what I do and what I hope to do, and I am sure Mamma will be fittingly grateful for any advice you may have offered with regard to me. But I feel obliged to say quite distinctly that I must manage my own affairs. Pray excuse this freedom, and believe me, yours truly,

                              ALMA FLORENCE FROTHINGHAM

He gasped, and with wide eyes read the missive again and again. As soon as his nerves were quieted, he sat down and replied thus: –

DEAR MISS FROTHINGHAM,
Your frankness can only be deemed a compliment. It is perhaps a triviality on my part, but I feel prompted to say that I have at no time discussed your position or prospects with Mrs Frothingham, and that I have neither offered advice on the subject nor have been requested to do so. If this statement should appear to you at all germane to the matter, I beg you will take it into consideration. – And I am, yours truly,

HARVEY RADCLIFFE ROLFE

## CHAPTER 10

This reply despatched, Harvey congratulated himself on being quits with Miss Frothingham. Her letter, however amusing, was deliberate impertinence; to have answered it in a serious tone would have been to encourage ill-mannered conceit which merited nothing but a snub.

But what had excited her anger? Had Mrs Frothingham been guilty of some indiscretion, or was it merely the result of hot-headed surmises and suspicions on the girl's part? Plainly, Alma had returned to England in no amiable mood; in all probability she resented her step-mother's behaviour, now that it had been explained to her; there had arisen 'unpleasantness' on the old, the eternal subject – money. Ignoble enough; but was it a new thing for him to discern ignoble possibilities in Alma's nature?

Nevertheless, his thoughts were constantly occupied with the girl. Her image haunted him; all his manhood was subdued and mocked by her scornful witchery. From the infinitudes of reverie, her eyes drew near and gazed upon him – eyes gleaming with mischief, keen with curiosity; a look now supercilious, now softly submissive; all the varieties of expression caught in susceptible moments, and stored by a too faithful memory. Her hair, her lips, her neck, grew present to him, and lured his fancy with a wanton seduction. In self-defence – pathetic stratagem of intellectual man at issue with the flesh – he fell back upon the idealism which ever strives to endow a fair woman with a beautiful soul; he endeavoured to forget her body in contemplation of the spiritual excellencies that might lurk behind it. To depreciate her was simpler, and had generally been his wont; but subjugation had reached another stage in him. He summoned all possible pleadings on the girl's behalf: her talents, her youth, her grievous trials. Devotion to classical music cannot but argue a certain loftiness of mind; it might, in truth, be somehow akin to 'religion'. Remembering his own follies and vices at the age of four-and-twenty, was it not reason, no less than charity, to see in Alma the hope of future good? Nay, if it came to that, did she not embody infinitely more virtue, in every sense of the word, than he at the same age?

One must be just to women, and, however paltry the causes, do honour to the cleanliness of their life. Nothing had suggested to him that Alma was unworthy of everyday respect. Even when ill-mannered, she did not lose her sexual dignity. And after all she had undergone, there would have been excuse enough for decline of character, to say nothing of a lapse from the articles of good breeding. This letter of hers, what did it signify but the revolt of a spirit of independence, irritated by all manner of sufferings, great and small? Ought he not to have replied in other terms? Was it worthy of him – man of the world, with passions, combats, experience multiform, assimilated in his long, slow growth – to set his sarcasm against a girl's unhappiness?

He was vexed with himself. He had not behaved as a gentleman. And how many a time, in how many situations, had he incurred this form of self-reproach!

When a week went by without anything more from Alma, Harvey ceased to trouble. As the fates directed, so be it. He began to pack the books which he would take with him into Wales.

One day he found himself at Kensington High Street, waiting for a City train. In idleness, he watched the people who alighted from carriages on the opposite side of the platform, and among them he saw Alma. On her way towards the stairs she was obliged to pass him; he kept his position, and only looked into her face when she came quite near. She bent her head with a half-smile, stopped, and spoke in a low voice, without sign of embarrassment.

'I was quite wrong. I found it out soon after I had written, and I have wanted to beg your pardon.'

'It is my part to do that,' Harvey replied. 'I ought not to have answered as I did.'

'Perhaps not – all things considered. I'm rather in a hurry. Good-morning!'

As a second thought, she offered her hand. Harvey watched her trip up the stairs.

Next morning he had a letter from her. 'Dear Mr Rolfe,' she wrote, 'did you let Mamma know of my hasty and foolish behaviour? If not – and I very much hope you didn't – please not to reply to this, but let us see you on Wednesday afternoon, just in the ordinary way. If Mamma *has* been told, still don't trouble to write, and in that case I dare say you will not care to come. If you are engaged this Wednesday, perhaps you could come next.' And she signed herself his sincerely.

He did not reply, and Wednesday saw him climbing once more to the little flat; ashamed of being here, yet unable to see how he could have avoided it, except by leaving London. For that escape he had no longer much mind. Quite consciously, and with uneasiness which was now taking a new form, he had yielded to Alma's fascination. However contemptible and unaccountable, this was the state of things with him, and, as he waited for the door to be opened, it made him feel more awkward, more foolish, than for many a long year.

Mrs Frothingham and her step-daughter were sitting alone, the elder lady occupied with fancy-work, at her feet a basket of many-coloured silks, and the younger holding a book; nothing could have been quieter or more home-like. No sooner had he entered than he overcame all restraint, all misgiving; there was nothing here today but peace and good feeling, gentle voices and quiet amiability. Whatever shadow had arisen between the two ladies must have passed utterly away; they spoke to each other with natural kindness, and each had a tranquil countenance.

Alma began at once to talk of their common friends, the Carnabys, asking whether Rolfe knew that they were in Australia.

'I knew they had decided to go,' he answered. 'But I haven't heard for at least two months.'

'Oh, then I can give you all the news; I had a letter yesterday.

When Mrs Carnaby wrote, they had spent a fortnight at Melbourne, and were going on to Brisbane. Mr Carnaby is going to do something in Queensland – something about mines. I'll read you that part.'

The letter lay in the book she was holding. Sibyl wrote indefinitely, but Harvey was able to gather that the mining engineer, Dando, had persuaded Carnaby to take an active interest in his projects. Discussion on speculative enterprises did not recommend itself to the present company, and Rolfe could only express a hope that his friend had at last found a pursuit in which he could interest himself.

'But fancy Sibyl at such places!' exclaimed Alma, with amusement. 'How curious I shall be to see her when she comes back! Before she left England, I'm sure she hadn't the least idea in what part of Australia Brisbane was, or Melbourne either. I didn't know myself; had to look at a map. You'll think that a shameful confession, Mr Rolfe.'

'My own ideas of Australian geography are vague enough.'

'Oh, but haven't you been there?'

'Not to any of the new countries; I don't care about them. A defect, I admit. The future of England is beyond seas. I would have children taught all about the Colonies before bothering them with histories of Greece and Rome. I wish I had gone out there myself as a boy, and grown up a sheep-farmer.'

Alma laughed.

'That's one of the things you say just to puzzle people. It contradicts all sorts of things I've heard you say at other times. – Do *you* think, Mamma, that Mr Rolfe missed his vocation when he didn't become a sheep-farmer?'

Mrs Frothingham gently shook her head. No trace of nervousness appeared in her today; manipulating the coloured silks, she only now and then put in a quiet word, but followed the talk with interest.

'But I quite thought you had been to Australia,' Alma resumed. 'You see, it's very theoretical, your admiration of the new countries. And I believe you would rather die at once in England than go to live in any such part of the world.'

'Weakness of mind, that's all.'

'Still, you admit it. That's something gained. You always smile at other people's confessions, and keep your own mind mysterious.'

'Mysterious? I always thought one of my faults was over-frankness.'

'That only shows how little we know ourselves.'

Harvey was reflecting on the incompleteness of his knowledge of Alma. Intentionally or not, she appeared to him at this moment in a perfectly new light; he could not have pictured her so simple of manner, so direct, so placid. Trouble seemed to have given her a holiday, and at the same time to have released her from self-consciousness.

'But you have never told us,' she went on, 'about your wanderings in France this summer. English people don't go much to that part, do they?'

'No. I happened to read a book about it. It's the old fighting-ground of French and English – interesting to any one pedantic enough to care for such things.'

'But not to people born to be sheep-farmers. And you had a serious illness. – Did Mr Rolfe tell you, Mamma dear, that he nearly died at some miserable roadside inn?'

Mrs Frothingham looked startled, and declared she knew nothing of it. Harvey, obliged to narrate, did so in the fewest possible words, and dismissed the matter.

'I suppose you have had many such experiences,' said Alma. 'And when do you start on your next travels?'

'I have nothing in view. I half thought of going for the winter to a place in North Wales – Carnarvonshire, on the outer sea.'

The ladies begged for more information, and he related how, on a ramble with a friend last spring (it was Basil Morton), he had come upon this still little town* between the mountains and the shore, amid a country shining with yellow gorse, hills clothed with larch, heathery moorland, ferny lanes, and wild heights where the wind roars on crag or cairn.

'No railway within seven miles. Just the place for a pedant to escape to, and live there through the winter with his musty books.'

'But it must be equally delightful for people who are not pedants!' exclaimed Alma.

'In spring or summer, no doubt, though even then the civilised person would probably find it dull.'

'That's your favourite affectation again. I'm sure it's nothing but affectation when you speak scornfully of civilised people.'

'Scornfully I hope I never do.'

'Really, Mamma,' said Alma, with a laugh, 'Mr Rolfe is in his very mildest humour today. We mustn't expect any reproofs for our good. He will tell us presently that we are patterns of all the virtues.'

Mrs Frothingham spoke in a graver strain.

'But I'm sure it is possible to be too civilised – to want too many comforts, and become a slave to them. Since I have been living here, Mr Rolfe, you can't think how I have got to enjoy the simplicity of this kind of life. Everything is so easy; things go so smoothly. Just one servant, who can't make mistakes, because there's next to nothing to do. No wonder people are taking to flats.'*

'And is that what you mean by over-civilisation?' Alma asked of Rolfe.

'I didn't say anything about it. But I should think many people in large and troublesome houses would agree with Mrs Frothingham. It's easy to imagine a time when such burdens won't be tolerated. Our misfortune is, of course, that we are not civilised enough.'

'Not enough to give up fashionable nonsense. I agree with that. We're wretched slaves, most of us.'

It was the first sentence Alma had spoken in a tone that Rolfe recognised. For a moment her face lost its placid smile, and Harvey hoped that she would say more to the same purpose; but she was silent.

'I'm sure,' remarked Mrs Frothingham, with feeling, 'that most happiness is found in simple homes.'

'Can we be simple by wishing it?' asked Alma. 'Don't you think we have to be born to simplicity?'

'I'm not sure that I know what you mean by the word,' said Harvey.

'I'm not sure that I know myself. Mamma meant poverty, I think. But there may be a simple life without poverty, I should say. I'm thinking of disregard for other people's foolish opinions; living just as you feel most at ease – not torturing yourself because it's the custom.'

'That's just what requires courage,' Rolfe remarked.

'Yes; I suppose it does. One knows people who live in misery just because they daren't be comfortable; keeping up houses and things they can't afford, when, if they only considered themselves, their income would be quite enough for everything they really want. If you come to think of it, that's too foolish for belief.'

Harvey felt that the topic was growing dangerous. He said nothing, but wished to have more of Alma's views in this direction. They seemed to strike her freshly; perhaps she had never thought of the matter in this way before.

'That's what I meant,' she continued, 'when I said you must be born to simplicity. I should think no one ever gave up fashionable extravagance just because they saw it to be foolish. People haven't the strength of mind. I dare say,' she added, with a bright look, 'anyone who *was* strong enough to do that kind of thing would be admired and envied.'

'By whom?' Rolfe asked.

'Oh, by their acquaintances who were still slaves.'

'I don't know. Admiration and envy are not commonly excited by merely reasonable behaviour.'

'But this would be something more than merely reasonable. It would be the beginning of a revolution.'

'My dear,' remarked Mrs Frothingham, smiling sadly, 'people would never believe that it didn't mean loss of money.'

'They might be made to believe it. It would depend entirely on the persons, of course.'

Alma seemed to weary of the speculation, and to throw it aside. Harvey noticed a shadow on her face again, which this time did not pass quickly.

He was so comfortable in his chair, the ladies seemed so entirely at leisure, such a noiseless calm brooded about them, unbroken by any new arrival, that two hours went by insensibly, and with lingering reluctance the visitor found it time to take his leave. On reviewing the afternoon, Harvey concluded that it was probably as void of meaning as of event. Alma, on friendly terms once more with her step-mother, felt for the moment amiably disposed towards everyone, himself included; this idle good humour and insignificant talk was meant, no doubt, for an apology, all he had to expect. It implied, of course, thorough indifference towards him as an individual. As a member of their shrunken circle, he was worth retaining. Having convinced herself of his innocence of undue pretensions, Alma would, as the children say, be friends again, and everything should go smoothly.

He lived through a week of the wretchedest indecision, and at the end of it, when Wednesday afternoon came round, was again climbing the many stairs to the Frothinghams' flat; even more nervous than last time, much more ashamed of himself, and utterly doubtful as to his reception. The maid admitted him without remark, and showed him into an empty room. When he had waited for five minutes, staring at objects he did not see, Alma entered.

'Mamma went out to lunch,' she said, languidly shaking hands with him, 'and hasn't come back yet.'

No greeting could have conveyed less encouragement. She seated herself with a lifeless movement, looked at him, and smiled as if discharging a duty.

'I thought' – he blundered into speech – 'that Wednesday was probably your regular afternoon.'

'There is nothing regular yet. We haven't arranged our life. We are glad to see our friends whenever they come. – Pray sit down.'

He did so, resolving to stay for a few minutes only. In the silence that followed, their eyes met, and, as though it were too much trouble to avert her look, Alma continued to regard him. She smiled again, and with more meaning.

'So you have quite forgiven me?' fell from her lips, just when Harvey was about to speak.

'As I told you at the station, I feel that there is more fault on my side. You wrote under such a strange misconception, and I ought to have patiently explained myself.'

'Oh no! You were quite right in treating me sharply. I don't quite remember what I said, but I know it must have been outrageous. After that, I did what I ought to have done before, just had a talk with Mamma.'

'Then you took it for granted, without any evidence, that I came here as a meddler or busybody?'

His voice was perfectly good-humoured, and Alma answered in the same tone.

'I *thought* there was evidence. Mamma had been talking about her affairs, and mentioned that she had consulted you about something – Oh, about Mrs Abbott.'

'Very logical, I must say,' remarked Rolfe, laughing.

'I don't think logic is my strong point.'

She sat far back in the easy chair, her head supported, her hands resting upon the chair arms. The languor which she hardly made an effort to overcome began to invade her companion, like an influence from the air; he gazed at her, perceiving a new beauty in the half-upturned face, a new seductiveness in the slim, abandoned body. A dress of grey silk, trimmed with black, refined the ivory whiteness of her flesh; its faint rustling when she moved affected Harvey with a delicious thrill.

'There's no reason, now,' she continued, 'why we shouldn't talk about it – I mean, the things you discussed with Mamma. You imagine, I dare say, that I selfishly objected to what she was doing. Nothing of the kind. I didn't quite see why she had kept it from me, that was all. It was as if she felt afraid of my greediness. But I'm not greedy; I don't think I'm more selfish than ordinary people. And I think Mamma is doing exactly what she ought; I'm very glad she felt about things in that way.'

Harvey nodded, and spoke in a subdued voice.

'I was only consulted about one person, whom I happened to know.'

'Yes – Mrs Abbott.'

Her eyes were again fixed upon him, and he read their curiosity. Just as he was about to speak, the servant appeared with tea. Alma slowly raised herself, and, whilst she plied the office of hostess, Harvey got rid of the foolish hat and stick that encumbered him. He had now no intention of hurrying away.

As if by natural necessity, they talked of nothing in particular whilst tea was sipped. Harvey still held his cup, when at the outer door sounded a rat-tat-tat, causing him silently to execrate the intruder, whoever it might be. Unheeding, and as if she had not heard, Alma chatted of trifles. Harvey's ear detected movements without, but no one entered; in a minute or two, he again breathed freely.

'Mrs Abbott—'

Alma just dropped the name, as if beginning a remark, but lapsed into silence.

'Shall I tell you all about her?' said Rolfe. 'Her husband's death left her in great difficulties; she had hardly anything. A friend of hers, a Mrs Langland, who lives at Gunnersbury, was very kind and helpful. They talked things over, and Mrs Abbott decided to take a house at Gunnersbury, and teach children; – she was a teacher before her marriage.'

'No children of her own?'

'No. One died. But unfortunately she has the care of two,

whose mother – a cousin of hers – is dead, and whose father has run away.'

'Run away?'

'Literally. Left the children behind in a lodging-house garret to starve, or go to the workhouse, or anything else. A spirited man; independent, you see; no foolish prejudices.'

'And Mrs Abbott has to support them?'

'No one else could take them. They live with her.'

'You didn't mention that to Mamma.'

'No. I thought it needless.'

The silence that followed was embarrassing to Harvey. He broke it by abruptly changing the subject.

'Have you practised long today?'

'No,' was the absent reply.

'I thought you looked rather tired, as if you had been working too hard.'

'Oh, I don't work too hard,' said Alma impatiently.

'Forgive me. I remember that it is a forbidden subject.'

'Not at all. You may ask *me* anything you like about myself. I'm not working particularly hard just now; thinking a good deal, though. Suppose you let me have your thoughts on the same subject. No harm. But I dare say I know them, without your telling me.'

'I hardly think you do,' said Rolfe, regarding her steadily. 'At all events' – his voice faltered a little – 'I'm afraid you don't.'

'Afraid? Oh' – she laughed – 'don't be afraid. I have plenty of courage, and quite enough obstinacy. It rather does me good when people show they have no faith in me.'

'You didn't understand,' murmured Harvey.

'Then make me understand,' she exclaimed nervously, moving in the chair as if about to stand up, but remaining seated and bent forward, her eyes fixed upon him in a sort of good-humoured challenge. 'I believe I know what you mean, all the time. You didn't discuss me with Mamma, as I suspected, but you think about me just as she does. – No, let me go on, then you shall confess I was right. You have no faith in my powers, to begin with. It seems to you very unlikely that an everyday sort of girl, whom you have met in society and know all about, should develop into a great artist. No faith – that's the first thing. Then you are so kind as to have fears for me – yes, it was your own word. You think that you know the world, whilst I am ignorant of it, and that it's a sort of duty to offer warnings.'

Harvey's all but angry expression, as he listened and fidgeted, suddenly stopped her.

'Well! Can you deny that these things are in your mind?'

'They are not in my mind at this moment, that's quite certain,' said Harvey bluntly.

'Then, what is?'

'Something it isn't easy to say, when you insist on quarrelling with me. Why do you use this tone? Do I strike you as a pedagogue, a preacher – something of that sort?'

His energy in part subdued her. She smiled uneasily.

'No. I don't see you in that light.'

'So much the better. I wanted to appear to you simply a man, and one who has – perhaps – the misfortune to see in *you* only a very beautiful and a very desirable woman.'

Alma sat motionless. Her smile had passed, vanishing in a swift gleam of pleasure which left her countenance bright, though grave. In the same moment there sounded again a rat-tat at the outer door. Through his whirling senses, Harvey was aware of the threatened interruption, and all but cursed aloud. That Alma had the same expectation appeared in her moving so as to assume a more ordinary attitude; but she uttered the word that had risen to her lips.

'The misfortune, you call it?'

Harvey followed her example in disposing his limbs more conventionally; also in the tuning of his voice to something between jest and earnest.

'I said *perhaps* the misfortune.'

'It makes a difference, certainly.' She smiled, her eyes turned to the door. '*Perhaps* is a great word; one of the most useful in the language. – Don't you think so, Mamma?'

Mrs Frothingham had just entered.

## CHAPTER 11

The inconceivable had come to pass. By a word and a look Harvey had made real what he was always telling himself could never be more than a dream, and a dream of unutterable folly. Mrs Frothingham's unconscious intervention availed him nothing; he had spoken, and must speak again. For a man of sensitive honour there could be no trifling in such a matter as this with a girl in Alma Frothingham's position. And did he not rejoice that wavering was no longer possible?

This was love; but of what quality? He no longer cared, or dared, to analyse it. Too late for all that. He had told Alma that he loved her, and did not repent it; nay, hoped passionately to hear from her lips the echoed syllable. It was merely the proof of madness. A shake of the head might cure him; but from that way to sanity all his blood shrank.

He must consider; he must be practical. If he meant to ask Alma to marry him, and of course he did, an indispensable preliminary was to make known the crude facts of his worldly position.

Well, he could say, with entire honesty, that he had over nine hundred pounds a year. This was omitting a disbursement of an annual fifty pounds, of which he need not speak – the sum he had insisted on paying Mrs Abbott that she might be able to maintain Wager's children. With all the difficulty in the world had he gained his point. Mrs Abbott did not wish the children to go into other hands; she made it a matter of conscience to keep them by her, and to educate them, yet this seemed barely possible with the combat for a livelihood before her. Mrs Abbott yielded, and their clasp of hands cemented a wholesome friendship – frank, unsuspicious – rarest of relations between man and woman. But all this there was certainly no need of disclosing.

At midnight he was penning a letter. It must not be long; it must not strike the lyrical note; yet assuredly it must not read like a commercial overture. He had great difficulty in writing anything that seemed tolerable. Yet done it must be, and done it was; and before going to bed he had dropped his letter into the post. He durst not leave it for reperusal in the morning light.

Then came torture of expectancy. The whole man aching, sore, with impatience; reason utterly fled, intellect bemused and baffled; a healthy, competent citizen of nigh middle age set all at once in the corner, crowned with a fool's cap, twiddling his thumbs in nervous fury. Dolorous spectacle, and laughable withal.

He waited four-and-twenty hours, then clutched at Alma's

reply. 'Dear Mr Rolfe, – Will you come again next Wednesday?' That was all. Did it amuse her to keep him in suspense? The invitation might imply a fulfilment of his hopes, but Alma's capriciousness allowed no certainty; a week's reflection was as likely to have one result as another. For him it meant a week of solitude and vacancy.

Or would have meant it, but for that sub-vigorous element in his character, that saving strain of practical rationality, which had brought him thus far in life without sheer overthrow. An hour after receiving Alma's enigmatical note, he was oppressed by inertia; another hour roused him to self-preservation, and supplied him with a project. That night he took the steamer from Harwich to Antwerp, and for the next four days wandered through the Netherlands, reviving his memories of a journey, under very different circumstances, fifteen years ago. The weather was bright and warm; on the whole he enjoyed himself; he reached London again early on Wednesday morning, and in the afternoon, with a touch of weather on his cheek, presented himself at Alma's door.

She awaited him in the drawing-room, alone. This time, he felt sure, no interruption was to be feared; he entered with confident step and a cheery salutation. A glance showed him that his common-sense had served him well; it was Alma who looked pale and thought-worn, who betrayed timidity, and could not at once command herself.

'What have you been doing?' she asked, remarking his appearance.

'Rambling about a little,' he replied good-humouredly.

'Where? You look as if you had been a voyage.'

'So I have, a short one.'

And he told her how his week had passed.

'So that's how you would like to spend your life – always travelling?'

'Oh no! I did it to kill time. You must remember that a week is something like a year to a man who is waiting impatiently.'

She dropped her eyes.

'I'm sorry to have kept you waiting. But I never thought you very impatient. You always seemed to take things philosophically.'

'I generally try to.'

There was a pause. Alma, leaning forward in her chair, kept her eyes down, and did not raise them when she again spoke.

'You have surprised and perplexed and worried me. I thought in a week's time I should know what to say, but – Doesn't it strike you, Mr Rolfe, that we're in a strange position towards each other? You know very little of me – very little indeed, I'm sure. And of you, when I come to think of it, all I really know is that you hardly care at all for what has always been my one great interest.'

'That is putting it in a matter-of-fact way – or you think so. I see things rather differently. In one sense, I care very much indeed for everything that really makes a part of your life. And simply because I care very much about you yourself. I don't know you; who knows any other human being? But I have formed an idea of you, and an idea that has great power over my thoughts, wishes, purposes – everything. It has made me say what I thought I should never say to any woman – and makes me feel glad that I have said it, and full of hope.'

Alma drew in her breath and smiled faintly. Still she did not look at him.

'And of course I have formed an idea of you.'

'Will you sketch the outline and let me correct it?'

'You think I am pretty sure to be wrong?' she asked, raising her eyes and regarding him for a moment with anxiety.

'I should have said "complete" it. I hope I have never shown myself to you in an altogether false light.'

'That is the one thing I have felt sure about,' said Alma, slowly and thoughtfully. 'You have always seemed the same. You don't change with circumstances – as people generally do.'

Harvey had a word on his lips, but checked it, and merely gazed at her till her eyes again encountered his. Then Alma smiled more naturally.

'There was something you didn't speak of in your letter. What kind of life do you look forward to?'

'I'm not sure that I understand. My practical aims – you mean?'

'Yes,' she faltered, with embarrassment.

'Why, I'm afraid I have none. I mentioned the facts of my position, and I said that I couldn't hope for its improvement—'

'No, no, no! You misunderstand me. I am not thinking about money. I hate the word, and wish I might never hear it again!'

She spoke with impetuosity. 'I meant – how and where do you wish to live? What thoughts had you about the future?'

'None very definite, I confess. And chiefly because, if what I desired came to pass, I thought of everything as depending upon you. I have no place in the world. I have no relatives nearer than cousins. Of late years I have been growing rather bookish, and rather fond of quietness – but of course that resulted from circumstances. When a man offers marriage, of course he usually says: My life is this and this; will you enter into it, and share it with me? I don't wish to say anything of the kind. My life may take all sorts of forms; when I ask you to share it, I ask you to share liberty, not restraint.'

'A gipsy life?' she asked, half playfully.

'Is your inclination to that?'

Alma shook her head.

'No, I am tired of homelessness. – And,' she added as if on an impulse, 'I am tired of London.'

'Then we agree. I, too, am tired of both.'

Her manner altered; she straightened herself, and spoke with more self-possession.

'What about my art – my career?'

'It is for me to ask that question,' replied Harvey, gazing steadfastly at her.

'You don't mean that it would all necessarily come to an end.'

'Why? I mean what I say when I speak of sharing liberty. Heaven forbid that I should put an end to any aim or hope of yours – to anything that is part of yourself. I want you to be yourself. Many people nowadays revolt against marriage because it generally means bondage, and they have much to say for themselves. If I had been condemned to a wearisome occupation and a very small income, I'm sure I should never have asked anyone to marry me; I don't think it fair. It may seem to you that I haven't much right to call myself an independent man as it is—'

Alma broke in, impatiently.

'Don't speak of money? You have enough – more than enough.'

'So it seems to me. You are afraid this might prevent you from becoming a professional musician?'

'I know it would,' she answered with quiet decision.

'I should never dream of putting obstacles in your way. Do

understand and believe me. I don't want to shape you to any model of my own; I want you to be your true self, and live the life you are meant for.'

'All the same, you would rather I did not become a professional musician. Now, be honest with me! Be honest before everything. You needn't answer, I know it well enough; and if I marry you, I give up my music.'

Rolfe scrutinised her face, observed the tremulous mouth, the nervous eyelid.

'Then,' he said, 'it will be better for you not to marry me.'

And silence fell upon the room, a silence in which Harvey could hear a deep-drawn breath and the rustle of silk. He was surprised by a voice in quite a new tone, softly melodious.

'You give me up very easily.'

'Not more easily than you give up your music.'

'There's a difference. Do you remember what we were saying, last Wednesday, about simplicity of living?'

'Last Wednesday? It seems a month ago. Yes, I remember.'

'I have thought a good deal of that. I feel how vulgar the life is that most people lead. They can't help it; they think it impossible to do anything else. But I should like to break away from it altogether – to live as I chose, and not care a bit what other people said.'

Harvey had the same difficulty as before in attaching much significance to these phrases. They were pleasant to hear, for they chimed with his own thoughts, but he could not respond with great seriousness.

'The wife of a man with my income won't have much choice, I fancy.'

'How can you say that?' exclaimed Alma. 'You know that most people would take a house in a good part of London, and live up to the last penny – making everyone think that their income must be two or three thousand pounds. I know all about that kind of thing, and it sickens me. There's the choice between vulgar display with worry, and a simple, refined life with perfect comfort. You fancied I should want a house in London?'

'I hardy thought anything about it.'

'But it would ease your mind if I said that I would far rather live in a cottage, as quietly and simply as possible?'

'What does ease my mind – or rather, what makes me very

happy, is that you don't refuse to think of giving me your companionship.'

Alma flushed a little.

'I haven't promised. After all my thinking about it, it came to this – that I couldn't make up my mind till I had talked over everything with you. If I marry, I must know what my life is going to be. And it puzzles me that you could dream of making anyone your wife before you had asked her all sorts of questions.'

In his great contentment, Harvey laughed.

'Admirable, theoretically! But how is a man to begin asking questions? How many would he ask before he got sent about his business?'

'That's the very way of putting his chance to the test!' said Alma brightly. 'If he *is* sent about his business, how much better for him than to marry on a misunderstanding.'

'I agree with you perfectly. I never heard anyone talk better sense on the subject.'

Alma looked pleased, as she always did when receiving a compliment.

'Will you believe, then, Mr Rolfe, that I am quite in earnest in hating show and pretences and extravagance, and wishing to live in just the opposite way?'

'I will believe it if you cease to address me by that formal name – a show and a pretence, and just a little extravagant.'

Her cheeks grew warm again

'That reminds me,' she said; 'I didn't know you had a second name – till I got that letter.'

'I had almost forgotten it myself, till I answered a certain other letter. I didn't know till then that *you* had a second name. Your "Florence" called out my "Radcliffe" – which sounds fiery, doesn't it? I always felt that the name over-weighted me. I got it from my mother.'

'And your first – Harvey?'

'My first I got from a fine old doctor, about whom I'll tell you some day – Alma.'

'I named your name. I didn't address you by it.'

'But you will?'

'Let us talk seriously. – Could you live far away from London, in some place that people know nothing about?'

'With you, indeed I could, and be glad enough if I never saw London again.'

An exaltation possessed Alma; her eyes grew very bright, gazing as if at a mental picture, and her hands trembled as she continued to speak.'

'I don't mean that we are to go and be hermits in a wilderness. Our friends must visit us – our real friends, no one else; just the people we really care about, and those won't be many. If I give up a public career – as of course I shall – there's no need to give up music. I can go on with it in a better spirit, for pure love of it, without any wish for making money and reputation. You don't think this a mere dream?'

Harvey thought more than he was disposed to say. He marvelled at her sudden enthusiasm for an ideal he had not imagined her capable of pursuing. If he only now saw into the girl's true character, revealed by the awakening of her emotions, how nobly was his ardour justified! All but despising himself for loving her, he had instinctively chosen the one woman whose heart and mind could inspire him to a life above his own. 'I should think it a dream,' he answered, 'if I didn't hear it from your lips.'

'But it is so easy! We keep all the best things, and throw off only the worthless – the things that waste time and hurt the mind. No crowded rooms, no wearying artificial talk, no worry with a swarm of servants, no dressing and fussing. The whole day to one's self, for work and pleasure. A small house – just large enough for order and quietness, and to keep a room for the friend who comes. How many people would like such a life, but haven't the courage to live it!'

'Where shall it be, Alma?'

'I have given no promise. I only say this is the life that I should like. Perhaps you would soon weary of it?'

'I? Not easily, I think.'

'There might be travel, too,' she went on fervently. 'We should be rich, when other people, living in the ordinary vulgar way, would have nothing to spare. No tours where the crowd goes; real travel in out-of-the-way parts.'

'You are describing just what I should choose for myself; but I shouldn't have dared to ask it of you.'

'And why? I told you that you knew so little of me. We are only just beginning to understand each other.'

'What place have you in mind?'

'None. That would have to be thought about. Didn't you say you were going to some beautiful spot in Wales?'

Harvey reflected.

'I wonder whether you would like that—'

'We are only supposing, you know. But show me where it is. If you wait a moment, I'll fetch a map.'

She rose quickly. He had just time to reach the door and open it for her; and as she rapidly passed him, eyes averted, the faintest and sweetest of perfumes was wafted upon his face. There he stood till her return, his pulses throbbing.

'This is my old school atlas,' she said gaily; 'I always use it still.'

She opened it upon the table and bent forward.

'North Wales, you said? Show me—'

He pointed with a finger that quivered. His cheek was not far from hers; the faint perfume floated all about him; he could imagine it the natural fragrance of her hair, of her breath.

'I see,' she murmured. 'That's the kind of place far off, but not too far. And the railway station?'

As he did not answer, she half turned towards him.

'The station? – Yes. – Alma!—'

## CHAPTER 12

Mrs Frothingham was overjoyed. In private talk with Harvey she sang the praises of her step-daughter, whom, she declared, any man might be proud to have won. For Alma herself had so much pride; the characteristic, said Mrs Frothingham, which had put dangers in her path, and menaced her prospects of happiness.

'There's no harm in saying, Mr Rolfe, that I never dared to hope for this. I thought perhaps that you – but I was afraid Alma wouldn't listen to any one. Just of late, she seemed to feel her position so much more than at first. It was my fault; I behaved so foolishly; but I'm sure you'll both forgive me. For months I really wasn't myself. It made the poor girl bitter against all of us. But how noble she is! How high-minded! And how much, much happier she will be than if she had struggled on alone – whatever she might have attained to.'

It was clear to Harvey that the well-meaning lady did not quite understand Alma's sudden enthusiasm for the 'simple life', that she had but a confused apprehension of the ideal for which Alma panted. But the suggestion of 'economy' received her entire approval.

'I feel sure you couldn't do better than to go and live in the country for a time. There are so many reasons why Alma will be happier there, at first, than in London. I don't know whether that place in North Wales would be *quite* – but I mustn't meddle with what doesn't concern me. And you will be thoroughly independent; at any moment you can make a change.'

To a suggestion that she should run down into Carnarvon-shire, and see her proposed home before any practical step was taken, Alma replied that she had complete faith in Harvey Rolfe's judgment. Harvey's only doubt was as to the possibility of finding a house. He made the journey himself, and after a few days' absence returned with no very hopeful report; at present there was nothing to be had but a cottage, literally a cotter's home, and this would not do. He brought photographs, and Alma went into raptures over the lovely little bay, with its grassy cliffs, its rivulet, its smooth sand, and the dark-peaked moun-tains sweeping nobly to a sheer buttress above the waves. 'There must be a house! There *shall* be a house!' Of course, said Harvey, one could build, and cheaply enough; but that meant a long delay. Regarding the date of the marriage nothing was as yet decided, but Harvey had made up his mind to be 'at home' for Christmas. When he ventured to hint at this, Alma evaded the question.

A correspondent would inform him if any house became tenantless. 'I shall bribe someone to quit!' he cried. 'One might advertise that all expenses would be paid, with one year's rent of a house elsewhere.' Harvey was in excellent spirits, though time hung rather heavily on his hands.

On an appointed day the ladies paid him a visit at his rooms. Mrs Handover, requested to prepare tea for a semi-ceremonious occasion, was at once beset with misgivings, and the first sight of the strangers plunged her into profound despondency. She consulted her indifferent relative, Buncombe; had he any inkling of the possibility that Mr Rolfe was about to change his condition? Buncombe knew nothing and cared nothing; his own domestic affairs were giving him more than usual anxiety just now. 'I didn't think he was fool enough' – thus only he replied to Mrs Handover's anxious questions.

Alma surveyed the book-shelves, and took down volumes with an air of interest; she looked over a portfolio of photographs, inspected mementoes of travel from Cyprus, Palestine, Bagdad. Mrs Frothingham noted to herself how dusty everything was.

'That woman neglects him scandalously,' she said afterwards to Alma. 'I wish I had to look after her when she is at work.'

'I didn't notice any neglect. The tea wasn't very well made, perhaps.'

'My dear child! the room is in a disgraceful state – never dusted, never cleaned – oh dear!'

Alma laughed.

'I'm quite sure, Mamma, you are much happier now – in one way – than when you never had to think of such things. You have a genius for domestic operations. When I have a house of my own I shall be rather afraid of you.'

'Oh, of course you will have good servants, my dear.'

'How often have I to tell you, Mamma, that we're not going to live in that way at all! The simplest possible furniture, the simplest possible meals – *everything* subordinate to the higher aims and pleasures.'

'But you must have servants, Alma! You can't sweep the rooms yourself, and do the cooking?'

'I'm thinking about it,' the girl answered gravely. 'Of course, I shall not waste my time in coarse labour; but I feel sure we shall need only one servant – a competent, trustworthy woman, after your own heart. It's snobbish to be ashamed of housework; there are all sorts of things I should like to do, and that every woman is better for doing.'

'That is very true indeed, Alma. I can't say how I admire you for such thoughts. But—'

'The thing is to reduce such work to the strictly necessary. Think of all the toil that is wasted in people's houses, for foolish display and luxury. We sweep all that away at one stroke! Wait till you see. I'm thinking it out, making my plans.'

In the pleasant little drawing-room, by the fireside (for it was now October and chilly), Harvey and Alma had long, long conversations. Occasionally they said things that surprised each other and led to explanations, debates, but harmony was never broken. Rolfe came away ever more enslaved; more impressed by the girl's sweet reasonableness, and exalted by her glowing idealism. Through amorous mists he still endeavoured to discern the real Alma; he reflected ceaselessly upon her character; yet, much as she often perplexed him, he never saw reason to suspect her of disingenuousness. At times she might appear to excite herself unduly, to fall into excess of zeal; it meant, no doubt, that the imaginative fervour she had been wont to expend on music was turned in a new quarter. Alma remained herself – impulsive, ardent, enthusiastic, whether yearning for public triumphs, or eager to lead a revolution in domestic life. Her health manifestly improved; languor was unknown to her; her cheeks had a warmer hue, a delicate carnation, subtly answering to her thoughts.

She abhorred sentimentality. This was one of her first intimate declarations, and Harvey bore it in mind. He might praise, glorify, extol her to the uttermost, and be rewarded by her sweetest smiles; but for the pretty follies of amatory transport she had no taste. Harvey ran small risk of erring in this direction; he admired and reverenced her maidenly aloofness; her dignity he found an unfailing charm, the great support of his own self-respect. A caress was not at all times forbidden, but he asserted the privilege with trembling diffidence. It pleased her, when he entered the room, to be stately and rather distant of manner, to greet him as though they were still on formal terms; this troubled Harvey at first, but he came to understand and like it. In Mrs Frothingham's presence, Alma avoided every sign of familiarity, and talked only of indifferent things.

Early in November there came news that a certain family in the little Welsh town would be glad to vacate their dwelling if a tenant could at once be found for it. The same day Harvey travelled northwards, and on the morrow he despatched a telegram to Alma. He had taken the house, and could have possession in a week or two. Speedily followed a letter of description. The house was stone-built and substantial, but very plain; it stood alone and unsheltered by the roadside, a quarter of a mile from the town, looking seaward; it had garden ground and primitive stabling. The rooms numbered nine, exclusive of kitchen; small, but not diminutive. The people were very friendly

(Harvey wrote), and gave him all aid in investigating the place, with a view to repairs and so on; by remaining for a few days he would be able to consult with a builder, so as to have necessary work set in train as soon as the present occupants were gone.

Alma's engagement had been kept strictly secret. When Harvey returned after a week of activity, he found her still reluctant to fix a day, or even the month, for their wedding. He did not plead, but wrote her a little letter, saying that the house could be ready by – at all events – the second week in December; that he would then consult with her about furniture, and would go down to superintend the final putting in order. 'After that, it rests with you to say when you will enter into possession. I promise not to speak of it again until, on coming into the room, I see your atlas lying open on the table; that shall be a sign unto me.'

On his return to London he received a note from Mrs Frothingham, requesting him to be at home at a certain hour, as she wished to call and speak privately with him. This gave him an uneasy night; he imagined all manner of vexatious or distracting possibilities; but Mrs Frothingham brought no ill news.

'Don't be frightened,' she began, reading his anxious face. 'All's well, and I am quite sure Alma will soon have something to say to you. I have come on a matter of business – strictly business.'

Harvey felt a new kind of uneasiness.

'Let me speak in a plain way about plain things,' pursued the widow, with that shadow on her face which always indicated that she was thinking of the mournful past. 'I know that neither Alma nor you would hear of her accepting money from me; I know I mustn't speak of it. All the better that you have no need of money. But now that you are my relative – will be so very soon – I want to tell you how my affairs stand. Will you let me? Please do!'

Impossible to refuse a hearing to the good little woman, who delighted in confidential gossip, and for a long time had been anxious to pour these details into Harvey's ear. So she unfolded everything. Her capital at Bennet Frothingham's death amounted to more than sixteen thousand pounds, excellently invested – no 'Britannia' stocks or shares! Of this, during the past six months, she had given away nearly six thousand to sufferers by the great catastrophe. Her adviser and administrator in this affair was an old friend of her husband's, a City man of honourable repute. He had taken great trouble to discover worthy recipients of her bounty, and as yet had kept the source of it unknown.

'I mustn't give very much more,' she said, looking at Harvey with a pathetic deprecation of criticism. 'I want to keep an income of three hundred pounds. I could live on less, much less; but I should like still to have it in my power to do a little good now and then, and I want to be able to leave something to my sister, or her children. The truth is, Mr Rolfe – no, I will call you Harvey, once for all – the truth is, I couldn't live now without giving a little help here and there to people poorer than myself. Don't think it foolish.' Her voice quivered. 'I feel that it will be done in the name of my poor husband as if he himself were doing it, and making amends for a wrong he never, never intended. If I had given up everything – as some people say I ought to have done – it wouldn't have seemed the same to me. I couldn't earn my own living, and what right had I to become a burden to my relatives? I hope I haven't done very wrong. Of course, I shall give up the flat as soon as Alma is married. In taking it I really thought more of her than of my own comfort. I shall live with my sister, and come up to town just now and then, when it is necessary.'

The listener was touched, and could only nod grave approval.

'There's another thing. Alma thinks with me in everything – but she says I ought to let it be known who has given that money. She says it would make many people less bitter against her father's memory. Now, what is your opinion? If she is right in that—'

Harvey would offer no counsel, and Mrs Frothingham did not press him. She must think about it. The disclosure, if wise, could be made at any time.

'That's all I had to say, Harvey. Now tell me about the house, and then go and see Alma. I have business in the City.'

He went, but only to be disappointed; Alma was not at home. To make amends, she sent him a note that evening, asking him to call at twelve the next day, and to stay to luncheon. When he entered the room, the first object his eye fell upon was the old school atlas, lying open on the table at the map of England and Wales.

And the day appointed was the twentieth of December.

The wedding was to be the simplest conceivable. No costume, no bridesmaid or hulking groomsman, no invitations; no announcement to anyone until the day had passed, save only to Dora Leach, who would be summoned as if for some ordinary occasion of friendship, and then be carried off to the church.

'It will insure my smiling all through the ordeal,' said Alma to her step-mother; 'Dora's face will be such a study!'

'My dear,' began Mrs Frothingham very earnestly, 'you are *quite* sure—'

'More than sure, if that's possible. And Harvey throws up his hat at being let off so easily. He dreaded the ceremony.'

Which was very true, though Rolfe had not divulged it.

His personal possessions were now to be made ready for removal. The books represented nearly all that he could carry away from his old rooms, but they were a solid addendum to the garnishing of home. For a moment he thought of selling a few score of volumes. Would he ever really want those monumental tomes – the six folios of Muratori,* for instance, which he liked to possess, but had never used? Thereby hung the great, the unanswerable question: How was he going to spend his life as a married man? Was it probable that he would be come a serious student, or even that he would study as much as heretofore? No foreseeing; the future must shape itself, even as the past had done. After all, why dismember his library for the sake of saving a few shillings on carriage? If he did not use the books himself—

A thought flashed through him which made his brain unsteady. If he did not use the books himself, perhaps—

He tried to laugh, but for five minutes was remarkably sober. No, no; of course he would keep his library intact.

And now there was a duty to perform: he must write to his friends, make known his marriage; the letters to be posted only on the day of fate. Dear old Basil Morton – how he would stare! Morton should soon come down into Wales, and there would be great quaffing and smoking and talking into the small hours; a jolly anticipation! And Hugh Carnaby! Hugh would throw up his great arms, clench his huge red fists, and roar with mocking laughter. Good old boy! out there on the other side of the world, perhaps throwing away his money, with the deft help of a swindler. And the poor lad, Cecil Morphew! who assuredly would never pay back that fifty pounds – to which he was heartily welcome. Morphew had kept his promise to quit the garret in Chelsea, but what was since become of him Harvey knew not; the project of their going together into Wales had, of course, fallen through.

Lastly, Mary Abbott – for so had Harvey come to name his friend's widow. Mary Abbott! how would she receive this news? It would come upon her as the strangest surprise; not the mere fact of his marrying, but that he had chosen for a wife, out of the whole world, the daughter of Bennet Frothingham. Would she be able to think kindly of him after this? Of Mrs Frothingham she could speak generously, seeming to have outlived natural bitterness; but the name must always be unwelcome to her ears. Alma would cease to bear that name, and perhaps, in days to come, Mary Abbott might forget it. He could only hope so, and that the two women might come together. On Alma's side, surely, no reluctance need be feared; and Mary, after her ordeal, was giving proof of sense and character which inspired a large trust. He would write to her in the most open-hearted way; indeed, no other tone was possible, having regard to the relations that had grown up between them.

How the aspect of his little world was changing! A year ago, what things more improbable than that he should win Alma Frothingham for a wife, and become the cordial friend of Mary Abbott?

When the revelation could be postponed no longer, he made known to Mrs Handover that he was about to be married. It cost him an extraordinary effort, for in a double sense he was shamed before the woman. Mrs Handover, by virtue of her sex, instinctively triumphed over him. He saw in her foolish eyes the eternal feminine victory; his head was bowed before her slatternly womanhood. Then again, he shrank from announcing to the poor creature that she could no longer draw upon him for her livelihood.

'I'm very sorry, Mr Rolfe,' she began, in her most despondent voice. 'That is, of course, I'm very glad you're going to be married, and I'm sure I wish you every happiness – I do indeed. But we are sorry to lose you – indeed we are.'

Of her sincerity herein there could be no sort of doubt.

Harvey coughed, and looked at the window – which had not been cleaned for some months.

'May I ask, without rudeness, whether it is the young lady who came—'

'Yes, Mrs, Handover.'

He was uncommonly glad that Alma's name had never been spoken. There, indeed, would have been matter for gossip.

'A very handsome young lady, Mr Rolfe, and I'm sure I wish her all happiness, as well as yourself.' She fidgeted. 'Of course, I don't know what your plans may be, sir, but – perhaps there's no harm if I mention it – if ever you should be in need of a housekeeper – you've known me a long time, sir—'

'Yes – yes – certainly.' Harvey perspired. 'Of course, I should bear you in mind.'

Thereupon he had to listen whilst Mrs Handover discoursed at large upon her dubious prospects. At the close of the interview, he gave her a cheque for ten pounds, concealed in an envelope. 'A little present – of course, I shall be hearing of you – every good wish—'

On the eve of his marriage day he stood in the dismantled rooms, at once joyful and heavy at heart. His books were hidden in a score of packing-cases, labelled, ready to be sent away. In spite of open windows, the air was still charged with dust; since the packing began, everyone concerned in it had choked and coughed incessantly; on the bare floor, footsteps were impressed in a thick flocky deposit. These rooms could have vied with any in London for supremacy of filthiness. Yet here he had known hours of still contentment; here he had sat with friends congenial, and heard the walls echo their hearty laughter; here he had felt at home – here his youth had died.

Where all else was doubtful, speculative, contingent, that one thing he certainly knew; he was no longer a young man. The years had passed like a shadow, unnoted, uncounted, and had brought him to this point of pause, of change momentous, when he must needs look before and after. In all likelihood much more than half his life was gone. His mother did not see her thirtieth year; his father died at little over forty; his grandparents were not long-lived; what chance had he of walking the earth for more than half the term already behind him? Did the life of every man speed by so mockingly? Yesterday a school-boy; tomorrow – 'Rolfe? you don't say so? Poor old fellow!'

And he was going to be married. Incredible, laughter-moving, but a fact. No more the result of deliberate purpose than any other change that had come about in his life, than the flight of years and the vanishment of youth. Fate so willed it, and here he stood.

Someone climbed the stairs, breaking upon his reverie. It was Buncombe, who smiled through a settled gloom.

'All done? I shan't be much longer here myself. House too big for me.'

'Ah! it is rather large.'

'I'm thinking of changes. – You know something about my affairs. – Yes – changes—'

Rolfe had never seen the man so dismal before; he tried to inspirit him, but with small result.

'It's the kids that bother me,' said Buncombe. Then he dropped his voice, and brought his head nearer.

'You're going to get married.' His eyes glinted darkly. 'I'm – going to get divorced.'

And with a grim nod the man moved away.

# PART THE SECOND

BOOK THE SECOND.

# CHAPTER I

A morning of April, more than two years after his marriage, found Harvey Rolfe in good health and very tolerable spirits. As his wont was, he came down at half-past eight, and strolled in the open air before breakfast. There had been rain through the night; a grey mist still clung about the topmost larches of Carn Bodvean, and the Eifel summits were densely wrapped. But the sun and breeze of spring promised to have their way; to drive and melt the clouds, to toss white wavelets on a blue sea, to make the gorse shine in its glory, and all the hills be glad.

A gardener was at work in front of the house; Harvey talked with him about certain flowers he wished to grow this year. In the small stable-yard a lad was burnishing harness; for him also the master had a friendly word, before passing on to look at the little mare amid her clean straw. In his rough suit of tweed and shapeless garden hat, with brown face and cheery eye, Rolfe moved hither and thither as though native to such a life. His figure had filled out; he was more robust, and looked, indeed, younger than on the day when he bade farewell to Mrs Handover and her abominations.

At nine o'clock he entered the dining-room, where breakfast was ready, though as yet no other person had come to table. The sun would not touch this window for several hours yet, but a crackling fire made the air pleasant, and brightened all within. Seats were placed for three. An aroma of coffee invited to the meal, which was characterised by no suggestion of asceticism. Nor did the equipment of the room differ greatly from what is usual in middle-class houses. The clock on the mantelpiece was flanked with bronzes; engravings and autotypes hung about the walls; door and window had their appropriate curtaining; the oak sideboard shone with requisite silver. Everything unpretentious; but no essential of comfort, as commonly understood, seemed to be lacking.

In a minute or two appeared Mrs Frothingham; alert, lightsome, much improved in health since the first year of her widowhood. She had been visiting here for a fortnight, and tomorrow would return to her home in the south. Movement, variety, intimate gossip, supported her under the affliction which still seemed to be working for her moral good. Her bounty (or restitution) had long ago ceased to be anonymous, but she did not unduly pride herself upon the sacrifice of wealth; she was glad to have it known among her acquaintances, because, in certain quarters, the fact released her from constraint, and restored her to friendly intercourse. For her needs and her pleasures a very modest income proved quite sufficient. To all appearances, she found genuine and unfailing satisfaction in the exercise of benevolent sympathies.

'Alma will not come down,' was her remark, as she entered. 'A little headache – nothing. We are to send her some tea and dry toast.'

'I thought she didn't seem quite herself last night,' said Harvey, as he cut into a ham.

Mrs Frothingham made no remark, but smiled discreetly, taking a place at the head of the table.

'We shall have to go somewhere,' Harvey continued. 'It has been a long winter. She begins to feel dull, I'm afraid.'

'A little, perhaps. But she's quite well – it's nothing—'

'Why won't she go on with her water-colours? She was beginning to do really good things – then all at once gives it up.'

'Oh, she must! I think those last sketches simply wonderful. Anyone would suppose she had worked at it all her life, instead of just a few months. How very clever she is!'

'Alma can do anything,' said Harvey, with genial conviction.

'Almost anything, I really think. Now *don't* let her lose interest in it, as she did in her music. You have only to show that you think her drawings good, and speak about them. She depends rather upon encouragement.'

'I know. But it wasn't for lack of *my* encouragement that she dropped her violin.'

'So unfortunate! Oh, she'll come back to it, I'm sure.'

When Mrs Frothingham paid her first visit to the newly-married couple, it amused her to find a state of things differing considerably from her anxious expectations. True, they had only one servant within doors, the woman named Ruth, but she did not represent the whole establishment. Having bought a horse and trap, and not feeling called upon to act as groom, Harvey had engaged a man, who was serviceable in various capacities; moreover, a lad made himself useful about the premises during the day. Ruth was a tolerable cook, and not amiss as a housemaid. Then, the furnishing of the house, though undeniably 'simple', left little to be desired; only such things were eschewed as serve no rational purpose and are mostly in people's way. Alma, as could at once be perceived, ran no risk of over-exerting herself in domestic duties; she moved about of mornings with feather-brush, and occasionally plied an unskilful needle, but kitchenward she never turned her steps. Imprudently, Mrs Frothingham remarked that this life, after all, much resembled that of other people; whereat Alma betrayed a serious annoy-ance, and the well-meaning lady had to apologise, to admit the absence of 'luxuries', the homeliness of their diet, the unmistak-able atmosphere of plain living and high thinking.*

She remained for nearly a month, greatly enjoying herself. Late in autumn, Alma begged her to come again, and this time the visit lasted longer; for in the first week of December the house received a new inhabitant, whose arrival made much commotion. Alma did not give birth to her son without grave peril. Day after day Harvey strode about the wintry shore under a cloud of dread. However it had been with him a year ago, he was now drawn to Alma by something other than the lures of passion; the manifold faults he had discerned in her did not seriously conflict with her peculiar and many-sided charm; and the birth of her child inspired him with a new tenderness, an emotion different in kind from any that he had yet conceived. That first wail of feeblest humanity, faint-sounding through the silent night, made a revolution in his thoughts, taught him on the moment more than he had learnt from all his reading and cogitation.

It seemed to be taken as a matter of course that Alma would not nurse the baby; only to Harvey did this appear a subject for regret, and he never ventured to speak of it. The little mortal was not vigorous; his nourishment gave a great deal of trouble; but with the coming of spring he took a firmer hold on life, and less persistently bewailed his lot. The names given to him were Hugh Basil. When apprised of this, the strong man out in Australia wrote a heart-warming letter, and sent with it a little lump of Queensland gold, to be made into something, or kept intact, as the parents saw fit. Basil Morton followed the old tradition, and gave a silver tankard with name and date of the new world-citizen engraved upon it.

Upon her recovery, Harvey took his wife to Madeira, where they spent three weeks. Alma's health needed nothing more than this voyage; she returned full of vitality. During her absence Mrs Frothingham superintended the household, the baby being in charge of a competent nurse. It occurred to Harvey that this separation from her child was borne by Alma with singular philosophy; it did not affect in the least her enjoyment of travel. But she reached home again in joyous excitement, and for a few days kept the baby much in view. Mrs Frothingham having departed, new visitors succeeded each other: Dora and Gerda Leach, Basil Morton and his wife, one or two of Alma's relatives. Little Hugh saw less and less of his mother, but he continued to thrive; and Harvey understood by now that Alma must not be expected to take much interest in the domestic side of things. It simply was not her forte.

She had ceased to play upon her violin, save for the entertainment and admiration of friends. After her return from Madeira she made the acquaintance of a lady skilled in water-colour drawing, and herewith began a new enthusiasm. Her progress was remarkable, and corresponded to an energy not less than that she had long ago put forth in music. In the pursuit of landscape she defied weather and fatigue; she would pass half the night abroad, studying moonlight, or rise at an unheard-of hour to catch the hues of dawn. When this ardour began to fail, her husband was vexed rather than surprised. He knew Alma's characteristic weakness, and did not like to be so strongly reminded of it. For about this time he was reading and musing much on questions of heredity.*

In a moment of confidence he had ventured to ask Mrs Frothingham whether she could tell him anything of Alma's mother. The question, though often in his mind, could hardly have passed his lips, had not Mrs Frothingham led up to it by speaking of her own life before she married: how she had enjoyed the cares of country housekeeping; how little she had dreamt of ever being rich; how Bennet Frothingham, who had known her in his early life, sought her out when he began to be prosperous, therein showing the fine qualities of his nature, for she had nothing in the world but gentle birth and a lady's education. Alma was then a young girl of thirteen, and had been motherless for eight years. Thus came Harvey's opportunity. Alma herself had already imparted to him all she knew: that her mother was born in England, emigrated early with her parents to Australia, returned to London as a young woman, married, and died at twenty-seven. To this story Mrs Frothingham could add little, but the supplement proved interesting. Bennet Frothingham spoke of his first marriage as a piece of folly; it resulted in unhappiness, yet, the widow was assured, with no glaring fault on either side. Alma's mother was handsome, and had some natural gifts, especially a good voice, which she tried to use in public, but without success. Her education scarcely went beyond reading and writing. She died suddenly, after an evening at the theatre, where, as usual, she had excited herself beyond measure. Mrs Frothingham had seen an old report of the inquest that was held, the cause of death being given as cerebral haemorrhage. In these details Harvey Rolfe found new matter for reflection.

Their conversation at breakfast this morning was interrupted by the arrival of letters; two of them particularly welcome, for they bore a colonial postmark. Hugh Carnaby wrote to his friend from an out-of-the-way place in Tasmania; Sibyl wrote independently to Alma from Hobart.

'Just as I expected,' said Harvey, when he had glanced over a few lines. 'He talks of coming home: – "There seems no help for it. Sibyl is much better in health since we left Queensland, but I see she would never settle out here. She got to detest the people at Brisbane, and doesn't like those at Hobart much better. I have left her there whilst I'm doing a little roaming with a very decent fellow I have come across, Mackintosh by name. He has been everywhere and done everything – not long ago was in the service of the Indo-European Telegraph Company at Tehran, and afterwards lived (this will interest you) at Bagdad, where he got a *date-boil*,* which marks his face and testifies to his veracity. He has been trying to start a timber business here; says some of the hard woods would be just the thing for street paving. But now his father's death is taking him back home, and I shouldn't wonder if we travel together. One of his ideas is a bicycle factory;* he seems to know all about it, and says it'll be the most money-making business in England for years to come. What do you think? Does this offer a chance for *me*?"'

Harvey interrupted himself with a laugh. Smelting of abandoned gold ores, by the method of the ingenious Dando, had absorbed some of Hugh's capital, with very little result, and his other schemes for money-making were numerous.

'"The fact is, I must get money somehow. Living has been expensive ever since we left England, and it's madness to go on till one's resources have practically run out. And Sibyl *must* get home again; she's wasting her life among these people. How does she write to your wife? I rather wish I could spy at the letters. (Of course, I don't seriously mean that.) She bears it very well, and, if possible, I have a higher opinion of her than ever."'

Again Harvey laughed.

'Good old chap! What a pity he can't be cracking crowns somewhere!'

'Oh! I'm sure I'd rather see him making bicycles.'

''Tisn't his vocation. He ought to go somewhere and get up a little war of his own – as he once told me he should like to. We can't do without the fighting man.'

'Will you bring Hughie up to it, then?'

Harvey fixed his eyes on a point far off.

'I fear he won't have the bone and muscle. But I should like him to have the pluck. I'm afraid he mayn't, for I'm a vile coward myself.'

'I should like a child never to hear or know of war,' said Mrs Frothingham fervently.

'And so should I,' Harvey answered, in a graver tone.

When Mrs Frothingham went upstairs with the letter for Alma, he broke open another envelope. It was from Mary Abbott, who wrote to him twice a year, when she acknowledged the receipt of his cheque. She sent the usual careful report concerning Wager's children – the girl now seven years old, and the boy nine. Albert Wager, she thought, was getting too old for her; he ought to go to a boys' school. Neither he nor his sister had as yet repaid the care given to them; never were children more difficult to manage. Harvey read this between the lines; for Mary Abbott never complained of the task she had undertaken. He rose and left the room with a face of anxious thoughtfulness.

The day was wont to pass in a pretty regular routine. From half-past nine to half-past one Harvey sat alone in his study, not always energetically studious, but on the whole making progress in his chosen field of knowledge. He bought books freely, and still used the London Library. Of late he had been occupying himself with the authorities on education; working, often impatiently, through many a long-winded volume. He would have liked to talk on this subject with Mary Abbott, but had not yet found courage to speak of her paying them a visit. The situation, difficult because of Alma's parentage, was made more awkward by his reticence with Alma regarding the payment he made for those luckless children. The longer he kept silence, the less easily could he acquaint his wife with this matter – in itself so perfectly harmless.

This morning he felt indisposed for study, and cared just as little to go out, notwithstanding the magnificent sky. From his windows he looked upon the larch-clad slopes of Carn Bodvean; their beauty only reminded him of grander and lovelier scenes in far-off countries. From time to time the wanderer thus awoke in him, and threw scorn upon the pedantries of a book-lined room. He had, moreover, his hours of regret for vanished conviviality; he wished to step out into a London street, collect his boon-companions, and hold revel in the bygone way. These, however, were still but fugitive moods. All in all, he regretted nothing. Destiny seemed to have marked him for a bookish man; he grew more methodical, more persistent, in his historical reading; this, doubtless, was the appointed course for his latter years. It led to nothing definite. His life would be fruitless—

Fruitless? There sounded from somewhere in the house a shrill little cry, arresting his thought, and controverting it without a syllable. Nay, fruitless his life could not be, if his child grew up. Only the chosen few, the infinitesimal minority of mankind, leave spiritual offspring, or set their single mark upon the earth; the multitude are but parents of a new generation, live but to perpetuate the race. It is the will of nature, the common lot. And if indeed it lay within his power to shape a path for this new life, which he, nature's slave, had called out of nothingness, – to obviate one error, to avert one misery, – to ensure that, in however slight degree, his son's existence should be better and happier than his own, – was not this a sufficing purpose for the years that remained to him, a recompense adequate to any effort, any sacrifice?

As he sat thus in reverie, the door softly opened, and Alma looked in upon him.

'Do I interrupt you?'

'I'm idling. How is your headache?'

She answered with a careless gesture, and came forward, a letter in her hand.

'Sibyl says she will certainly be starting for home in a few weeks. Perhaps they're on the way by now. You have the same news, I hear.'

'Yes. They must come to us straight away,' replied Harvey, knocking the ash out of his pipe 'Or suppose we go to meet them? If they come by the Orient Line, they call at Naples. How would it be to go overland, and make the voyage back with them?'

Alma seemed to like the suggestion, and smiled, but only for a moment. She had little colour this morning, and looked cold, as she drew up to the fire, holding a white woollen wrap about her shoulders. A slow and subtle modification of her features was tending to a mature beauty which would make bolder claim than the charm that had characterised her in maidenhood. It was still remote from beauty of a sensual type, but the outlines, in becoming a little more rounded, more regular, gained in common estimate what they lost to a more refined apprehension. Her eyes appeared more deliberately conscious of their depth and gleam; her lips, less responsive to the flying thought, grew to an habitual expression – not of discontent, but something akin unto it; not of selfwill, but something that spoke a spirit neither tranquil nor pliant.

'Had you anything else?' she asked, absently.

'A letter from Mrs Abbott.'

Alma smiled, with a shade of pleasantry not usual upon her countenance. Harvey generally read her extracts from these letters. Their allusion to money imposed the reserve; otherwise they would have passed into Alma's hands. From his masculine point of view, Harvey thought the matter indifferent; nothing in his wife's behaviour hitherto had led him to suppose that she attached importance to it.

'The usual report of progress?'

'Yes. I fancy those two children are giving her a good deal of trouble. She'll have to send the boy to a boarding school.'

'But can she afford it?'

'I don't know.'

'I've never understood yet why you take so much interest in those children.'

Her eyes rested upon him with a peculiarly keen scrutiny, and Harvey, resenting the embarrassment due to his own tactics, showed a slight impatience.

'Why, partly because I wish to help Mrs Abbott with advice, if I can: partly because I'm interested in the whole question of education.'

'Yes, it's interesting, of course. She has holidays, I suppose?'

'It's holiday time with her now.'

'Then why don't you ask her to come and see us?'

'I would at once,' Harvey replied, with hesitation, 'if I felt sure that—' He broke off, and altered the turn of his sentence. 'I don't know whether she can leave those children.'

'You were going to make a different objection. Of course there's a little awkwardness. But you said long ago that all that sort of thing would wear away, and surely it ought to have done by now. If Mrs Abbott is as sensible as you think, I don't see how she can have any unpleasant feeling towards me.'

'I can't suppose that she has.'

'Then now is the opportunity. Send an invitation. – Why shouldn't I write it myself?'

Alma had quite shaken off the appearance of lassitude; she drew herself up, looked towards the writing-table, and showed characteristic eagerness to carry out a project. Though doubtful of the result, Harvey assented without any sign of reluctance, and forthwith she moved to the desk. In a few minutes she had penned a letter, which was held out for her husband's perusal.

'Admirable!' he exclaimed. 'Couldn't be better. *Nihil quod tetigit non ornavit.*'*

'And pray what does that mean?' asked Alma, her countenance a trifle perturbed by the emotions which blended with her delight in praise.

'That my wife is the most graceful of women, and imparts to all she touches something of her own charm.'

'All that?'

'Latin, you must know, is the language of compression.'

They parted with a laugh. As she left the study, Alma saw her little son just going out; the nurse had placed him in his mail-cart, where he sat smiling and cooing. Mrs Frothingham, who delighted in the child, had made ready for a walk in the same direction, and from the doorway called to Alma to accompany them.

'I may come after you, perhaps,' was the reply. 'Ta-ta, Hughie!'

With a wave of her hand, Alma passed into the sitting-room, where she stood at the window, watching till Mrs Frothingham's sunshade had disappeared. Then she moved about, like one in search of occupation; taking up a book only to throw it down again, gazing vacantly at a picture, or giving a touch to a bowl of flowers. Here, as in the dining-room, only the absence of conventional superfluities called for remark; each article of furniture was in simple taste; the result, an impression of plain elegance. On a little corner table lay Alma's colour-box, together with a drawing-board, a sketching-block, and the portfolio which contained chosen examples of her work. Not far away, locked in its case, lay her violin, the instrument she had been wont to touch caressingly; today her eyes shunned it.

She went out again into the little hall. The front door stood open; sunshine flooded the garden; but Alma was not tempted to go forth. All the walks and drives of the neighbourhood had become drearily familiar; the meanest of London streets shone by contrast as a paradise in her imagination. With a deep sigh of ennui, she turned and slowly ascended the stairs.

Above were six rooms; three of them the principal chambers (her own, Harvey's, and the guest-room), then the day-nursery, the night nursery, and the servant's bedroom. On her first coming, she had thought the house needlessly spacious; now it often seemed to her oppressively small, there being but one spare room for visitors. She entered her own room. It could not be called disorderly, yet it lacked that scrupulous perfection of arrangement, that dainty finish, which makes an atmosphere for the privacy of a certain type of woman. Ruth had done her part, preserving purity unimpeachable; the deficiency was due to Alma alone. To be sure, she had neither dressing-room nor lady's-maid; and something in Alma's constitution made it difficult for her to dispense with such aids to the complete life.

She stood before the mirror, and looked at herself, blankly, gloomily. Her eyes fell a little, and took a new expression, that of anxious scrutiny. Gazing still, she raised her arms, much as though she were standing to be measured by a dressmaker; then she turned, so as to obtain a view of her figure sideways. Her arms fell again, apathetically, and she moved away.

Somehow, the long morning passed. In the afternoon she drove with Harvey and Mrs Frothingham, conversing much as usual, giving no verbal hint of her overwhelming ennui. No reference was made to Mrs Abbott. Harvey had himself written her a letter, supporting Alma's invitation with all possible cordiality; but he gravely feared that she would not come.

At tea, according to custom, little Hugh was brought into the room, to be fondled by his mother, who liked to see him when he was prettily dressed, and to sit upon his father's knee. Hugh, aged sixteen months, began to have a vocabulary of his own, and to claim a share in conversation; he had a large head, well formed, and slight but shapely limbs; the sweet air of sea and mountain gave a healthful, though very delicate, colouring to his cheeks; his eyes were Alma's, dark and gleaming, but with promise of a keener intelligence. Harvey liked to gaze long at the little face, puzzled by its frequent gravity, delighted by its flashes of mirth. Syllables of baby-talk set him musing and philosophising. How fresh and young, yet how wondrously old! Babble such as this fell from a child's lips thousands of years ago, in the morning of the world; it sounded on through the ages, infinitely reproduced; eternally a new beginning; the same music of earliest human speech, the same ripple of innocent laughter, renewed from generation to generation. But he, listening, had not the merry, fearless pride of fathers in an earlier day. Upon him lay the burden of all time; he must needs ponder anxiously on his child's heritage, use his weary knowledge to cast the horoscope of this dawning life.

'Why are you looking at him in that way?' exclaimed Alma. 'You'll frighten him.'

'How did I look?'

'As if you saw something dreadful.'

Harvey laughed, and ran his fingers through the soft curls, and bade himself be of good heart. Had he not thrown scorn upon people who make a 'fuss' about their children. Had he not despised and detested chatter about babies? To his old self what a simpleton would he have seemed!

On the morrow Mrs Frothingham took her departure; leaving it, as usual, uncertain when she would come again, but pleasantly assured that it could not be very long. She thought Harvey the best of husbands; he and Alma, the happiest of married folk. In secret, no doubt, she sadly envied them. If her own lot had fallen in such tranquil places!

Two more days, and Alma received a reply to her invitation. Yes, Mrs Abbott would come, and be with them for a week; longer she could not. Her letter was amiable and well-worded as Alma's own. Harvey felt a great relief, and it pleased him not a little to see his wife's unfeigned satisfaction. This was Monday; the visitor promised to arrive on Tuesday evening.

'Of course you'll drive over with me to meet her,' said Harvey.

'I think not. I dislike making acquaintance at railway stations. If it should rain, you'll have to have a covered carriage, and imagine us three shut up together!'

Alma laughed gaily at the idea. Harvey, though at a loss to interpret her merriment, answered it with a smile, and said no more. Happily, the weather was settled; the sun shone gallantly each morning; and on Tuesday afternoon Harvey drove the seven miles, up hill and down, between hedges of gorse and woods of larch, to the little market-town where Mary Abbott would alight after her long journey.

## CHAPTER 2

Half an hour after sunset Alma heard the approach of wheels. She had long been ready to receive her visitor, and when the horse stopped, she stood by the open door of the sitting-room, commanding her nervousness, resolute to make an impression of grace and dignity. It would have eased her mind had she been able to form some idea of Mrs Abbott's personal appearance; Harvey had never dropped a hint on the subject, and she could not bring herself to question him. The bell rang; Ruth hastened to answer it; Harvey's voice sounded.

'It turns chilly after the warm sunshine. I'm afraid we ought to have had a covered carriage.'

'Then I should have seen nothing,' was replied in softer tones. 'The drive was most enjoyable.'

There came into the lamplight a rather tall figure in plain, serviceable travelling-costume. Alma discerned a face which

gave her a shock of surprise, so unlike was it to anything she
had imagined; the features regular and of intelligent expression,
but so thin, pallid, worn, that they seemed to belong to a woman
of nearly forty, weighted by years of extreme suffering. The
demeanour which Alma had studiously prepared underwent an
immediate change; she stepped forward with an air of frank
kindliness, of cordial hospitality.

'Wasn't your train late? How tired you must be – and how
cold! In these fine spring days we have been living as if it were
midsummer, but I'm sure you oughtn't to have had that long
drive in the open trap so late. Harvey thinks everybody as robust
as himself—'

But the guest was in very good spirits, though manifestly
fatigued. She spoke with pleasure of the beautiful wild country,
glowing in sunset. A little tired, yes; she had not travelled so far
for a long time; but the air had braced her wonderfully, and
after a night's rest—

At dinner Alma behaved with the same friendliness, closely
observing her guest, and listening to all she said, as if anxious
not to miss a word. Mrs Abbott conversed in a very low voice;
her manner was marked by a subdual which might partly be
attributable to weariness, but seemed in a measure the result of
timidity under novel circumstances. If she looked at either of her
companions, her eyes were instantly withdrawn. A smile never
lingered on her features; it came and passed, leaving the set
expression of preoccupied gravity. She wore a dress of black
silk, close at the neck; and Alma perceived that it was by no
means new.

An hour after the meal she begged permission to retire to her
room. The effort to talk had become impossible; she was at the
end of her strength, and could hold up no longer.

When Alma came down again, she stood for a minute before
the fire, smiling and silent. Harvey had picked up a newspaper;
he said nothing.

'How very nice she is!' fell at length from Mrs Rolfe's lips.

'Astonishingly altered,' was her husband's murmured reply.

'Indeed? In what way?'

'Looks so wretchedly ill, for one thing.'

'We must take her about. What do you think of doing
tomorrow?'

By feminine device of indirect question, Alma obtained some

understanding of the change that had come upon Mrs Abbott during the past three years. Harvey's disclosures did not violate the reticence imposed upon him by that hour in which he had beheld a woman's remorseful anguish; he spoke only of such things as were manifest to everyone who had known Mary Abbott before her husband's death; of her social pleasures, her intellectual ambitions, suddenly overwhelmed by a great sorrow.

'I suppose she ought to be doing much better things than teaching children,' said Alma.

'Better things?' repeated Harvey, musing. 'I don't know. It all depends how you regard it.'

'Is she very clever?'

'Not appallingly,' he answered, with a laugh. 'It's very possible she is doing just what she ought to be – neither more nor less. Her health seems to be the weak point.'

'Do you think she has enough to live upon?'

Harvey knitted his brows and looked uneasy.

'I hope so. Of course it must be a very small income; but I dare say those friends of hers at Gunnersbury make life a little easier.'

'I feel quite sorry for her,' said Alma, with cheerfulness. 'I hadn't realised her position. We must make her stay as long as she can. Yes, if it's fine again, we might drive to Tre'r Caeri. That would interest her, no doubt. She likes history, doesn't she? – the same things that you are fond of.'

At breakfast Mrs Abbott appeared with a much brighter countenance; refreshed in body and mind, she entered gladly into the plans that had been made for the day, talked with less restraint, and showed an interest in all her surroundings. But her demeanour still had the air of self-subdual which seemed at moments to become a diffidence bordering on humility. This was emphasised by its contrast with the bearing of her hostess. Alma had never shown herself to more brilliant advantage; kind interpretation might have thought that she had set herself to inspirit the guest in every possible way. Her face was radiant with good humour and vivacity; she looked the incarnation of joyous, healthy life. The flow of her spirited talk seemed to aim at exhibiting the joys and privileges of existence in places such as this. She represented herself as glorying in the mountain heights, and in solitary tracts of shore. Here were no social burdens, or restrictions, or extravagances; one lived naturally, simply, without regrets for wasted time, and without fear of the morrow. To all this Mary Abbott paid the tribute of her admiration, perhaps of her envy; and Alma grew the more animated, the more she felt that she had impressed her hearer.

Harvey wondered at this sudden revival of his wife's drooping energies. But he did not consider the phenomenon too curiously; enough that Alma was brilliant and delightful, that she played her part of hostess to perfection, and communicated to their guest something of her own vitality.

They had an exhilarating drive through the mountains to Tre'r Caeri, a British fastness on a stern bare height; crumbled dwellings amid their great protecting walls, with cairn and cromlech and mystic circles; where in old time the noise of battle clanged amid these grey hills, now sleeping in sunlight. And from Tre'r Caeri down into the rocky gloom of the seaward chasm, Nant Gwrtheyrn,* with its mound upon the desolate shore, called by legend the burial-place of Vortigern.* Here Mrs Abbott spoke of the prehistoric monuments she had seen in Brittany, causing Alma to glance at her with a sudden surprise. The impulse was very significant. Thinking of her guest only as a poverty-stricken teacher of children, Alma forgot for the moment that this subdued woman had known happier days, when she too boasted of liberty, and stored her mind in travel. After all, as soon appeared, the travels had been of very modest extent; and Alma, with her knowledge of many European countries, and her recent ocean voyage, regained the confident superiority which kept her in such admirable humour.

Mary Abbott, reluctant to converse on things that regarded herself, afforded Alma every opportunity of shining. She knew of Mrs Rolfe's skill as a musician, and this same evening uttered a hope that she might hear her play. The violin came forth from its retirement. Playing, it seemed at first, without much earnestness, as though it were but a pastime, Alma presently chose one of her pageant pieces, and showed of what she was capable. Lack of practice had told upon her hand, but the hearers were uncritical, as she well knew.

'That's magnificent,' said Harvey, with a mischievous smile. 'But do condescend now to the primitive ear. Let us have something of less severity.'

Alma glanced at Mrs Abbott, who had softly murmured her

thanks; then turned an eye upon her husband, saying wickedly, 'Home, Sweet Home?'

'I've no doubt you could play it wonderfully – as you would "Three Blind Mice".'

Alma looked good-natured disdain, and chose next a Tarantelle of Schubert.* The exertion of playing brought warm colour into her face; it heightened her beauty, and she was conscious of it; so that when she chanced to find Mrs Abbott's look fixed upon her, a boundless gratification flashed from her own dark eyes, and spoke in the quiver of her lips.

Next evening, when again requested to play, she sat down to the piano. On this instrument Alma had not the same confidence as with the violin; but she could not refrain from exhibiting such skill as she possessed, Mrs Abbott having declared that her own piano-playing was elementary. Meantime, the portfolio of water-colours had of course been produced for exhibition. In this art, though she did not admit it, Mrs Abbott had formerly made some progress; she was able to form a judgment of Alma's powers, and heard with genuine surprise in how short a time this point had been attained. Alma again glowed with satisfaction.

She found a new source of pride in her motherhood. Not having been told, or having forgotten, that Mrs Abbott had lost a child, she playfully offered assurance that the guest should not be worried with nursery talk.

'Children are anything but a delight to you, I'm afraid; you must have too much of them.'

'They often give me trouble,' Mrs Abbott replied. 'But I wish I had one more to trouble me. My little girl would have been six years old by now.'

Alma gave one of those looks which occasionally atoned for many less amiable glances.

'I'm so sorry – I didn't know –'

Mrs Abbott did not dwell on the subject. Her reserve was still unbroken, though there never appeared the least coldness in her manner; she talked with perfect freedom of everything that contained no allusion to herself. The change was manifestly doing her good; even by the second day she showed an increase of vigour, and no longer wore the preoccupied, overstrained look. Becoming familiar with her face, Alma thought it more attractive than at first, and decidedly younger. She still had a great deal of curiosity to satisfy with regard to Mrs Abbott; especially it seemed strange to her that Harvey and his friend were so little inclined for conversation; they talked only of formal, uninteresting things, and she wondered whether, after all, they really had much in common.

'Take Mrs Abbott for a walk tomorrow morning,' she said in private; 'you must have so many things to talk about – by yourselves.'

'I don't know that we have,' Harvey returned, looking at her with some surprise. 'I want to hear a little more about those youngsters, that's all.'

Mrs Abbott wished to climb Carn Bodvean* the great hill, clad in tender green of larch-woods, which overlooked the town. For the toil of this ascent Alma had no mind; pleasantly excusing herself, she proposed at breakfast that Harvey and Mrs Abbott should go alone; they might descend on the far side of the mountain, and there, at a certain point known to her husband, she would meet them with the dogcart. Harvey understood this to mean that the man would drive her; for Alma had not yet added the art of driving to her various accomplishments; she was, indeed, timid with the reins. He readily assented to the plan, which, for some reason, appeared to amuse and exhilarate her.

'Don't be in a hurry,' she said. 'There'll be a good view on a day like this, and you can have a long rest at the top. If you meet me at half-past one, we shall be back for lunch at two.'

When they started, Alma came out to the garden gate, and dismissed them with smiling benignity; one might have expected her to say 'Be good!' as when children are trusted to take a walk without superintendence. On re-entering, she ran quickly to an upper room, where from the window she could observe them for a few minutes, as they went along in conversation. Presently she bade her servant give directions for the dogcart to be brought round at one o'clock.

'Williams to drive, ma'am?' said Ruth, who had heard something of the talk at breakfast.

'No,' Alma replied with decision. 'I shall drive myself.'

The pedestrians took their way along a winding road, between boulder walls thick-set with the new leaves of pennywort; then crossed the one long street of the town (better named a village), passing the fountain, overbuilt with lichened stone, where women and children filled their cans with sweet water, sparkling in the golden light. Rolfe now and then received a respectful greeting. He had wished to speak Welsh, but soon abandoned the endeavour. He liked to hear it, especially on the lips of children at their play. An old, old language, symbol of the vitality of a race; sounding on those young lips as in the time when his own English, composite, hybrid, had not yet begun to shape itself.*

Beyond the street and a row of cottages, they began to climb; at first a gentle ascent, on either hand high hedges of flowering blackthorn, banks strewn with primroses and violets, and starred with the white stitchwort; great leaves of foxglove giving promise for future days. The air was bland, yet exquisitely fresh; scented from innumerable sources in field and heath and wood. When the lane gave upon open ground, they made a pause to look back. Beneath them lay the little grey town, and beyond it the grassy cliffs, curving about a blue bay. Near by rose the craggy slopes of a bare hill, and beyond it, a few miles to the north, two lofty peaks, wreathed against the cloudless heaven with rosy mist.

'Sure it won't be too much for you?' said Harvey looking upwards to the wooded height.

'I feel equal to anything,' answered his companion brightly. 'This air has given me new life.'

There was a faint colour on her cheeks, and for the first time Harvey caught an expression which reminded him of the face he had known years ago, when Mrs Abbott looked upon life much as Alma did now.

They entered upon a rising heath, green with mosses where the moisture of a hidden stream drew downwards, brown with dead bracken on dry slopes. Just above was a great thicket of flowering gorse; a blaze of colour, pure, aerial, as that of the sky which illumined it. Through this they made their way, then dropped into a green nook of pasture, among sheep that raised their heads distrustfully, and loud-bleating lambs, each running to its mother.

'If you can scale this wall, it will save us a quarter of an hour.'

'If you can, I can,' was the laughing reply.

Protruding boulders made it an easy clamber. They were then at the base of Carn Bodvean, and before them rose steep mountain glades. Mrs Abbott gazed upwards with unspoken delight.

'There are no paths,' said Harvey. 'It's honest woodland. Some day it will be laid out with roads and iron benches, with finger-posts, "To the summit".'

'You think so?'

'Why, of course. It's the destiny of every beautiful spot in Britain. There'll be a pier down yonder, and a switchback railway, and leagues of lodging-houses, and brass bands.'

'Let us hope we shall be dead.'

'Yes – but those who come after us? What sort of a world will it be for Hugh? I often think I should be wrong if I taught him to see life as I do. Isn't it only preparing misery for him? I ought to make him delight in piers, and nigger minstrels, and switch-backs. A man should belong to his time.'

'But a man helps to make his time,' replied Mary Abbott.

'True. You are hopeful, are you?'

'I try very hard to be. What use am I, if I don't put a few thoughts into children's heads which will help to make their lives a little better?'

Harvey nodded.

Their feet sank in the mossy ruin of immemorial summers. Overhead, the larch-boughs dangled green tresses, or a grove of beech shook sunlight through branches decked with translucent gold. Now and then they came out into open spaces, where trees rent from the soil, dead amid spring's leafage, told of a great winter storm; new grass grew thickly about the shattered trunks, and in the hollows whence the roots had been torn. One moment they stood in shadow; the next, moved upward into a great splash of sunshine, thrown upon moss that still glistened with the dews of the night, and on splints of crag painted green and gold with lichen. Sun or shadow; the sweet fir-scents breathed upon their faces, mingled with many a waft of perfume from little woodland plants.

More than once Mrs Abbott had to pause. Midway she was tempted by a singular resting-place. It was a larch tree, perhaps thirty feet high; at the beginning of its growth, the stem had by some natural means been so diverted as to grow horizontally for a yard or more at a couple of feet above the ground; it had then made a curve downwards, and finally, by way of a perfect loop across itself, had shot again in the true direction, growing at last, with straight and noble trunk, like its undistorted neighbours. Much wondering at so strange a deformity, Mrs Abbott seated herself on the level portion, and Harvey, as he stood before her, told a fancy that had come to him when for the first time he chanced to climb this way. Might not the tree represent some human life? A weak, dubious, all but hopeless beginning; a check; a return upon itself; a laboured circling; last a healthful maturity, upright, triumphing. He spoke with his eyes on the ground. Raising them at the end, he was astonished to see that his companion had flushed deeply; and only then it occurred to him that this parable might be applied by the hearer to herself.

'To make a confession,' he added at once, 'it forcibly reminded me of my own life – except that I can't pretend to be "triumphing".'

His laugh did not cover the embarrassment with which he discovered that, if anything, he had made matters worse. Here was an instance of his incorrigible want of tact; much better to have offered no application of the fable at all, and to have turned the talk. He had told a simple truth, but with the result of appearing to glorify himself, and possibly at his friend's expense. Vexed beyond measure, he crushed his heel into the soft ground.

'That is a very striking thought,' said Mary Abbott, her look still downcast. 'I shall never forget it.'

And she rose to move onward. They climbed in silence, the flank of the mountain growing steeper.

'I should have brought you my old alpenstock,' jested Harvey. 'Go slowly; we have plenty of time.'

'I like to exert myself. I feel so well, and it does me good!'

He ventured to look at her again. All her confusion had passed away; she had the light of enjoyment in her eyes, and returned his look with a frankness hitherto lacking.

'You must stay a second week. Alma won't let you go.'

'Go, I must. The two children can't be left longer at Mrs Langland's – it would be presuming upon her kindness.'

'I want to talk about them, but one hasn't much breath here. When we get to the top—'

Last of all came a slippery scramble on broken stones, to where a shapeless cairn rose above tree-tops, bare to the dazzling sky. As they issued from the shelter of the wood, a breeze buffeted about them, but only for a moment; then the air grew still, and nothing was audible but a soft whispering among the boughs below. The larches circling this stony height could not grow to their full stature; beaten, riven, stunted, by fierce blasts from mountain or from wave, their trunks were laden, and their branches thickly matted, with lichen so long and hoary that it gave them an aspect of age incalculable. Harvey always looked upon them with reverence, if not with awe.

In the sunny stillness their eyes wandered far and wide, around a vast horizon. On two sides lay the sea; to the west, bounded only where it met the blue sky above (though yonder line of cloud might perchance be the hills of Wicklow); eastward, enfolded by the shores of a great bay, with mountains on the far side, faintly visible through silvery vapour. Northward rose a noble peak, dark, stern, beautiful in the swift fall of curving rampart to the waves that broke at its foot; loftier by the proximity of two summits, sharp-soaring like itself, but unable to vie with it. Alone among the nearer mountains, this crest was veiled; smitten by sea-gusts, it caught and held them, and churned them into sunny cloudlets, which floated away in long fleecy rank, far athwart the clear depths of sky. Farther inland, where the haze of the warm morning hung and wavered, loomed at moments some grander form, to be imagined rather than descried; a glimpse of heights which, as the day wore on, would slowly reveal themselves and bask in the broad glow under crowning Snowdon.

'We have time! We can stay here!' said Mrs Abbott, moved with a profound delight.

'We have an hour at least. The sun is too hot; you must sit on the shadowed side of the cairn.'

The great silence had nothing of that awesomeness which broods in the mountain calm of wilder solitudes. Upon their ear fell the long low hushing of the wood, broken suddenly from time to time by a fitful wind, which flapped with hollow note around the great heap of stones, whirled as if in sport, and was gone. Below, in leafy hollows, sounded the cry of a jay, the laugh of a woodpecker; from far heath and meadow trembled the bleat of lambs. Nowhere could be discovered a human form; but man's dwellings, and the results of his labour, painted the wide landscape in every direction. On mountain sides, and across the undulating lowland, wall or hedge mapped his conquests of nature, little plots won by the toil of successive generations for pasture or for tillage, won from the reluctant wilderness, which loves its fern and gorse, its mosses and heather. Near and far were scattered the little white cottages, each a gleaming speck, lonely, humble; set by the side of some long-winding, unfrequented road, or high on the green upland, trackless save for the feet of those who dwelt there.

From talk of the scenery they passed, by no agreeable transition, to the subject which as yet they had not found an opportunity of discussing. It was necessary to arrive at some new arrangement regarding Wager's children; for the boy, Albert, would soon be nine years old, and, as Mrs Abbott confessed, he had given her a great deal of trouble. Both the children were intractable, hated lessons, and played alarming pranks; Master Albert's latest feat might have cost him his life, for he struck furiously through a pane of glass at a child mocking him from the other side, and was all but fainting from loss of blood when Mrs Abbott came to his help. Plainly this youngster must be sent to a boarding-school. Minnie, his sister, would be more easily managed after he had gone.

'He'll grow up a fighter,' said Harvey. 'We can't do without fighters. I'll make inquiry at once about a school for him, and in a year or two we'll take counsel with his teachers. Perhaps he might go into the navy.'

'The cost of it all,' fell from his companion in a nervous undertone.

'We had that out long ago. Don't think about it.'

'Of course, you will send only half the money when Albert leaves me,' said Mrs Abbott earnestly. 'I shall be in no difficulty. I have had letters from several people, asking me to take their little children to live with me. Albert's place will be filled at once. I can't take more into the house; there's no room. With them, and my kindergarten, and the lessons I give in the evening, I can live very well.'

Harvey mused. Wishing to feel himself in complete sympathy with his friend, he knew that something of the old criticism still tempered his liking. Mary Abbott had fine qualities, but lacked the simplicity, the directness, which would have made her courage wholly admirable. He suspected that she continually mourned over what seemed to her a waste of life. Proud of her 'culture', remembering her distinction as a teacher of grown-up girls, she had undertaken as a penitence the care of little children, and persevered in it with obstinacy rather than with inspired purpose. Mary Abbott, doubtless, had always regarded life as a conflict; she had always fought for her own hand. When such a nature falls into genuine remorse, asceticism will inevitably follow; with it comes the danger of more or less conscious embitterment. Harvey had a conviction of his friend's sincerity, and believed her in every way a better woman than in the days before her great sorrow; but he could not yet assure himself that she had found her true vocation.

They spoke of the people who were so anxious to be relieved of their children.

'One lady wrote to me that she would pay almost anything if I would take her little boy and keep him all the year round; she has only a small house, and the child utterly upsets her life. Of course, I understand her; I should have sympathised with her once.'

'It's intelligible enough,' replied Harvey, with a laugh. 'Presently there will be huge establishments for the young children of middle-class people. Naturally, children are a nuisance; especially so if you live in a whirlpool.'

'Yes, I know it too well, the whirlpool way of life,' said Mrs Abbott, her eyes on the far mountains. 'I know how easily one is drawn into it. It isn't only idle people.'

'Of course not. There's the whirlpool of the furiously busy. Round and round they go; brains humming till they melt or explode. Of course, they can't bother with children.'

'One loses all sense of responsibility.'

'Rather, they have never had it, and it has no chance of developing. You know, it isn't a matter of course for people to see that they are under an enormous obligation to the children they bring into the world; except in a parent here and there, that comes only with very favourable circumstances. When there's no leisure, no meditation, no peace and quietness, – when, instead of conversing, people just nod or shout to each other as they spin round and round the gulf, – men and women practically return to the state of savages in all that concerns their offspring. The brats have come into existence, and must make the best of it. Servants, governesses, schoolmasters – anybody but the parents – may give thought to children. Well, it's a matter for the individual. I shouldn't feel comfortable myself.'

'It's a matter for the world, too,' said Mary.

Harvey nodded. As he sat at the foot of the piled stones, his hand touched a sprig of last year's heather; the stem was hung with dry, rustling, colourless bells, which had clung there all through the cold, stormy months, telling of beauty that was past, and of beauty that was to come. He broke it off, and showed it to his companion. Until the time for moving, they talked of simpler things, and Mary Abbott recovered her spirits.

## CHAPTER 3

Turning regretfully from the place of rest, with its lulling sounds and noble prospects, they began to descend the other side of the mountain, which was more rugged than that by which they had come up. Harvey timed the walk so well, that they reached the point of the road where Alma would meet them, at a few minutes before the time agreed upon. No one was in sight. The road in its inland direction could be scanned for a quarter of a mile; the other way it curved rapidly, and was soon hidden by gorse-bushes.

'I hear nothing,' said Rolfe, when they had stood silent for a little. 'A mistake is impossible; the man has driven to meet us here before. Shall we walk on?'

They proceeded slowly, stopping from time to time. Harvey was puzzled by this unpunctuality; it would soon be a quarter to two. He began to feel hungry, and his companion looked tired. Of a sudden they heard the sound of a vehicle approaching behind them.

'It can't be Alma. She wouldn't have gone farther than—'

But the horse appeared round the curve of the road, and behind it was a dogcart, and in the dogcart sat Alma, alone. At sight of them she pulled up abruptly, so abruptly that the horse reared a little. Harvey walked forward.

'You've been driving yourself?'

'Of course. Why not?' replied Alma in a strangely high key.

'How have we missed you?'

As he put this question he became aware of something very unusual in his wife's appearance. Alma was pallid and shaking; her small felt hat had got out of position, and her hair was disordered, giving her a wild, rakish aspect. He saw, too, that the horse dripped with sweat; that it glared, panted, trembled, and could not for a moment stand still.

'What on earth have you been doing? She's run away with you!'

'No, no!' cried Alma, laughing, as she looked at Mrs Abbott, who had just come up. 'She was rather fresh, and I gave her a good run, that's all. I'm sorry I missed you at the place—'

'Why didn't Williams drive?' asked Harvey in a voice turning to anger.

'Williams? Why should Williams drive?' Alma returned, her eyes flashing. 'I'm only a few minutes late; I don't see anything to make a fuss about!'

This temper was as strange in Alma as the personal appearance she presented. Harvey said no more, but, after quickly examining the horse, helped Mrs Abbott to a seat at the back of the vehicle; he then jumped up to his wife's side, and without a word took the reins from her hand. Alma made no remark as she surrendered them.

'Put your hat straight,' he said to her in a low voice.

'My hat? What's the matter with it The wind, I suppose. Did you enjoy it, Mrs Abbott?'

She turned, in speaking, so as to have her back towards Harvey, and kept this position all the way, talking with her guest as if nothing had happened. Rolfe, his face grimly set, uttered only a word or two. He had to drive very slowly and with all caution, for the animal shied every other minute, and he felt heartily glad when they all alighted. Williams, who ran out from the stable, stood in astonishment at sight of the horse's condition.

'Rather fresh this morning,' said Harvey, as the ladies went in. 'Mrs Rolfe had a little trouble with her.'

This mild explanation by no means satisfied the coachman, though he pretended to acquiesce. Seeing him give a look at the horse's knees, Harvey did the same; nothing was wrong there. Williams pointed to marks on one of the wheels; the cart had evidently grazed against a wall. Alma must have lost control of the horse, and have been carried a considerable distance before, somehow, it was stopped. Without doubt, she had had a very narrow escape. Her anger seemed to be the result of nerves upset and mortified vanity; she wished to show Mrs Abbott that she could drive – the explanation of the whole matter. Harvey was vexed at such a piece of childishness; irritated, too, by the outbreak of temper with which Alma had replied to his very natural alarm. Of course, he would say nothing more; it would be interesting to await the outcome of his wife's mature reflection on her folly.

As he stepped into the house, something like a cry for help sounded from above stairs. He shouted, 'What's that?' and in the same moment Mary Abbott called to him that Mrs Rolfe had fainted. On rushing up, he found Mary with difficulty supporting Alma's unconscious form.

'I saw she could hardly get upstairs,' said Mrs Abbott. 'Just here on the landing she gave a moan and fell back. I was luckily close by her.'

They carried her into her room, and gave what help they could whilst the doctor was being summoned. In a few minutes Alma regained consciousness, and declared herself quite well again; but when she tried to rise, strength failed her; she began to moan in physical distress. Harvey went downstairs, whilst Mrs Abbott and Ruth tended the sufferer.

Their ordinary medical man was far away among the hills; his assistant had to be searched for, and came only after the lapse of two hours, by which time Rolfe had worked himself into a fever. Whilst Mrs Abbott, faint with agitation and weariness, took a hurried meal, he went to the bedside, and tried to learn whether Alma was suffering merely from shock, or had sustained an actual injury; but she still nursed her grievance against him, and would say very little. Why did not the doctor come? She wished to see the doctor; no one else was of any use.

'Go down and have lunch with Mrs Abbott properly. Do go, please; I hate all this fuss, and it's quite unnecessary. Let me be alone till the doctor comes.'

Before the arrival of Dr Evans's assistant she again fainted, and upon that followed an attack of hysteria. When at length the medical man had seen her, Harvey received an adequate, but far from reassuring, explanation of the state of things. At nightfall Dr Evans came in person, and was with the patient for a long time. He spoke less gravely of the case, offered a lucid diagnosis,* and thought that the services of an ordinary nurse for a few days would meet every necessity. Williams was sent with a hired vehicle to the market town, seven miles away, and late at night returned with the woman recommended. Alma meanwhile had lain quietly, and the household at length went to rest without renewal of alarms.

Twice before dawn Harvey left his room and stepped silently to Alma's door. The first time, he heard low voices; the second, there was no sound. When, about eight o'clock, he went down and out into the garden, he was surprised to meet Mrs Abbott. She had already seen the nurse this morning, and reported that all was going well. Rolfe talked cheerfully again, and would not listen to his guest's timid suggestion that she should take leave today. Not a bit of it; she was to go down to the seashore and enjoy the sunshine, and worry herself just as little as possible. At breakfast-time came a message from Alma to the same effect. Mrs Abbott was on no account to cut short her visit, and Harvey was to do his duty as host. She herself, said Mrs Rolfe, would be as well as ever in a day or two.

For all that, when the appointed day for the guest's departure came, Alma still lay blanched and feeble, not likely to leave her bed for another week. She was, however, in a remarkably cheerful frame of mind. Having to start on her journey as early as half-past eight, Mrs Abbott bade good-bye to her hostess the evening before, and nothing could have been kinder or more amiable than Alma's behaviour.

'Don't bear a grudge against me for spoiling your holiday,' she said, holding her guest's hand and smiling brightly. 'If I say all is for the best, perhaps you'll understand me, and perhaps you won't; it sounds pious at all events, doesn't it? We must see each other again, you know – here or somewhere else. I'm quite sure we can be friends. Of course, Harvey will go with you in the morning.'

Mrs Abbott begged he would do nothing of the kind, but Alma was imperative.

'Of course he will! If it rains, a covered carriage will be here in time. And write to me – mind you write to me; not only to say you've got safe home, but in future. You promise?'

In the morning it did rain, and heavily, so Harvey and his friend drove to the station shut up together, with scarce a glimpse of anything beyond the boulder walls and gorse hedges and dripping larch-trees. They spoke a good deal of Alma. As soon as she was well again, said Rolfe, he must take her for a thorough change. In truth, he was beginning, he said, to doubt whether she could live in this out-of-the-world place much longer. She liked it – oh yes, she liked it – but he feared the solitude was telling upon her nerves. Mrs Abbott admitted that there might be something in this.

'Should you return to London?' she asked.

Whereupon Harvey stared before him, and looked troubled, and could only answer that he did not know.

When, two days after, the promised letter came from Mrs Abbott, Harvey took it up to the invalid's room, and sat by her whilst she read it.

'She writes so nicely,' said Alma, who never in her life had showed such sweetness of disposition as during this convalescence. 'Read it for yourself, Harvey. Isn't it a nice letter? I feel so sorry we haven't known each other before. But we're going to be friends now.'

'I'm sure I'm very glad.'

'Nothing from Mamma? I almost think I could write to her to-day. Of course, she'll fall into a dreadful state of mind, and want to know why she wasn't sent for, and lament over – everything. But it's no use her coming here now. When we go away we must manage to see her.'

'Yes. Have you thought where you would like to go?'

'Not yet. There's plenty of time.'

Not a word had passed between them with reference to the perilous drive. Alma spoke as if her illness were merely natural, due to nothing in particular; but her husband fancied that she wished to atone, by sweet and affectionate behaviour, for that unwonted ill-usage of him. He saw, too, beyond doubt, that the illness seemed to her a blessing; its result, which some women would have wept over, brought joy into her eyes. This, in so far as it was unnatural, caused him some disturbance; on the other hand, he was quite unable to take a regretful view of what had happened, and why should he charge upon Alma as a moral fault that which he easily condoned in himself?

A few days more and the convalescent was allowed to leave her room. As if to welcome her, there arrived that morning a letter from Melbourne, with news that Sibyl and her husband would sail for England in a fortnight's time after the date of writing, by the Orient Line steamer *Lusitania*.

'You know what you suggested?' cried Alma delightedly. 'Shall we go?'

'What – to Naples? We should have to be off immediately. If they come by the next ship after the one that brought this letter, they are now only a fortnight from the end of the voyage. That means – allowing for their nine days from Naples to London – that we should have to be at Naples in four or five days from now.'

'Well? That's easily managed, isn't it?'

'Not by anyone in your state of health,' replied Harvey gently.

'I am perfectly well! I could travel night and day. Why not? One eats and sleeps as usual. Besides, are you quite sure They may be longer than you think. Telegraph to the London office and ask when the *Lusitania* will reach Naples.'

'If you like. But, for one thing, it's quite certain you oughtn't to travel in less than a week; and then – what about Hughie?'

Alma's face darkened with vexation.

'It doesn't matter,' she said coldly. 'I had counted on it; but, of course, that's nothing. There's the baby to be considered first.'

Harvey had never been so near the point of answering his wife in rough, masculine fashion. This illness of hers had unsettled his happy frame of mind, perturbing him with anxious thoughts, and making confusion of the quiet, reasonable prospect that lay before him only a week or two ago. He, too, could much have enjoyed the run to Naples and the voyage back, and disappointment taxed his patience. Irritated against Alma, and ashamed of himself for not being better tempered, he turned and left the room. A few minutes afterwards he walked to the post-office, where he addressed a telegram of inquiry to the Orient Line people in London. It was useless, of course; but he might as well satisfy Alma.

The reply telegram was delivered to him as he sauntered about in the garden. It merely confirmed his calculation; there might possibly be a clear five days before the *Lusitania* touched at Naples – most likely not more than four. He went into the sitting-room, but Alma was not there; he looked into the study, and found it vacant. As Ruth happened to pass, he bade her take the telegram to Mrs Rolfe upstairs.

He had no mind for reading or for any other occupation. He shut his door, and began to smoke. In the whiffs curling from his pipe he imagined the smoke of the great steamer as she drove northward from Indian seas; he heard the throb of the engines, saw the white wake. Naples; the Mediterranean; Gibraltar frowning towards the purple mountains of Morocco; the tumbling Bay; the green shores of Devon; – his pulses throbbed as he went voyaging in memory. And he might start this very hour, but for the child, who could not be left alone to servants. With something like a laugh, he thought of the people who implored Mary Abbott to relieve them of their burdensome youngsters. And at that moment Alma opened the door.

Her face, thinned a little by illness, had quite recovered its amiable humour.

'Of course you are quite right, Harvey. We can't rush across Europe at a moment's notice.'

He rose up, the lover's light in his eyes again, and drew her to him, and held her in a laughing embrace.

'What has been wrong between us? It's a new thing for you and me to be scowling and snarling.'

'I hope I neither scowled nor snarled, dear boy, though I'm not sure that *you* didn't. No doubt, Mrs Abbott went away thinking we lead rather a cat and dog life.'

'Hang it, no! How could she have any such thoughts?'

'Oh, the drive home that day.'

'Why, whose fault was that? I should have been all right, except that I couldn't understand why you had run the chance of killing yourself.'

'I don't think I should have cared very much that morning,' said Alma idly. 'I was more miserable than you can imagine.'

'Why?'

'Oh, I don't know – foolishness. But you never gave me a word of praise, and I'm sure I deserved it. Why, she galloped with me like mad for nearly two miles, and I never lost hold of the reins, and I pulled her up by myself and got her round, and drove back to meet you as if nothing had happened. I told Mrs Abbott all about it, and she was astonished at my pluck.'

'Must have been. So am I.'

'I doubt it. I doubt whether you ever think much of anything I do.'

'That's rather unkind, because you know it isn't true.'

'I always thought very much the same, you know.'

'Rubbish! But come, what are we going to do? Naples seems out of the question; but there's no reason why we shouldn't go to meet them in London.'

'You would much rather wait here, and let them come,' said Alma. 'I don't care particularly about going away. So long as we keep on good terms with each other – that's the chief thing.'

'There has never been a dream of anything else. We are on good terms as a matter of course. It's part of the order of the universe.'

'I'm very sorry, dear, that I threatened the universe with catastrophe; but I won't do it again – indeed I won't. I will watch your face, and be on my guard. And really, you know, under ordinary circumstances, I am good-tempered enough.'

'What's all this about?' cried Harvey. For she seemed to be in earnest, and spoke with a soft humility, such as might have become the least original of wives. 'Watch my face, and be on your guard? Since when have I desired you to be a simpleton?'

'I'm quite serious. It isn't foolish at all. I want to please you; that's all I mean, dear.'

He gazed at her, wondering, inclined to laugh, yet withheld from it by an uneasy feeling.

'This kind of talk means defective circulation, lost appetite, and so on,' was his half-joking answer. 'The way to please me is to get some colour into your cheeks again, and snub me for my ignorance of music, and be your own arrogant self. But listen. You're quite mistaken in thinking I want to stay here till Hugh and his wife come. It won't do. You're getting far too sweet and docile, and everything detestable. I had no idea of marrying an angel; it's too bad if you turn seraphic upon my hands. I wonder, now, whether, by way of pleasing me, you would answer a plain question?'

'I'll try.'

'Have you been wanting to get away from this place – I mean, to live somewhere else?'

'I? What can have made you think so?'

'That isn't trying to answer a question, you know.'

Alma, after looking keenly at him, had turned her face to the window. She kept silence, and wore a look of calm reflectiveness.

'Have you been bored and wearied by this life?' Harvey asked in his most good-natured tone.

'I don't think I have ever for a moment shown a sign of it,' replied Alma, with grave conviction.

'So much the worse, if it meant that you concealed your thoughts.'

'I shall always be content, Harvey, so long as I see you are living the kind of life that suits you.'

He uttered a shout of humorous, yet half-genuine, exasperation.

'Do you want me to swear it's a long time since I lost the habit, but it might strike you as manly, and perhaps I had better practise again. What has it to do with *you*, the kind of life that suits *me*? Don't you remember my talking about that before we were married? I've had a suspicion that you were getting rather into that state of mind. You dropped your music, and partly, I've no doubt, because you didn't find enough intelligent sympathy in me. You went in for painting, and you've dropped that—'

'It was winter, you see,' Alma interrupted.

'Yes, but that wasn't the only reason. It meant general failure of energy — the kind of thing I've known myself, only too well.'

'What — here?' asked Alma, with some alacrity.

'I meant now and again, all through my life. No; here I've gone on right enough, with a tolerably even mind; and for that very reason I haven't noticed any signs of the other thing in you — till just now, when you lost your head. Why haven't you been frank with me?'

'You take it for granted that I had anything to be frank about,' Alma remarked.

'Yes — and you don't contradict me.'

'Then what were you going to say, Harvey?'

She bent towards him, with that air of sweet reasonableness which showed her features at their best: eye tranquil and intelligent, lips ingenuously smiling; a countenance she wore not thrice in a twelvemonth, but by Harvey well remembered amid all changes, and held to express the true being of the woman he loved.

'Why, I was going to say, dear,' he replied tenderly, 'that no good can come of sacrificing your instincts. You have not to ask yourself whether I am lazily comfortable — for that's what it amounts to — but what you are making of your life. Remember, for one thing, that I am considerably older—'

'Please!' She checked him with an extended hand. 'I don't want to remember anything of the kind.'

'There's no harm in it, I hope.' He laughed a little. 'The difference isn't distressing, but just enough to be taken into account. At forty, or near it, a man who is happily married gets used to his slippers and his pipe – especially if comfort, and all the rest of it, have come after half a lifetime of homelessness. I might often say to myself that I was wasting time, rusting, and so on; but the next day I should fall back into the easy-chair again, and hate the thought of changes. But you, with thirty still far ahead, slippers and pipe have no particular attraction for you.'

He saw a thought in her eyes, and paused.

'Hughie will soon be able to talk,' fell from Alma, her look no longer that of ingenuous sweetness, but of virtue just a trifle self-conscious. And her husband, though he read this meaning in the change, was yet pleased by the words that accompanied it.

'Yes; and then there will be more for you to do, you were going to say. But that won't occupy you entirely, and it doesn't bind you to any particular spot.'

'Perhaps not.'

She had become almost demure. Harvey took his eyes away.

'It comes to this – you're not to subordinate your life to mine. That's the old idea, and it still works well with some people. Yet I don't know; perhaps it doesn't, really; one knows little enough about people's lives. At all events, it won't work in our case, and remember that we never thought it would. We talked it all over, with no humbug on either side – rather an unusual sort of talk, when one comes to think of it. I liked you for the common-sense you showed, and I remember patting myself on the back for a rational bit of behaviour at a time when I felt rather crazy.'

Alma laughed in her gayest key.

'You were delicious. I didn't quite know what to make of you. And perhaps that was the very reason—'

'Reason for what?' asked Harvey, when she broke off and looked not quite so pale as a moment before.

'I forget what I was going to say. But please go on. It's very interesting – as your talk always is.'

'I've said about all. You're not to be dutiful and common-place; that's the matter in a nutshell.'

'I don't think you can accuse me of ever being commonplace.'

'Perhaps not,' said Harvey.

'And as for dutiful, our duty is to be consistent, don't you think?'

'Yes – if by consistency you mean the steady resolve to make the most of yourself. That's what you had in mind when you came here. As soon as you begin to grow limp, it's time to ask what is the matter. I don't offer any advice; you know yourself better than I can know you. It's for you to tell me what goes on in your mind. What's the use of our living together if you keep your most serious thoughts to yourself?'

Harvey Rolfe glowed with a sense of his own generous wisdom. He had never felt so keen a self-approval. Indeed, that emotion seldom came to solace him; for the most part he was the severest critic of his own doings and sayings. But for once it appeared to him that he uttered golden words, the ripe fruit of experience and reflection. That personal unrest had anything to do with the counsel he offered to his wife, he did not for the moment even suspect. Alma had touched him with her unfamiliar note of simple womanhood, and all at once there was revealed to him a peril of selfishness, from which he strongly recoiled. He seemed to be much older, and Alma much more youthful, than he was wont to perceive. Very gently and sweetly she had put him in mind of this fact; it behoved him to consider it well, and act upon the outcome of such reflection. Heavens! was he in danger of becoming the typical husband – the man who, as he had put it, thinks first of his pipe and slippers? From the outside, no man would more quickly or more contemptuously have noted the common-sense moral of this present situation. Being immediately concerned, he could see nothing in his attitude but a wise and noble disinterestedness.* And thus, at a moment when he wittingly held the future in his hands, he prided himself on leaving to Alma an entire responsibility – making her, in the ordinary phrase, mistress of her own fate, and waiting upon her decisions.

'I will think a little longer,' said Alma, sighing contentedly, 'and then we'll talk about it again. It's quite true I was getting a little run down, and perhaps – but we'll talk about it in a day or two.'

'Could we decide anything for the present? Would you care to go and meet the steamer at Plymouth?'

'And take Hughie? Suppose I wrote very nicely to Mamma, and asked if we might leave Hughie with her, in Hampshire, for a few days? I dare say she would be delighted, and the other people too. The nurse could be with him, I dare say. We could call there on our way. And Ruth would look after the house very well.'

'Write and ask.'

'Then you and I' – Alma began to talk joyously – 'might ramble about Devonshire till the ship comes. Let me see – if we travelled on Monday, that would give us several days, wouldn't it? And the Carnabys might either land at Plymouth, or we go on with them in the ship to London. That's a very good plan. But why lose time by writing? Send a telegram to Mamma – "Could we leave Hughie and nurse with you for a day or two?"'

Harvey again turned his steps to the post-office, and this message was despatched. A few hours elapsed before the reply came, but it was favourable.

'Then we'll leave on Monday!' exclaimed Alma, whose convalescence was visibly proceeding. 'Just send another telegram – a word or two, that they may be ready.'

'Might as well have mentioned the day in the other,' said Harvey, though glad to have something more to do.

'Of course; how thoughtless!'

And they laughed, and were in the best of tempers.

On the morrow, Sunday, they walked together as they had used to do in the first spring after their marriage; along the grassy cliffs, then down to the nook where the sand is full of tiny shells, and round the little headland into the next bay, where the quaint old fishing-village stands upon the edge of the tide. And Alma was again in love, and held her husband's hand, and said the sweetest things in the most wonderful voice. She over-tired herself a little, so that, when they ascended the cliff again, Harvey had to support her; and in the sunny solitude she thanked him with her lips – in two ways.

It was a second honeymoon.


CHAPTER 4


Mrs Frothingham's sister, who lived near Basingstoke,* gave a warm welcome to little Hugh Rolfe; and Mrs Frothingham, who had all but forgotten that the child was not really her grandson, took charge of him with pride and joy. He stayed a week; he stayed a fortnight; – he stayed two months.

For when the Carnabys – who landed at Plymouth* and rested there for a couple of days – made known their intention of straightway taking a flat in town, it seemed to Alma that the very best thing for her health would be to spend a week or two in London, and see her old friends, and go to a few concerts. The time was favourable, for June had only just set in. Harvey, nothing loath, took his wife to a quiet hotel in the Portman Square region, whither also went their friends from abroad; his project being to look for furnished rooms, where child and nurse could join them. But Mrs Frothingham thought it a pity of pities to take little Hugh into the town, when all was so pleasantly arranged for him down in Hampshire; and, as Alma evidently inclined to the same view, the uninviting thought of 'apartments' was laid aside. They might as well remain at the hotel, said Harvey. Alma, with a pretty show of economical hesitation, approved the plan, saying that she would be quite ready to go home again when Sibyl had established herself in a flat. This event came to pass in about three weeks; the Carnabys found a flat which suited them very well at Oxford and Cambridge Mansions, and thither, with the least possible delay, transferred a portion of their furniture, which had lain in warehouse. Thereupon, sweetly reasonable, Mrs Rolfe made known that it was time to fetch her baby and return to Carnarvonshire. She felt incalculably better; the change had been most refreshing; now for renewed enjoyment of her dear home!

But Harvey wore his wisest countenance; no owl could have surpassed it for sage gravity.

'You are very much better, and don't you think you would be better still after another week or two? The concerts are in full swing; it seems a pity – now you are here—'

Alma looked gracefully reluctant. Were not the hotel expenses rather heavy?

'Pooh! You must remember that at home we live on half our income, or less. If that's all that troubles you—'

'You are very kind, Harvey!'

'Why, as for that, I'm enjoying myself. And I like to see you in such capital spirits.'

So, with a happy sigh, Alma gave up the packing of her trunk, and wrote to Mrs Frothingham that if baby *really* was not a trouble, they might stay for another fortnight. 'Harvey is in such capital spirits, and does so enjoy himself, that I don't think he ought to go home whilst all the life of the season is in full swing. Of course, I could leave him here, but – if you will credit it – he seems really to wish to have me with him. If I tried to say how thoroughly good and kind he is, I should make you laugh. It amuses me to see him turned into a sort of bachelor again. This is no contradiction; I mean that here, among his men friends, he shows a new side of himself, seems younger (to tell the truth), and has a kind of gaiety quite different from his good humour at home. You can't think how he enjoys a dinner at the club, for instance, quite in a boyish way; and then he comes back with all sorts of stories and bits of character and I don't know what; we forget the time, and sit talking till I daren't tell you when. But I am doing the same thing now, for it is half-past twelve (noon), and I have promised to lunch with Sibyl at half-past one. Her flat is just finished, and looks very pretty indeed. A thousand kisses to my little darling! Try and make him understand that *mum-mum* has not gone for ever.'

She dressed with care (her wardrobe had undergone a complete renewal), and drove off in a hansom to Oxford and Cambridge Mansions. It was to be a luncheon of intimacy, for Sibyl had not yet gathered her acquaintances. When Alma entered, Mrs Carnaby was sitting just as in the days before her great migration, perfectly at ease, admirably self-possessed, her beauty arrayed with all the chastity of effect which distinguished her among idle and pleasure-loving women. She had found a new way of doing her hair, a manner so young, so virginal, that Alma could not but gaze with wonder and admiration.

'You do look sweet today!'

'Do I? I'm glad you think so. – I want your opinion. Would you have the piano there, or *there*?'

This matter was discussed, and then they obeyed the tuneful gong that summoned them to the dining-room. Alma surveyed everything, and felt a secret envy. Here was no demonstration of the simple life; things beautiful and luxurious filled all available space, and indeed over-filled it, for Sibyl had tried to use as much as possible of the furniture formerly displayed in Hamilton Terrace, with such alterations and novelties as were imposed by the fashion of today. She offered her guest a most dainty little meal; a luncheon such as Alma could not possibly have devised, in spite of all her reminiscences.

'Civilisation is a great thing,' Sibyl remarked. 'It's good to have been in savagery, just to appreciate one's privileges.'

'But you liked Honolulu?'

'Honolulu – yes. I was thinking of Queensland. There's no barbarism at Honolulu, if you keep out of sight of the Americans and Europeans. Yes, I enjoyed myself there. I think I could go back and live out my life at Waikiki.'

'It astonished me that you didn't make an effort to go with Hugh to that great volcano. I have read about it since, and I'm sure I should have faced anything.'

'Kilauea,' murmured Sibyl, with a dreamy air, as she raised the wine-glass to her lips. 'I was lazy, no doubt. The climate, you know; and then I don't care much about bubbling lava. It was much nicer to watch the gold-fish at Waikiki. – Where is your husband today?'

'Of all things in the world, gone to Lord's!* He says he never saw a cricket match in his life, and it struck him this morning that it really was a defect in his education. Of course, he was thinking of Hughie. He wants Hughie to be a cricketer and horseman and everything that's robust.'

'Just like Hugh,' replied Sibyl, laughing. 'I should feel the same if I had a boy. I like open-air men – though I shouldn't care always to live among them.'

'Hugh at Coventry still?' Alma inquired.

Her hostess gave a nod, with a look intimating that she would say more when the servant left them free to talk. She added –

'Do you know Mrs Strangeways?'

'I seem to remember a Mr Strangeways,' replied Alma, 'but I can't think how or where.'

'Yes, he's a man who goes about a good deal. His wife was the widow of that artist who promised so well, and got into a scrape, and died miserably – Edward – no, Egbert Dover. Don't you know that big landscape that hangs in Mrs Holt's boudoir? – that was one of his. He hid himself away, and died in a garret or a workhouse – something cheerful. I met Mrs Strangeways at Brisbane; she and her husband were globe-trotting. She might look in this afternoon. I don't know whether you would care for her; she's rather – rapid, you know. But she remembers hearing you play somewhere – spoke of you with great admiration.'

Alma's eyes shone.

'Oh, I should be glad to meet her! Are you going to let me stay with you all the afternoon, then?'

'If you have nothing better to do. I suppose I shall be losing you presently. I'm very sorry. I wish you lived in London.'

'On this one account,' replied Alma, 'I wish I did. But I've got so out of it. Don't you think I carry a rustic atmosphere about with me?'

Sibyl laughed, in the tone her friend wished to hear. Alma would have been profoundly mortified if Mrs Carnaby had seemed ever so little to agree with her.

For all that, they were not quite so well attuned to each other as when the young married woman, indifferent seemingly to social distinction, patronised the ambitious girl, and, by the mere bestowal of confidence, subtly flattered her. In those days Alma did not feel it as patronage, for Sibyl's social position was perhaps superior to her own, and in things of the intellect (apart from artistic endowment) she sincerely looked up to her friend. Together they trod ground above the heads of ordinary women in their world. But changes had been at work. Alma now felt herself, to say the least, on equal terms with Mrs Carnaby. Economically, she was secure; whereas Sibyl, notwithstanding the show she made, drew daily nearer to a grave crisis, and might before long find herself in a very unpleasant situation. Intellectually, Alma saw herself in a less modest light than before marriage; the daily companionship of such a man as her husband had been to her as a second education; she had quite overtaken Sibyl, if not gone a little beyond her. The deference she still showed was no longer genuine, and this kind of affectation, hard to support and readily perceived, is very perilous to friendship. Conscious of thoughts she must not utter, Alma naturally attributed to her friend the same sort of reticence. She feared that Sibyl must often have in mind the loss she had suffered three years ago, and would contrast her own precarious circumstances with the comfort of Bennet Frothingham's daughter. Moreover, Mrs Carnaby was not in all respects her own self; she had lost something on her travels; was it a shade of personal delicacy, of mental refinement? She seemed more inclined to self-assertion, to aim somewhat at worldly success, to be less careful about the friends she made. Alma felt this difference, though not clear as to its nature, and insensibly it helped to draw them apart.

'Yes, Hugh is at Coventry,' said Sibyl, when the servant had withdrawn. 'He'll go backwards and forwards, you know. I don't think he'll have very much to do practically with the business; but just at first he likes to see what's going on.'

'I hope it will prosper.'

'Oh, no doubt it will. It was a very good idea.'

Sibyl spoke as though she had never contemplated the possibilities which were in Alma's mind. Her husband, as Alma knew from Rolfe, was in anything but a sanguine mood; he saw his position in all its gravity, and could hardly rest for fear that this latest enterprise should not succeed. Sibyl, however, enjoyed her lunch with complete tranquillity. She had the air of being responsible for nothing.

'I'm not at all sorry we went away for a time. Travelling suits Hugh; it has done him a great deal of good. I believe he would have liked to stay in Tasmania; but he saw it wouldn't do for me, and the good fellow could think of nothing else but my comfort. I have a great admiration for Hugh,' she added, with a smile, not exactly of superiority or condescension, but of approval distinct from tenderness. 'Of course, I always had, and it has increased since I've travelled with him. He shows to far more advantage on a ship than in a drawing-room. On this last voyage we had some very bad weather, and then he was at his best. I admired him immensely!'

'I can quite imagine how he would be,' said Alma.

'And how glad I was when I heard you had married his best friend! It had crossed my mind more than once. Perhaps you don't remember – you didn't notice it at the time – but I ventured a discreet hint before we parted. You couldn't have done a more sensible thing, Alma.'

Though quite willing to believe this, Alma, for some reason, did not care to hear it thus asserted. The manner of the remark, for all its friendliness, reminded her that marriage had signified her defeat, the end of high promises, brave aspirations.

'I couldn't tell you how it happened,' she said, with a little awkwardness. 'And I dare say you would say the same about your own marriage.'

'Of course. So would every woman. One never does know how it happens.'

And Sibyl laughed with quiet merriment which had a touch of cynicism. Alma had not yet spoken of the impulse which carried her away to the little house in Carnarvonshire, to the life of noble simplicity and calm retirement, and she had no disposition now to touch on the matter. Even in her early letters to Sybil not much was said of it, for she felt that her friend might have a difficulty in sympathising with such enthusiasm. She would have liked to make Sibyl understand that her rustication was quite voluntary; but the subject embarrassed her, and she preferred to keep silence.

'I didn't hear very much about your time in Germany,' Mrs Carnaby resumed. 'Nothing much to tell, I suppose.'

'Very little.'

'Any – any adventures?'

'Oh no!'

Alma felt herself grow warm, less at the thought of the adventures which really had befallen her than from vexation at the feeling of insignificance. She understood very well what Sibyl meant by her smiling question, and it would almost have been a relief to tell certain stories, in proof that she had not utterly fallen out of sight and mind on her self-banishment from society. There was no reason, indeed, why she should not make fun of Felix Dymes and his proposal; but the episode seemed idle in comparison with another, on which she had never ceased to reflect. Perhaps a certain glory attached to that second incident; Sibyl might be impressed alike with the character of the temptation and with her friend's nobility in scorning it. But the opportunity had gone by.

On rising from table, Sibyl remarked that she wished to make one or two purchases; would Alma accompany her to the shop? They went forth, and drove as far as Regent Street. Mrs Carnaby's requirements were one or two expensive trifles, which she chose with leisurely gratification of her taste. It surprised Alma to see this extravagance; one would have thought the purchaser had never known restricted means, and dreamt of no such thing; she bought what she happened to desire, as a matter of course. And this was no ostentation for Alma's benefit. Evidently Sibyl had indulged herself with the same freedom throughout her travels; for she had brought back a museum of beautiful and curious things, which must have cost a good deal. Perhaps for the first time in her life Alma experienced a sense of indignation at the waste of money. She was envious withal, which possibly helped to explain the other impulse.

They returned in an hour's time. Sibyl then withdrew for a few minutes, and reappeared in an exquisite tea-gown, which made her friend's frock, though new and handsome, look something less than suitable to the occasion. Alma, glancing about the room, spoke as if in pursuance of a train of thought.

'People *do* make a lot of money out of bicycles, I think?'

'I have heard so,' answered her hostess indifferently. 'Will you play me something? The piano has been tuned; I should like to know if you think it all right.'

'I have quite given up playing the piano.'

'Indeed? And the violin too?'

'No, no; the violin is my instrument. Whose is that little water-colour, Sibyl? I tried for just that effect of sun through mist not long ago.'

'Oh yes, to be sure, you have gone in for water-colours; you told me in a letter. I must see some of your things. Of course, I shall be coming—'

The door opened, and a small page, very smartly equipped, announced Mrs Herbert Strangeways. The page was a surprise to Alma; she had not as yet seen this functionary; but Mrs Strangeways drew her attention. A lady of perhaps thirty-five, with keen, thin face, and an artificial bloom on her hollow cheeks; rather overdressed, yet not to the point of vulgarity; of figure very well proportioned, slim and lissom. Her voice was a trifle hard, but pleasant; her manner cordial in excess.

'So here you are, *chez vous*. Charming! Charming! The prettiest room I have seen for a long time. Mrs Rolfe? Oh, Mrs Rolfe, the name put me out for a moment; but I remember you perfectly, perfectly. It was at the Wigrams'; you played the violin wonderfully!'

Alma did not much care to be reminded of this. Mr Wigram, one of her father's co-directors, was lying at this moment in durance vile,* and his wife lived somewhere or other on charity. But Mrs Strangeways uttered the name without misgiving, and behaved as though nothing conceivable could have afforded her more delight than to meet Alma again. It was her habit to speak in superlatives, and to wear a countenance of corresponding ecstasy. Any casual remark from either of the ladies she received with a sort of rapture; her nerves seemed to be in a perpetual thrill. If she referred to herself, it was always with depreciation, and not at all the kind of depreciation which invites compliment, but a tremulous self-belittlement, such as might be natural in a person who had done something to be ashamed of, and held her place in society only on sufferance.

'You still play, of course?' she said to Mrs Rolfe presently. 'I so hope I may have the pleasure of hearing you again. I wonder whether I could persuade you to come next Wednesday? We have a little house in Porchester Terrace.* Of course, I don't mean to ask you to play; I shouldn't venture to. Just a few friends in the evening – if you didn't think it tiresome? I'll send you a card.'

There entered a tall young man of consumptive features, accompanied by a stout, florid woman, older than himself; and upon this couple followed half-a-dozen miscellaneous callers, some of whom Alma knew. These old acquaintances met her with a curiosity they hardly troubled to disguise; she herself was reserved, and took no part in the general chatter. Mrs Strangeways withdrew into a corner, as if wishing to escape observation. When Mrs Rolfe took a chair by her side, she beamed with gratitude, and their gossip grew quite intimate. Alma could not understand why Sibyl had stigmatised this woman as 'rapid' – that is to say, 'fast'; she gabbled, indeed, at a great rate, but revealed no startling habits of life or thought, and seemed to have rather an inclination for childish forms of amusement. Before they parted, Alma gave a promise that she would go to Mrs Strangeways 'at home' next Wednesday.

'And your husband, if he would care to come. I should be so delighted to know him. But perhaps he doesn't care about that kind of thing. I hate to bore anyone – don't you? But then, of course, you're never in danger of doing it. So very, *very* glad to have met you! And so exceedingly kind of you to promise! – so *very* kind!'

As Sibyl also was going to Porchester Terrace, they arranged to chaperon each other, and to start from Mrs Rolfe's hotel.

'It's no use making Harvey uncomfortable,' said Alma. 'He would go if I asked him, but sorely against the grain. He always detested 'at homes' – except when he came to admire *me*! And he likes to see me going about independently.'

'Does he?' said Sibyl, with an inquiring look.

'Yes – seriously. We do our best not to encumber each other. Don't you think it's the best way?'

'No doubt whatever.'

Mrs Carnaby smiled, and the smile grew to a laugh; but she would not explain what she meant by it.

On the Wednesday evening, they reached Mrs Strangeways' house at ten o'clock. Carriages and cabs made a queue up to the door, and figures succeeded each other rapidly on the red cloth laid down across the pavement. Alma was nervous. More than three years had passed since the fatal evening when, all unconsciously, she said goodbye to social splendours; from then till now she had taken part in no festivity. The fact that her name was no longer Frothingham gave her some encouragement; but she must expect to be recognised, perhaps to be stared at. Well, and would it be so very disagreeable? An hour before, the mirror had persuaded her that she need not shrink from people's eyes; her dress defied criticism, and she had not to learn how to bear herself with dignity. Sibyl was unusually lavish of compliments, and in a matter such as this Sibyl's judgment had weight. As soon as she found herself on the stairs, amid perfumes and brilliances, she breathed freely; it was the old familiar atmosphere; her heart leaped with a sudden joy, as in a paradise regained.*

Already the guests were very numerous, and they continued to arrive. The drawing-rooms filled; a crowd of men smoked in the 'library' and the billiard-room; women swarmed in passages and staircase. After welcoming Mrs Rolfe with the ardour of a bosom friend and the prostration of a devotee, the hostess turned to the next comer with scarcely less fervency. And Alma passed on, content for the present to be lost amid thronging strangers.

'Who are all these people?' she asked of Sibyl, who had moved along by her side.

'Nobodies, most of them, I should imagine. There's no need to stay very long, you know. That's Mr Strangeways, the little man with a red face talking to that mountain of a woman in green. Mercy, what a dress! He's coming this way; I'll introduce him to you.'

The host had a jovial carriage and a bluff way of speaking, both obviously affected. His eyes wandered as he talked, and never met anyone else's with a steady look. Alma thought him offensively familiar, but he did not inflict himself upon her for long.

When the hostess began to go hither and thither, she pounced eagerly on Mrs Rolfe, and soon made her the centre of a group. Alma began to taste the old delight of homage, though she perceived that her new acquaintances were not of the world in which she had formerly shone. About midnight, when she was a little tired of the crush, and thought of going, there fell upon her ear a voice which startled and aroused her like an unexpected grasp. On the instant she saw an open place in Munich; the next, a lake and mountains.

'I wasn't in town then. I got out of sorts, and ran away to a little place I have on the Lake of Garda.'

The speaker was immediately behind her. She all but turned her head, and grew hot in the effort to command herself. Amid the emotions naturally excited in her she was impressed by a quality in the voice, a refinement of utterance, which at once distinguished it from that of the men with whom she had been talking. It belonged to a higher social grade, if it did not express a superiority of nature. For some moments she listened, catching now and then a word; then other voices intervened. At length, turning where she stood, she let her eyes range, expressionless, over the faces near by. That which she sought was not discoverable, but at the same moment the hostess came up to her.

Mrs Rolfe, do you know Mr Cyrus Redgrave?'

'Mr Redgrave—?'

The confused, hesitating repetition of the name was taken by Mrs Strangeways for a reply in the negative.

'A charming man, and a great friend of mine – oh, a very old friend. Let me bring him.'

She rustled away, and Mrs Rolfe sank back on to the *causeuse** from which she had newly risen. Quickly the hostess returned, and, in the track she made through crowded clusters of people who stood talking, there followed a gentleman of easy carriage, with handsome features and thin hair. He was looking for Alma, and as soon as his eyes perceived her, they fell. Of what Mrs Strangeways said, Alma heard not a syllable; she bowed mechanically, clutching her fan as though in peril of a fall and this the only thing within reach; she knew that Redgrave bent solemnly, silently; and then, with sudden relief, she saw the hostess retire.

'I beg your pardon.' The voice was addressing her in a respectful undertone. 'I had no choice. I did not feel justified in saying I knew you.'

'You were quite right,' she replied coldly, her fingers now relaxed upon the fan. 'Mrs Strangeways is a little impulsive; she gave me no opportunity of preventing the introduction.'

'Will you let me say, Mrs Rolfe, that I am glad to have been presented to you as a stranger? I should be happy indeed if our acquaintance might begin anew.'

It was polite in terms, but sounded to Alma very like the coolest impertinence. She bent her head, ever so little. The second seat of the *causeuse* being unoccupied, Redgrave hereupon took possession of it. No sooner had he done so than Alma rose, let a smile of indifference just fall upon him, and lost herself amid the buzzing assembly.

Ten minutes later, Redgrave and Mrs Carnaby were lounging in these same seats, conversing with perfect mutual intelligence. They had not met for three years, but the interval signified very little in their lives, and they resumed conversation practically at the point where it had broken off in Mrs Frothingham's drawing-room. A tactful question assured the man of the world that Mrs Carnaby knew nothing of certain passages at Munich and Bregenz.

'I'm afraid,' he added, 'Mrs Rolfe has become a little reserved. Natural, no doubt.'

'She lives in a wild part of Wales,' Sibyl answered, smiling tolerantly. 'And her husband detests society.'

'Indeed? Odd choice for her to have made, don't you think? – And so your Odyssey is over? We shall have some chance of seeing you again.'

'But your own Odyssey is perpetually going on. Are you ever in town except for a few weeks of the season?'

'Oh, I go about very little now; I'm settling down. – You never met my sister, I think? She has a house at Wimbledon with a good-sized garden – sort of little park, in fact, – and I have persuaded her to let me build myself a bungalow among the trees.'

'Splendid idea!'

'Not bad, I think. One is free there; a member of the family whenever one likes; domesticated; all that's respectable; and only a few steps away, the bachelor snuggery, with all that's – . No, no! I was *not* going to complete the antithesis, though by your smiling you seem to say so.'*

'The suggestion was irresistible,' said Sibyl, with the composure, the air of security, which always covered her excursions on to slippery ground.

'When the weather is good, I ask a few of my friends to come and sit there in the shade. They may or may not be my sister's friends also; that doesn't matter. I have a separate entrance from the road. – But I wish you knew Mrs Fenimore. She lived a year or two at Stuttgart, for her children to learn German. Her husband's in India. She tried it, but couldn't stand the climate.'

'And you really live in the bungalow?' inquired Mrs Carnaby, disregarding this information about Redgrave's sister.

'Yes, it's my headquarters in England. Let me send you a card, will you, when I have my next afternoon? It might amuse you, and I assure you it *is* perfectly respectable.'

'How could I doubt it, if you invite me?'

Alma drove home by herself in a hansom. She liked this disregard of conventionalities; all the more because Harvey, who, of course, had sat up for her, seemed a trifle anxious. Her spirits were exuberant; she gave a merry, mocking account of the evening, but it included no mention of Cyrus Redgrave.

At the end of June her friends the Leaches moved from their old house in Elgin Road to a new one out at Kingsbury-Neasden, and when the removal was completed Alma went there to make a call, taking her husband. Harvey had never been beyond Swiss Cottage on this extension of the Metropolitan Railway;* he looked with interest at the new districts springing up towards Harrow, and talked of them with Mrs Leach. A day or two after, he travelled by himself to a greater distance on the same line, making a survey of the country from Harrow to Aylesbury. At his next meeting with Hugh Carnaby, which took place about the middle of July, he threw out a suggestion that for anyone who wished to live practically in London and yet away from its frenzy, the uplands towards Buckinghamshire were convenient ground.

'I wish you were thinking of it yourself,' replied Hugh. 'Your wife is about the only woman Sibyl cares to see much of, and the only woman I know that she'll get any good from.'

The strong man did not look very cheerfully on the world just now, and it was evident that he felt some sort of trouble with regard to his wife. For her sake solely he had returned to England, where he was less than ever at his ease. He wished Sibyl to live in her own way, grudged her nothing, admired and cherished her with undiminished fervour; but in Oxford and Cambridge Mansions it cost him a great effort to pretend to be at home. The years of wandering had put him hopelessly out of touch with what Sibyl called society. Little as he understood about manufactures, or cared for the details of commerce, he preferred to stay down at Coventry with his partner Mackin-tosh, living roughly, smoking his pipe and drinking his whisky in the company of men who had at least a savour of sturdy manhood. His days of sport were gone by; he was risking the solid remnant of his capital; and if it vanished – But of that possibility he would not speak, even with Harvey Rolfe. As he meditated, his teeth were set, his eyes darkened. And it appeared to Harvey that the good fellow drank a little more whisky than was needful, even in these warm days.

'I want to see the little chap, my namesake,' he said. 'Why don't you have him up here? Doesn't your wife feel she wants him?'

'Alma will think more of him in a year or two,' Harvey replied.

'Yes. I've noticed that women – one sort of women – don't care much about babies nowadays. I dare say they're right. The fewer children people have, the better. It's bad to see the poor little squalling brats in the filth and smoke down yonder, and worse still in this damned London. Great God! when there's so much of the world clean and sweet, here we pack and swelter together, a million to the square mile! What eternal fools we are!'

Harvey growled his heartiest agreement. None the less, a day or two after, he was holding a conversation with Alma which encouraged her secret weariness of the clean and sweet places of the earth. They had come home from a Richter concert,* and Alma uttered a regret that she had not her violin here. A certain *cadenza* introduced by a certain player into a certain violin solo did not please her; why, she could extemporise a *cadenza* far more in keeping with the spirit of the piece. After listening, with small attention to the matter, but much to the ardent speech and face of enthusiasm, Harvey made a quiet remark.

'I want you to decide very soon what we are going to do.'

'Going to do?'

'About the future – where we are to live.'

Alma strummed lightly with her finger-tips upon the table, and smiled, but did not look up.

'Do you really think of making any change?'

'I leave it entirely to you. You remember our last talk before we came away. You have simply to ask yourself what your needs are. Be honest with yourself and with me. Don't sacrifice life to a whim, one way or the other. You have had plenty of time to think; you have known several ways of life; you're old enough to understand yourself. Just make up your mind, and act.'

'But it's ridiculous, Harvey, to speak as if I had only myself to consider.'

'I don't want you to do so. But supposing that were your position, now, after all your experience, where would you choose to live?'

He constrained her to answer, and at length she spoke, with a girlish diffidence which seemed to him very charming.

'I like the concerts – and I like to be near my musical friends – and I don't think it's at all necessary to give up one's rational way of living just because one is in London instead of far away.'

'Precisely. That means we ought to come back.'

'Not if you do it unwillingly.'

'I'll be frank in my turn. For Hughie's sake, I don't think we ought to live in the town; but it's easy enough to find healthy places just outside.'

'I shouldn't wish to be actually in the town,' said Alma, her voice tremulous with pleasure. 'You know where the Leaches are living?'

'Yes. Or just a little farther away, on the higher ground. Very well, let us regard *that* as settled.'

'But you, dear – could you live there?'

'Well enough. It's all the same to me if I have my books, and a field to walk in – and if you don't want me to see too many women.'

Alma laughed gaily, and had done with semblance of hesitation.

They began to search for a house, and in a week's time had found one, newly built, which seemed to answer their requirements. It was at Pinner, not many minutes by rail from Alma's friends at Kingsbury-Neasden, and only about half an hour from Baker Street – 'so convenient for the concerts'. A new house might be damp, but the summer months were hastening to dry it, and they would not enter into residence before the end of autumn. 'We must go and enjoy our heather,' said Alma brightly. The rent was twice what Harvey had been paying; there was no stabling, but Alma agreed that they ought not to keep a horse, for naturally there would be 'other expenses'.

Other expenses, to be sure. But Harvey signed the three years' lease without misgiving. A large surplus lay in hand after the 'simple life' in Carnarvonshire, and his position was not that of men who have extravagant wives.

## CHAPTER 5

The Leach family gave it to be understood by their friends that they had moved out of town because of Mrs Leach's health. Other explanations were suspected; for the new establishment seemed to be on a more modest footing than that in Elgin Road, and the odd arrangement whereby Mr Leach came home only on Saturday could not be without significance. Mrs Leach, it was true, suffered from some obscure affection of the nerves, which throughout the whole of her married life had disabled her from paying any continuous regard to domestic affairs; this debility had now reached such a point that the unfortunate lady could do nothing but collapse in chairs and loll on sofas. As her two daughters, though not debilitated, had never dreamt of undertaking household management, all such matters were left to a cook-housekeeper, changed every few months, generally after a quarrel, wherein Mrs Leach put forth, for an invalid, very surprising energy. Mr Leach, a solicitor, had no function in life but to toil without pause for the support of his family in genteel leisure; he was a mild man, dreading discord, and subservient to his wife. For many years he had made an income of about £2000, every penny of which, excepting a small insurance premium, had been absorbed by expenses of the house. At the age of fifty, prematurely worn by excessive labour, he was alarmed to find his income steadily diminishing, with no corresponding diminution – but rather the opposite – in the demands made upon him by wife and daughters. In a moment of courage, prompted by desperation, he obtained the consent of Dora and Gerda to this unwelcome change of abode. It caused so much unpleasantness between himself and Mrs Leach, that he was glad to fit up a sleeping-room at his office and go home only once a week; whereby he saved time, and had the opportunity of starving himself as well as of working himself to death.

Dora and Gerda, having grown up in such domestic circumstances, accepted them with equanimity. When their father spoke nervously of retrenchment, saying that he grew old and must save money to provide for their future, they made no objection, but were as far as ever from perceiving the sordid tragedy of his lot. Dora lived for her music; Gerda sang a little, but was stronger on the social side, delighting in festivities and open-air amusements. They were amiable and intelligent girls, and would have been amazed had anyone charged them with selfishness; no less if it had been suggested to them that they personally might rectify the domestic disorder of which at times they were moved to complain. They had no beauty, and knew it; neither had received an offer of marriage, and they looked for nothing of the kind. That their dresses cost a great deal, was taken as a matter of course; also that they should go abroad when other people did, and have the best places at concert or theatre, and be expansively 'at home'. With all sincerity they said of themselves that they lived a quiet life. How could it be quieter? – unless one followed the example of Alma Rolfe; but Alma was quite an exceptional person – to be admired and liked, not to be imitated.

Yet even Alma, it seemed, had got tired of her extraordinary freak. She was back again within the circle of civilisation; or, as she put it in her original, amusing way, 'on the outer edge of the whirlpool'. She had a very nice little house, beautifully furnished; everyone knew Alma's excellent taste. She came frequently to Kingsbury-Neasden, and ran up to town at least as often as they (Dora and Gerda) did. Like them she found it an annoyance to have to rush to the station before midnight; but, being married, she could allow herself more freedom of movement than was permissible to single young women, and having once missed the last train, she simply went to a hotel where she was known, and quietly returned to Pinner next morning. That Mrs Rolfe had such complete liberty and leisure seemed to them no subject for remark; being without cares, she enjoyed life; a matter of course. And she was so very clever. No wonder Mr Rolfe (charming man) always had admiration in his eyes when he looked at her. Some husbands (miserable churls) can see nothing in their wives, and never think of encouraging what talent they may have. But when Alma grew a little dissatisfied with her violin (a 'Vuillaume',* which poor Mr Bennet Frothingham had given her in the days gone by), Mr Rolfe did not hesitate to spend fifty pounds on an instrument more to her liking; and the dear girl played on it divinely.

There was no shadow of envy in Dora Leach. 'I don't play quite badly,' she said to Alma. 'Goodness knows, I oughtn't to, after all the lessons I've had and the pains I've given. But with you it's different, dear. You know very well that, if you liked, you could become a professional, and make a name.'

'I *might* have done,' Alma admitted; 'but marriage put an end to that. You have too much sense to think I mean that I repent it.'

'I don't see why marriage should put an end to it,' urged Dora. 'I'm quite sure your husband would be very proud if you came out and had a great success.'

'But if I came out and made a fiasco?'

'You wouldn't.'

That was in the summer of 1890,* when the Rolfes had been living at Pinner for eight months. The new violin (new to her, old and mellow in itself) had inspired Alma to joyous exertions. Again she took lessons from Herr Wilenski, who was sparing of compliment, but, by the mere fact of receiving her at all, showed his good opinion. And many other people encouraged her in a fine conceit of herself. Mrs Strangeways called her 'an unrecognised genius', and worshipped at her feet. To be sure, one did not pay much attention to Mrs Strangeways, but it is sweet to hear such phrases, and twice already, though against her better judgment, Alma had consented to play at that lady's house.

On both these occasions Cyrus Redgrave was present. Choosing his moment, he approached her, looked in her face with a certain timidity to which Alma was not insensible, and spoke as an ordinary acquaintance. There was no helping it; the man had been formally introduced, and, as he suggested, they had begun to know each other afresh. Alma liked to remember how severely she had treated him at that first encounter; perhaps that was enough for dignity. Mr Redgrave would hardly forget himself again. For the rest, she could not pretend, within herself, to dislike him; and if he paid homage to her beauty, to her social charm, to her musical gifts (all of which things Alma recognised and tabulated), it might be only just to let him make amends for something known to both of them. The insult Alma was far from forgiving. But when she had talked twice with Redgrave – distantly, as a stranger to all his affairs – it began to steal upon her mind that there would be a sweetly subtle satisfaction in allowing the man to imagine that her coldness was not quite what it seemed; that so, perchance, he might be drawn on and become enslaved. She had never been able to congratulate herself on a conquest of Cyrus Redgrave. The memory of Bregenz could still, at moments, bring the blood to her face; for it was a memory of cool, calculating outrage, not of passion that had broken bounds. To subdue the man in good earnest would be another thing, and a peculiarly delicious morsel of revenge. Was it possible? Not long ago she would have scoffed at the thought, deeming Redgrave incapable of love in any shape. But her mind was changing in an atmosphere of pleasure and flattery, and under the influence of talk such as she heard in this house and one or two others like it.

To her husband, she represented Mrs Strangeways as a very pleasant woman with a passion for all the arts; formerly wife of a painter, and now married to a wealthy man who shared her tastes. This satisfied Harvey; but Alma had not deceived herself, and could not be quite comfortable with Mrs Strangeways. She no longer puzzled over the flow of guests to the house in Porchester Terrace, having discovered not only that most of these were people, as Sibyl said, of no account, who had few houses open to them, but that several would not be admitted to any circle of scrupulous respectability. The fact was that Mrs Strangeways largely entertained the *demi-monde*,* to use in its true sense a term persistently misapplied. Not impossibly she thought the daughter of Bennet Frothingham might, from one point of view, be included among such persons; on the other hand, her warmth proved that she regarded Mrs Rolfe as a social acquisition, if indeed she was not genuinely attracted to her. What circumstances had led, or forced, Mrs Strangeways into this peculiar position, Alma could not discover; it might be simply one result of an unfortunate marriage, for undoubtedly there was something sinister in the husband, a coarseness varnished with sham geniality, which made Alma dislike to be near him. In the woman herself she found little that was objectionable; her foolish effusiveness, and her artificial complexion, seemed to indicate merely a weak character; at times her talk was interesting, and she knew many people of a class superior to that represented in her drawing-room. But for the illumination she had received, Alma would have felt surprised at meeting Cyrus Redgrave in these assemblies; formerly she had thought of him as belonging to a sphere somewhat above her own, a quasi-aristocratic world, in which Sibyl Carnaby, the daughter of Mrs Ascott Larkfield, also moved by right of birth and breeding. Sibyl, however, was not above accepting Mrs Strangeways' invitations, though she continued to speak of her slightingly; and Redgrave had known the lady for a long time – even, it appeared, before her first marriage.

In a year's time Alma had made and renewed a large number of acquaintances. She spoke of herself as living 'in the country', and still professed a dislike of mere gaiety, a resolve to maintain her simple, serious mode of existence. At half-an-hour's journey from town, she was protected against the time-wasting intrusion of five-o'clock babblers; a luncheon or two in the season, and a modest dinner at long intervals, would discharge her social liabilities; and she had the precious advantage of being able to use London for all legitimate purposes, without danger of being drawn into the vortex of its idle temptations. Once more she was working earnestly at her music – much, it seemed, to Harvey's satisfaction. He wanted her to go on also with water-colours, but she pointed out to him that one art was all she had time for.

'It's all very well for mere amateurs to take up half-a-dozen things. I aim at more than that. You would like me, wouldn't you, to become really *something* as a violinist?'

Harvey assented.

'And you understand,' she pursued, regarding him with her

bright smile, 'that the life of an artist can't be quite like that of other women?'

'Of course, I understand it. You know I don't wish to put the least restraint upon you.'

'My one fear was, that you might think I went about rather too much – didn't pay enough attention to home—'

'We manage pretty well, I think. You needn't have any such fear.'

'Of course, when Hughie gets older – when I can really begin to teach him—'

The child was now approaching the close of his third year, and, in Harvey's opinion, needed more than the attention of an ordinary nursemaid. They had recently engaged a nursery-governess, her name Pauline Smith; a girl of fair education and gentle breeding, who lived as a member of the family. It appeared to Rolfe that Hughie was quite old enough to benefit by his mother's guidance and companionship; but he had left himself no ground for objection to Alma's ordering of her life. The Welsh servant, Ruth, still remained with them, acting to a great extent as housekeeper, and having under her a maid and a boy. Ruth, a trustworthy woman, was so well paid that they had not to fear her desertion. Regularity and comfort prevailed to a much greater extent than might have been looked for under the circumstances. Expenditure had of course greatly increased, and now touched the limit of Harvey's ordinary income; but this was a matter which did not immediately concern Mrs Rolfe. For domestic and private purposes she had a bank-account of her own; an arrangement made on their removal to Pinner, when Harvey one morning handed her a pass-book and a cheque-book, remarking that she would find to her credit a couple of hundred pounds. Alma pretended to think this unnecessary, but her countenance betrayed pleasure. When he thought the fund must be nearly exhausted, he made a new payment to the account, without saying anything; and Alma preserved an equally discreet silence.

One of her new acquaintances was Mrs Rayner Mann, a lady who desired to be known as the patroness of young people aiming at success on the stage or as musicians. Many stories were told of Mrs Mann's generosity to struggling artists, and her house at Putney swarmed with the strangest mingling of people, some undoubtedly in society, others no less decidedly out of it. Here Alma encountered Felix Dymes, whose reputation and prosperity had much advanced since their meeting at Munich. The comic opera of which he then spoke had been brought out at a provincial theatre with considerable success, and was shortly to be produced in London; his latest songs, 'The Light of Home', and 'Where the Willow Dips', had caught the ear of the multitude. Alma ridiculed these compositions, mocking at the sentimentalism of the words, and declaring that the airs were mere popular tinkle; but people not inferior to her in judgment liked the music, which certainly had a sweetness and pathos not easy to resist. The wonder was how such a man as Felix Dymes could give birth to such tender melody. The vivacity of his greeting when of a sudden he recognised Alma, contrasted markedly with Cyrus Redgrave's ill-concealed embarrassment in the like situation. Dymes had an easy conscience, and in the chat that followed he went so far as to joke about his ill-luck some four years ago.

'You didn't think much of me. But I'm going ahead, you know. You have to admit I'm going ahead.'

Prosperity was manifest in his look and voice. He had made no advance in refinement, and evidently thought himself above the necessity of affecting suave manners; his features seemed to grow even coarser; his self-assertion was persistent to the point of grotesque conceit.

'Is your husband musical?' he asked.

'Not particularly.'

'Well, there's something to be said for that. One doesn't always want to be talking shop. – I can't help looking at you; you've altered in a queer sort of way. You were awfully fetching, you know, in those days.'

'You were awfully impertinent,' replied Alma, with a laugh. 'And I don't see that you've altered at all in that respect.'

'Do you play still?'

'A good deal better than I used to.'

'Really? If it's true, why don't you come out? I always believed in you – I did really. There's no better proof of it than what I said at Munich; you were the only girl that could have brought me to that, you know; it was quite against my principles. Have you heard of Ada Wellington? – a girl I'm going to bring out next spring – a pianist; and she'll make a hit. I should like you to know her.'

'How do you mean you are going to bring her out?'

'Do all the business for her, you know; run the show. Not as a speculation; I don't want to make anything out of it, more than expenses. I know her people; they're very badly off, and I shall be glad if I can do them a good turn. There's nothing between us; just friends, that's all. If ever you come out, put the business into my hands, will you?'

'I won't promise,' replied Alma, 'until I see how you succeed with Miss Wellington.'

'Shall it be an understanding? If I float Ada, you'll let me have a try with you?'

'We'll talk of it, Mr Dymes, when you have learnt the elements of good manners.'

She nodded in a friendly way, and left him.

Their next meeting was at a music-shop, where Dymes came in whilst Alma was making purchases. The composer, clad in a heavy fur overcoat, entered humming a tune loudly, by way of self-advertisement; he was at home here, for the proprietors of the business published his songs. On perceiving Alma, he dropped his blustering air, bowed with exaggerated politeness, and professed himself overjoyed.

'I looked in just to try over a thing I've got in my head. Do come and listen to it – will you? It would be so kind of you to give me your opinion.'

He pointed to a room at the back, visible between plush curtains. Alma, wishing to refuse, murmured that she had very little time; but Dymes prevailed, and she followed him. They passed into the pleasant warmth of a blazing fire. The musician flung off his coat, and at once sat down at the grand piano, open for the convenience of such favoured persons as himself; whilst Alma seated herself in an easy-chair, which she had pushed forward so as to allow of her being seen from the shop. After some preliminary jingling, Dymes played an air which the listener could not but like; a dainty, tripping melody, fit for a fairy song, with strange little echoes as of laughter, and a half-feigned sadness in the close. With hands suspended, Dymes turned to see the effect he had produced.

'Is that your own?' Alma asked.

'I'm under that impression. Rather good, I think – don't you?'

'Very pretty.'

She hardly believed his assurance, so strong was the contrast between that lightsome lyric and the coarse vanity of the man himself. He played it again, and she liked it still better, uttering a more decided word of praise.

'Dicky must write me patter for that!' Dymes exclaimed, when he saw that she smiled with pleasure. 'You don't know Dicky Wellington? A cousin of Ada's. By-the-bye, her concert will be at the end of May – Prince's Hall,* most likely. You shall have a ticket.'

'Very kind of you.'

'You know that Mrs Rayner Mann is giving a charity concert next week?'

'I have been asked to take part in it,' said Alma quietly.

'I'm awfully glad of that!' shouted Dymes. 'So I shall hear you again. The fact is, you know, I don't think of you as an amateur. I can't stand amateurs, except one or two. I've got it into my head that you've been one of us, and retired. Queer thing, isn't it?'

Alma enjoyed the flattery. Comfortable in her chair, she showed no disposition to move. Dymes asked her what she thought of playing, and she told him, Hauser's 'Rhapsodie Hongroise'.*

'I'm always being bored by amateurs,' he resumed. 'A silly woman who belongs to a Symphony Society asked me yesterday to go and hear her play in the C minor!* I begged to be told what harm I had ever done her, and she said I was very rude. But I always am to people of that sort; I can't help it. Another of them asked me to tell her of a nice piece for the piano – a really *nice* piece. At once I suggested Chopin's A flat major Polonaise.* Do you know it?'

'Of course I do. Could you play it yourself?'

'I? Of course not. You don't imagine that because one is a successful composer he must be a brilliant virtuoso. I hardly ever touch a musical instrument. Wagner was a very poor player, and Berlioz simply couldn't play at all. I'm a musical dreamer. Do you know that I literally dreamt "The Light of Home"? Now, that's a proof of genius.'

Alma laughed.

'But it is! Do you know how most songs get made nowadays? There's Sykes' "Come when the Dawn" – you remember it? I happen to know all about that. A fellow about town somehow got hold of an idea for a melody; he didn't know a note, but he whistled it to Sykes, and Sykes dotted it down. Now, Sykes knows no more of harmony than a broomstick, so he got another man to harmonise it, and then a fourth fellow wrote an orchestral accompaniment. That's the kind of thing – division of labour in art.'

'You're quite sure you do everything for yourself?' said Alma mischievously, rising at length.

'I forgive you, because you're really one of us – you are, you know. You haven't the look of an amateur. Now, when you've gone out, I'll ask Sammy, behind the counter there, who he thinks you are, and I'll give Mrs Rayner Mann a guinea for her charity if he doesn't take you for a professional musician.'

'You will be good enough, Mr Dymes,' said Alma severely, 'not to speak of me at all to anyone behind a counter.'

'It was only a joke. Of course, I shouldn't have done anything of the kind. Goodbye; shall see you at Putney.'

For all that, no sooner was Mrs Rolfe gone than Dymes did talk of her with the salesman, and in a way peculiar to his species, managing, with leers and half-phrases, to suggest not only that the lady was a performer of distinction, but that, like women in general, she had found his genius and his person fatally attractive. Dymes had the little weaknesses of the artistic temperament.

As usual, Mrs Rayner Mann's concert was well attended, and Alma's violin solo, though an audience more critical than she had yet faced made her very nervous to begin with, received much applause. Felix Dymes, not being able to get a seat at her side, stood behind her, and whispered his admiration.

'You've gone ahead tremendously. That isn't amateur playing. All the others are not fit to be heard in the same day. Really, you know, you ought to think of coming out.'

Many other persons were only less complimentary, and one, Mrs Strangeways, was even more so; she exhausted herself in terms of glowing eulogy. At the end of the concert this lady drew Alma apart.

'Dear Mrs Rolfe, I wonder whether I could ask you to do me a kindness? Are you in any hurry to get home?

It was six o'clock, on an evening of January. Delighted with her success, Alma felt very much like a young man whose exuberant spirits urge him to 'make a night of it'. She declared that she was in no hurry at all, and would be only too glad to do Mrs Strangeways any kindness in her power.

'It will sound rather odd to you,' pursued the lady in a low voice, 'but I would rather trust you than anyone else. You know that Mr Redgrave and I are very old friends – such old friends that we are really almost like brother and sister.'

Alma nodded.

'You've heard us speak of his bungalow at Wimbledon. Just now he is in Paris, and he happens to want a portrait, a photograph, out of an album in the bungalow. Naturally he would have asked his sister to look for it and send it, but Mrs Fenimore is also away from home; so he has written to me, and begged me to do him the kindness. I know exactly where the photo is to be looked for, and all I have to do is to drive over to Wimbledon, and a servant will be waiting to admit me. Now, you will think it childish, but I really don't like to go alone. Though Mr Redgrave and I are such great friends, of course I have only been to the bungalow when he had people there – and – of course it's very foolish at my age – but I'm sure you understand me—'

'You mean you would like me to go with you?' said Alma, with uncertain voice.

'Dare I ask it, dear Mrs Rolfe? There will be *no* one but the servant, who is told to expect a friend of her master's. I am *very* foolish, but one cannot be too careful, you know, and with *you* I shall feel everything so simple and natural and straightforward. I'm sure you understand me.'

'Certainly,' faltered Alma. 'Yes – I will go—'

'Oh, how sweet of you, dear! Need I say that I should never breathe a word to Mr Redgrave? He will think I went alone – as of course I very well might—'

'But – if the servant should mention to him—?'

'My dear, keep your fall* down. And then it is perfectly certain he will never ask a question. He thinks it such a trivial matter—'

Alma did not entertain the least doubt of her friend's veracity, and the desire to have a companion on such an expedition seemed to her natural enough; yet she felt so uneasy at the thought of what she had consented to do, that even whilst descending the stairs she all but stopped and begged to be excused. The thought of stealing into Redgrave's bachelor home, even with Mrs Strangeways, startled and offended her self-respect; it seemed an immodesty. She had never been invited to the bungalow; though Mrs Carnaby had received and accepted such an invitation for an afternoon in the summer, when Mrs Strangeways did the honours. Redgrave was now scrupulously respectful; he would not presume so far on their revived acquaintance as to ask her to Wimbledon. For this very reason – and for others – she had a curiosity about the bungalow. Its exotic name affected her imagination; as did the knowledge that Cyrus Redgrave, whom she knew so particularly well, had built it for his retreat, his privacy. Curiosity and fear of offending Mrs Strangeways overcame her serious reluctance. On entering the carriage she blushed hotly. It was the first time in her life that she had acted with deliberate disregard of grave moral compunction, and conscience revenged itself by lowering her in her own eyes.

Mrs Strangeways talked all the way, but not once of Redgrave; her theme was the excellence of Alma's playing, which, she declared, had moved everyone with wonder and delight.

'Several people took it for granted that you were a professional violinist. I heard one man saying, "How is it I don't know her name?" Of course, your playing in an amateur is altogether exceptional. Did it ever occur to you to come forward professionally?'

'I thought of it once, before my marriage.'

'Ah! you really did? I'm not at all surprised. Would Mr Rolfe look with disapproval—?'

'I hardly know,' replied Alma, who was not mistress of herself, and paid little attention to what she was saying. 'I dare say he wouldn't mind much, one way or another.'

'Indeed?'

The intimate significance of this word warned Alma that she had spoken too carelessly. She hastened to add that, of course, in such a matter, her husband's wish would be final, and that she had never thought of seeking his opinion on the subject.

'If ever you *should* take that step, my dear, it will mean a great triumph for you – oh! a great triumph! And there is room just now for a lady violinist – don't you think? One has to take into account other things besides mastery of the instrument; with the public naturally, a beautiful face and a perfect figure—'

This was too much even for Alma's greediness of flattery; she interrupted the smooth, warm adulation with impatient protest and told herself – though she did not quite know the reason – that after that day she would see less of Mrs Strangeways.

The carriage stopped. Glancing to either side, Alma saw that they were in a country road, its darkness broken at this spot by the rays of two gas-lamps which flanked a gateway. The footman had alighted; the gate was thrown open; the carriage passed through on to a gravel drive. Her nerves strung almost beyond endurance, and even now seeking courage to refuse to enter the house, Alma felt the vehicle turn on a sharp curve, and stop.

'We shall not be more than a minute,' said Mrs Strangeways, just above her breath, as though she spoke with effort.

Involuntarily, Alma laid a hand on her arm

'I will – wait for you here – please—'

'But, dear, your promise! Oh, you wouldn't fail me?'

The carriage door had opened; the footman stood beside it. Scarce knowing what she did, Alma stepped out after her companion, and in the same moment found a glow of light poured suddenly about her; it came from the entrance-hall of a house, where a female servant had presented herself. A house of unusual construction, with pillars and a veranda; nothing more was observable by her dazzled and confused senses. Mrs Strangeways said something to the servant; they entered, crossed a floor of smooth tiles, under electric light ruby-coloured by glass shades, and were led into a room illumined only by a fire until the servant turned on a soft radiance like that in the hall.

Mrs Strangeways glanced about her as if surprised.

'You are not expecting Mr Redgrave?' she said quickly.

'No, madam. We always have fires against the damp.'

Thereupon the woman withdrew, closing the door, and Mrs Strangeways, who was very pale save for her rouge spots, said in a low tone of great relief –

'I began to fear there might be some mistake. Put up your veil for a moment, dear, and glance at the pictures. Every one has cost a small fortune. Oh, he is immensely rich – and knows so well what to buy!'

Alma's agitation did not permit her to examine details. The interior of Redgrave's house was very much what she had imagined; its atmosphere of luxurious refinement, its colour, perfume, warmth, at once allured and alarmed her. She wished to indulge her senses, and linger till she had seen everything; she wished to turn at once and escape. Mrs Strangeways, meanwhile, seemed to be looking for the album of which she had spoken, moving hither and thither, with a frequent pause as of one who listens, or a glance towards the door.

'You won't be long?' said Alma, turning abruptly to her.

'It's my silly nervousness, dear. I thought I remembered perfectly where the album lay. How foolish of me! I quite tremble – anyone would think we were burglars.'

She laughed, and stood looking about the room.

'Is that it?' asked Alma, pointing to a volume on a table near her.

'Yes! – no – I'm not sure.'

An album it was; Mrs Strangeways unclasped it, and turned over a few pages with quivering hand.

'No, I thought not. It's a smaller one. Oh, what a good photo of Mrs Carnaby! Have you seen this one?'

Alma stepped forward to look, strangely startled by the name of her friend; it was as though Sibyl herself had suddenly entered the room and found her here. The photograph she already knew; but its eyes seemed to regard her with the very look of life, and at once she drew back.

'Do find the right one, Mrs Strangeways,' she spoke imploringly. 'It must be—What bell was that?'

An electric bell had rung within the house; it still trembled in her ears, and she turned sick with fright. Mrs Strangeways, flushing red, stammered a reassurance.

'There – here is the right one – in a minute—'

The door opened. As she saw it move, a dreadful certainty of what was about to happen checked Alma's breath, and a sound like a sob escaped her; then she was looking straight into the eyes of Cyrus Redgrave. He, wearing an ulster and with a travelling-cap in his hand, seemed not to recognise her, but turned his look upon her companion, and spoke with mirthful friendliness.

'What! I have caught you, Mrs Strangeways? Police! Oh, I am so sorry I didn't send you a wire. I thought you would come tomorrow, or the day after. How very kind of you to take this trouble immediately. I had to run over at a moment's notice. – Mrs Rolfe! Forgive me; for the moment I didn't know you, coming out of the darkness. So glad to see you.'

He had shaken hands with both of them, behaving as though Mrs Rolfe's presence were the most natural thing in the world. But Alma's strength failed her; she trembled towards the nearest chair, and sank upon it. Mrs Strangeways, who had watched her with anxiety, took a step to her side, speaking hurriedly.

'Mr Redgrave, I took the liberty to use your house as if it were my own. Mrs Rolfe has over-tired, over-excited herself. She has been playing this afternoon at a concert at Mrs Rayner Mann's. We were to drive back together, and came this way that I might call here – for the photo. But Mrs Rolfe became faint – after her exertions—'

Redgrave surpassed himself in graceful courtesy. How could Mrs Strangeways dream of offering excuses? Why had she not called for tea – or anything? He would give orders at once, and the ladies would permit him to get rid of his travelling attire, whilst they rested. He was turning to leave the room when Alma rose and commanded her voice.

'I am perfectly well again – thank you so much, Mr Redgrave – indeed I mustn't stay—'

With admirable suavity Redgrave overcame her desire to be gone. Pleading, he passed playfully from English into French, of which he had a perfect command; then, in his own language, declared that French alone permitted one to make a request without importunity, yet with adequate fervour. Alma again seated herself. As she did so, her host and Mrs Strangeways exchanged a swift glance of mutual intelligence.

'How can I hope you will forgive me?' the lady murmured at Alma's ear as soon as they were alone.

'It's very annoying, and there's nothing more to be said,' was the cold reply.

'But it isn't of the least importance – do believe me. We are such old friends. And no one can ever know – though it wouldn't matter if all the world did.'

'I dare say not. But, please, let our stay be as short as possible.'

'We will go, dear, as soon as ever we have had a cup of tea. I am *so* sorry; it was all my foolishness.'

The tea was brought, and Mrs Strangeways, her nervousness having quite passed away, began to talk as if she were in her own drawing-room. Alma, too, had recovered control of herself, held the teacup in an all but steady hand, and examined the room at her leisure. After ten minutes' absence, Redgrave rejoined them, now in ordinary dress; his face warm from rapid ablution, and his thin hair delicately disposed. He began talking in a bright, chatty vein. So Mrs Rolfe had been playing at a concert; how he regretted not having been there! What had she played? Then, leaning forward with an air of kindness that verged on tenderness –

'I am sure it must be very exhausting to the nerves; you have so undeniably the glow, the fervour, of a true artist; it is inspiring to watch you as you play, no less than to hear you. You do feel better now?'

Alma replied with civility, but did not meet his look. She refused another cup of tea, and glanced so meaningly at her friend that in a few moments Mrs Strangeways rose.

'You won't leave me yet to my solitude?' exclaimed Redgrave. With a sigh he yielded to the inevitable, inquired gently once more whether Mrs Rolfe felt quite restored, and again overwhelmed Mrs Strangeways with thanks. Still the ladies had to wait a few minutes for their carriage, which, at Redgrave's direction, had made a long detour in the adjacent roads; and during this delay, as if the prospect of release inspirited her, Alma spoke a few words in a more natural tone. Redgrave had asked what public concerts she usually attended.

'None regularly,' was her reply. 'I should often go on Saturdays to the Crystal Palace,* if it were not so far for me. I want to get there, if possible, on Saturday week, to hear Sterndale Bennett's new concerto.'*

'Ah, I should like to hear that!' said Redgrave. 'We may perhaps see each other.'

This time she did not refuse to encounter his look, and the smile with which she answered it was so peculiarly expressive of a self-confident disdain that he could scarcely take his eyes from her. Cyrus Redgrave knew as well as most men the signals of challenge on a woman's features; at a recent meeting he had detected something of the sort in Alma's behaviour to him, and at this moment her spirit could not be mistaken. Quite needlessly she had told him where he might find her, if he chose. This was a great step. To be defied so daringly meant to him no small encouragement.

'It's fortunate,' said Alma, as the carriage bore her away, 'that we had this adventure with a *gentleman*.'

The remark sounded surprising to Mrs Strangeways.

'I'm so glad you have quite got over your annoyance, dear,' she replied.

'It was as bad for you as for me, under the circumstances. But I'm sure Mr Redgrave won't give it another thought.'

And Alma chatted very pleasantly all the way back to town, where she dined with Mrs Strangeways. At eleven o'clock she reached home. Her husband, who was recovering from a sore throat, sat pipeless and in no very cheerful mood by the library fire; but the sight of Alma's radiant countenance had its wonted effect upon him; he stretched his arms, as if to rouse himself from a long fit of reverie, and welcomed her in a voice that was a little husky.

'Well, how did it go?'

'Not badly, I think. And how have you been getting on, poor old boy?'

'So so; swearing a little because I couldn't smoke. But Hughie has a cold tonight; caught mine, I dare say, confound it! Miss Smith took counsel with me about it, and we doctored him a little.'

'Poor dear little man! I wish I had been back in time to see him. But there was no getting away – had to stay to dinner—'

Alma had not the habit of telling falsehoods to her husband, but she did it remarkably well – even better, perhaps, than when she deceived her German friend, Fraulein Steinfeld, in the matter of Cyrus Redgrave's proposal; the years had matured her, endowing her with superior self-possession, and a finish of style in dealing with these little difficulties. She was unwilling to say that she had dined in Porchester Terrace, for Harvey entertained something of a prejudice against that household. His remoteness nowadays from the world in which Alma amused herself made it quite safe to venture on a trifling misstatement.

'I have a note from Carnaby,' said Rolfe. 'He wants to see me in town tomorrow. Says he has good news – "devilish good news", to be accurate. I wonder what it is.'

'The lawsuit won, perhaps.'

'Afraid not; that'll take a few more years. Odd thing, I have another letter – from Cecil Morphew, and he, too, says that he has something hopeful to tell me about.'

Alma clapped her hands, an unusual expression of joy for her.

'We are cheering up all round!' she exclaimed. 'Now, if only *you* could light on something fortunate.'

He gave her a quick look.

'What do you mean by that?'

'Only that you haven't seemed in very good spirits lately.'

'Much as usual, I think. – Many people at Putney?'

'About a hundred and twenty. Compliments showered on me; I do so wish you could have heard them. Somebody told me that some man asked her how it was he didn't know my name – he took me for a professional violinist.'

'Well, no doubt you are as good as many of them.'

'You really think that?' said Alma, pulling her chair a little nearer to the fire and looking eagerly at him.

'Why shouldn't you be? You have the same opportunities, and make all possible use of them.'

Alma was silent for a few ticks of the clock. Once, and a second time, she stole a glance at Harvey's face; then grasping with each hand the arms of her chair, and seeming to string herself for an effort, she spoke in a half-jesting tone.

'What should you say if I proposed to come out – to *be* a professional?'

Harvey's eyes turned slowly upon her; he read her face with curiosity, and did not smile.

'Do you mean you have thought of it?'

'To tell you the truth, it is so often put into my head by other people. I am constantly being asked why I'm content to remain an amateur.'

'By professional musicians?'

'All sorts of people.'

'It reminds me of something. You know I don't interfere; I don't pretend to have you in surveillance, and don't wish to begin it. But are you quite sure that you are making friends in the best class that is open to you?'

Alma's smile died away. For a moment she recovered the face

of years gone by; a look which put Harvey in mind of Mrs Frothingham's little drawing-room at Swiss Cottage, where more than once Alma had gazed at him with a lofty coldness which concealed resentment. That expression could still make him shrink a little and feel uncomfortable. But it quickly faded, giving place to a look of perfectly amiable protest.

'My dear Harvey, what has caused you to doubt it?'

'I merely asked the question. Perhaps it occurred to me that you were not exactly in your place among people who talk to you in that way.'

'You must allow for my exaggeration,' said Alma softly. 'One or two have said it – just people who know most about music. And there's a *way* of putting things.'

'Was Mrs Carnaby there today?'

'No.'

'You don't see her very often now?'

'Perhaps not *quite* so often. I suppose the reason is that I am more drawn to the people who care about music. Sibyl really isn't musical – though, of course, I like her as much as ever. Then – the truth is, she seems to have grown rather extravagant, and I simply don't understand how she can keep up such a life – if it's true that her husband is only losing money. Last time I was with her I couldn't help thinking that she ought to – to deny herself rather more. It's habit, I suppose.'

Harvey nodded – twice, thrice; and kept a grave countenance.

'And you don't care to see much of Mrs Abbott?' he rather let fall than spoke.

'Well, you know, dear, I don't mean to be at all disagreeable, but we have so little in common. Isn't it so? I am sure Mrs Abbott isn't anxious for my society.'

Again Rolfe sat silent, and again Alma stole glances at him.

'Shall I tell you something I have in mind?' he said at length, with deliberation. 'Hughie, you know, is three years old. Pauline does very well with him, but it is time that he had companions – other children. In half a year or so he might go to a kindergarten, and' – he made an instant's pause – 'I know only of one which would be really good for him. I think he will have to go to Mrs Abbott.'

Their eyes met, and the speaker's were steadily fixed.

'But the distance?' objected Alma.

'Yes. If we want to do that, we must go to Gunnersbury.'

Alma's look fell. She tapped with her foot and meditated, slightly frowning. But, before Harvey spoke again, the muscles of her face relaxed, and she turned to him with a smile, as though some reflection had brought relief.

'You wouldn't mind the bother of moving?'

'What is that compared with Hughie's advantage? And if one lives in London, it's in the nature of things to change houses once a year or so.'

'But we don't live in London!' returned Alma, with a laugh.

'Much the same thing. At Gunnersbury you would be nearer to everything, you know.'

'Then you would send away Pauline?'

Harvey made a restless movement, and gave a husky cough.

'Well, I don't know. You see, Hughie would be with Mrs Abbott only a few hours each day. Who is to look after the little man at other times? I suppose I can't very well undertake it myself – though I'm glad to see as much of him as possible; and I won't let him be with a servant. So—'

Alma was gazing at the fire, and seemed to give only a divided attention to what her husband said. Her eyes grew wide; their vision, certainly, was of nothing that disturbed or disheartened her.

'You have given me two things to think about, Harvey. Will you reflect on the *one* that I suggested?'

'Then you meant it seriously?'

'I meant that I should like to have your serious opinion about it. Only we won't talk now. I am very tired, and you, I'm sure, oughtn't to sit late with your bad throat. I promise to consider *both* the things you mentioned.'

She held her hands to him charmingly, and kissed his cheek as she said goodnight.

Harvey lingered for another hour, and – of all people in the world – somehow found himself thinking of Buncombe. Buncombe, his landlord in the big dirty house by Royal Oak. What had become of Buncombe? It would be amusing, some day to look at the old house and see if Buncombe still lived there.

They never talked about money. Alma took it for granted that Harvey would not allow their expenditure to outrun his income, and therewith kept her mind at rest. Rolfe had not thought it necessary to mention that he derived about three hundred pounds from debenture stock* which was redeemable, and that the date of redemption fell early in this present year, 1891.* He himself had all along scarcely regarded the matter. When the stock became his, 1891 seemed very remote; and on settling in North Wales he felt financially so secure that the question of re-investment might well be left for consideration till it was pressed upon him.

As now it was. He could no longer disregard percentages; he wanted every penny that his capital would yield. Before marriage he would have paid little heed to the fact that his canal shares (an investment which he had looked upon as part of the eternal order of things) showed an inclination to lose slightly in value; now it troubled him day and night. As for the debenture stock, he might, if he chose, 'convert' it without withdrawal, but that meant a lower dividend, which was hardly to be thought of. Whither should he turn for a security at once sound and remunerative? He began to read the money article in his daily paper, which hitherto he had passed over as if it did not exist, or turned from with contemptuous impatience. He picked up financial newspapers at railway bookstalls, and in private struggled to comprehend their jargon, taking care that they never fell under his wife's eyes. At the Metropolitan Club – of which he had resumed membership, after thinking that he would never again enter clubland – he talked with men who were at home in City matters, and indirectly tried to get hints from them. He felt like one who meddles with something forbidden – who pries, shamefaced, into the secrets of an odious vice. To study the money-market gave him a headache. He had to go for a country walk, to bathe and change his clothes, before he was at ease again.

Two only of his intimates had any practical acquaintance with methods of speculation, and their experiences hitherto were not such as to suggest his seeking advice from them. Hugh Carnaby might or might not reap profit from his cycle factory;

as yet it had given him nothing but worry and wavering hopes. Cecil Morphew had somehow got into better circumstances, had repaid the loan of fifty pounds, and professed to know much more about speculation than in the days when he made money only to lose it again; but it was to be feared that Cecil associated with people of shady character, and might at any moment come to grief in a more or less squalid way. He confessed that there was a mystery in his life – something he preferred not to speak of even with an old friend.

Oddly enough, Carnaby and Morphew wrote both at the same time, wishing to see him, and saying that they had cheering news to impart. Amid his perplexities, which were not concerned with money alone, Harvey welcomed this opportunity of forgetting himself for a few hours. He agreed to lunch with Hugh at a restaurant (Carnaby would have nothing to do with clubs), and bade Morphew to dinner at the Metropolitan.

It was a day of drizzle and slush, but Harvey had got over his sore throat, and in ordinary health defied the elements. Unlike himself, Carnaby came a little late for his appointment, and pleaded business with a 'blackguard' in the City. Rheums and bronchial disorders were to him unknown; he had never possessed an umbrella, and only on days like this donned a light overcoat to guard himself against what he called 'the sooty spittle' of a London sky. Yet he was not the man of four or five years ago. He had the same appearance of muscularity, the same red neck and mighty fists; but beneath his eyes hung baggy flesh that gave him a bilious aspect, his cheeks were a little sunken, and the tone of his complexion had lost its healthy clearness. In temper, too, he had suffered; perhaps in manners. He used oaths too freely; intermingled his good bluff English – the English of a country gentleman – with recent slang; tended to the devil-may-care rather than to the unconsciously breezy and bold.

'Let us find a corner,' he said, clutching his friend by the shoulder, 'out of the damned crowd.'

'Lawsuit finished?' asked Harvey, when they had found a place and ordered their meal.

Hugh answered with a deep rolling curse.

When he returned to England, in the summer of 1889,* he entered at once into partnership with the man Mackintosh, taking over an established business at Coventry, with which his partner already had some connection. Not a week passed before they found themselves at law with regard to a bicycle brake – a patent they had begun by purchasing, only to find their right in it immediately contested. The case came on in November; it occupied nine days, and was adjourned. Not until July of the following year, 1890, was judgment delivered; it went for Mackintosh & Co, the plaintiffs, whose claim the judge held to be proved. But this by no means terminated the litigation. The defendants, who had all along persisted in manufacturing and selling this patent brake, now obtained stay of injunction until the beginning of the Michaelmas term, with the understanding that, if notice of appeal were given before then, the injunction would be stayed until the appeal was settled. And notice *was* given, and the appeal would doubtless be heard some day or other; but meanwhile the year 1891 had come round, and Mackintosh & Co. saw their rivals manufacturing and selling as gaily as ever. Hugh Carnaby grew red in the face as he spoke of them; his clenched fist lay on the tablecloth, and it was pretty clear how he longed to expedite the course of justice.

Still, he had good news to communicate, and he began by asking whether Harvey saw much of Redgrave.

'Redgrave?' echoed the other in surprise. 'Why, I hardly know him.'

'But your wife knows him very well.'

'Yes; I dare say she does.'

Carnaby did not observe his friend's countenance; he was eating with great appetite. 'Redgrave isn't at all a bad fellow. I didn't know him much till lately. Used to see him at B. F.'s, you know, and one or two other places where I went with Sibyl. Thought him rather a snob. But I was quite mistaken. He's a very nice fellow when you get near to him.'

Harvey's surprise was increased. For his own part, he still thought of Redgrave with the old prejudice, though he had no definite charge to bring against the man. He would have supposed him the last person either to seek or to obtain favour with Hugh Carnaby.

'Sibyl has known him for a long time,' Hugh continued. 'Tells me he did all sorts of kindnesses for her mother at Ascott Larkfield's death; fixed up her affairs – they were in a devil of a state, I believe. Last autumn we met him in Scotland; he was with his sister and her family – Mrs Fenimore. Her husband's in India, and he seems to look after her in a way that does him credit. In fact, I saw a new side of the fellow. We got quite chummy, and I happened to speak about Mackintosh & Co. Well, now, what do you think? Two days ago, at Coventry, I got a note from him: he was coming through, and would like to see me; would I lunch with him at a hotel? I did, and he surprised me by beginning to talk about business. The fact was, he had some money lying loose, wanted to place it somewhere, and had faith in cycles. Why shouldn't he make an offer to a friend? Would Mackintosh & Co. care to admit a new partner? Or – anyhow – could we make use of a few thousand pounds?'

Rolfe had ceased to eat, and was listening intently. The story sounded very strange to him; it did not fit at all with his conception of Cyrus Redgrave.

'I suppose a few thousands would come very handy?' he remarked.

'Well, old man, to tell you the truth, – I can do it now, – for me it means a jump out of a particularly black hole. You must understand that we're not doing downright badly; we pay our way, but that was about all. I, individually, shouldn't have paid my way for many months longer. God! how I clutched at it! You don't know what it is, Rolfe, to see your damned account at the bank slithering away, and not a cent to pay in. I've thought of all sorts of things – just stopping short of burglary, and I shouldn't have stopped at that long.'

'You mean that this new capital will give such a push to the business—'

'Of course! It was just what we wanted. We couldn't advertise – couldn't buy a new patent – couldn't move at all. Now we shall make things hum.'

'Does Redgrave become a partner, then?'

'A sleeping partner. But Redgrave is wide enough awake. Mackintosh says he never met a keener man of business. You wouldn't have thought it, would you? I should fancy he manages all his own property, and does it devilish well, too. Of course, he has all sorts of ways of helping us on. He's got ideas of his own, too, about the machines; I shouldn't wonder if he hits on something valuable. I never half understood him before. He doesn't shoot much, but knows enough about it to make pleasant talk. And he has travelled a good deal. Then, of course, he goes in for art, music – all that sort of thing. There's really no humbug about him. He's neither prig nor cad, though I used to think him a little of both.'

Harvey reflected; revived his mental image of the capitalist, and still found it very unlike the picture suggested by Hugh.

'Who *is* Redgrave?' he asked. 'How did he get his money?'

'I know nothing about that. I don't think he's a university man. He hinted once that he was educated abroad. Seems to know plenty of good people. Mrs Fenimore, his sister, lives at Wimbledon. Sibyl and I were over there not long ago, dining; one or two titled people, a parson, and so on; devilish respectable, but dull – the kind of company that makes me want to stand up and yell. Redgrave has built himself what he calls a bungalow, somewhere near the house; but I didn't see it.'

'You're a good deal at Coventry?' asked Rolfe.

'Off and on. Just been down for ten days. If it were possible, I should go steadily at the business. I used to think I couldn't fit into work of that sort, but a man never knows what he can do till he tries. I can't stand doing nothing; that floors me. I smoke too much, and drink too much, and get quarrelsome, and wish I was on the other side of the world. But it's out of the question to live down yonder; I couldn't ask Sibyl to do it.'

'Do you leave her quite alone, then?'

Carnaby made an uneasy movement.

'She has been visiting here and there for the last month; now her mother wants her to go to Ventnor. Much better she shouldn't; they hate each other – can't be together a day without quarrelling. Pretty plain on which side the fault lies. I shouldn't think there are many women better tempered than Sibyl. All the time we've been married, and all we've gone through, I have never once seen an unpleasant look on her face – to *me*, that is. It's something to be able to say that. Mrs Larkfield is simply intolerable. She's always either whining or in a fury. Can't talk of anything but the loss of her money.'

'That reminds me,' interposed Harvey. 'Do you know that there seems to be a chance of getting something out of the great wreck?'

'What? Who says so?'

'Mrs Frothingham. The creditors come first, of course. Was your wife creditor or shareholder?'

'Why, both.'

'Then she may hear something before long. I don't pretend to understand the beastly affair, but Mrs Frothingham wrote to us about it the day before yesterday, with hints of eighteenpence in the pound, which she seemed to think very glorious.'

Carnaby growled in disgust.

'Eighteenpence be damned! Well, perhaps it'll buy her a hat. I tell you, Rolfe, when I compare Sibyl with her mother, I almost feel she's too good for the world. Suppose she had turned out *that* sort of woman! What would have been the end of it? Murder, most likely. But she bore the loss of all her money just as she did the loss of her jewellery and things when our house was burgled – never turned a hair. There's a girl to be proud of, I tell you!'

He insisted upon it so vehemently that one might have imagined him in conflict with secret doubts as to his wife's perfection.

'It's a very strange thing,' said Rolfe, looking at his wine, 'that those thieves got clean away – not a single thing they stole ever tracked. There can't be many such cases.'

'I have a theory about that.' Hugh half-closed his eyes, looking at once shrewd and fierce. 'The woman herself – the housekeeper – is at this moment going about in society, somewhere. She was no Whitechapel thief. There's a gang organised among the people we live with. If I go out to dine, as likely as not I sit next to a burglar or a forger, or anything you like. The police never get on the scent, and it's the same in many another robbery. Some day, perhaps, there'll be an astounding disclosure, a blazing hell of a scandal – a dozen men and women marched from Belgravia and Mayfair to Newgate.* I'm sure of it! What else can you expect of such a civilisation as ours? Well, I should know that woman again, and if ever I find myself taking her down to dinner—'

Harvey exploded in laughter.

'I tell you I'm quite serious,' said the other angrily. 'I *know* that's the explanation of it! There are plenty of good and honest people still, but they can't help getting mixed up among the vilest lot on the face of the earth. That's why I don't like my wife to make new acquaintances. *She* won't get any harm, but I hate to think of the people she perhaps meets. Mackintosh was telling me of a woman in London who keeps up a big house and entertains all sorts of people – and her husband knows where the money comes from. He wouldn't mention her name, because, by Jove, he had himself contributed to the expenses of the establishment! It was three or four years ago, when he had his money and ran through it. For all I know, Sibyl may go there – I can't tell her about such things, and she wouldn't believe me if I did. She's an idealist – sees everything through poetry and philosophy. I should be a brute if I soiled her mind. And, I say, old man, why don't your wife and she see more of each other? Is it just the distance?'

'I'm afraid that has something to do with it,' Harvey replied, trying to speak naturally.

'I'm sorry. They're both of them too good for ordinary society. I wish to God we could all four of us go out to a place I know in Tasmania, and live honest, clean, rational lives! Can't be managed. Your wife has her music; Sibyl has her books and so on –'

'By-the-bye, you know Mrs Strangeways?'

'I know *of* her.'

'And not much good?'

'No particular harm. Sibyl saw a little of her, but I don't think they meet now. Your wife know her?'

'She has met her here and there: you and I are alike in that. We can't stand the drawing-room, so our wives have to go about by themselves. The days are past when a man watched over his wife's coming and going as a matter of course. We should only make fools of ourselves if we tried it on. It's the new world, my boy; we live in it, and must make the best of it.'

Hugh Carnaby drank more wine than is usually taken at luncheon. It excited him to boisterous condemnation of things in general. He complained of the idleness that was forced upon him, except when he could get down to Coventry.

'I hang about for whole days doing literally nothing. What *should* I do? I'm not the man for books; I can't get much sport nowadays; I don't care for billiards. I want to have an axe in my hand!'

Gesticulating carelessly, he swept a wine-glass off the table.

'There – damn it! shows we've sat long enough. Come and talk to Sibyl, and let her give you a cup of tea. You never see her – never; yet she thinks better of you than of any other man we know. Come, let's get out of this beastly air. The place reeks of onions.'

They went to Oxford and Cambridge Mansions, where Rolfe

spent the time until he had to leave for his appointment with Cecil Morphew. Sibyl was very kind, but gently reproachful. Why had Alma forsaken her? Why did Harvey himself never drop in?

'I'm often quite lonely, Mr Rolfe, and as one result of it I'm getting learned. Look at these books. Won't you give me a word of admiration?'

There was a volume of Crowe and Cavalcaselle, one of Symonds's 'Renaissance', Benvenuto's 'Memoirs' in the original.*

'I can't help clinging to the old world,' she said sweetly. 'Hugh forgives me, like a good boy; and you, I know, not only forgive, but sympathise.'*

Of course, not a word passed with reference to Hugh Carnaby's business; Redgrave's name was not mentioned. Sibyl, one felt, would decline to recognise, in her own drawing-room, the gross necessities of life. Had bankruptcy been impending, she would have ignored it with the same perfection of repose. An inscrutable woman, who could look and smile at one without conveying the faintest suggestion of her actual thoughts.

On his way to the club, Harvey puzzled over what seemed to him Redgrave's singular behaviour. Why should a man in that position volunteer pecuniary aid to an obscure and struggling firm? Could it be genuine friendship for Hugh Carnaby? That sounded most improbable. Perhaps Redgrave, like the majority of people in his world, appeared much wealthier than he really was, and saw in Mackintosh's business a reasonable hope of profit. In that case, and if the concern began to flourish, might not an older friend of Carnaby's find lucrative employment for his capital?

He had always thought with uttermost contempt of the man who allows himself to be gripped, worried, dragged down, by artificial necessities. Was he himself to become a victim of this social disease? Was he, resistless, to be drawn into the muddy whirlpool, to spin round and round among gibbering phantoms, abandoning himself with a grin of inane conceit, or clutching in desperation at futile hopes? He remembered his tranquil life between the mountains and the sea; his earlier freedom, wandering in the sunlight of silent lands. Surely there needed but a little common-sense, a little decision, to save himself from this rushing current. One word to Alma – would it not suffice? But of all things he dreaded to incur the charge of meanness, of selfishness. That had ever been his weak point: in youth, well-nigh a cause of ruin; in later life, impelling him to numberless insincerities and follies.

However, the danger as yet only threatened. He was solvent; he had still a reserve. It behoved him merely to avoid the risks of speculation, and to check, in natural, unobtrusive ways, that tendency to extravagance of living which was nowadays universal. Could he not depend upon himself for this moderate manliness?

Cecil Morphew, though differing in all other respects from Hugh Carnaby, showed a face which, like Hugh's, was growing prematurely old; a fatigued complexion, sunken eyes; an expression mingled of discontent and eagerness, now furtive, now sanguine, yet losing the worse traits in a still youthful smile as he came forward to meet his friend. Year after year he clung to the old amorous hope, but he no longer spoke of it with the same impulsive frankness; he did not shun the subject – brought it, indeed, voluntarily forward, but with a shamefaced hesitance. His declaration in a letter, not long ago, that he was unworthy of any good woman's love, pointed to something which had had its share in the obvious smirching of his character; something common enough, no doubt; easily divined by Harvey Rolfe, though he could not learn how far the man's future was compromised. Today Morphew began with talk of a hopeful tenor. He had got hold of a little money; he had conceived a project for making more. When the progress of their eating and drinking cleared the way for confidential disclosures, Morphew began to hint at his scheme.

'You've heard me speak of Denbow?' This was a man who had given him lessons in photography; a dealer in photographic apparatus, with a shop in Westminster Bridge Road. 'He's a very decent fellow, but it's all up with him. His wife drinks, and he has lost money in betting, and now he wants to clear out – to sell his business and get away. He came to me to apologise for spoiling some negatives – he does a little printing for me now and then and told me what he meant to do. Did I know of anyone likely to take his shop?'

Harvey laughed.

'You're in with a queer lot of people, it seems to me.'

'Oh, Denbow is all but a gentleman, I assure you. He was

educated at Charterhouse, but made a fool of himself, I believe, in the common way. But about his business. I've seen a good deal of it, going in and out, and talking with them, and I know as much about photography as most amateurs – you'll admit that, Rolfe?'

It was true that he had attained more than ordinary skill with the camera. Indeed, but for this resource, happily discovered in the days of his hopelessness, he would probably have sunk out of sight before now.

'Denbow's salesman is a thoroughly honest and capable fellow – Hobcraft, his name. He's been at the shop three or four years, and would be only too glad to carry on the business, but he can't raise money, and Denbow must have cash down. Now the fact is, I want to buy that business myself.'

'I see. What does the man ask for it?'

Morphew fidgeted a little.

'Well, just at present there isn't much stock – nothing like what there ought to be. Denbow has been coming down the hill; he's stopped himself only just in time. When I first knew him he was doing reasonably well. It's a good position for that kind of shop. Swarms of men, you know, go backwards and forwards along the Westminster Bridge Road, and just the kind of men, lots of them, that take up photography – the better kind of clerk, and the man of business who lives in the south suburbs. And photography is going ahead so.* I have all sorts of ideas. One might push the printing branch of the business – and have dark rooms for amateurs – and hit on a new hand-camera – and perhaps even start a paper, call it *Camera Notes*, or something of that kind. Don't smile and look sceptical – '

'Not at all. It seems to me the best suggestion I've heard from you yet.'

'Think so? I'm awfully glad of that. You know, Rolfe, a fellow like myself – decent family, public school, and that kind of thing – naturally fights shy of shopkeeping. But I've got to the point that I don't care what I do, if only it'll bring me a steady income in an honest way. I ought to be able to make several hundreds a year, even at starting, out of that business.'

'Have you spoken of it in the usual quarter?'

'No, I haven't.' Cecil's countenance fell. 'I should if I made a successful start. But I've talked of so many things, I'm ashamed.

And she mightn't quite understand; perhaps she would think I
was going down – down – '

'How is her father?'

'Neither better nor worse. That man will take another ten
years over his dying – see if he doesn't. Well, we've got used to
it. We're neither of us young any longer; we've lost the best part
of our lives. And all for what? Because we hadn't money enough
to take a house three times bigger than we needed! Two lives
wasted because we couldn't feed fifty other people for whom we
didn't care a damn! Doesn't it come to that?'

'No doubt. What does Denbow ask?'

'For the stock, two hundred pounds; shop-fittings, fifty;
business as it stands, say three hundred. The rent is ninety-five.
Floor above the shop let to a family, who pay twenty-four
shillings a week – a substantial set-off against the rent; but I
should like to get rid of the people, and use the whole house for
business purposes. There's three years of Denbow's lease to run,
but this, he says, the landlord would be willing to convert into a
seven years' lease to a new tenant. Then one must allow
something for repairs and so on at the fresh start. Well, with
purchase of a little new stock, say another hundred and fifty
pounds. Roughly speaking, I ought to have about five hundred
pounds to settle the affair.'

'And you have the money?'

'Not quite; I've got – well, I may say three hundred. I'm not
speaking of my own private income; of course, that goes on as
usual, and isn't a penny too much for – for ordinary expenses.'
He fidgeted again. 'Would you care to know how I made this
bit of capital?'

'If you care to tell me.'

'Yes, I will, just to show you what one is driven to do. Two
years ago I was ill – congestion of the lungs – felt sure I should
die. You were in Wales then. I sent for Tripcony, to get him to
make my will – he used to be a solicitor, you know, before he
started the bucket-shop.* When I pulled through, Trip came one
day and said he had a job for me. You'll be careful, by-the-bye,
not to mention this. The job was to get the City editor of a
certain newspaper (a man I know very well) to print a damaging
rumour about a certain company. You'll wonder how I could
manage this. Well, simply because the son of the chairman of
that company was a sort of friend of mine, and the City editor

knew it. If I could get the paragraph inserted, Tripcony would –
not pay me anything, but give me a tip to buy certain stock
which he guaranteed would be rising. Well, I undertook the job,
and I succeeded, and Trip was as good as his word. I bought as
much as I dared – through Trip, mind you, and he wouldn't let
me of the cover,* which I thought suspicious, though it was
only habit of business. I bought at 75, and on settling day the
quotation was par. I wanted to go at it again, but Trip shook
his head. Well, I netted nearly five hundred. The most caddish
affair I ever was in; but I wanted money. Stop, that's only half
the story. Just at that time I met a man who wanted to start a
proprietary club. He had the lease of a house near Golden
Square, but not quite money enough to furnish it properly and
set the club going. Well, I joined him, and put in four hundred
pounds; and for a year and a half we didn't do badly. Then
there was a smash; the police raided the place one night, and my
partner went before the magistrates. I trembled in my shoes, but
my name was never mentioned. It only ended in a fifty-pound
fine, and of course I went halves. Then we sold the club for two
hundred, furniture and all, and I found myself with – what I
have now, not quite three hundred.'

'My boy, you've been going it,' remarked Rolfe, with a
clouded brow.

'That's what I tell you. I want to get out of all that kind of
thing. Now, how am I to get two or three hundred honestly? I
think Denbow would take less than he says for cash down. But
the stock, I guarantee, is worth two hundred.'

'You have the first offer?'

'Till day after tomorrow – Monday.'

'Tomorrow's Sunday – that's awkward. Never mind. If I come
over in the morning, will you take me to the place, and let me
look over it with you, and see both Denbow and the shopman?'

'Of course I will!' said Morphew delightedly. 'It's all above-
board. There's a devilish good business to be made; it depends
only on the man. Why, Denbow has made as much as two
hundred in a year out of printing for amateurs alone. It's his
own fault that he didn't keep it up. I swear, Rolfe, that with
capital and hard work and acuteness, that place can be made
*the* establishment of the kind south of the Thames. Why, there's
no reason why one shouldn't net a thousand a year in a very
short time.'

'Is Denbow willing to exhibit his books?'

'Of course he is. I've seen them. It isn't speculative, you know; honest, straightforward business.'

'What part do you propose to take in it yourself?'

'Why, Denbow's part – without the betting. I shall go in for the business for all I'm worth; work day and night. And look here, Rolfe. It isn't as if I had no security to offer. You see, I have my private income; that gives me a pull over the ordinary man of business just starting. Suppose I borrow three – four – five hundred pounds; why, I can afford to make over stock or receipts – anything in that way – to the lender. Four per cent, that's what I offer, if it's a simple loan.'

'You would keep the man – what's his name?'

'Hobcraft. Decidedly. Couldn't do without him. He has been having thirty-five shillings a week.'

Harvey rose, and led the way to the smoking-room. His companion had become a new man; the glow of excitement gave him a healthier look, and he talked more like the Cecil Morphew of earlier days, whom Rolfe had found and befriended at the hotel in Brussels.

'There's nothing to be ashamed of in a business of this kind. If only her father was dead, I'm sure *she* wouldn't mind it. – Ah, Rolfe, if only she and I, both of us, had had a little more courage! Do you know what I think? It's the weak people that do most harm in the world. They suffer, of course, but they make others suffer as well. If I were like *you* – ah, if I were like *you*!' Harvey laughed.


# CHAPTER 8


To Alma, on his return, he gave a full account of all he had heard and done. The story of Hugh Carnaby's good fortune interested her greatly. She elicited every detail of which Harvey had been informed; asked shrewd questions; and yet had the air of listening only for her amusement.

'Should you have thought Redgrave likely to do such a thing?' Rolfe inquired.

'Oh, I don't know him at all well. He has been a friend of Sibyl's for a long time – so, of course – '

Her voice dropped, but in a moment she was questioning again.

'You say that Mr Redgrave went to see him at Coventry?'

'Yes. Redgrave must have heard he was there, from Sibyl, I suppose.'

'And that was two days ago?'

'So Carnaby said – Why?'

'Somebody – oh, I think it was Mrs Rayner Mann, yesterday – said Mr Redgrave was in Paris.'

Cecil Morphew's affairs had much less interest for her; but when Harvey said that he was going to town again tomorrow, to look at the shop in Westminster Bridge Road, she regarded him with an odd smile.

'You surely won't get mixed up in things of that kind?'

'It might be profitable,' he answered very quietly; 'and – one doesn't care to lose any chance of that kind – just now – '

He would not meet her eyes; but Alma searched his face for the meaning of these words, so evidently weighted.

'Are you at all uneasy, Harvey?'

'Not a bit – not a bit,' answered the weak man in him. 'I only meant that, if we are going to remove – '

They sat for more than five minutes in silence. Alma's brain was working very rapidly, as her features showed. When he entered, she looked rather sleepy; now she was thrilling with vivid consciousness; one would have thought her absorbed in the solution of some exciting problem. Her next words came unexpectedly.

'Harvey, if you mean what you say about letting me follow my own instincts, I think I shall decide to try my fortune – to give a public recital.'

He glanced at her, but did not answer.

'We made a sort of bargain – didn't we?' she went on, quickly, nervously, with an endeavour to strike the playful note. 'Hughie shall go to Mrs Abbott's, and I will attend to what you said about the choice of acquaintances.'

'But surely neither of those things can be a subject of bargaining between us? Isn't your interest in both at least equal to my own?'

'Yes – I know – of course. It was only a joking way of putting it.'

'Tell me plainly' – he looked at her now – 'have you the slightest objection, on any ground, to Hughie's being taught by Mrs Abbott? If so, do let us clear it up.'

'Dear, I have not a shadow of objection,' replied Alma, straightening herself a little, and answering his gaze with excessive frankness. 'How could I have? You think Mrs Abbott will teach him much better than I could, and in that you are quite right. I have no talent for teaching. I haven't much patience – except in music. It's better every way, that he should go to Mrs Abbott. I feel perfect confidence in her, and I shouldn't be able to in a mere stranger.'

Harvey gave a slow nod, and appeared to have something more of importance to say; but he only asked how the child's cold had been tonight. Alma replied that it was neither better nor worse; she spoke absently.

'On whose encouragement do you principally rely?' was Rolfe's next question.

'On that of twenty people!'

'I said "principally".'

'Herr Wilenski has often praised me; and he doesn't throw his praise away. And you yourself, Harvey, didn't you say last might that I was undoubtedly as good as most professionals?'

'I don't think I used quite those words; and, to tell you the truth, it had never entered my head that you would take them for encouragement to such a step as this.'

Alma bent towards him, smiling.

'I understand. You don't think me good enough. Now the truth, the truth!' and she held up a finger – which she could not succeed in keeping steady.

'Yes, you shall have the truth. It's too serious a matter for making pretences. My own judgment is worthless, utterly; it should neither offend nor encourage you. But it's very plain to me that you shouldn't dream of coming before the public unless Wilenski, and perhaps some one else of equal or better standing, actually urges you to it. Now, has he done anything like that?'

She reddened, and hardly tried to conceal her vexation.

'This only means, Harvey, that you don't want me to come out.'

'Come now, be more reasonable. It does not *only* mean that;

in fact, I can say honestly it doesn't mean that at all. If Wilenski tells you plainly that you ought to become a professional violinist, there's no one will wish you luck half so heartily as I. But if it's only the encouragement of "twenty people" – that means nothing. I'm speaking simply as the best friend you have. Don't run the risk of a horrible disappointment. I know you wouldn't find that easy to bear – it would be bad for you, in every way.'

Impelled by annoyance – for the project seemed to him delusive, and his sense of dignity rose against it – Harvey had begun with unwonted decision, but he was soon uncomfortably self-conscious and self-critical; he spoke with effort, vainly struggling against that peculiar force of Alma's personality which had long ago subdued him. When he looked at her, saw her distant smile, her pose of the head as in one who mildly rebukes presumption, he was overcome with a feeling of solemn ineptitude. Quite unaware that his last sentence was to Alma the most impressive – the only impressive – part of his counsel, suddenly he broke off, and found relief in unexpected laughter.

'There now, I've done my duty – I've discharged the pedagogue. Get rid of your tragic mask. Be yourself; do as you wish. When the time comes, just tell me what you have decided.'

So, once more, did he oust common-sense with what he imagined a riper wisdom. One must not take things funereally. Face to face with a woman in the prime of her beauty, he heard a voice warning him against the pedantic spirit of middle age, against formalism and fogeyishness.

'Now I know you again,' said Alma, softening, but still reserved; for she did not forget that he had thrown doubt upon her claims as an artist – an incident which would not lose its importance as she pondered it at leisure.

Harvey sat late. On going upstairs, instead of straightway entering his own room, he passed it with soft step and paused by another door, that of the chamber in which Hughie slept under the care of Miss Smith. The child had coughed in the night during this last week. But at present all was quiet, and with comfortable reassurance the father went to rest.

Alma had matters to occupy her more important than a child's passing ailment. As she slowly unrobed herself by the fire, combed out her warm, fragrant, many-rippled tresses, or held mute dialogue with her eyes in the glass, from a ravel of uneasy thoughts there detached itself, first and foremost, the discovery that Redgrave had not been in Paris when Mrs Strangeways said he was. What was the meaning of this contradiction? Thereto hung the singular coincidence of Redgrave's return home exactly at the time when she and Mrs Strangeways happened to be there. She had thought of it as a coincidence and nothing more; but if Redgrave had deceived Mrs Strangeways as to his movements, the unlooked-for arrival took a suspicious significance. There remained a dark possibility: that Mrs Strangeways knew what was about to happen. Yet this seemed inconceivable.

Was it inconceivable? Why should a woman of that age, and of so much experience, feel nervous about going alone to her friend's house on such a simple mission? It appeared odd at the time, and was more difficult to understand the more she thought of it. And one heard such strange stories – in society of a certain kind – so many whispered hints of things that would not bear to be talked about.

Redgrave had not been in Paris, but at Coventry. There again was a puzzling circumstance. Harvey himself declared his surprise at hearing that Redgrave had entered into partnership with Hugh Carnaby. Had Sibyl anything to do with this? Could she have hinted to her friend the millionaire that her husband's financial position was anything but satisfactory, and had Redgrave, out of pure friendship – of course, out of pure friendship – hastened to their succour?

This perplexity was almost as disturbing as that which preceded it. Knowing the man of money as she did, Alma found it disagreeable to connect his name thus closely with Sibyl's. Disagreeable in a complicated sense; for she had begun to think of Cyrus Redgrave as intimately associated with her own ambitions, secret and avowed. He was to aid her in winning fame as a violinist; and, to this end, all possible use (within certain limits) was to be made of the power she had over him. Alma viewed the position without the least attempt at disguising its true nature. She was playing with fire; knew it; enjoyed the excitement of it; trusted herself with the completest confidence to come out of the game unscorched. But she felt assured that other women, in similar circumstances, had engaged in much the same encounter with Cyrus Redgrave; and could it be imagined that Sibyl Carnaby was one of them – Sibyl, the woman of culture, of high principle, the critic of society – Sibyl, to whom she had so long paid homage, as to one of the chosen of her sex? That Redgrave might approach Sibyl with lawless thought, she could well believe, and such a possibility excited her indignation; that Sibyl would meet him on his own terms, she could not for a moment have credited, but for a traitor-voice that spoke in her for the first time, the voice of jealousy.

Where and how often did they meet? To ask this question was to touch another motive of discontent. Ever since the return to London life, Alma had felt dissatisfied with her social position. She was the wife of a gentleman of independent means; in theory, all circles should be open to her. Practically, she found herself very much restricted in the choice of acquaintances. Harvey had hinted that she should be careful where she went, and whom she knew; that she recognised the justice of this warning served merely to irritate her against its necessity. Why, then, did not her husband exert himself to obtain better society for her? Plainly, he would never take a step in that direction; he had his two or three friends, and found them sufficient; he would have liked to see her very intimate with Mrs Abbott – perhaps helping to teach babies on the kindergarten system! Left to her own resources, she could do little beyond refusing connections that were manifestly undesirable. Sibyl, she knew, associated with people of much higher standing, only out of curiosity taking a peep at the world to which her friend was restricted. There had always been a slight disparity in this respect between them, and in former days Alma had accepted it without murmuring; but why did Sibyl, just when she could have been socially helpful, show a disposition to hold aloof? 'Of course, you care nothing for people of that kind,' Mrs Carnaby had said, after casually mentioning some 'good' family at whose country house she had been visiting. It was intended, perhaps, as a compliment, with allusion to Alma's theories of the 'simple life'; but, in face of the very plain fact that such theories were utterly abandoned, it sounded to Alma a humiliating irony.

Could it be that Sibyl feared inquiries, shrank from having it known that she was on intimate terms with the daughter of the late Bennet Frothingham – a name still too often mentioned in newspapers and elsewhere? The shadow of this possibility had ere now flitted over Alma's mind; she was in the mood to establish it as a certainty, and to indulge the resentment that naturally ensued. For on more than one occasion of late, at Mrs Rayner Mann's or in some such house, she had fancied that one person and another had eyed her in a way that was not quite flattering, and that remarks were privately exchanged about her. Perhaps Harvey himself saw in the fact of her parentage a social obstacle, which made him disinclined to extend their circle of common acquaintances. Was that what he meant by his grave air this evening? Was he annoyed at the thought of a publicity which would reveal her maiden name?

These currents of troubled feeling streamed together and bore her turbidly onwards whither her desires pointed. In one way, and one way only, could she hope to become triumphantly conspicuous, to raise herself quite above petty social prejudices, to defeat ill-wishers and put to shame faint-hearted friends. She had never been able to endure the thought of mediocrity. One chance there was; she must grasp it energetically and without delay. And she must make use of all subsidiary means to her great conquest – save only the last dishonour.

That on her own merit she might rise to the first rank of musicians, Alma did not doubt. Her difficulty lay in the thought that it might require a long time, a wearisome struggle, to gain the universal recognition which alone would satisfy her. Therefore must Cyrus Redgrave be brought to the exertion of all his influence, which she imagined would assist her greatly. Therefore, too, must Felix Dymes be retained as her warm friend, probably (his own suggestion) as her man of business.

It was January. Her 'recital' must take place in the coming season, in May or June. She would sketch a programme at once – tomorrow morning – and then work, work, work terrifically!

Saved by the fervour of this determination from brooding over mysteries and jealousies, Alma lay down with a contented sigh, and was soon asleep, thanks to the health she still enjoyed. Her excitability was of the imagination rather than of the blood, and the cool, lymphatic flow, characteristically feminine, which mingled with the sanguine humour, traceable perhaps to a paternal source, spared her many an hour of wakefulness, as it guarded her against much graver peril.

On Sunday morning she generally went to church – not because of any spiritual impulse, but out of habit. In Wales, Harvey often accompanied her; at Pinner he ceased to do so; but neither then nor now had any talk on the subject passed between them. Alma took it for granted that her husband was very 'broad' in matters of faith. She gathered from her reading that every man of education nowadays dispensed with dogmas, and, for her own part, it was merely an accident that she had not sought to attract attention by pronounced freethinking. Sibyl Carnaby went to church as a matter of course, and never spoke for or against orthodoxy. Had Sibyl been more 'advanced' in this direction, undoubtedly Alma would long ago have followed her example. Both of them, in girlhood, had passed through a great deal of direct religious teaching – and both would have shrunk amazed if called upon to make the slightest sacrifice in the name of their presumed creed.

This morning, however, Alma remained at home, and one of the first things she did was to write to Sibyl, asking when it would be convenient for her friend to give her half-an-hour's private talk. Then she wrote to Felix Dymes, addressing the letter to the care of his publishers. At midday, as Harvey had gone to town on his business with Cecil Morphew, she decided to run over to Kingsbury-Neasden and ask her friends for lunch, in return for which she would make known to them her startling project. It was a wretched day; Hughie must not go out, and Pauline – good creature – would amuse him in one way and another all the afternoon.

As it chanced, her surprise visit could not have been worse timed, for Mrs Leach was in a state of collapse after a violent quarrel, the day before, with her cook-housekeeper, who quitted the house at a moment's notice. Luncheon, in the admissible sense of the word, there was none to be had. Mr Leach, finding the house intolerable when he arrived on Saturday afternoon, had gone back to his bachelor quarters, and the girls, when Alma presented herself, were just sitting down alone to what the housemaid chose to give them. But such an old friend could not be turned away because of domestic mishap.

Not until they had despatched the unsatisfactory meal, and were cosy in the drawing-room, did Alma reveal her great purpose. Dora Leach happened to have a slight acquaintance with a professional pianist who had recently come before the public, and Alma began by inquiring whether her friend could obtain information as to the expenses of the first 'recital' given by that lady.

'I'm afraid I don't know her quite well enough,' replied Miss

Leach. 'What's it for? Are you thinking – ? Really? You *really* are?'

The sisters became joyously excited. Splendid idea! They had feared it was impossible. Oh, she might count with certainty upon a brilliant success! They began to talk about the programme. And what professionals would she engage to take part in the concert? When Alma mentioned that the illustrious Felix Dymes had offered to undertake the management of her business, interest rose to the highest point. Felix Dymes would of course be a tower of strength. Though tempted to speak of the support she might expect from another great man, Alma refrained; her reason being that she meant to ask Dora to accompany her to the Crystal Palace next Saturday. If, as was almost certain, Redgrave met them there, it would be unpleasant to let Dora surmise that the meeting was not by chance.

They chattered for two or three hours, and, among other things, made merry over a girl of their acquaintance (struggling with flagrant poverty), who aimed at a professional career. 'It really would be kindness,' said Dora, 'to tell her she hasn't the least chance; but one can't do that. She was here the other day playing to us – oh, for *such* a time! She said her bow would have to be rehaired, and when I looked at it, I saw it was all greasy and black near the frog, from her dirty fingers; it only wanted washing. I just managed to edge in a hint about soap and water. But she's very touchy; one has to be so careful with her.'

'It's dreadfully awkward, you know,' put in Gerda, 'to talk to people who are so *poor* – isn't it? It came out one day that she had been peeling potatoes for their dinner! It makes one so uncomfortable – she really need not have mentioned it.'

The public halls were discussed. Which would Alma select? Then again the programme. Would she play the Adagio? – meaning, of course, that in Spohr's Concerto 9. No, no; *not* the Adagio – not on any account the Adagio! Something of Bach's? – yes; perhaps the Chaconne. And Brahms? There was the Sonata in A for violin and piano. A stiff piece, but one must not be too popular – Heaven forbid that one should catch at cheap applause! How about a trio? What was that thing of Dvořák's, at St James's Hall not long ago? Yes, the trio in B flat – piano, violin, and 'cello. At least a score of pieces were jotted down, some from memory, some picked out of old programmes, of which Dora produced a great portfolio. Interruption came at length – a servant entering to say that Mrs Leach felt so ill, she wished the doctor to be summoned.

'Oh, bother Mamma and her illnesses!' exclaimed the vivacious Gerda when the intruder was waved off. 'It's all nonsense, you know. She will quarrel with servants and get herself into a state. It'll have to be a boarding-house; I see it coming nearer every day.'

Having made an appointment with Dora for next Saturday, Alma took leave, and went home in excellent spirits. Everything seemed to plan itself; the time had come, the moment of destiny. Doubtless she had been wise in waiting thus long. Had she come forward only a year or so after her father's tragedy, people might have said she was making profit of a vulgar sensation; it would have seemed in bad taste; necessity would have appeared to urge her. Now, such remarks were impossible. Mrs Harvey Rolfe sounded much better than Miss Alma Frothingham. By-the-bye, was it to be 'Mrs', or ought she to call herself 'Madame'? People did use the Madame, even with an English name. Madame Rolfe? Madame Harvey Rolfe? That made her laugh; it had a touch of the ridiculous; it suggested millinery rather than music. Better to reject such silly affectations and use her proper name boldly.

It was to be expected, of course, that people in general would soon discover her maiden name. Whispers would go round; facts might even get into the newspapers. Well? She herself had done nothing to be ashamed of, and if curiosity helped her to success, why, so much the better. In all likelihood it *would* help her; but she did not dwell upon this adventitious encouragement. A more legitimate source of hope revealed itself in Mrs Strangeways' allusion to her personal advantages. She was not ill-looking; on that point there needed no flatterer's assurance. Her looks, if anything, had improved, and possibly she owed something to her experiment in 'simplicity', to the air of mountain and of sea. Felix Dymes, Cyrus Redgrave, not to speak of certain other people – no matter. For all that, she must pay grave attention to the subject of dress. Her recital would doubtless be given in the afternoon, according to custom; so that it was not a case of *grande tenue*\*; but her attire must be nothing short of perfection in its kind. Could she speak about it with Sibyl?

Perhaps – yet perhaps not. She was very anxious to see Sibyl, and felt that a great deal depended upon their coming interview.

This took place on Tuesday; for Sibyl replied at once to the note, and begged her to come without delay. 'Tuesday at twelve. I do little in these gloomy days but read – am becoming quite a bookworm. Why have you been silent so long? I was on the very point of writing to you, for I wish to see you particularly.'

And, when the servant opened her door, Sibyl was discovered in the attitude of a severe student, bending over a table on which lay many volumes. She would not have been herself had there appeared any neglect or unbecomingness in her costume, but she wore the least pretentious of morning gowns, close at throat and wrist, which aided her look of mental concentration and alertness. She rose with alacrity, and the visitor, using her utmost keenness in scrutiny of countenance, found that her own eyes, not Sibyl's, were the first to fall.

'Yes – working as if I had an examination to pass. It's the best thing in weather such as this – keeps one in health, I believe. You, of course, have your music, which answers the same purpose. I'm going in for the Renaissance; always wished to make a thorough study of it. Hugh is appalled; he never imagined I had so much energy. He says I shall be writing a book next – and why not?'

'Of course you could,' replied Alma. 'You're clever enough for anything.'

Her suspicions evaporated in this cosy cloister. She wondered how she could have conceived such a thought of Sibyl, who, dressed so simply, had a girlish air, a beauty as of maidenhood. Exhilarated by her ambitious hopes, she turned in heart to the old friendship, felt her admiration revive, and spoke it freely.

'I know I'm not stupid,' said Sibyl, leaning back as if a little weary; 'and there's the pity of it, that I've never made more use of my brains. Of course, those years abroad were lost, though I suppose I got to know a little more of the world. And since we came back I have had no peace of mind. Did you guess that? Perhaps your husband knew about things from Hugh?'

'I was afraid you might be getting rather anxious; but as you never said anything yourself—'

'I never should have done – I hate talking about money. And you know that things are looking better?'

Sibyl's confident smile drew one of like meaning from Alma.

'Your husband had good news, I know, when Harvey met him on Saturday.'

'It sounds good,' said Sibyl, 'and I take it for granted it will be as good as it sounds. If that's complicated, well, so is business, and I don't profess to understand the details. I can only say that Hugh seems to be a good deal shrewder and more practical than I thought him. He is always making friends with what I consider the wrong kind of people; now at last he has got hold of just the right man, and it very much puzzles me how he did it. I have known Mr Redgrave – you've heard it's Mr Redgrave? – I've known him for several years now, and, between ourselves, I never expected to benefit by the acquaintance.'

Her laugh was so significant that Alma had much ado to keep a steady face.

'I know – things are said about him,' she murmured.

'Things *are* said about him, as you discreetly put it, my dear Alma.' The voice still rippled with laughter. 'I should imagine Hugh has heard them, but I suppose a man of the world thinks nothing of such trifles. And after all' – she grew serious – 'I would rather trust Hugh's judgment than general gossip. Hugh thinks him a "very good fellow". They were together a little in Scotland last autumn, you know, and – it's very wrong to make fun of it, and I shouldn't repeat the story to anyone but you – Mr Redgrave confided to him that he was a blighted being, the victim of an unhappy love in early life. Can you quite picture it?'

'It has an odd sound,' replied Alma, struggling with rather tense nerves. 'Do you believe the story?'

'I can't see why in the world such a man should invent it. It seems he wanted to marry someone who preferred someone else; and since then he has—'

Sibyl rippled off again.

'He has – what?'

'Been blighted, my dear! Of course, people have different ways of showing blight. Mr Redgrave, it is rumoured, hides his head in a hermitage, somewhere in the north of Italy, by one of the lakes. No doubt he lives on olives and macaroni, and broods over what *might* have been. Did you ever hear of that hermitage?'

Alma's colour heightened ever so little, and she kept her eyes on the questioner with involuntary fixedness. The last shadow of doubt regarding Sibyl having disappeared (no woman with an uneasy conscience, she said to herself, could talk in this way), she had now to guard herself against the betrayal of suspicious sensibilities. Sibyl, of course, meant nothing personal by these jesting allusions – how could she? But it was with a hard voice that Alma declared her ignorance of Mr Redgrave's habits, at home, or in retreat by Italian lakes.

'It doesn't concern us,' agreed her friend. 'He has chosen to put his money into Hugh's business, and, from one point of view, that's a virtuous action. Hugh says he didn't suggest anything of the kind, but I fancy the idea must have been led up to at some time or other. The poor fellow has been horridly worried, and perhaps he let fall a word or two he doesn't care to confess. However it came about, I'm immensely glad, both for his sake and my own. My mind is enormously relieved – and that's how I come to be working at the Renaissance.'

Alma took the first opportunity of giving the conversation a turn. It was not so easy as she had anticipated to make her announcement; for, to her own mind, Cyrus Redgrave and the great ambition were at every moment suggestive of each other, and Sibyl, in this peculiar mood, might throw out disturbing remarks or ask unwelcome questions. Only one recent occurrence called for concealment. Happily, Sibyl no longer met Mrs Strangeways (whose character had taken such a doubtful hue), and Redgrave himself could assuredly be trusted for discretion, whatever his real part in that perplexing scene at the bungalow.

'I feel the same want as you do,' said Alma, after a little transitional talk, 'of something to keep me busy. Of course, it must be music; but music at home, and at other people's homes, isn't enough. You know my old revolt against the bonds of the amateur. I'm going to break out – or try to. What would you give for my chances?'

'My dear, I am no capitalist,' replied her friend, with animation. 'For such a bargain as that you must go among the great speculators. Hugh's experience seems to point to Mr Redgrave.'

'Sibyl, please be serious.'

'So I am. I should like to have the purchase of your chances for a trifle of a few thousand pounds.'

Alma's flush of discomposure (more traitorous than she imagined) transformed itself under a gratified smile.

'You really think that I might do something worth the

trouble? – I don't mean money-making – though, of course, no one despises money – but a real artistic success?'

Sibyl made no half-hearted reply. She seemed in thorough agreement with those other friends of Alma's who had received the project enthusiastically. A dozen tickets, at least a dozen, she would at once answer for. But, as though an unwelcome word must needs mingle with her pleasantest talk today, she went on to speak of Alma's husband; what did he think of the idea?

'He looks on, that's all,' Alma replied playfully. 'If I succeed, he will be pleased; if I don't, he will have plenty of consolation to offer. Harvey and I respect each other's independence – the great secret of marriage, don't you think? We ask each other's advice, and take it or not, as we choose. I fancy he doesn't quite like the thought of my playing for money. But if it were *necessary* he would like it still less. He finds consolation in the thought that I'm just amusing myself.'

'I wish you would both come over and dine with us quietly,' said Sibyl, after reflecting, with a smile. 'It would do us all good. I don't see many people nowadays, and I'm getting rather tired of ordinary society; after all, it's great waste of time. I think Hugh is more inclined to settle down and be quiet among his friends. What day would suit you?'

Alma, engrossed in other thoughts, named a day at random. Part of her scheme was still undisclosed: she had a special reason for wishing Sibyl to know of her relations with Felix Dymes, yet feared that she might not hit exactly the right tone in speaking of him.

'Of course, I must have a man of business – and who do you think has offered his services?'

Sibyl was not particularly impressed by the mention of Dymes's name; she had only a slight personal acquaintance with him, and cared little for his reputation as a composer.

'I had a note from him this morning,' Alma continued. 'He asks me to see him today at the Apollo – the theatre, you know. They're going to produce his comic opera, "Blue Roses" – of course, you've heard of it. I shall feel rather nervous about going there – but it'll be a new experience. Or do you think it would be more discreet if I got him to come to Pinner?'

'I didn't think artists cared about those small proprieties,' answered Sibyl, laughing.

'No – of course, that's the right way to regard it. Let me show you his letter.' She took it from her little seal-skin bag. 'A trifle impudent, don't you think? Mr Dymes has a great opinion of himself, and absolutely no manners.'

'Well – if you can keep him in hand – '

They exchanged glances, and laughed together.

'No fear of that,' said Alma 'And he's just the kind of man to be very useful. His music – ah well! But he has popularity, and a great many people take him at his own estimate. Impudence does go a long way.'

Sibyl nodded, and smiled vaguely.

Dymes had suggested a meeting at three o'clock, and to this Alma had already given her assent by telegraph. She lunched with Mrs Carnaby, – who talked a great deal about the Renaissance, – left immediately after, to visit a few shops, and drove up to the Apollo Theatre at the appointed time. Her name sufficed; at once she was respectfully conducted to a small electric-lighted room, furnished only with a table and chairs, and hung about with portraits of theatrical people, where Dymes sat by the fire smoking a cigarette. The illustrious man apologised for receiving her here, instead of in the manager's room, which he had hoped to make use of.

'Littlestone is in there, wrangling about something with Sophy Challis, and they're likely to slang each other for an hour or two. Make yourself comfortable. It's rather hot; take off those furry things.'

'Thank you,' replied Alma, concealing her nervousness with malapert vivacity, 'I shall be quite comfortable in my own way. It *is* rather hot, and your smoke is rather thick, so I shall leave the door a little open.'

Dymes showed his annoyance, but could offer no objection.

'We're getting into shape for this day week. Littlestone calls the opera "Blue Noses" – it has been so confoundedly cold at rehearsals.'

Alma was seized by the ludicrous suggestion, and laughed without restraint; her companion joined in, his loud neigh drowning her more melodious merriment. This put them on natural terms of comradeship, and then followed a long, animated talk. Dymes was of opinion that the hiring of a hall and the fees of supplementary musicians might be defrayed out of the sale of tickets; but there remained the item of advertisement, and on this subject he had large ideas. He wanted 'to do the thing properly'; otherwise he wouldn't do it at all. But Alma was to take no thought for the cost; let it all be left to him.

'You want to succeed? All right; let your fiddling be up to the mark, and I answer for the public. It's all between you and me; you needn't say who is doing the job for you. Ada Wellington comes off on May the 10th; I shall put you down for a fortnight later. That gives you nearly four months to prepare. Don't overdo it; keep right in health; take plenty of exercise. You look very well now; keep it up, and you'll *knock 'em*. I only wish it was the stage instead of the platform – but no use talking about that, I suppose?'

'No use whatever,' Alma replied, flushing with various emotions.

In the course of his free talk, it happened that he addressed her as 'Alma'. She did not check him; but when the name again fell from his lips, she said quietly, with a straight look –

'I think not. The proper name, if you please.'

Dymes took the rebuke good-humouredly. When their conversation was over, he wished her to go with him to a restaurant for tea; but Alma insisted on catching a certain train at Baker Street, and Dymes had to be satisfied with the promise of another interview shortly.

## CHAPTER 9

A visit was due from Mrs Frothingham, who had not been seen at Pinner for more than six months. She would have come at New Year, but an attack of influenza upset her plans. Now she wrote to announce her arrival on Saturday.

'I wish it had been Monday,' said Alma; 'I have to go to the Crystal Palace.'

'Is it imperative?' asked her husband.

'Yes; there's something new of Sterndale Bennett's, and I've asked Dora.'

It seemed to Harvey that this arrangement might have been put aside without great inconvenience, but, as usual, he made no comment. As he would be in town on Saturday, he promised to meet their visitor at Waterloo. Alma, he thought, had never shown much gratitude for her step-mother's constant kindness; during the past half-year she had now and then complained of the trouble of answering Mrs Frothingham's letters, and the news of illness at Basingstoke drew from her only a few words of conventional sympathy. To Hughie, who frequently received presents from 'Grandmamma', she rarely spoke of the affectionate giver. A remark of hers recently on some piece of news from Mrs Frothingham bore an obvious suggestion.

'I wonder,' she said, 'if a single person has been really benefited by all the money Mamma has given away? Isn't it likely she has done much more harm than good?'

There was truth in his surmise that Alma sometimes thought with jealousy of Mrs Frothingham's having had control of a fortune, whilst she, the only child of him who made the money, possessed nothing of her own. The same trend of feeling appeared in a word or two of Alma's, when a daily paper, in speaking of a paltry dividend offered at last to the creditors in one branch of Bennet Frothingham's speculations, used a particularly bitter phrase.

'I should have felt that once; now – '

In these days Alma suffered from a revival of the indignation which had so perturbed her in the time just before her marriage. If now she had possessed even a little money, it would have made her independent in a sense far more tangible than that of the friendly understanding with her husband. She strongly disliked the thought of making Harvey responsible for the expenses of her 'recital'. Had it been possible to procure a small sum by any honest means, she would eagerly have turned to it; but no method seemed discoverable. On her journey homeward after the interview with Felix Dymes, her mind was full of the money question. What did Dymes mean by bidding her take no thought for expenses? Could it have occurred to his outrageous vanity that she might be persuaded to become his debtor, with implied obligation of gratitude?

Not with impunity could her thought accustom itself to stray in regions forbidden, how firm soever her resolve to hold bodily aloof. Alma's imagination was beginning to show the inevitable taint. With Cyrus Redgrave she had passed from disdainful resentment, through phases of tolerance, to an interested flirtation, perilous on every side. In Felix Dymes she easily, perhaps not unwillingly, detected a motive like to Redgrave's, and already, for her own purposes, she was permitting him to regard her as a woman not too sensitive, not too scrupulous. These tactics might not be pleasant or strictly honourable, but she fancied they were forced upon her. Alma had begun to compassionate herself – a dangerous situation. Her battle had to be fought alone; she was going forth to conquer the world by her mere talents, and can a woman disregard the auxiliary weapons of beauty? If Dymes chose to speculate in hopes ludicrously phantasmal, was that her affair? She smiled at the picture of two men, her devoted servants, exerting themselves to the utmost for her advantage, yet without a syllable of express encouragement, and foredoomed to a disappointment which would be perfectly plain to them could they but use their common-sense.

Throughout this week Harvey did not behave quite as usual to her; or so Alma thought. He had not the customary jocoseness when they met at the close of day; he asked no questions about how she had spent her time; his manner was preoccupied. One evening she challenged him.

'You are worrying about what you think my foolishness.'

'Foolishness? Of what folly are you guilty?'

'My ambition, then.'

'Oh no!' He laughed as if the thought genuinely amused him. 'Why should I worry about it? Don't work too hard, that's all. No, I was thinking of a squalid little ambition of my own. I have an idea Morphew may make something of that business; and I want him to, for the fellow's own good. It's wonderful how near he has been to going to the devil, once for all. I fancy I've got him now by the coat-tail; I may hold him.'

'You can't call that a squalid ambition,' said Alma, wishing to be amiable.

'Not that side of it – no. But I've decided to put a little money into the business – nothing that matters, but it may just as well be made safe, if a little trouble will do it. I was wondering how it would be if I worked a little down yonder – kept Morphew in sight. Distance is the chief objection.'

'But you think of moving to Gunnersbury?'

'Yes, I do. I'm thinking of it seriously. Will you go over with me one day next week! Better be Saturday – Mrs Abbott will be free.'

It was unfortunate that Alma had not been able to establish

an intimacy with Mary Abbott. They saw each other very rarely, and, as Harvey perceived, made no progress in friendship. This did not surprise him; they were too unlike in temper, intellect, and circumstances. Whether to these obstacles should be added another more serious, Harvey could not quite assure himself. He had suspected that Alma entertained a slight jealousy – natural, perhaps, though utterly without substantial cause. He even reckoned with this when proposing to put the child under Mrs Abbott's care, thinking that, in revolt against such an alternative, Alma might be impelled to take the duty upon herself. That nothing of the kind had resulted, seemed to prove that, whatever feeling might occasionally have arisen in Alma, she did not regard his friend with any approach to hostility. For his own part, he had always felt that the memory of Bennet Frothingham must needs forbid Mrs Abbott to think with unrestrained kindliness of Alma, and, but for Alma herself, he would scarce have ventured to bring them together. That they were at least on amiable terms must be held as much as could be hoped for. With regard to Mary's efficiency as a teacher, his opinion had grown more favourable since he had seen her in her own home. Time and experience were moulding her, he thought, to a task undertaken first of all in a spirit of self-discipline. She appeared to be successful in winning the confidence of parents, and she no longer complained of inability to make herself liked by her little pupils. Best of all, she was undoubtedly devoting herself to the work with all the powers of her mind, making it the sole and sufficient purpose of her life. Harvey felt no misgiving; he spoke his true thought when he said that he would rather trust Hughie to Mrs Abbott than to any other teacher. It was with surprise, therefore, and some annoyance, that he received Alma's reply to his proposal for their going over to Gunnersbury next week.

'Are you quite sure,' she said, rather coldly, 'that Mrs Abbott will teach better than Pauline?'

'It isn't only that. Hughie must have companions. I thought we had agreed about it.'

'Have you inquired who his companions will be?'

'Oh – the ordinary children of ordinary people,' he replied, with some impatience. 'I don't know that babies are likely to corrupt each other. But, of course, you will ask Mrs Abbott all about that kind of thing – or anything else you wish.'

Alma shook her head, laughing carelessly.

'No, no. That is all in *your* hands. You have discussed it with her, haven't you?'

'I haven't so much as mentioned it. But, of course, I am quite willing to relieve you of all trouble in the matter.'

His tone seemed to startle Alma, for she looked up at him quickly, and spoke in a more serious voice.

'I don't think we quite understand each other about Hughie. Why should you be so anxious? He seems to me to be doing very well. Remember, he's only a little more than three years old – quite a baby, as you say. I don't think he would feel the want of companions for another year at least.'

Harvey met her look, and replied quietly.

'It isn't that I'm anxious about him. I have to plan for his education, that's all.'

'You're beginning rather early. Fathers don't generally look after their children so young.'

'Unfortunately, they don't,' said Harvey, with a laugh. 'Mothers do, here and there.'

'But surely you don't mean that I am neglectful, Harvey?'

'Not at all. Teaching isn't your métier, Alma.'

'I have always confessed that. But, then, the time for teaching Hughie has hardly come. What can Pauline do but just see that he doesn't get into mischief?'

'That's the very reason why he would be better for two or three hours a day with some one who knows *how* to teach a child of his age. It isn't as unimportant as you think. Pauline does very well, but Mrs Abbott will do better.'

Vexed at his own cowardliness – for he could not utter the words that leaped to his tongue – Harvey fell into a perverse insistence on Mrs Abbott's merits. He had meant to confine himself within the safe excuse that the child needed companionship. Forbidden the natural relief of a wholesome, hearty outburst of anger – which would have done good in many ways – his nerves drove him into smothered petulance, with the result that Alma misread him, and saw in his words a significance quite apart from their plain meaning.

'I have not the least intention of interfering, Harvey,' she said, with her distant smile. 'For the next few months I shall be very busy indeed. Only one thing I would ask – you don't think of leaving this house before midsummer?'

'No.'

'Because I shall probably give my recital in May, and it would be rather inconvenient – '

'Everything shall be arranged to suit you.'

'Not at all, not at all!' she exclaimed cheerfully. 'I don't ask so much as that; it would be unreasonable. We are neither of us to stand in the other's way – isn't that the agreement? Tell me your plans, and you shall know mine, and I'm sure everything will be managed very well.'

So the conversation ended, satisfactorily to neither. Harvey, aware of having spoken indiscreetly, felt that he was still more to blame for allowing his wife a freedom of which she threatened to make absurd use; and Alma, her feelings both as wife and mother sensibly perturbed, resented the imputation which seemed to have been thrown upon her conduct. This resentment was of course none the less enduring because conscience took her husband's side. She remembered her appointment tomorrow (practically an appointment) with Cyrus Redgrave at the Crystal Palace; would not that be more difficult to confess than anything she could reasonably suppose to have happened between Harvey and Mary Abbott? Yet more than ever she hoped to meet Redgrave, to hold him by a new link of illusory temptation, that he might exert himself to the utmost in promoting her success. For among the impulses which urged her forward, her reasons for desiring a public triumph, was one which Harvey perhaps never for a moment imagined – a desire to shine gloriously in the eyes of her husband. Harvey would never do her justice until constrained by the voice of the world. Year after year he held her in less esteem; he had as good as said that he did not think her capable of taking a place among professional violinists. Disguise it how he might, he secretly wished her to become a mere domestic creature, to abandon hopes that were nothing better than a proof of vanity. This went to Alma's heart, and rankled there. He should see! He should confess his error, in all its injurious and humiliating extent! At whatever cost – at all but *any* cost – the day of her triumph should come about! Foreseeing it, she had less difficulty in keeping calm when the excellencies of Mrs Abbott were vaunted before her, when Harvey simply ignored all that in herself compensated the domestic shortcoming. Of course, she was not a model of the home-keeping virtues; who expected an artist to be that? But

Harvey denied this claim; and of all the motives contributing to her aspiration, none had such unfailing force as the vehement resolve to prove him wrong.

Next morning the weather was so bad that Harvey asked whether she had not better give up her expedition to the Crystal Palace. Alma smiled and shook her head.

'You think I go only for amusement. It's so difficult to make you understand that these things are serious.'

'Congestion of the lungs is serious. I don't think Mrs Frothingham will face it. There'll probably be a telegram from her.'

But by midday the fierce wind and driving sleet had abated, though the outlook remained cheerless enough. After an early lunch, Alma set forth. Dora Leach joined her in the train, and thus they travelled, through sooty gloom, under or above ground, from the extreme north to the farthest south of London; alighting at length with such a ringing of the ears, such an impression of roar and crash and shriek, as made the strangest prelude to a feast of music ever devised in the world's history. Their seats having been taken in advance, they entered a few moments before the concert began, and found themselves amid a scanty audience; on either side of them were vacant places. Alma did not dare to glance round about. If Redgrave were here, and looked for her, he would have no difficulty in discovering where she sat; probably, too, he could manage to take possession of the chair at her side. And this was exactly what happened, though not until the first piece had been performed.

'I congratulate you on your zeal,' spoke the voice which always put her in mind of sunny mountains and a blue lake.

'Inviting a compliment in return,' said Alma, with a sudden illumination of her features. 'Are you one of the regular attendants?'

'Don't you remember?' His voice dropped so low that he hardly seemed to address her. 'I promised myself the pleasure—'

Alma pretended not to hear. She turned to her companion, spoke a word, and renewed the very slight acquaintance which had existed a few years ago between Redgrave and Miss Leach. Then the sound of an instrument imposed silence.

It was not the first time that Alma affected to be absorbed in music when not consciously hearing it at all. Today the circumstances made such distraction pardonable; but often enough she

had sat thus, with countenance composed or ecstatic, only
seeming to listen, even when a master played. For Alma had no
profound love of the art. Nothing more natural than her laying
it completely aside when, at home in Wales, she missed her
sufficient audience. To her, music was not an end in itself. Like
numberless girls, she had, to begin with, a certain mechanical
aptitude, which encouraged her through the earlier stages, until
vanity stepped in and urged her to considerable attainments.
Her father's genuine delight in music of the higher kind served
as an encouragement whenever her own energies began to fail;
and when at length, with advancing social prospects, the
thought took hold of her that, by means of her violin, she might
maintain a place of distinction above ordinary handsome girls
and heiresses, it sufficed to overcome her indolence and lack of
the true temper. She founded her Quartet Society, and queened
it over amateurs, some of whom were much better endowed
than herself. Having set her pride on winning praise as a
musician, of course she took pains, even working very hard
from time to time. She had first-rate teachers, and was clever
enough to profit by their lessons. With it all, she cared as little
for music as ever; to some extent it had lost even that power
over her sensibilities which is felt by the average hearer. Alma
had an emotional nature, but her emotions responded to
almost any kind of excitement sooner than to the musical. So
much had she pretended and posed, so much had she struggled
with mere manual difficulties, so much lofty cant and sounding
hollowness had she talked, that the name of her art was
grown a weariness, a disgust. Conscious of this, she was irritated whenever Harvey begged her to play simple things; for
indeed, if she must hear music at all, it was just those simple
melodies she would herself have preferred. And among the
self-styled musical people with whom she associated, were
few, if any, in whom conceit did not sound the leading motive.
She knew but one true musician, Herr Wilenski. That the
virtuoso took no trouble to bring her in touch with his own
chosen circle, was a significant fact which quite escaped Alma's
notice.

Between the pieces Redgrave chatted in a vein of seductive
familiarity, saying nothing that Dora Leach might not have
heard, but frequently softening his voice, as though to convey
intimate meanings. His manner had the charm of variety; he

was never on two occasions alike; today he seemed to relax in a luxurious mood, due in part to the influence of sound, and in part, as his eyes declared, to the sensuous pleasure of sitting by Alma's side.

'What an excellent fellow Carnaby is!' he remarked unexpectedly. 'I have been seeing a good deal of him lately – as you know, I think?'

'So I have heard.'

'I like him all the better because I am rather sorry for him.'

'Why?'

'Don't you feel that he is very much out of place? He doesn't belong to our world at all. He ought to be founding a new civilisation in some wild country. I can sympathise with him; I have something of the same spirit.'

'I never observed it,' said Alma, allowing her glance to skim his features.

'Perhaps because you yourself represent civilisation in its subtlest phase, and when I am with you I naturally think only of that. I don't say I should have thriven as a backwoodsman; but I admire the type in Carnaby. That's one of *our* privileges, don't you think? We live in imagination quite as much as in everyday existence. You, I am sure, are in sympathy with infinite forms of life* – and,' he added, just above his breath, 'you could realise so many of them.'

'I shall be content with one,' replied Alma.

'And that – ?'

She nodded towards the concert platform, where, at the same moment, a violinist stepped forward. Redgrave gazed inquiringly at her, but she kept silence until the next interval. Then, in reply to his direct question, she told him, with matter-of-fact brevity, what her purpose was. He showed neither surprise nor excessive pleasure, but bent his head with a grave approving smile.

'So you feel that the time has come. Of course I knew that it would. Are any details arranged? – or perhaps I mustn't ask?'

'I wanted to talk it over with you,' she answered graciously.

After the concert they had tea together. Redgrave was very attentive to Miss Leach, whom his talk amused and flattered. Alma's enterprise was discussed with pleasant freedom, and Redgrave learnt that she had decided to employ Mr Felix Dymes as her agent. The trio set forth at length on their homeward journey in a mood of delightful animation, and travelled together as far as Victoria.

'I haven't said that you can rely on me for all possible assistance,' Redgrave remarked, as he walked along the roaring platform by Alma's side. 'That is a matter of course. We shall meet again before long?'

'No doubt.'

'In Porchester Terrace perhaps?'

'Perhaps.'

Alma met his eyes, and took away with her the consciousness of having dared greatly. But the end was a great one.

In spite of the bad weather, Mrs Frothingham had travelled up from Basingstoke. Alma found her in the drawing-room, and saw at a glance that there had been conversation on certain subjects between her and Harvey; but not until the next day did Mrs Frothingham speak of what she had heard, and make her private comments for Alma's benefit.

'I thought Harvey was joking, dear. Have you reflected how many reasons there are why you *shouldn't* – ?'

The pathetic gaze of appeal produced no effect.

'Did Harvey ask you to talk about it, Mamma?'

'No. He takes it in the kindest way. But, Alma, you surely see that it pains him?'

'Pains him? That shows you don't understand us, dear Mamma. We could neither of us possibly do anything that would pain the other. We are in perfect harmony, yet absolutely independent. It has all been talked over and settled. You must have misunderstood Harvey altogether.'

From this position Alma could not be moved, and Mrs Frothingham, too discreet to incur the risk of interference, spoke no more of the matter as it concerned man and wife. But another objection she urged with almost tearful earnestness. Did Alma forget that her appearance in public would give occasion to most disagreeable forms of gossip? And even if she disregarded the scandal of a few years ago, would not many of her acquaintances say and believe that necessity had driven her into a professional career?

'They may say what they like, and think what they like,' was Alma's lofty reply. 'If artists had always considered such trivial difficulties, where should we have been? Suppose gossip does its worst – it's all over in a few months; then I stand by my own merit. Dear Mamma, *don't* be old fashioned! You look so young and so charming – indeed you do – that I can't bear to hear you talk in that early Victorian way. Art is art, and all these other things have nothing whatever to do with it. There, it's all over. Be good, and amuse yourself whilst you are with us. I assure you we are the most reasonable and the happiest people living.'

Mrs Frothingham smiled at the compliment to herself; then sighed, and held her peace.

## CHAPTER 10

So day by day Alma's violin sounded, and day after day Harvey heard it with a growing impatience. As is commonly the case with people of untrained ear, he had never much cared for this instrument; he preferred the piano. Not long ago he would have thought it impossible that he could ever come to dislike music, which throughout his life had been to him a solace and an inspiration; but now he began to shrink from the sound of it. As Alma practised in the morning, he was driven at length to alter his habits, and to leave home after breakfast. Having no other business, he went to Westminster Bridge Road, met Cecil Morphew at the shop, watched the progress of alterations that seemed advisable, picked up a little knowledge of photography, talked over prices, advertisements, and numerous commercial matters of which he had hitherto been contentedly ignorant. Before long, his loan to Morphew was converted into an investment; he became a partner in the concern, which, retaining the name of the old proprietor, they carried on as Denbow & Co.

The redemption of his debentures kept him still occupied with a furtive study of the money-market. He did not dare to face risk on a large scale; the mere thought of a great reduction of income made him tremble and perspire. So in the end he adopted the simple and straightforward expedient of seeking an interview with his banker, by whom he was genially counselled to purchase such-and-such stock, a sound security, but less productive than that he had previously held. An unfortunate necessity, seeing that his expenses increased and were likely to do so. But he tried to hope that Westminster Bridge Road would eventually reimburse him. With good luck, it might do more.

His days of quietude were over. He, too, was being drawn into the whirlpool. No more dreaming among his books; no more waking to the ordinary duties and cares of a reasonable life. As a natural consequence of the feeling of unsettlement, of instability, he had recourse more often than he wished to the old convivial habits, gathering about him once again, at club or restaurant, the kind of society in which he always felt at ease – good, careless, jovial, and often impecunious fellows, who, as in days gone by, sometimes made a demand upon his purse which he could not resist, though he had now such cause for rigid economy. Was it that he grew old? – he could no longer take his wine with disregard of consequence. The slightest excess, and too surely he paid for it on the morrow, not merely with a passing headache, but with a whole day's miserable discomfort. Oh, degeneracy of stomach and of brain! Of will, too; for he was sure to repeat the foolish experience before a week had passed.

It was not till Mrs Frothingham had left them after a fortnight's visit that he reminded Alma of her promise to go with him to Gunnersbury.

'Did I promise?' she said. 'I thought we agreed that you should settle all that yourself.'

'I had rather you came with me to see Mrs Abbott. Shall it be Saturday?'

'Can't,' replied Alma, with a shake of the head and a smile. 'I have to see Mr Dymes.'

'Dymes? Who is he?'

'My agent.'

'Oh! very well; then I'll go alone.'

He would not permit himself any further inquiry. Alma had never spoken to him of Dymes, her 'agent'. Harvey pictured an ill-shaven man in a small office, and turned from the thought with disgust. Too late to interpose, to ask questions; anything of that kind would but make him seem small, ridiculous, fussy. He had chosen his course, and must pursue it.

Not that Alma behaved in such a way as to suggest estrangement; anything but so. Her manner was always amiable, frequently affectionate. When they spent an evening together – it did not often happen – she talked delightfully; avoiding, as did

Harvey himself, the subjects on which they were not likely to agree. Her gaze had all the old directness, her smile was sweet as ever, and her laugh as melodious. If ever he felt uneasy during her long absences in town, one of these evenings sufficed to reassure him. Alma was Alma still, and could he but have reconciled himself to the thought of her playing in public, she would have been yet the wife he chose, frankly self-willed, gallantly independent.

Until a certain day at the end of March, when something happened of which Harvey had no suspicion, but which affected Alma in a way he soon perceived.

That morning he had left home early, and would not return till late. Alma practised as usual, had luncheon alone, and was thinking of going out, when the post delivered two letters – one for herself from Dymes, the other for her husband. A glance showed her that Harvey's correspondent was Mrs Abbott, and never till today had one of Mrs Abbott's letters come into her hand. She regarded it with curiosity, and the longer she looked the stronger her curiosity became. Harvey would of course tell her what his friend wrote about – as he always did; but the epistle itself she would not be asked to read. And did she, as a matter of fact, always know when Harvey heard from Mrs Abbott? A foolish question, probably; for if the correspondence were meant to be secret, it would be addressed to Harvey at his club, not to the house. All the same, a desire of years concentrated itself in this moment. Alma wished vehemently to read one of Mary Abbott's letters with her own eyes.

She turned the envelope. It was of very stout paper, and did not look quite securely gummed. Would not a touch of the finger – almost – ? Why, there, just as she thought; a mere touch, and the envelope came open. 'Now, if I ever wrote a dangerous word,' mused Alma – 'which I don't, and never shall – this would be a lesson to me.'

Well, it was open, and, naturally enough, the letter came forth. What harm? There could be nothing in it that Harvey would wish to hide from her. So, with hands that trembled, and cheeks that felt warm, she began to read.

The letter was Mrs Abbott's acknowledgment of the quarterly cheque she received from Rolfe. Alma was surprised at the mention of money in the first line, and read eagerly on. As Mary Abbott and her friend had seen each other so recently, there was no need of a full report concerning Minnie Wager (her brother had long since gone to a boarding-school), but the wording allowed it to be understood that Harvey paid for the child, and, what was more, that he held himself responsible for her future. What could this mean? Alma pondered it in astonishment; gratified by the discovery, but disturbed beyond measure by its mysterious suggestiveness. The letter contained little more, merely saying, towards the end, how very glad the writer would be to give her utmost care to little Hugh when presently he came into her hands. Last of all – 'Please remember me kindly to Mrs Rolfe.'

At this point of her life Alma had become habitually suspicious of any relation between man and woman which might suggest, however remotely, dubious possibilities. Innocence appeared to her the exception, lawlessness the rule, where man and woman were restrained by no obvious barriers. It was the natural result of her experience, of her companionship, of the thoughts she deliberately fostered. Having read the letter twice, having mused upon it, she leaped to a conclusion which seemed to explain completely the peculiar intimacy subsisting between Harvey and Mary Abbott. These two children, known as Albert and Minnie Wager, were Harvey's offspring, the result of some *liaison* before his marriage; and Mrs Abbott, taking charge of them for payment, had connived at the story of their origin, of their pitiful desertion. What could be clearer?

She did not go further in luminous conjectures. Even with her present mind, Alma could not conceive of Mary Abbott as a wanton, of Harvey Rolfe as a shameless intriguer; but it stung her keenly to think that for years there had been this secret between them. Probably the matter was known to Mrs Abbott's husband, and so, at his death, it had somehow become possible for Harvey to suggest this arrangement, whereby he helped the widow in her misfortunes, and provided conscientiously for his own illegitimate children. Harvey was so very conscientious about children!

Did they resemble him? She had seen the little girl, but only once, and without attention. She would take an early opportunity of going over to Gunnersbury, to observe. But no such evidence was necessary; the facts stared one in the face.

That Harvey should have kept this secret from her was intelligible enough; most men, no doubt, would have done the same. But it seemed to Alma only another proof of her husband's inability to appreciate her. He had no faith in her as artist; he had no faith in her as woman. Had she not felt this even from the very beginning of their intimate acquaintance? Perhaps the first thing that awakened her interest in Harvey Rolfe was the perception that he did not, like other men, admire her unreservedly, that he regarded her with something of criticism. She could attract him; she could play upon his senses; yet he remained critical. This, together with certain characteristics which distinguished him from the ordinary drawing-room man, suggestions of force and individuality, drew her into singular relations with him long before she dreamt that he would become her husband. And his attitude towards her was unchanged, spite of passionate love-making, spite of the tenderness and familiarity of marriage; still he viewed her with eyes of tolerance, rather than of whole-hearted admiration. He compared, contrasted her with Mary Abbott, for whose intellect and character he had a sincere respect. Doubtless he fancied that, if this secret became known to her, she would sulk or storm, after the manner of ordinary wives. What made him so blind to her great qualities? Was it that he had never truly loved her? Had it been owing to mere chance, mere drift of circumstances, that he offered her marriage, instead of throwing out a proposal such as that of Cyrus Redgrave at Bregenz?

Though but darkly, confusedly, intermittently conscious of the feeling, Alma was at heart dissatisfied with the liberty, the independence, which her husband seemed so willing to allow her. This, again, helped to confirm the impression that Harvey held her in small esteem. He did not think it worth while to oppose her; she might go her frivolous way, and he would watch with careless amusement. At moments, it was true, he appeared on the point of ill-humour; once or twice she had thought (perhaps had hoped) that he could lay down the law in masculine fashion; but no – he laughed, and it was over. When, at the time of her misery in Wales—her dim jealousy of Mrs Abbott, and revolt against the prospect of a second motherhood – she had subdued herself before him, spoken and behaved like an everyday dutiful wife, Harvey would have none of it. He wished – was that the reason? – to be left alone, not to be worried with her dependence upon him. That no doubt of her fidelity ever seemed to enter his mind, was capable of anything but a complimentary interpretation; he simply took it for granted that she would be faithful – in other words, that she had not spirit or originality enough to defy conventional laws. To himself, perhaps, he reserved a much larger liberty. How could she tell where, in what company, his evenings were spent? More than once he had been away from home all night – missed the last train, he said. Well, it was nothing to her; but his incuriousness as to her own movements began to affect her sensibly, now that she imagined so close a community of thoughts and interests between Harvey and Mary Abbott.

Before his return tonight other letters had arrived for him, and all lay together, as usual, upon his desk. Alma, trying to wear her customary face, waited for him to mention that he had heard from Gunnersbury, but Harvey said nothing. He talked, instead, of a letter from Basil Morton, who wanted him to go to Greystone in the spring, with wife and child.

'You mustn't count on me,' said Alma.

'But after your concert – recital – whatever you call it; it would be a good rest.'

'Oh, I shall be busier than ever. Mr Dymes hopes to arrange for me at several of the large towns.'

Harvey smiled, and Alma observed him with irritation she could scarcely repress. Of course, his smile meant a civil scepticism.

'By-the-bye,' he asked, 'is Dymes the comic opera man?'

'Yes. I rather wondered, Harvey, whether you would awake to that fact. He will be one of our greatest composers.'

She went on with enthusiasm, purposely exaggerating Dymes's merits, and professing a warm personal regard for him. In the end, Harvey's eye was upon her, still smiling, but curiously observant.

'Why hasn't he been here? Doesn't he think it odd that you never ask him?'

'Oh, you know that I don't care to ask people. They are aware' – she laughed – 'that my husband is not musical.'

Harvey's countenance changed.

'Do you mean that you tell them so?'

'Not in any disagreeable way, of course. It's so natural, now, for married people to have each their own world.'

'So it is,' he acquiesced.

Alma would have gone to Gunnersbury the very next day, but

she feared to excite some suspicion in her husband's mind. He
little imagined her capable of opening his letters, and to be
detected in such a squalid misdemeanour would have overwhelmed her with shame. In a day or two she would be going
to Mrs Rayner Mann's, to meet a certain musical critic 'of great
influence', and by leaving home early she could contrive to make
a call upon Mrs Abbott before lunching at Putney. This she did.
She saw little Minnie Wager, scrutinised the child's features, and
had no difficulty whatever in discerning Harvey's eyes, Harvey's
mouth. Why should she have troubled herself to come? It was
very hard to control her indignation. If Mrs Abbott thought her
rather strange, rather abrupt, what did it matter?

At Mrs Rayner Mann's she passed into a soothing and
delicious atmosphere. The influential critic proved to be a very
young man, five-and-twenty at most; he stammered with nervousness when first addressing the stranger, but soon gave her
to understand, more or less humorously, that his weekly article
was 'quite' the most important thing in latter-day musical
criticism, and that he panted for the opportunity of hearing a
new violinist of real promise. But Alma had not brought her
violin; lest she should make herself cheap, she never played now
at people's houses. The critic had to be satisfied with hearing
her talk and gazing upon her beauty. Alma was become a very
fluent talker, and her voice had the quality which fixes attention.
At luncheon, whilst half-a-dozen persons lent willing ear, she
compared Sarasate's playing of Beethoven's Concerto with that
of Joachim,* and declared that Sarasate's *cadenza* in the first
movement, though marvellous for technical skill, was not at all
in the spirit of the work. The influential writer applauded,
drawing her on to fresh displays of learning, taste, eloquence.
She had a great deal to say about somebody's 'technique of the
left hand', of somebody else's 'tonal effects', of a certain pianist's
'warmth of touch'. It was a truly musical gathering; each person
at table had some exquisite phrase to contribute. The hostess,
who played no instrument, but doted upon all, was of opinion
that an executant should 'aim at mirroring his own nature in his
interpretation of a tone-poem'; whereupon another lady threw
out remarks on 'subjective interpretation', confessing her preference for a method purely 'objective'. The influential critic
began to talk about Liszt, with whom he declared that he had

been on intimate terms; he grew fervent over the master's rhapsodies, with their 'clanging rhythm and dithyrambic fury'.

'I don't know when I enjoyed myself so much,' said Alma gaily, as the great young man pressed her hand at parting and avowed himself her devoted admirer.

'My dear Mrs Rolfe,' said the hostess privately, 'you were simply brilliant! We are all looking forward *so* eagerly!'

And as soon as Alma was gone, the amiable lady talked about her to the one remaining guest.

'*Isn't* she delightful! I do so hope she will be a success. I'm afraid so much depends upon it. Of course, you know that she is the daughter of Bennet Frothingham? Didn't you know? Yes, and left without a farthing. I suppose it was natural she should catch at an offer of marriage, poor girl, but it seems to have been *most* ill-advised. One never sees her husband, and I'm afraid he is anything but kind to her. He *may* have calculated on her chances as a musician. I am told they have little or nothing to depend upon. Do drum up your friends – will you? It is to be at Prince's Hall, on May the 16th – I think. I feel, don't you know, personally responsible; she would never have come out but for my persuasion, and I'm *so* anxious for a success!'

The day drew near for Ada Wellington's début. Alma met this young lady, but they did not take to each other; Miss Wellington was a trifle 'loud', and, unless Alma mistook, felt fiercely jealous of any one admired by Felix Dymes. As she could not entertain at their own house (somewhere not far south of the Thames), Mrs Wellington borrowed Dymes's flat for an afternoon, and there, supported by the distinguished composer, received a strange medley of people who interested themselves in her daughter's venture. Alma laughed at the arrangement, and asked Dymes if he expected her congratulations.

'Don't make fun of them,' said Felix. 'Of course, they're not *your* sort, Alma. But I've known them all my life, and old Wellington did me more than one good turn when I was a youngster. Ada won't make much of it, but she'll squeeze in among the provincial pros after this send off.'

'You really are capable of generosity?' asked Alma.

'I swear there's nothing between us. There's only one woman living that I have eyes for – and I'm afraid she doesn't care a rap about me; at all events, she treats me rather badly.'

This dialogue took place in a drawing-room the evening

before Miss Wellington's day. Alma had declined to meet her agent a second time at the Apollo Theatre; they saw each other, by arrangement, at this and that house of common friends, and corresponded freely by post, Dymes's letters always being couched in irreproachable phrase. Whenever the thing was possible, he undisguisedly made love, and Alma bore with it for the sake of his services. He had obtained promises from four musicians of repute to take part in Alma's concert, and declared that the terms they asked were lower than usual, owing to their regard for him. The expenses of the recital, without allowing for advertisements, would amount to seventy or eighty pounds; and Dymes guaranteed that the hall should produce at least that. Alma, ashamed to appear uneasy about such paltry sums, always talked as though outlay mattered nothing.

'Don't stint on advertisements,' she said.

'No fear! Leave that to me,' answered Felix, with a smile of infinite meaning.

Ada Wellington could not afford to risk much money, and Alma thought her announcements in the papers worth nothing at all. However, the pianist was fairly successful; a tolerable audience was scraped together (at Steinway Hall),* and press notices of a complimentary flavour, though brief, appeared in several quarters. With keen anxiety Alma followed every detail. She said to herself that if *her* appearance in public made no more noise than this, she would be ready to die of mortification. There remained a fortnight before the ordeal; had they not better begin to advertise at once? Thus she wrote to Dymes, who replied by sending her three newspapers, in each of which a paragraph of musical gossip informed the world that Mrs Harvey Rolfe was about to give her first public violin recital at Prince's Hall. Mrs Rolfe, added the journalists in varying phrase, was already well known to the best musical circles as an amateur violinist, and great interest attached to her appearance in public, a step on which she had decided only after much persuasion of friends and admirers. Already there was considerable demand for tickets, and the audience would most certainly be both large and distinguished. Alma laughed with delight.

The same day, by a later post, she received a copy of a 'society' journal, addressed in a hand unknown to her. Guided by a red pencil mark, she became aware of no less than a quarter of a column devoted to herself. From this she might learn (if she did not already know it) that Mrs Harvey Rolfe was a lady of the utmost personal and social charm; that her beauty was not easily described without the use of terms that would sound extravagant; that as a violinist she had stood for a year or two *facile princeps** amid lady amateurs; that she had till of late lived in romantic seclusion 'amid the noblest scenery of North Wales', for the sole purpose of devoting herself to music; and that only with the greatest reluctance had she consented to make known to the public a talent – nay, a genius – which assuredly was 'meant for mankind'. She was the favourite pupil of that admirable virtuoso, Herr Wilenski. At Prince's Hall, on the sixteenth of May, all lovers of music would have, &c, &c.

This batch of newspapers Alma laid before dinner on Harvey's desk, and about an hour after the meal she entered the library. Her husband, smoking and meditating, looked up constrainedly.

'I have read them,' he remarked, in a dry tone.

Alma's coldness during the last few weeks he had explained to himself as the result of his failure to take interest in her proceedings. He knew that this behaviour on his part was quite illogical; Alma acted with full permission, and he had no right whatever to 'turn grumpy' just because he disliked what she was doing. Only today he had rebuked himself, and meant to make an effort to restore goodwill between them; but these newspaper paragraphs disgusted him. He could not speak as he wished.

'This is your agent's doing, I suppose?'

'Of course. That is his business.'

'Well, I won't say anything about it. If *you* are satisfied, I have no right to complain.'

'Indeed, I don't think you have,' replied Alma, putting severe restraint upon herself to speak calmly. Thereupon she left the room.

Harvey rose to follow her. He took a step forward – stood still – returned to his chair. And they did not see each other again that night.

In the morning came a letter from Dymes. He wrote that a certain newspaper wished for an 'interview' with Mrs Rolfe, to be published next week. Should the interviewer call upon her, and, if so, when? Moreover, an illustrated paper wanted her portrait with the least possible delay. Were her new photographs ready? If so, would she send him a dozen? Better still if he could see her today, for he had important things to speak of. Might he look for her at Mrs Littlestone's at about four o'clock?

At breakfast Alma was chatty, but she directed her talk almost exclusively to Pauline Smith and to little Hugh, who now had his place at table – a merry, sunny-haired little fellow, dressed in a sailor suit. Harvey also talked a good deal – he, too, with Pauline and the child. When Alma rose he followed her, and asked her to come into the library for a moment.

'I'm a curmudgeon,' he began, facing her with nervous abruptness. 'Forgive me for that foolery last night, will you?'

'Of course,' Alma replied distantly.

'No, but in the same spirit, Alma. I'm an ass! I know that if you do this thing at all, you must do it in the usual way. I wish you success heartily, and I'll read with pleasure every scrap of print that praises you.'

'I'm hurrying to town, Harvey. I have to go to the photographer, and see Mr Dymes, and all sorts of things.'

'The photographer? I hope they'll be tolerable; I know they won't do you justice. Will you sit to a painter if I arrange it? Unfortunately, I can't afford Millais,* you know; but I want a good picture of you.'

'We'll talk about it,' she replied, smiling more pleasantly than of late. 'But I really haven't time now.'

'And you forgive me my idiotics?'

She nodded and was gone.

In the afternoon she met Dymes at Mrs Littlestone's, a house of much society, for the most part theatrical. When they had moved aside for private talk, he began by asking a brusque question.

'Who got that notice for you into the *West End*?'

'Why, didn't you?'

'Know nothing about it. Come, who was it?'

'I have no idea. I took it for granted—'

'Look here, Alma, I think I'm not doing badly for you, and the least you can do is to be straight with me.'

Alma raised her head with a quick, circuitous glance, then fixed her eyes on the man's heated face, and spoke in an undertone: 'Please, behave yourself, or I shall have to go away.'

'Then you won't tell me? Very well. I chuck up the job. You can run the show yourself.'

Alma had never looked for delicacy in Felix Dymes, and his

motives had from the first been legible to her, but this revelation of brutality went beyond anything for which she was prepared. As she saw the man move away, a feeling of helplessness and of dread overcame her anger. She could not do without him. The only other man active on her behalf was Cyrus Redgrave, and to seek Redgrave's help at such a juncture, with the explanation that must necessarily be given, would mean abandonment of her last scruple. Of course, the paragraph in the *West End* originated with him; since Dymes knew nothing about it, it could have no other source. Slowly, but very completely, the man of wealth and social influence had drawn his nets about her; at each meeting with him she felt more perilously compromised; her airs of command served merely to disguise defeat in the contest she had recklessly challenged. Thrown upon herself, she feared Redgrave, shrank from the thought of seeing him. Not that he had touched her heart or beguiled her senses; she hated him for his success in the calculated scheme to which she had consciously yielded step by step; but she was brought to the point of regarding him as inseparable from her ambitious hopes. Till quite recently her thought had been that, after using him to secure a successful début, she could wave him off, perhaps tell him in plain words, with a smile of scorn, that they were quits. She now distrusted her power to stand alone. To the hostility of such a man as Dymes – certain, save at intolerable cost – she must be able to oppose a higher influence. Between Dymes and Redgrave there was no hesitating on whatever score. This advertisement in the fashionable and authoritative weekly paper surpassed Dymes's scope; his savage jealousy was sufficient proof of that. All she could do for the moment was to temporise with her ignobler master, and the humiliation of such a necessity seemed to poison her blood.

She rose, talked a little of she knew not what with she knew not whom, and moved towards the hostess, by whom her enemy was sitting. A glance sufficed. As soon as she had taken leave, Dymes followed her. He came up to her side at a few yards from the house, and they walked together, without speaking, until Alma turned into the first quiet street.

'I give you my word,' she began, 'that I know nothing whatever about that paper.'

'I believe you, and I'm sorry I made a row,' Dymes replied.

'There's no harm done. I dare say I shall be hearing more about it.'

'I have some photographs here,' said Alma, touching her seal-skin bag. 'Will you take them?'

'Thanks. But there's a whole lot of things to be arranged. We can't talk here. Let's go to my rooms.'

He spoke as though nothing were more natural. Alma, the blood throbbing at her temples, saw him beckon a crawling hansom.

'I can't come – now. I have a dreadful headache.'

'You only want to be quiet. Come along.'

The hansom had pulled up. Alma, ashamed to resist under the eyes of the driver, stepped in, and her companion placed himself at her side. As soon as they drove away he caught her hand and held it tightly.

'I can't go to your rooms,' said Alma, after a useless resistance. 'My head is terrible. Tell me whatever you have to say, and then take me to Baker Street Station. I'll see you again in a day or two.'

She did not feign the headache. It had been coming on since she left home, and was now so severe that her eyes closed under the torture of the daylight.

'A little rest and you'll be all right,' said Dymes.

Five minutes more would bring them to their destination. Alma pulled away her hand violently.

'If you don't stop him, I shall.'

'You mean it? As you please. You know what I—'

Alma raised herself, drew the cabman's attention, and bade him drive to Baker Street. There was a short silence, Dymes glaring and muttering inarticulately.

'Of course, if you really have a bad headache,' he growled at length.

'Indeed I have – and you treat me very unkindly.'

'Hang it, Alma, don't speak like that! As if I *could* be unkind to you!'

He secured her hand again, and she did not resist. Then they talked of business, settled one or two matters, appointed another meeting. As they drew near to the station, Alma spoke impulsively, with a bewildered look.

'I shouldn't wonder if I give it up, after all.'

'Rot!' was her companion's amazed exclamation.

'I might. I won't answer for it. And it would be your fault.'

Stricken with alarm, Dymes poured forth assurances of his good behaviour. He followed her down to the platform, and for a quarter of an hour she had to listen, in torment of mind and body, to remonstrances, flatteries, amorous blandishments, accompanied by the hiss of steam and the roar of trains.

On reaching home she could do nothing but lie down in the dark. Her head ached intolerably; and hour after hour, as often happens when the brain is over-wearied, a strain of music hummed incessantly on her ear, till inability to dismiss it made her cry in half-frenzied wretchedness.

With sleep she recovered; but through the next day, dull and idle, her thoughts kept such a gloomy colour that she well-nigh brought herself to the resolve with which she had threatened Felix Dymes. But for the anticipation of Harvey's triumph, she might perhaps have done so.

## CHAPTER II

For several days she had not touched the violin. There was no time for it. Correspondence, engagements, intrigues, whirled her through the waking hours and agitated her repose. The newspaper paragraphs resulted in a shower of letters, inquiring, congratulating, offering good wishes, and all had to be courteously answered, lest the writers should take offence. Invitations to luncheon, to dinner, to midnight 'at homes', came thick and fast. If all this resulted from a few preliminary 'puffs' what, Alma asked herself, would be the consequence of an actual success? How did the really popular musicians contrive to get an hour a day for the serious study of their art? Her severe headache had left behind it some nervous disorder, not to be shaken off by any effort – a new distress, peculiarly irritating to one who had always enjoyed good health. When she wrote, her hand was unsteady, and sometimes her eyes dazzled. This would be alarming if it went on much longer; the day approached, the great day, the day of fate, and what hope was there for a violinist who could not steady her hand?

The 'interviewer' called, and chatted for half an hour, and

took his leave with a flourish of compliments. The musicians engaged to play with her at Prince's Hall's came down to try over pieces, a trio, a duet; so that at last she was obliged to take up her instrument – with results that did not reassure her. She explained that she was not feeling quite herself; it was nothing; it would pass in a day or two. Sibyl Carnaby had asked her and Harvey to dine next week, to meet several people; Mrs Rayner Mann had arranged a dinner for another evening; and now Mrs Strangeways, whom she had not seen for some weeks, sent an urgent request that she would call in Porchester Terrace as soon as possible, to speak of something 'very important'.

This summons Alma durst not disregard. Between Mrs Strangeways and Cyrus Redgrave subsisted an intimacy which caused her frequent uneasiness. It would not have surprised her to discover that this officious friend knew of all her recent meetings with Redgrave – at the Crystal Palace and elsewhere; and, but for her innocence, she would have felt herself at the woman's mercy. That she had not transgressed, and was in no danger of transgressing, enabled her to move with head erect among the things unspeakable which always seemed to her to be lurking in the shadowed corners of Mrs Strangeways' house. The day was coming when she might hope to terminate so undesirable an acquaintance, but for the present she must show a friendly face.

She made this call at three o'clock, and was received in that over-scented, over-heated boudoir, which by its atmosphere invariably turned her thoughts to evil. The hostess rose languidly, with a pallid, hollow-eyed look of illness.

'Only my neuralgic something or other,' she said, in reply to a sympathetic inquiry. 'It's the price one pays for civilisation. I've had two terrible days and nights, but it's over for the present. But for that I should have written to you before. Why, *you* don't look quite so well as usual. Be careful – do be careful!'

'I mean to be, if people will let me.'

'You have eight days, haven't you? Yes, just eight days. You ought to keep as quiet as possible. We are all doing our best; but, after all, success depends greatly upon yourself, you know.'

The voice, as always, seemed to fondle her, but Alma's ear detected the usual insincerity. Mrs Strangeways spoke in much the same way to numbers of people, yet not quite so caressingly. Some interest she undoubtedly had to serve by this consistent

display of affection, and with all but certainty Alma divined it.
She shrank from the woman; it cost her an unceasing effort not
to betray dislike, or even hostility.

'Of course, you saw last week's *West End*?' pursued the
hostess, smiling. 'You know whose doing that was?'

'I only guessed that it *might* be Mr Redgrave's kindness.'

'I have the same suspicion. He was here the other day – we
talked about you. You haven't seen him since then?'

'No.'

'He hinted to me – just a little anxiety. I hardly know whether
I ought to speak of it.'

Alma looked an interrogation as unconcerned as she could
make it, but did not open her lips.

'It was with reference to – your man of business. It seems he
has heard something – I really don't know what – not quite
favourable to Mr Dymes. I shall not offend you, dear?'

'I don't take offence, Mrs Strangeways,' Alma answered, with
a slight laugh to cover her uneasiness. 'It's so old-fashioned.'

The hostess uttered a thin trill of merriment.

'One is always safe with people who have humour, dear. It
*does* make life easier, doesn't it? Oh, the terrible persons who
take everything with tragic airs! Well, there's not a bit of harm
in it. Between ourselves, it struck me that our friend was just a
little inclined to be – yes, you understand.'

'I'm afraid I don't.'

'I hate the word – well, just a trifle jealous.'

Alma leaned back in her chair, glanced about her, and said
nothing.

'Of course, he would never allow *you* to suspect anything of
the kind. It will make no difference. You can count upon his
utmost efforts. But when one thinks how very much he has it in
his power to do – . That bit of writing in the *West End*, you
know – only the highest influence can command that kind of
thing. The *West End* can't be bought, I assure you. And one has
to think of the future. A good beginning is much, but how many
musicians are able to follow it up? My dear Alma, let me
implore you not to imagine that you will be able to dispense
with this kind of help.'

'Do you mean that Mr Redgrave is likely to withdraw it?'

'Impossible for me to say, dear. I am only telling you how his
conversation struck me. He appeared to think – to be apprehen-

sive that you might in future look to Mr Dymes rather than to him. Of course, I could say nothing – I would not venture a syllable.'

'Of course not,' Alma murmured mechanically, her eyes wandering.

'Are you likely, I wonder, to see him in the next few days?'

'I hardly know – I think not.'

'Then let me – will you? – let me contrive a *chance* meeting here.'

Loathing herself, and burning with hatred of the woman, in whose hands she felt powerless, Alma gave an assenting nod.

'I am sure it will be a measure of prudence, dear. I thought possibly you might be seeing him at Mrs Carnaby's. He is there sometimes, I believe?'

Alma looked at the speaker, detecting some special significance in her inquiry. She replied that Redgrave of course called upon Mrs Carnaby – but not often, she thought.

'No?' threw out Mrs Strangeways. 'I fancied he was there a good deal; I don't quite know why.'

'Have you met him there?'

'No. It's quite a long time since I called – one has so many people to see.'

Alma knew that Sibyl was now holding aloof from Mrs Strangeways, and it seemed not improbable that this had excited some ill-feeling in the latter. But her own uneasiness regarding Sibyl's relations with Redgrave, uneasiness never quite subdued, made her quick to note, and eager to explore, any seeming suspicion on that subject in another's mind. Mrs Strangeways was a lover of scandal, a dangerous woman, unworthy of confidence in any matter whatsoever. Common prudence, to say nothing of loyalty to a friend, bade Alma keep silence; but the subtly-interrogating smile was fixed upon her; hints continued to fall upon her ear, and an evil fascination at length compelled her to speak.

'You know,' she said, as if mentioning an unimportant piece of news, 'that Mr Redgrave has joined Mr Carnaby in business?'

The listener's face exhibited a surprise of which there was no mistaking the sincerity. Her very features seemed to undergo a change as the smile vanished from them; they became on the instant hard and old, lined with sudden wrinkles, the muscles tense, every line expressive of fierce vigilance.

'In business? – what business?'

'Oh, I thought you would have heard of it. Perhaps Mr Redgrave doesn't care to have it known.'

'My dear, I am discretion itself.'

Everything was told, down to the last detail of which Alma had any knowledge. As she listened and questioned, Mrs Strangeways resumed her smiling manner, but could not regain the perfect self-command with which she had hitherto gossiped. That she attached great importance to this news was evident, and the fact of its being news to her brought fresh trouble into Alma's thoughts.

'How very interesting!' exclaimed Mrs Strangeways at length. 'Another instance of Mr Redgrave's kindness to his friends. Of course, it was done purely out of kindness, and that is why he doesn't speak of it. Quite amusing, isn't it, to think of him as partner in a business of that kind. I wonder whether—'

She broke off with a musing air.

'What were you wondering?' asked Alma, whose agitation increased every moment, though the seeming tendency of her companion's words was to allay every doubt.

'Oh, only whether it was *Mr* Carnaby who first made known his difficulties.'

'I am told so.'

'By Mrs Carnaby? Yes, no doubt it was so. I don't think Mrs Carnaby could quite have – I mean she is a little reserved, don't you think? She would hardly have spoken about it to – to a comparative stranger.'

'But Mr Redgrave can't be called a stranger,' said Alma. 'They have been friends for a long time. Surely you know that.'

'Friends in *that* sense? The word has such different meanings. You and Mr Redgrave are friends, but I don't think you would care to tell him if your husband were in difficulties of that kind – would you?'

'But Sibyl – Mrs Carnaby didn't tell him,' replied Alma, with nervous vehemence.

'No, no; we take that for granted. I don't think Mr Carnaby is – the kind of man –'

'What kind of man?'

'I hardly know him; we have met, that's all. But I should fancy he wouldn't care to know that his wife talked about such things to Mr Redgrave or any one else. There *are* men' – her voice sank, and the persistent smile became little better than an ugly grin – 'there *are* men who don't mind it. One hears stories I shouldn't like to repeat to you, or even to hint at. But those are very different people from the Carnabys. Then, I suppose,' she added, with abrupt turn, 'Mr Carnaby is very often away from home?'

Trying to reply, Alma found her voice obstructed.

'I think so.'

'How very kind of Mr Redgrave, wasn't it! Has he spoken about it to *you*?'

'Of course not.'

'Naturally, he wouldn't. – Oh, don't go yet, dear. Why, we have had no tea; it isn't four o'clock. Must you really go? Of course, you are overwhelmed with engagements. But do – do take care of your health. And remember our little scheme. If Mr Redgrave could look in – say, the day after tomorrow? You shall hear from me in time. I feel – I really feel – that it wouldn't be wise to let him think – you understand me.'

With scarce a word of leave-taking, Alma hastened away. The air of this room was stifling her, and the low cooing voice had grown more intolerable than a clanging uproar. From Porchester Terrace she walked into Bayswater Road, her eyes on the pavement. It was a sunny afternoon, but there had been showers, and now again large spots of rain began to fall. As she was opening her umbrella, a cabman's voice appealed to her, and fixed her purpose. She bade him drive her to Oxford and Cambridge Mansions.

Sibyl was not at home. The maid-servant could not say when she might return; she had been absent since yesterday morning. Unable to restrain herself, Alma inquired whether Mr Carnaby was in town. He was not; he had been away for several days.

On the morrow a letter from Sibyl came to Pinner. She was grieved to hear that Alma had called during her absence. Was it anything of importance, or would it keep till she and Harvey came to dine on Saturday? 'I have been down to Weymouth\* – not to enjoy myself, but to see my mother. She *says* she is very ill, and thinks it monstrous that I don't feel inclined to devote myself to the care of her. Her illness, I am sure, is nothing but discontent and bad temper, just because she feels herself dropping out of society. She must get used to it. In any case, we could never endure each other; and how can I be expected to make any sacrifice for a mother who never gave me an hour of motherly care from the day of my birth? But you know all about this, and don't want to hear of it again just when you are so busy. If there is anything in the world I can do for you, let me know at once.'

But for her conversation with Mrs Strangeways, it would not have occurred to Alma to doubt the truth of what Sibyl wrote; as it was, she tortured herself with dark surmises. Jealousy without love, a passion scarcely intelligible to the ordinary man, is in woman common enough, and more often productive of disaster than the jealousy which originates in nobler feeling. To suspect that she was the plaything of Sibyl's subtlety, and that Redgrave smiled at her simplicity in never having discovered an obvious rival, fired her blood to the fever point. She could no longer balance probabilities; all the considerations which hitherto declared for Sibyl's innocence lost their weight. Her overexcited mind, her impaired health, were readily receptive of such poison as distilled from the lips of Mrs Strangeways. What she now desired was proof. Only let evidence be afforded her, cost what it might! After that, she saw her way.

No! Hugh Carnaby was assuredly not one of the men who wink at their wives' dishonour, nor one of the men who go slinking for a remedy to courts of law – or she mistook him strangely

At receipt of the expected note from Porchester Terrace – it said merely, 'Pray be here, if possible, at three tomorrow afternoon' – she quivered with anticipation of seeing Redgrave. How it was to come about, she did not ask, but Redgrave should not part from her before she had obtained light upon his relations with Sibyl. She believed herself irresistible if she chose to put forth all her power. With two men, dangerous both of them, she had played the game of her own interests, played it safely, and for a long time; she made them her instruments, mocking at their hopes, holding them at arm's-length, in spite of all their craft and their vehemence. Only a very clever woman could do this. In giddiness of self-admiration, she felt everything to be possible. Boldness was necessary – far more boldness than she had yet dared to use. The rivalry of such a woman as Sibyl could not be despised; it threatened her ambitions. But in the struggle now to be decided she had a supreme advantage; for Sibyl, having gained her object, assuredly had paid its price.

Hence her pretended absorption in study, hence the revival of her friendliness; what were these things but blinds to mislead the only woman whose observation she had much reason to fear?

How astonishing it now seemed to her that she could have accepted such shallow explanations of Redgrave's partnership with Hugh Carnaby! Why, Harvey himself, least suspicious of men, was perplexed, and avowed his inability to understand it. As for Mrs Strangeways – a woman of the world, if there was one – the fact had but to be mentioned to her, and on the moment she saw its meaning. No wonder the matter had been kept so quiet. But for the honesty of the duped husband no one at all would have heard of it.

Arriving at the house a little before her time, she found her hostess a prey to vexation.

'My dear, he can't come. It's most annoying. Only an hour ago I had a telegram – look – '

The despatch was from Coventry: 'Don't expect me. Detained on business. Redgrave.' It rustled in Alma's hand, and she had much ado to keep herself from tears of angry chagrin.

'He had promised to be here,' went on Mrs Strangeways. 'I thought nothing would have kept him away.'

'Do you mean,' asked Alma bluntly, 'that he knew I was coming?'

'I had said that I half expected you. Don't be vexed, dear. I did so wish you to meet.'

'If he's at Coventry,' Alma continued, 'it must be on *that* business.'

'It seems likely. Do sit down. You still look anything but yourself. Pray, pray remember that you have only a day or two—'

'Don't worry me, please,' said Alma, with a contemptuous gesture.

She had thrown off reserve, caring only, now the first step was taken, to make all possible use of this woman whom she detested. Her voice showed the change that had been wrought in her; she addressed her hostess almost as though speaking to an inferior.

'What do you think it means, his keeping away?'

'Business, possibly. More likely – the other thing I spoke of.'

In this reply Mrs Strangeways modified her tone, discarding

mellifluous tenderness, yet not going quite so far as Alma in neglect of appearances. She was an older woman, and had learnt the injudiciousness of impulsive behaviour.

'Speak plainly – it saves time. You think he won't care to meet me at all again?'

'I don't say that. I should be very sorry indeed to think it. But – to speak as plainly as you wish, dear – I know that someone must have said unpleasant things to him about your – your friendship with Mr Dymes.'

'Are you hinting at anyone in particular?' Alma asked, salving her self-respect with a poor affectation of haughtiness.

'Ask yourself, my dear, who is at all likely to give him such information.'

'Information?' Alma's eyes flashed. 'That's a strange word to use. Do you imagine there is any information of that kind to be given?'

'I spoke carelessly,' answered the other, smiling. 'Do sit down, dear Mrs Rolfe. I'm sure you will overtax your strength before Tuesday. I meant nothing whatever, I assure you.'

Reluctantly Alma became seated, and the conversation was prolonged. Without disguise they debated the probability that Redgrave was being estranged from Alma by Sibyl Carnaby; of course, taking for granted Sibyl's guilt, and presuming that she feared rivalry. From time to time Alma threw out scornful assertion of her own security; she was bold to the point of cynicism, and recklessly revealed herself. The other listened attentively, still smiling, but without constraint upon her features; at moments she appeared to feel something of admiration.

'There are several things in your favour,' she remarked deliberately, when Alma had declared a resolve to triumph at all hazards. 'Above all – but one need not mention it.'

'What? I don't understand.'

'Oh, I'm sure you do! You alluded to it the other day. Some women have such tiresome husbands.'

The look which accompanied this struck Alma cold. She sat motionless, staring at the speaker.

'What do you mean? You think that my husband – ?'

'I meant only to encourage you, my dear.'

'You think that my husband has less sense of honour than Mr Carnaby?'

Mrs Strangeways looked wonderingly at her.

'How strange you are! Could I have dreamt of saying anything so ill-mannered?'

'You implied it!' exclaimed Alma, her voice thrilling on the note of indignation. 'How dare you so insult me! Is it possible that you have such thoughts?'

Overcome by what seemed to her the humour of the situation, Mrs Strangeways frankly laughed.

'I beg your pardon a thousand times, my dear Mrs Rolfe! I have misunderstood, I am afraid. You *are* quite serious? Yes, yes, there has been a misunderstanding. Pray forgive me.'

Alma rose from her chair. 'There *has* been a misunderstanding. If you knew my husband – if you had once met him – such a thought could never have entered your mind. You compare him to his disadvantage with Mr Carnaby? What right have you to do that? I believe in Mr Carnaby's honesty, and do you know why? – because he is my husband's friend. But for *that*, I should suspect him.'

'My dear,' replied Mrs Strangeways, 'you are wonderful. I prophesy great things for you. I never in my life met so interesting a woman.'

'You may be as sarcastic as you please,' Alma retorted, in a low, passionate voice. 'I suppose you believe in no one?'

'I have said, dear, that I believe in *you*; and I shall think it the greatest misfortune if I lose your friendship for a mere indiscretion. Indeed, I was only trying to understand you completely.'

'You do – now.'

They did not part in hostility. Mrs Strangeways had the best of reasons for averting this issue, at any cost to her own feelings, which for the moment had all but escaped control. Though the complications of Alma's character puzzled her exceedingly, she knew how to smooth over the trouble which had so unexpectedly arisen. Flattery was the secret of her influence with Mrs Rolfe, and it still availed her. With ostentation of frankness, she pointed a contrast between Alma and her presumed rival. Mrs Carnaby was the corrupt, unscrupulous woman, who shrank from nothing to gratify a base selfishness. Alma was the artist, pursuing a legitimate ambition, using, as she had a perfect right to do, all her natural resources, but pure in soul.

'Yes, I understand you at last, and I admire you more than ever. You will go far, my dear. You have great gifts, and, more than that, you have principle. It is character that tells in the long run. And depend upon me. I shall soon have news for you. Keep quiet; prepare yourself for next Tuesday. As for all *that* – leave it to me.'

Scarcely had Alma left the house, when she suddenly stood still, as though she had forgotten something. Indeed she had. In the flush of loyal resentment which repelled an imputation upon her husband's honour, she had entirely lost sight of her secret grievance against Harvey. Suddenly revived, the memory helped her to beat down that assaulting shame which took advantage of reaction in mind and blood. Harvey was not honest with her. Go as far as she might, short of the unpardonable, there still remained to her a moral superiority over the man she defended. And yet – she was glad to have defended him; it gave her a sense of magnanimity. More than that, the glow of an honest thought was strangely pleasant.

She had sundry people to see and pieces of business to transact. What a nuisance that she lived so far from the centre of things! It was this perpetual travelling that had disordered her health, and made everything twice as troublesome as it need be. Today, again, she had a headache, and the scene with Mrs Strangeways had made it worse.

In Regent Street she met Dymes. She was not afraid of him now, for she had learnt how to make him keep his distance; and after the great day, if he continued to trouble her, he might be speedily sent to the right-about. He made an inspiriting report: already a considerable number of tickets had been sold – enough, he said, or all but enough, to clear expenses.

'What, advertising and all?' asked Alma.

'Oh, leave that to me. Advertising is a work of art. If you like just to come round to my rooms, I'll—'

'Haven't time today. See you at the Hall on Monday.'

A batch of weekly newspapers which arrived next morning, Saturday, proved to her that Dymes was sufficiently active. There were more paragraphs; there were two reproductions of her portrait; and as for advertisements, she tried, with some anxiety, to conjecture the cost of these liberal slices of page, with their eye-attracting type. Naturally the same question would occur to her husband, but Harvey kept his word; whatever he thought, he said nothing. And Alma found it easier to be good-humoured with him than at any time since she had read Mary Abbott's letter; perhaps yesterday's event accounted for it.

They dined at the Carnabys', the first time for months that they had dined from home together. Harvey would have shirked the occasion, had it been possible. With great relief, he found that the guests were all absolute strangers to him, and that they represented society in its better sense, with no suggestion of the 'half-world' – no Mrs Strangeways or Mrs Rayner Mann. Alma, equally conscious of the fact, viewed it as a calculated insult. Sibyl had brought her here to humiliate her. She entered the doors with jealous hatred boiling in her heart, and fixed her eyes on Sibyl with such fire of malicious scrutiny that the answer was a gaze of marked astonishment. But they had no opportunity for private talk. Sibyl, as hostess, bore herself with that perfect manner which no effort and no favour of circumstance would ever enable Mrs Rolfe to imitate. Envying every speech and every movement, knowing that her own absent behaviour and forced talk must produce an unpleasant impression upon the well-bred strangers, she longed to expose the things unspeakable that lay beneath this surface of social brilliancy. What was more, she would do it when time was ripe. Only this consciousness of power to crush her enemy enabled her to bear up through the evening.

At the dinner-table she chanced to encounter Sibyl's look. She smiled. There was disquiet in that glance – furtive inquiry and apprehension.

No music. Alma would have doubted whether any of these people were aware of her claim to distinction, had not a lady who talked with her after dinner hinted, rather than announced, an intention of being present at Prince's Hall next Tuesday. None of the fuss and adulation to which she was grown accustomed; no underbred compliments; no ambiguous glances from men. It angered her to observe that Harvey did not seem at all wearied; that he conversed more naturally than usual in a mixed company, especially with the hostess. One whisper – and how would Harvey look upon his friend's wife? But the moment had not come.

She left as early as possible, parting from Sibyl as she had met her, with eyes that scarce dissembled their malignity.

When Hugh and his wife were left together, Sibyl abstained

from remark on Alma; it was Carnaby who introduced the subject. 'Don't you think Mrs Rolfe looked seedy?'

'Work and excitement,' was the quiet answer. 'I think it more than likely she will break down.'

'It's a confounded pity. Why, she has grown old all at once. She's losing her good looks. Did you notice that her eyes were a little bloodshot?'

'Yes, I noticed it. I didn't like her look at all.'

Hugh, as his custom was, paced the floor. Nowadays he could not keep still, and he had contracted an odd habit of swinging his right arm, with fist clenched, as though relieving his muscles after some unusual constraint.

'By Jove, Sibyl, when I compare her with you! – I feel sorry for Rolfe; can't help it. Why didn't you stop this silly business before it went so far?'

'That's a characteristic question, dear boy,' Sibyl replied merrily. 'There are more things in life – particularly woman's life – than your philosophy ever dreamt of. Alma has quite outgrown me, and I begin to suspect that she won't honour me with her acquaintance much longer.'

'Why?'

'For one thing, we belong to different worlds, don't you see; and the difference, in future, will be rather considerable.'

'Well, I'm sorry. Rolfe isn't half the man he was. Why on earth didn't *he* stop it? He hates it, anyone can see. Why, if I were in his place—'

Sibyl interrupted with her mellow laughter.

'You wouldn't be a bit wiser. It's the fate of men – except those who have the courage to beat their wives. You know you came back to England at my heels when you didn't want to. Now, a little energy, a little practice with the horsewhip –'

Carnaby made pretence of laughing. But he turned away his face; the jest had too serious an application. Yes, yes, if he had disregarded Sibyl's wishes, and stayed on the other side of the world! It seemed to him strange that she could speak of the subject so lightly; he must have been more successful than he thought in concealing his true state of mind.

'Rolfe tells me he has got a house at Gunnersbury.'

'Yes; he mentioned it to me. Why Gunnersbury? There must be some reason they don't tell us.'

'Ask his wife,' said Hugh, impatiently. 'No doubt the choice is hers.'

'No doubt. But I don't think,' added Sibyl musingly, 'I shall ask Alma that or anything else. I don't think I care much for Alma in her new development. For a time I shall try leaving her alone.'

'Well, I'm sorry for poor old Rolfe,' repeated Hugh.


## CHAPTER 12

On Monday morning Hugh Carnaby received a letter from Mrs Ascott Larkfield. It was years since Sibyl's mother had written to him, and the present missive, scrawled in an unsteady hand, gave him some concern. Mrs Larkfield wrote that she was very ill, so ill that she had abandoned hope of recovery. She asked him whether, as her son-in-law, he thought it right that she should be abandoned to the care of strangers. It was the natural result, no doubt, of her impoverished condition; such was the world; had she still been wealthy, her latter days would not have been condemned to solitude. But let him remember that she still had in her disposal an income of about six hundred pounds, which, under ordinary circumstances, would have passed to Sibyl; by a will on the point of being executed, this money would benefit a charitable institution. To him this might be a matter of indifference; she merely mentioned the fact to save Sibyl a possible disappointment.

Hugh and his wife, when both had read the letter, exchanged uneasy glances.

'It isn't the money,' said Carnaby. 'Hang the money! But – after all, Sibyl, she's your mother.'

'And what does *that* mean?' Sibyl returned coldly. 'Shall I feel the least bit of sorrow if she dies? Am I to play the hypocrite just because this woman brought me into the world? We have always hated each other, and whose fault? When I was a child, she left me to dirty-minded, thieving servants; they were my teachers, and it's wonderful enough that – that nothing worse came of it. When I grew up, she left me to do as I pleased –

anything so that I gave her no trouble. Do you wish me to go and pretend—'

'I tell you what – I'll run down to Weymouth myself, shall I? Perhaps I might arrange something – for her comfort, I mean.'

Sibyl carelessly assented. Having business in town, Hugh could not start till afternoon, but he would reach Weymouth by half-past six, and might manage to be back again in time for Mrs Rolfe's concert tomorrow.

'I shouldn't put myself to any inconvenience on that account,' said Sibyl, smiling.

'Out of regard for Rolfe, that's all.'

He left home at eleven, transacted his business, and at half-past one turned in for lunch at a Strand restaurant before proceeding to Waterloo. As he entered, he saw Mrs Rolfe, alone at one of the tables; she was drawing on her gloves, about to leave. They met with friendly greeting, though Hugh, from the look with which Mrs Rolfe recognised him, had a conviction that his growing dislike of her was fully reciprocated. In the brief talk before Alma withdrew, he told her that he was going down into the country.

'To Coventry?' she asked, turning her eyes upon him.

'No; to Weymouth. Mrs Larkfield is no better, I'm afraid, and – Sibyl wants me to see her.'

'Then you won't be back—'

'For tomorrow? – oh yes, I shall certainly be back in time, unless anything very serious prevents me. There's a good train from Weymouth at 10.10 – gets in about half-past two. I shall easily get to Prince's Hall by three.'

Alma again regarded him, and seemed on the point of saying something, but she turned her head, rose, and rather hastily took leave. Hugh remarked to himself that she looked even worse by daylight than in the evening; decidedly, she was making herself ill – perhaps, he added, the best thing that could happen.

For his luncheon he had small appetite. The journey before him was a nuisance, and the meeting at the end of it more disagreeable than anything he had ever undertaken. What a simple matter life would be, but for women! That Sibyl should detest her mother was perhaps natural enough, all things considered; but he heartily wished they were on better terms. He felt that Sibyl must have suffered in character, to some extent, by this abnormal antipathy. He did not blame her; her self-defence this morning proved that she had ground for judging her mother sternly; and perhaps, as she declared, only by her own strength and goodness had she been saved from the worst results of parental neglect. Hugh did not often meditate upon such things, but just now he felt impatience and disgust with women who would not care properly for their children. Poor old Rolfe's wife, for instance, what business had she to be running at large about London, giving concerts, making herself ill and ugly, whilst her little son was left to a governess and servants! He had half a mind to write a letter to old Rolfe. But no; that kind of thing was too dangerous, even between the nearest friends. Men must not quarrel; women did more than enough of that. Sibyl and Alma had as good as fallen out; the less they saw of each other the better. And now he had to face a woman, perhaps dying, who would doubtless rail by the hour at her own daughter.

O heaven! for a breath of air on sea or mountain or prairie! Could he stand this life much longer?

Driving to Waterloo, he thought of Mrs Larkfield's bequest to the charitable institution. Six hundred pounds might be a paltry income, but one could make use of it. A year ago, to be sure, he would have felt more troubled by the loss; at present he had reason to look forward hopefully, so far as money could represent hope. The cycle business was moving; as likely as not, it would ultimately enrich him. There was news, too, from that fellow Dando in Queensland, who declared that his smelting process, gradually improved, had begun to yield results, and talked of starting a new company. Hugh's business of the morning had been in this connection: by inquiry in the City he had learnt that Dando's report might be relied upon, and that capital which had seemingly vanished would certainly yield a small dividend this year. He was thankful that he could face Mrs Larkfield without the shame of interested motives. Let her do what she liked with her money; he went to see the woman merely out of humane feeling, sense of duty; and assuredly no fortune-hunter had ever imposed upon himself a more distasteful office.

On alighting at the station, he found that the only coin, other than gold, which he had in his pocket was a shilling. In accordance with usage, he would have given the cabman an extra sixpence, had he possessed it. When the man saw a tender of his legal fare, he, also in accordance with usage, broadened his mouth, tossed the coin on his palm, and pointedly refrained from thanks. At another time Hugh might have disregarded this professional suavity, but a little thing exasperated his present mood.

'Well?' he exclaimed, in a voice that drew the attention of everyone near. 'Is it your fare or not? Learn better manners, vicious brute!'

Before the driver could recover breath to shout a primitive insult, Hugh walked into the station. Here, whilst his wrath was still hot, a man tearing at full speed to catch a train on another platform bumped violently against him. He clenched his fist, and, but for the gasped apology, might have lost himself in blind rage. As it was, he inwardly cursed railway stations, cursed England, cursed civilisation. His muscles were quivering; sweat had started to his forehead. A specialist in nervous pathology would have judged Hugh Carnaby a dangerous person on this Monday afternoon.

He took his ticket, and, having some minutes to wait, moved towards the bookstall. By his side, as he scanned the papers, stood a lady who had just made a purchase; the salesman seemed to have handed her insufficient change, for she said to him, in a clear, business-like voice, 'It was half-a-crown that I gave you.'

At the sound of these words, Hugh turned sharply and looked at the speaker. She was a woman of thirty-five, solidly built, well dressed without display of fashion; the upper part of her face was hidden by a grey veil, through which her eyes shone. Intent on recovering her money, she did not notice that the man beside her was looking and listening with the utmost keenness; nor, on turning away at length, was she aware that Hugh followed. He pursued her, at a yard's distance, down the platform, and into the covered passage which leads to another part of the station. Here, perhaps because the footstep behind her sounded distinctly, she gave a backward glance, and her veiled eyes met Carnaby's. At once he stepped to her side. 'I don't think I can be mistaken,' were his low, cautiously-spoken words, whilst he gazed into her face with stern fixedness. 'You remember me, Mrs Maskell, no doubt.'

'I do not, sir. You certainly *are* mistaken.'

She replied in a voice which so admirably counterfeited a French accent that Hugh could not but smile, even whilst setting his teeth in anger at her impudence.

'Oh! that settles it. As you have two tongues, you naturally have two names – probably more. I happened to be standing by you at the bookstall a moment ago. It's a great bore; I was just starting on a journey; but I must trouble you to come with me to the nearest police station. You have too much sense to make any fuss about it.'

The woman glanced this way and that. Two or three people were hurrying through the passage, but they perceived nothing unusual.

'You have a choice,' said Carnaby, 'between my companionship and that of the policeman. Make up your mind.'

'I don't think you will go so far as that, Mr Carnaby,' said the other, with self-possession and in her natural voice.

'Why not?'

'Because I can tell you something that will interest you very much – something that nobody else can.'

'What do you mean?' he asked roughly.

'It refers to your wife; that's all I need say just now.'

'You are lying.'

'As you please. Let us go.'

She moved on with unhurried step, and turned towards the nearest cab-rank. Pausing within sight of the vehicles, she looked again at her companion.

'Would you rather have a little quiet talk with me in a four-wheeler, or drive straight to – ?'

Hugh's brain was in commotion. The hint of secrets concerning his wife had not its full effect in the moment of utterance; it sounded the common artifice of a criminal. But Mrs Maskell's cool audacity gave significance to her words; the two minutes' walk had made Hugh as much afraid of her as she could be of him. He stared at her, beset with horrible doubts.

'Won't it be a pity to miss your train?' she said, with a friendly smile. 'I can give you my address.'

'No doubt you can. Look here – it was a toss-up whether I should let you go or not, until you said *that*. If you had begged off, ten to one I should have thought I might as well save myself trouble. But after that cursed lie—'

'That's the second time you've used the word, Mr Carnaby.

I'm not accustomed to it, and I shouldn't have thought you would speak in that way to a lady.'

He was aghast at her assurance, which, for some reason, made him only the more inclined to listen to her. He beckoned a cab.

'Where shall we drive to?'

'Say Clapham Junction.'

They entered the four-wheeler, and, as soon as it began to move out of the station, Mrs Maskell leaned back. Her claim to be considered a lady suffered no contradiction from her look, her movements, or her speech; throughout the strange dialogue she had behaved with remarkable self-command, and made use of the aptest phrases without a sign of effort. In the years which had elapsed since she filled the position of housekeeper to Mrs Carnaby, she seemed to have gained in the externals of refinement; though even at that time her manners were noticeably good.

'Raise your veil, please,' said Hugh, when he had pulled up the second window.

She obliged him, and showed a face of hard yet regular outline, which would have been almost handsome but for its high cheek-bones and coarse lips.

'And you have been going about all this time, openly?'

'With discretion. I am not perfect, unfortunately. Rather than lose sixpence at the bookstall, I forgot myself. That's a woman's weakness; we don't easily get over it.'

'What put it into your head to speak of my wife?'

'I had to gain time, had I not?'

In a sudden burst of wrath, Hugh banged the window open; but, before he could call to the cabman, a voice sounded in his ear, a clear quick whisper, the lips that spoke all but touching him.

'Do you know that your wife is Mr Redgrave's mistress?'

He fell back. There was no blood in his face; his eyes stared hideously.

'Say that again, and I'll crush the life out of you!'

'You look like it, but you won't. My information is too valuable.'

'It's the vilest lie ever spoken by whore and thief.'

'You are not polite, Mr Carnaby.'

She still controlled herself, but in fear, as quick glances

showed. And her fear was not unreasonable; the man glared murder.

'Stop that, and tell me what you have to say.'

Mrs Maskell raised the window again.

'You have compelled me, you see. It's a pity. I don't want to make trouble.'

'What do you know of Redgrave?'

'I keep house for him at Wimbledon.'

'You?'

'Yes. I have done so for about a year.'

'And does he know who you are?'

'Well – perhaps not quite. He engaged me on the Continent. A friend of his (and of mine) recommended me, and he had reason to think I should be trustworthy. Don't misunderstand me. I am housekeeper – *rien de plus*. It's a position of confidence. Mr Redgrave – but you know him.'

The listener's face was tumid and discoloured, his eyes bloodshot. With fearful intensity he watched every movement of Mrs Maskell's features.

'How do you know I know him?'

'You've been at his place. I've seen you, though you didn't see me; and before I saw you I heard your voice. One remembers voices, you know.'

'Go on. What else have you seen or heard?'

'Mrs Carnaby has been there too.'

'I know that!' Hugh shouted rather than spoke. 'She was there with Mrs Fenimore – Redgrave's sister – and several other people.'

'Yes; last summer. I caught sight of her as she was sitting in the veranda, and it amused me to think how little she suspected who was looking at her. But she has been there since.'

'When?'

Mrs Maskell consulted her memory, and indicated a day in the past winter. She could not at this moment recall the exact date, but had a note of it. Mrs Carnaby came at a late hour of the evening, and left very early the next day.

'How are you going to make this lie seem probable?' asked Hugh, a change of voice betraying the dread with which he awaited her answer; for the time of which she spoke was exactly that when Redgrave had offered himself as a partner in the firm of Mackintosh & Co. 'Do you want me to believe that she came and went so that every one could see her?'

'Oh no. I was new to the place then, and full of curiosity. I have my own ways of getting to know what I wish to know. Remember, once more, that it's very easy to recognise a voice. I told you that I was in a position of confidence. Whenever Mr Redgrave wishes for quietness, he has only to mention it; our servants are well disciplined. I, of course, am never seen by visitors, whoever they may be, and whenever they come; but it happens occasionally that I see *them*, even when Mr Redgrave doesn't think it. Still, he is sometimes very careful indeed, and so he was on that particular evening. You remember that his rooms have French windows – a convenient arrangement. The front door may be locked and bolted, but people come and go for all that.'

'That's the bungalow, is it?' muttered Carnaby. 'And how often do you pretend you have heard *her* voice?'

'Only that once.'

It was worse than if she had answered 'Several times.' Hugh looked long at her, and she bore his gaze with indifference.

'You don't pretend that you *saw* her?'

'No, I didn't see her.'

'Then, if you are not deliberately lying, you have made a mistake.'

Mrs Maskell smiled and shook her head.

'What *words* did you hear?'

'Oh – talk. Nothing very particular.'

'I want to know what it was.'

'Well, as far as I could make out, Mrs Carnaby was going to get a bicycle, and wanted to know what was the best. Not much harm in that,' she added, with a silent laugh.

Hugh sat with his hands on his knees, bending forward. He said nothing for a minute or two, and at length looked to the window.

'You were going back to Wimbledon?'

'Yes. I have only been in town for an hour or two.'

'Is Redgrave there?'

'No; he's away.'

'Very well; I am going with you. You will find out for me on what date that happened.'

'Certainly. But what is the understanding between us?'

Hugh saw too well that any threat would be idle. Whether this woman had told the truth or not, her position in Redgrave's house, and the fact of Redgrave's connection with the firm of Mackintosh – of which she evidently was not aware – put it in her power to strike a fatal blow at Sibyl. He still assured himself that she was lying – how doubt it and maintain his sanity? – but the lie had a terrible support in circumstances. Who could hear this story without admitting the plausibility of its details? A man such as Redgrave, wealthy and a bachelor; a woman such as Sibyl, beautiful, fond of luxurious living; her husband in an embarrassed position – how was it that he, a man of the world, had never seen things in this light? Doubtless his anxiety had blinded him; that, and his absolute faith in Sibyl, and Redgrave's frank friendliness. Even if he obtained (as he would) complete evidence of Sibyl's honesty, Mrs Maskell could still dare him to take a step against her. How many people were at her mercy? He might be sure that she would long ago have stood in the dock but for her ability to make scandalous and ruinous revelations. Did Redgrave know that he had a high-class criminal in his employment? Possibly he knew it well enough. There was no end to the appalling suggestiveness of this discovery. Hugh remembered what he had said in talk with Harvey Rolfe about the rottenness of society. Never had he felt himself so much a coward as in face of this woman, whose shameless smile covered secrets and infamies innumerable.

The cabman was bidden drive on to Wimbledon, and, with long pauses, the dialogue continued for an hour. Hugh interrogated and cross-examined his companion on every matter of which she could be induced to speak, yet he learned very little in detail concerning either her own life or Redgrave's; Mrs Maskell was not to be driven to any disclosure beyond what was essential to her own purpose. By dint of skilful effrontery she had gained the upper hand, and no longer felt the least fear of him.

'If I believed you,' said Carnaby, at a certain point of their conversation, 'I should have you arrested straight away. It wouldn't matter to me how the thing came out; it would be public property before long.'

'Where would you find your witnesses?' she asked. 'Leave me alone, and I can be of use to you as no one else can. Behave shabbily, and you only make yourself look foolish, bringing a charge against your wife that you'll never be able to prove. You would get no evidence from me. Whether you want it kept quiet or want to bring it into court, you depend upon my goodwill.'

They reached the end of the road in which was the approach to Redgrave's house.

'You had better wait here,' said the woman. 'I shall be ten minutes or a quarter of an hour. You needn't feel uneasy; I haven't the least intention of running away. Our interests are mutual, and if you do your part you can trust me to do mine.'

She stopped the cab, alighted, told the driver to wait, and walked quickly down the by-road. Hugh, drawn back into a corner, sat with head drooping; for a quarter of an hour he hardly stirred. Twenty minutes, thirty minutes, passed, but Mrs Maskell did not show herself. At length, finding it impossible to sit still any longer, he sprang out, and paced backwards and forwards. Vastly to his relief, the woman at length appeared.

'He is there,' she said. 'I couldn't get away before.'

'Is he alone?'

'Yes. Don't do anything foolish.' Carnaby had looked as if he would move towards the house. 'The slightest imprudence, and you'll only harm yourself.'

'Tell me that date.'

She named it.

'I can't stay longer, and I advise you to get away. If you want to write to me, you can do so without fear; my letters are quite safe. Address to Mrs Lant. And remember – !'

With a last significant look she turned and left him. Hugh, mentally repeating the date he had learnt, walked back to the cab, and told the man to drive him to the nearest railway station, whichever it was.

When he reached home, some four hours had elapsed since his encounter with Mrs Maskell (or Mrs Lant) at Waterloo; it seemed to him a whole day. He had forgotten all about his purposed journey to Weymouth. One sole desire had possession of him to stand face to face with Sibyl, and to *see* her innocence, rather than hear it, as soon as he had brought his tongue to repeat that foul calumny. He would then know how to deal with the creature who thought to escape him by slandering his wife.

He let himself in with his latchkey, and entered the drawing-room; it was vacant. He looked into other rooms; no one was there. He rang, and a servant came.

'Has Mrs Carnaby been out long?'

She had left, was the reply, at half-past two. Whilst she sat at luncheon a telegram arrived for her, and, soon after, she prepared to go out, saying that she would not return tonight.

Not return tonight? Hugh scarcely restrained an exclamation, and had much ado to utter his next words.

'Did she mention where she was going?'

'No, sir. I took the dressing-bag down to the cab, and the cabman was told to drive to the post-office.'

'Very well. That will do.'

'Shall you dine at home, sir?'

'Dine? No.'

Sibyl gone away for the night? Where could she have gone to? He began to look about for the telegram she had received; it might be lying somewhere, and possibly would explain her departure. In the waste-paper basket he found the torn envelope lying at the top; but the despatch itself was not to be discovered.

Gone for the night? and just when he was supposed to have left town? The cabman told to drive to the post-office? This might be for the purpose of despatching a reply. Yet no; the reply would have been written at once and sent by the messenger in the usual way. Unless – unless Sibyl, for some reason, preferred to send the message more privately? Or again, she might not care to let the servant know whither the cab was really to convey her.

Sheer madness, all this. Had not Sibyl fifty legitimate ways of spending a night from home? Yet there was the fact that she had never before done so unexpectedly. Never before – ?

He looked at his watch; half-past six. He rang the bell again.

'Has any one called since Mrs Carnaby left home?'

'Yes, sir; there have been three calls. Mrs Rolfe—'

'Mrs Rolfe?'

'Yes, sir. She seemed very disappointed. I told her Mrs Carnaby would not be back tonight.'

'And the others?'

Two persons of no account. Hugh dismissed them, and the servant, with a wave of the hand.

He felt a faintness such as accompanies extreme hunger, but had no inclination for food. The whisky bottle was a natural resource; a tumbler of right Scotch restored his circulation, and in a few minutes gave him a raging appetite. He could not eat here; but eat he must, and that quickly. Seizing his hat, he ran down the stairs, hailed a hansom, and drove to the nearest restaurant he could think of.

After eating without knowledge of the viands, and drinking a bottle of claret in like unconsciousness, he smoked for half an hour, his eyes vacantly set, his limbs lax and heavy, as though in the torpor of difficult digestion. When the cigar was finished, he roused himself, looked at the time, and asked for a railway guide. There was a train to Wimbledon at ten minutes past eight; he might possibly catch it. Starting into sudden activity, he hastily left the restaurant, and reached Waterloo Station with not a moment to spare.

At Wimbledon he took a cab, and was driven up the hill. Under a clouded sky, dusk had already changed to darkness; the evening was warm and still. Impatient with what he thought the slow progress of the vehicle, Hugh sat with his body bent forward, straining as did the horse, on which his eyes were fixed, and perspiring in the imaginary effort. The address he had given was Mrs Fenimore's; but when he drew near he signalled to the driver: 'Stop at the gate. Don't drive up.'

From the entrance to Mrs Fenimore's round to the by-road which was the direct approach to Redgrave's bungalow would be a walk of some ten minutes. Hugh had his reasons for not taking this direction. Having dismissed his cab, he entered by the lodge-gate, and walked up the drive, moving quickly, and with a lighter step than was natural to him. When he came within view of the house, he turned aside, and made his way over the grass, in the deep shadow of leafy lime-trees, until the illumined windows were again hidden from him. He had seen no one, and heard no sound. A path which skirted the gardens would bring him in a few minutes to Redgrave's abode; this he found and followed.

The bungalow was built in a corner of the park where previously had stood a gardener's cottage; round about it grew a few old trees, and on two sides spread a shrubbery, sheltering the newly-made lawn and flower-beds. Here it was very dark; Hugh advanced cautiously, stopping now and then to listen. He reached a point where the front of the house became visible. A light shone at the door, but there was no movement, and Hugh could hear only his own hard breathing.

He kept behind the laurels, and made a half-circuit of the house. On passing to the farther side, he would come within view of those windows which opened so conveniently, as Mrs Maskell had said – the windows of Redgrave's sitting-room, drawing-room, study, or whatever he called it. To this end it was necessary to quit the cover of the shrubs and cross a lawn. As he stepped on to the mown grass, his ear caught a sound, the sound of talking in a subdued tone; it came, he thought, from that side of the building which he could not yet see. A few quick silent steps, and this conjecture became a certainty: someone was talking within a few yards of him, just round the obstructing corner, and he felt sure the voice was Redgrave's. It paused; another voice made reply, but in so low a murmur that its accents were not to be recognised. That it was the voice of a woman the listener had no doubt. Spurred by a choking anguish, he moved forward. He saw two figures standing in a dim light from the window-door – a man and a woman; the man bareheaded, his companion in outdoor clothing. At the same moment he himself was perceived. He heard a hurried 'Go in!' and at once the woman disappeared.

Face to face with Redgrave, he looked at the window; but the curtain which dulled the light from within concealed everything.

'Who was that?'

'Why – Carnaby? What the deuce—?'

'Who was *that*?'

'Who? – what do you mean?'

Carnaby took a step; Redgrave laid an arresting hand upon him. There needed but this touch. In frenzied wrath, yet with the precision of trained muscle, Hugh struck out; and Redgrave went down before him – thudding upon the door of the veranda like one who falls dead.

## CHAPTER 13

He forced the window; he rushed into the room, and there before him, pallid, trembling, agonising, stood Alma Rolfe.

'You?'

She panted incoherent phrases. She was here to speak with Mr Redgrave on business – about her concert tomorrow. She had not entered the house until this moment. She had met Mr Redgrave in the garden—'

'What is that to me?' broke in Hugh, staring wildly, his fist still clenched. 'I am not your husband.'

'Mr Carnaby, you *will* believe me? I came for a minute or two – to speak about—'

'It's nothing to me, Mrs Rolfe,' he again interrupted her, in a hoarse, faint voice. 'What have I done?' He looked to the window, whence came no sound. 'Have I gone mad? By God, I almost fear it!'

'You believe me, Mr Carnaby?' She moved to him and seized his hand. 'You know me too well – you know I couldn't – say you believe me! Say one kind, friendly word!'

She looked distracted. Clinging to his hand, she burst into tears. But Hugh hardly noticed her; he kept turning towards the window, with eyes of unutterable misery.

'Wait here; I'll come back.'

He stepped out from the window, and saw that Redgrave lay just where he had fallen – straight, still, his face turned upwards. Hugh stooped, and moved him into the light; the face was deathly – placid, but for its wide eyes, which seemed to look at his enemy. No blood upon the lips; no sign of violence.

'Where did I hit him? He fell with his head against something, I suppose.'

From the parted lips there issued no perceptible breath. A fear, which was more than half astonishment, took hold upon Carnaby. He looked up – for the light was all at once obstructed – and saw Alma gazing at him.

'What is it?' she asked in a terrified whisper. 'Why is he lying there?'

'I struck him – he is unconscious.'

'Struck him?'

He drew her into the room again.

'Mrs Rolfe, I shall most likely have to send for help. You mustn't be seen here. It's nothing to me why you came – yes, yes, I believe you – but you must go at once.'

'You won't speak of it?'

Her appeal was that of a child, helpless in calamity. Again she caught his hand, as if clinging for protection. Hugh replied in thick, hurried tones.

'I have enough trouble of my own. This is no place for you. For your own sake, if not for your husband's, keep away from here. I came because someone was telling foul lies – the kind of lies that drive a man mad. Whatever happens – whatever you hear – don't imagine that *she* is to blame. You understand me?'

'No word shall ever pass my lips!'

'Go at once. Get home as soon as you can.'

Alma turned to go. Outside, she cast one glance at the dark, silent, unmoving form, then bowed her head, and hastened away into the darkness.

Again Hugh knelt by Redgrave's side, raised his head, listened for the beating of his heart, tried to feel his breath. He then dragged him into the room, and placed him upon a divan; he loosened the fastenings about his neck; the head drooped, and there was not a sign of life. Next he looked for a bell; the electric button caught his eye, and he pressed it. To prevent any one from coming in, he took his stand close by the door. In a moment there was a knock, the door opened, and he showed his face to the surprised maid-servant.

'Is Mrs Lant in the house?'

'Yes, sir.'

'Mr Redgrave wants her at once; he is ill.'

The servant vanished. Keeping his place at the door, and looking out into the hall, Hugh, for full two minutes, heard no movement; then he was startled by a low voice immediately behind him.

'What are you doing here?'

The housekeeper, who had entered from the garden, and approached in perfect silence, stood gazing at him; not unconcerned, but with full command of herself.

'Look!' he replied, pointing to the figure on the divan. 'Is he only insensible – or dead?'

She stepped across the room, and made a brief examination by the methods Carnaby himself had used.

'I never saw any one look more like dead,' was her quiet remark. 'What have you been up to? A little quiet murder?'

'I met him outside. We quarrelled, and I knocked him down.'

'And why are you here at all?' asked the woman, with fierce eyes, though her voice kept its ordinary level.

'Because of you and your talk – curse you! Can't you do something? Get some brandy; and send someone for a doctor.'

'Are you going to be found here?' she inquired meaningly.

Hugh drew a deep breath, and stared at the silent figure. For an instant his face showed irresolution; then it changed, and he said harshly – 'Yes, I am. Do as I told you. Get the spirits, and send someone – sharp!'

'Mr Carnaby, you're a great blundering thickhead – if you care for my opinion of you. You deserve all you've got and all you'll get.'

Hugh again breathed deeply. The woman's abuse was nothing to him.

'Are you going to do anything!' he said. 'Or shall I ring for someone else?'

She left the room, and speedily returned with a decanter of brandy. All their exertions proved useless; the head hung aside, the eyes stared. In a few minutes Carnaby asked whether a doctor had been sent for.

'Yes. When I hear him at the door I shall go away. You came here against my advice, and you've made a pretty job of it. Well, you'll always get work at a slaughter-house.'

Her laugh was harder to bear than the words it followed. Hugh, with a terrible look, waved her away from him.

'Go – or I don't know what I may do next. Take yourself out of my sight! – out!'

She gave way before him, backing to the door; there she laughed again, waved her hand in a contemptuous farewell, and withdrew.

For half an hour Carnaby stood by the divan, or paced the room. Once or twice he imagined a movement of Redgrave's features, and bent to regard them closely; but in truth there was no slightest change. Within doors and without prevailed unbroken silence; not a step, not a rustle. The room seemed to grow intolerably hot. Wiping the sweat from his forehead, Hugh went to the window and opened it a few inches; a scent of vegetation and of fresh earth came to him with the cool air. He noticed that rain had begun to fall, large drops pattering softly on leaves and grass and the roof of the veranda. Then sounded the rolling of carriage wheels, nearer and nearer. It was the doctor's carriage, no doubt.

Uncertainty soon came to an end. Cyrus Redgrave was beyond

help: he must have breathed his last – so said the doctor – at the moment when he fell. Not as a result of the fall; the blow of Carnaby's fist had killed him. There is one stroke which, if delivered with sufficient accuracy and sufficient force, will slay more surely than any other: it is the stroke which catches an uplifted chin just at the right angle to drive the head back and shatter the spinal cord. This had plainly happened. The man's neck was broken, and he died on the spot.

Carnaby and the doctor stood regarding each other. They spoke in subdued voices.

'It was not a fight, you say?'

'One blow from me, that was all. He said something that maddened me.'

'Shall you report yourself?'

'Yes. Here is my card.'

'A sad business, Mr Carnaby, Can I be of any use to you?'

'You can – though I hesitate to ask it. Mrs Fenimore should be told at once. I can't do that myself.'

'I know Mrs Fenimore very well. I will see her – if she is at home.'

On this errand the doctor set forth. As soon as he was gone, Hugh rang the bell; the same domestic as before answered it, and again he asked for Mrs Lant. He waited five minutes; the servant came back, saying that Mrs Lant was not in the house. This did not greatly surprise him, but he insisted on a repetition of the search. Mrs Lant could not be found. Evidently her disappearance was a mystery to this young woman, who seemed ingenuous to the point of simple-mindedness.

'You are not to go into that room,' said Hugh. (They were talking in the hall.) 'The doctor will return presently.'

And therewith he left the house. But not the grounds; for in rain and darkness he stood watching from a place of conceal-ment, watching at the same time Redgrave's curtained window and the front entrance. His patience was not overtaxed. There sounded an approaching vehicle; it came up the drive and stopped at the front door, where at once alighted the doctor and a lady. Hugh's espial was at an end. As the two stepped into the house he walked quickly away.

Yes, he would 'report himself', but not until he had seen Sibyl. To that end he must go home and wait there. The people at Wimbledon, who doubtless would communicate with the police, might cause him to be arrested before his wife's return. He feared this much more than what was to follow. Worse than anything that could befall him would be to lose the opportunity of speaking in private with Sibyl before she knew what had happened.

In the early hours of the morning he lay down upon his bed and had snatches of troubled sleep. Knowing that he was wrong in the particular surmise which led him to Redgrave's house, Sibyl's absence no longer disturbed him with suspicions; a few hours would banish from his mind the last doubt of her, if any really remained. He had played the madman, bringing ruin upon himself and misery incalculable upon his wife, just because that thieving woman lied to him. She, of course, had made her speedy escape; and was it not as well? For, if the whole story became known, what hope was there that Sibyl would come out of it with untarnished fame? Merely for malice' sake, the woman would repeat and magnify her calumnies. If she successfully concealed herself, it might be possible to avoid a mention of Sibyl's name. He imagined various devices for this purpose, his brain plotting even when he slept.

To Alma Rolfe he gave scarcely a thought. If the worst were true of her, Rolfe had only to thank his own absurdity, which allowed such a conceited simpleton to do as she chose. The case looked black against her. Well, she had had her lesson, and in *that* quarter could come to no more harm. What sort of an appearance was she likely to make at Prince's Hall today? – feather-headed fool!

Before five o'clock the sunlight streamed into his bedroom. Sparrows twittered about the window, and somewhere close by, perhaps in a neighbour's flat, a caged throstle piped as though it were in the fields. Then began the street noises, and Hugh could lie still no longer. Remembering that at any moment his freedom might come to an end, he applied himself to arranging certain important matters. The housemaid came upon him with surprise; he bade her get breakfast, and, when the meal was ready, partook of it with moderate appetite.

The postman brought letters; nothing of interest for him, and for Sibyl only an envelope which, as one could feel, contained a mere card of invitation. But soon after nine o'clock there arrived a telegram. It was from Sibyl herself, and – from Weymouth.

'Why are you not here? She died yesterday. If this reaches you, reply at once.'

He flung the scrap of paper aside and laughed. Of all natural explanations, this, of course, had never occurred to him. Yesterday's telegram told of Mrs Larkfield's serious condition, and Sibyl had started at once for Weymouth, expecting to meet him there. One word of hers to the servant and he would simply have followed her. But Sibyl saw no necessity for that word. She was always reserved with domestics.

By the messenger, he despatched a reply. He would be at Weymouth as soon as possible.

He incurred the risk of appearing to run away; but that mattered little. Sibyl could hardly return before her mother's burial, and by going yonder to see her he escaped the worse danger, probably the certainty, of arrest before any possible meeting with her in London. Dreading this more than ever, he made ready in a few minutes; the telegraph boy had hardly left the building before Hugh followed. A glance at the timetables had shown him that, if he travelled by the Great-Western, he could reach Weymouth at five minutes past four; whereas the first train he could catch at Waterloo would not bring him to his destination until half an hour later; on the other hand, he could get away from London by the South-Western forty minutes sooner than by the other line, and this decided him. Yesterday, Waterloo had been merely the more convenient station on account of his business in town; today he chose it because he had to evade arrest on a charge of homicide. So comforted was he by the news from Sibyl, that he could reflect on this joke of destiny, and grimly smile at it.

At the end of his journey he betook himself to an hotel, and immediately sent a message to Sibyl. Before her arrival he had swallowed meat and drink. He waited for her in a private room, which looked seaward. The sight of the blue Channel, the smell of salt breezes, made his heart ache. He was standing at the window, watching a steamer that had just left port, when Sibyl entered; he turned and looked at her in silence.

'What are these mysterious movements?' she asked, coming forward with a smile. 'Why did you alter your mind yesterday?'

'I wasn't well.'

He could say nothing more, yet. Sibyl's face was so tranquil, and she seemed so glad to rejoin him, that his tongue refused to

utter any alarming word; and the more he searched her countenance, the more detestable did it seem that he should insult her
by the semblance of a doubt.

'Not well? Indeed, you look dreadfully out of sorts. How long
had I been gone when you got home again?'

'An hour or two. But tell me first about your mother. She died
before you came?'

'Very soon after they sent the telegram.'

Gravely, but with no affectation of distress, she related the
circumstances; making known, finally, that Mrs Larkfield had
died intestate.

'You are quite sure of that?' asked Hugh, with an eagerness
which surprised her.

'Quite. Almost with her last breath she talked about it, and
said that she *must* make her will. And she had spoken of it
several times lately. The people there knew all about her affairs.
She kept putting it off – and as likely as not she wished the
money to be mine, after all. I am sure she must have felt that
she owed me something.'

Carnaby experienced a profound relief. Sibyl was now provided for, whatever turn his affairs might take. She had seated
herself by the window, and, with her gloved hands crossed upon
her lap, was gazing absently towards the sea. How great must
be *her* relief! thought Hugh. And still he looked at her smooth,
pure features; at her placid eyes, in which, after all, he seemed
to detect a little natural sadness; and the accusation in his mind
assumed so grotesque an incredibility that he asked himself how
he should dare to hint at it.

'Sibyl – '

'Isn't there something you haven't told me?' she said, regarding him with anxiety, when he had just uttered her name and
then averted his look. 'I never saw you look so ill.'

'Yes, dear, there is something.'

It was not often he spoke so gently. Sibyl waited, one of her
hands clasping the other, and her lips close set.

'I was at Wimbledon last night – at Redgrave's.'

He paused again, for the last word choked him. Unless it were
a tremor of the eyelids, no movement betrayed itself in Sibyl's
features; yet their expression had grown cold, and seemed upon
the verge of a disdainful wonder. The pupils of her eyes
insensibly dilated, as though to challenge scrutiny and defy it.

'What of that?' she said, when his silence urged her to speak.

'Something happened between us. We quarrelled.'

Her lips suddenly parted, and he heard her quick breath; but the look that followed was of mere astonishment, and in a moment, before she spoke, it softened in a smile.

'This is your dreadful news? You quarrelled – and he is going to withdraw from the business. Oh, my dear boy, how ridiculous you are! I thought all sorts of horrible things. Were you afraid I should make an outcry? And you have worried yourself into illness about *this*? Oh, foolish fellow!'

Before she ceased, her voice was broken with laughter – a laugh of extravagant gaiety, of mocking mirth, that brought the blood to her face and shook her from head to foot. Only when she saw that her husband's gloom underwent no change did this merriment cease. Then, with abrupt gravity, which was almost annoyance, her eyes shining with moisture and her cheeks flushed, she asked him –

'Isn't that it?'

'Worse than that,' Hugh answered.

But he spoke more freely, for he no longer felt obliged to watch her countenance. His duty now was to soften the outrage involved in repeating Mrs Maskell's fiction by making plain his absolute faith in her, and to contrive his story so as to omit all mention of a third person's presence at the fatal interview.

'Then do tell me and have done!' exclaimed Sibyl, almost petulantly.

'We quarrelled – and I struck him – and the blow was fatal.'

'Fatal? – you mean he was killed?'

The blood vanished from her face, leaving pale horror.

'A terrible accident – a blow that happened to – I couldn't believe it till the doctor came and said he was dead.'

'But tell me more. What led to it? How could you strike Mr Redgrave?'

Sibyl had all at once subdued her voice to an excessive calmness. Her hands were trembling; she folded them again upon her lap. Every line of her face, every muscle of her body, declared the constraint in which she held herself. This, said Hugh inwardly, was no more than he had expected; disaster made noble proof of Sibyl's strength.

'I'll tell you from the beginning.'

He recounted faithfully the incidents at Waterloo Station, and the beginning of Mrs Maskell's narrative in the cab. At the disclosure of her relations with Redgrave, he was interrupted by a short, hard laugh.

'I couldn't help it, Hugh. That woman! – why, you have always said you were sure to meet her somewhere. Housekeeper at Mr Redgrave's! We know what the end of that would be!'

Sibyl talked rapidly, in an excited chatter – the kind of utterance never heard upon her lips.

'It was strange,' Hugh continued. 'Seems to have been mere chance. Then she began to say that she had learnt some of Redgrave's secrets – about people who came and went mysteriously. And then – Sibyl, I can't speak the words. It was the foulest slander that she could have invented. She meant to drive me mad, and she succeeded – curse her!'

Drops of anguish stood upon his forehead. He sprang up and crossed the room. Turning again, he saw his wife gazing at him, as if in utmost perplexity.

'Hugh, I don't in the least understand you. What *was* the slander? Perhaps I am stupid – but – '

He came near, but could not look her in the eyes.

'My dearest' – his voice shook – it was an infamous lie about *you* – that *you* had been there—'

'Why, of course I have! You know that I have.'

'She meant more than that. She said you had been there secretly – at night – '

Hugh Carnaby – the man who had lived as high-blooded men do live, who had laughed by the camp-fire or in the club smoking-room at many a Rabelaisian story and capped it with another, who hated mock modesty, was all for honest openness between man and woman – stood in guilty embarrassment before his own wife's face of innocence. It would have been a sheer impossibility for him to ask her where and how she spent a certain evening last winter; Sibyl, now as ever, was his ideal of chaste womanhood. He scorned himself for what he had yet to tell.

Sibyl was gazing at him, steadily, inquiringly.

'She made you believe this?' fell upon the silence, in her softest, clearest tones.

'No! She couldn't make me *believe* it. But the artful devil had such a way of talking—'

'I understand. You didn't know whether to believe or not. Just tell me, please, what proof she offered you.'

Hugh hung his head.

'She had heard you talking – in the house – on a certain – '

He looked up timidly, and met a flash of derisive scorn.

'She heard me talking? Hugh, I really don't see much art in this. You seem to have been wrought upon rather easily. It never occurred to you, I suppose, to ask for a precise date?'

He mentioned the day, and Sibyl, turning her head a little, appeared to reflect.

'It's unfortunate; I remember nothing whatever of that date. I'm afraid, Hugh, that I couldn't possibly prove an alibi.'

Her smiling sarcasm made the man wince. His broad shoulders shrank together; he stood in an awkward, swaying posture.

'Dear, I told her she lied!'

'That was very courageous. But what came next? You had the happy idea of going to Wimbledon to make personal inquiries?'

'Try to put yourself in my place, Sibyl,' he pleaded. 'Remember all the circumstances. Can't you see the danger of such a lie as that? I went home, hoping to find you there. But you had gone, and nobody knew where – you wouldn't be back that night. A telegram had called you away, I was told. When I asked where you told the cabman to drive you to – the post-office.'

'Oh, it looked very black! – yes, yes, I quite understand. The facts are so commonplace that I'm really ashamed to mention them. At luncheon-time came an urgent telegram from Weymouth. I sent no reply then, because I thought I knew that you were on your way. But when I was ready to start, it occurred to me that I should save you trouble by wiring that I should join you as soon as possible – so I drove to the post-office before going to Paddington. – Well, you rushed off to Wimbledon?'

'Not till later, and because I was suffering damnably. If I hadn't – been what would it have meant? When a man thinks as much of his wife as I do of you—'

'He has a right to imagine anything of her,' she interrupted in a changed tone, gently reproachful, softening to tenderness. A singularity of Sibyl's demeanour was that she seemed utterly forgetful of the dire position in which her husband stood. One would have thought that she had no concern beyond the refutation of an idle charge, which angered her indeed, but afforded scope for irony, possibly for play of wit. For the moment, Hugh himself had almost forgotten the worst; but he was bidden to proceed, and again his heart sank.

'I went there in the evening. Redgrave happened to be outside – in that veranda of his. I saw him as I came near in the dark, and I fancied that – that he had been talking to someone in the room – through the folding windows. I went up to him quickly, and as soon as he saw me he pulled the window to. After that – I only remember that I was raving mad. He seemed to want to stop me, and I struck at him – and that was the end.'

Sibyl shuddered.

'You went into the room?'

'Yes. No one was there.'

Both kept silence. Sibyl had become very grave, and was thinking intently. Then, with a few brief questions, vigilant, precise, she learnt all that had taken place between Hugh and Mrs Maskell, between Hugh and the doctor; heard of the woman's disappearance, and of Mrs Fenimore's arrival on the scene.

'What shall you do now?'

'Go back and give myself up. What else *can* I do?'

'And tell everything – as you have told it to me?'

Hugh met her eyes and moved his arms in a gesture of misery.

'No! I will think of something. He is dead, and can't contradict; and the woman will hide – trust her. Your name shan't come into it at all. I owe you that, Sibyl. I'll find some cause for a quarrel with him. Your name shan't be spoken.'

She listened, her eyes down, her forehead lined in thought.

'I know what!' Hugh exclaimed, with gloomy resolve. 'That woman – of course, there'll be a mystery, and she'll be searched for. Why' – he blustered against his shame – 'why shouldn't *she* be the cause of it? Yes, that would do.'

His hoarse laugh caused a tremor in Sibyl; she rose and stepped close to him, and laid a hand upon his shoulder.

'So far you have advised yourself. Will you let me advise you now, dear?'

'Wouldn't that seem likely?'

'I think not. And if it *did* – what is the result? You will be dealt with much more severely. Don't you see that?'

'What's that to me? What do I care so long as you are out of the vile business? You will have no difficulties. Your mother's money; and then Mackintosh—'

'And is that all?' asked Sibyl, with a look which seemed to wonder profoundly. 'Am I to think only of my own safety?'

'It's all my cursed fault – just because I'm a fierce, strong brute, who ought to be anywhere but among civilised people. I've killed the man who meant me nothing but kindness. Am I going to drag *your* name into the mud – to set people grinning and winking – '

'Be quiet, Hugh, and listen. I have a much clearer head than yours, poor boy. There's only one way of facing this scandal, and that is to tell everything. For one thing, I shall not let you shield that woman – we shall catch her yet. I shall not let you disgrace yourself by inventing squalid stories. Don't you see, too, that the disgrace would be shared by – by the dead man? Would that be right? And another thing – if shame comes upon you, do you think I have no part in it? We have to face it out with the truth.'

'You don't know what that means,' he answered, with a groan. 'You don't know the world.'

Sibyl did not smile, but her lips seemed only to check themselves when the smile was half born.

'I know enough of it, Hugh, to despise it; and I know you much better than you know yourself. You are not one of the men who can tell lies and make them seem the truth. I don't think my name will suffer. I shall stand by you from first to last. The real true story can't possibly be improved upon. That woman had every motive for deceiving you, and her disappearance is all against her. You have to confess your hot-headedness – that can't be helped. You tell everything – even down to the mistake about the telegram. I shall go with you to the police-station; I shall be at the inquest; I shall be at the court. It's the only chance.'

'Good God! how can I let you do this?'

'You had rather, then, that I seemed to hide away? You had rather set people thinking that there is coldness between us? We must go up tonight. Look out the trains, quick.'

'But your mother, Sibyl—'

'She is dead; she cares nothing. I have to think of my husband.'

Hugh caught her and crushed her in his arms.

'My darling, worse than killing a man who never harmed me was to think wrong of you!'

Her face had grown very pale. She closed her eyes, smiled faintly as she leaned her head against him, and of a sudden burst into tears.

## CHAPTER 14

'It shows one's ignorance of such matters,' said Harvey Rolfe, with something of causticity in his humour, when Alma came home after midnight. 'I should have thought that, by way of preparing for tomorrow, you would have quietly rested today.'

He looked round at her. Alma had entered the study as usual, and was taking off her gloves; but the effort of supporting herself seemed too great, she trembled towards the nearest chair, and affected to laugh at her feebleness as she sank down.

'Rest will come *after*,' she said, in such a voice as sounds from a parched and quivering throat.

'I'll take good care of that,' Harvey remarked. 'To look at you is almost enough to make me play the brutal husband, and say that I'll be hanged if you go out tomorrow at all.'

She laughed – a ghostly merriment.

'Where have you been?'

'Oh, at several places. I met Mr Carnaby at lunch,' she added quickly. 'He told me he was going somewhere – I forget – oh, to Weymouth, to see Mrs Larkfield.'

Harvey was watching her, and paid little attention to the news.

'Do you know, it wouldn't much surprise me if you couldn't get up tomorrow morning, let alone play at a concert. Well, I won't keep you talking. Go to bed.'

'Yes.'

She rose, but instead of turning to the door, moved towards where Harvey was sitting.

'Don't be angry with me,' she murmured in a shamefaced way. 'It wasn't very wise – I've over-excited myself but I shall be all right tomorrow; and afterwards I'll behave more sensibly – I promise – '

He nodded; but Alma bent over him, and touched his forehead with her lips.

'You're in a fever, I suppose you know?'

'I shall be all right tomorrow. Goodnight, dear.'

In town, this morning, she had called at a chemist's, and purchased a little bottle of something in repute for fashionable disorder of the nerves.* Before lying down she took the prescribed dose, though with small hope that it would help her to a blessed unconsciousness. Another thing she did which had not occurred to her for many a night: she knelt by the bedside, and half thought, half whispered through tearless sobs, a petition not learnt from any book, a strange half-heathen blending of prayer for moral strength, and entreaty for success in a worldly desire. Her mind shook perilously in its balance. It was well for Alma that the fashionable prescription did not fail her. In the moment of despair, when she had turned and turned again upon her pillow, haunted by a vision in the darkness, tortured by the never-ending echo of a dreadful voice, there fell upon her a sudden quiet; her brain was soothed by a lulling air from dreamland; her limbs relaxed, and forgot their aching weariness; she sighed and slept.

'I am much better this morning,' she said at breakfast. 'Not a trace of fever – no headache.'

'And a face the colour of the table-cloth,' added Harvey.

There was a letter from Mrs Frothingham, conveying good wishes not very fervently expressed. She had decided not to come up for the concert, feeling that the excitement would be too much for her; but Alma suspected another reason.

She had not asked her husband whether he meant to have a seat in Prince's Hall this afternoon; she still waited for him to speak about it. After breakfast he asked her when she would start for town. At noon, she replied. Every arrangement had been completed; it would be enough if she reached the Hall half an hour before the time of the recital, and after a light luncheon at a neighbouring restaurant.

'Then we may as well go together,' said her husband.

'You mean to come, then?' she asked dreamily.

'I shall go in at the last moment – a seat at the back.'

Anything but inclined for conversation, Alma acquiesced. For the next hour or two she kept in solitude, occasionally touching her violin, but always recurring to an absent mood, a troubled reverie. She could not fix her thoughts upon the trial that was before her. In a vague way she feared it; but another fear, at times amounting to dread, dimmed the day's event into insignificance. The morning's newspapers were before her, sent, no doubt, by Dymes's direction, and she mused over the eye-attracting announcements of her début. 'Mrs Harvey Rolfe's First Violin Recital, Prince's Hall, this afternoon, at 3.' It gave her no more gratification than if the name had been that of a stranger.

The world had grown as unreal as a nightmare. People came before her mind, people the most intimately known, and she seemed but faintly to recognise them. They were all so much changed since yesterday. Their relations to each other and to her were altered, confused. Scarce one of them she could regard without apprehension or perplexity.

What faces would show before her when she advanced upon the platform? Would she behold Sibyl, or Hugh Carnaby, or Cyrus Redgrave? Their presence would all but convince her that she had passed some hours of yesterday in delirium. They might be present; for was not she – she herself – about to step forward and play in public? Their absence – what would it mean? Where were they at this moment? What had happened in the life of each since last she saw them?

When it was time to begin to dress, she undertook the task with effort, with repugnance. She would have chosen to sit here, in a drowsy idleness, and let the hours go by. On her table stood the little vial with its draught of oblivion. Oh to drink of it again, and to lay her head upon the pillow and outsleep the day!

Nevertheless, when she had exerted herself, and was clad in the fresh garments of spring, the mirror came to her help. She was pale yet; but pallor lends distinction to features that are not commonplace, and no remark of man or woman had ever caused her to suspect that her face was ordinary. She posed before the glass, holding her violin, and the picture seemed so effective that she began to regain courage. A dreadful thing had happened – perhaps more dreadful than she durst imagine – but her own part in it was nothing worse than folly and misfortune. She had no irreparable sin to hide. Her moment of supreme peril was past, and would not return. If now she could but brace her nerves, and pass successfully through the ordeal of the next few hours, the victory for which she had striven so hard, and had risked so much, would at length be won. Everything dark and doubtful she must try to forget. Success would give her new strength; to fail, under any circumstances ignominious, would at this crisis of her life be a disaster fraught with manifold and intolerable shame.

She played a few notes. Her hand was steady once more; she felt her confidence revive. Whenever she had performed before an audience, it had always seemed to her that she must inevitably break down; yet at the last minute came power and self-control. So it would be today. The greater the demand upon her, so much the surer her responsive energy. She would not see faces. When all was over, let the news be disclosed, the worst that might be waiting; between now and then lay an infinity of time.

So, when she went downstairs to meet Harvey, the change in her appearance surprised him. He had expected a bloodless countenance, a tremulous step; but Alma came towards him with the confident carriage of an earlier day, with her smile of superiority, her look that invited or demanded admiration.

'Well? You won't be ashamed of me?'

'To tell the truth,' said Harvey, 'I was going because I feared someone would have to look after you in the middle of the affair. If there's no danger of that, I think I shall not go into the place at all.'

'Why?'

'I don't care for it. I prefer to hear you play in private.'

'You needn't have the least fear for me,' said Alma loftily.

'Very well. We'll lunch together, as we arranged, and I'll be at the door with a cab for you after the people have gone.'

'Why should you trouble?'

'I had rather, if you don't mind.'

They drove from Baker Street to the Hall, where Alma alighted for a minute to leave her instrument, and thence to a restaurant not far away. Alma felt no appetite, but the necessity of supporting her strength obliged her to choose some suitable refreshment. When their order had been given, Harvey laid his hand upon an evening newspaper, just arrived, which the waiter had thrown on to the next table. He opened it, not with any intention of reading, but because he had no mind to talk; Alma's name, exhibited in staring letters at the entrance of the public building, had oppressed him with a sense of degradation; he felt ignoble, much as a man might feel who had consented to his own dishonour. As his eyes wandered over the freshly-printed sheet, they were arrested by a couple of bold headlines: 'Sensational Affair at Wimbledon – Mysterious Death of a Gentleman'. He read the paragraph, and turned to Alma with a face of amazement.

'Look there – read that –'

Alma took the paper. She had an instantaneous foreboding of what she was to see; her heart stood still, and her eyes dazzled, but at length she read. On the previous evening (said the report), a gentleman residing at Wimbledon, and well known in fashionable circles, Mr Cyrus Redgrave, had met his death under very strange and startling circumstances. Only a few particulars could as yet be made public; but it appeared that, about nine o'clock in the evening, a medical man had been hastily summoned to Mr Redgrave's house, and found that gentleman lying dead in a room that opened upon the garden. There was present another person, a friend of the deceased (name not mentioned), who made a statement to the effect that, in consequence of a sudden quarrel, he had struck Mr Redgrave with his fist, knocking him down, and, as it proved, killing him on the spot. Up to the present moment no further details were obtainable, but it was believed that the self-accused assailant had put himself in communication with the police. There was a rumour, too, which might or might not have any significance, that Mr Redgrave's housekeeper had suddenly left the house and could not be traced.

'Dead?'

The word fell from her lips involuntarily.

'And who killed him?' said Harvey, just above his breath.

'It isn't known – there's no name –'

'No. But I had a sudden thought. Absurd – impossible –'

As Harvey whispered the words, a waiter drew near with the luncheon. It was arranged upon the table, but lay there disregarded. Alma took up the newspaper again. In a moment she leaned towards her husband.

'What did you think?'

'Nothing – don't talk about it.'

Two glasses of wine had been poured out; Harvey took his and drank it off.

'It's a pity I saw this,' he said; 'it has shaken your nerves. I ought to have kept it to myself.'

Alma dipped a spoon in the soup before her, and tried to swallow. Her hand did not tremble; the worst had come and gone in a few seconds; but her palate refused food. She drank wine, and presently became so collected, so quiet, that she wondered at herself. Cyrus Redgrave was dead – dead! – the word kept echoing in her mind. As soon as she understood and believed the fact of Redgrave's death, it became the realisation of a hope which she had entertained without knowing it. Only by a great effort could she assume the look of natural concern; had she been in solitude, her face would have relaxed like that of one who is suddenly relieved from physical torment. She gave no thought to wider consequences: she saw the event only as it affected herself in her relations with the dead man. She had feared him; she had feared herself; now all danger was at an end. Now – now she could find courage to front the crowd of people and play to them. Her conscience ceased from troubling; the hope of triumph no longer linked itself with dread of a fatal indebtedness. No touch of sorrow entered into her mood; no anxiety on behalf of the man whose act had freed her. He, her husband's friend, would keep the only secret which could now injure her. Cyrus Redgrave was dead, and to her it meant a renewal of life.

Harvey was speaking; he reminded her of the necessity of taking food.

'Yes, I am going to eat something.'

'Look here, Alma,' – he regarded her sternly, – 'if you have any fear, if you are unequal to this, let me go and make an excuse for you.'

'I have not the *least* fear. Don't try to make me nervous.'

She ate and drank. Harvey, the while, kept his eyes fixed on the newspaper.

'Now I must go,' she said in a few minutes, after looking at her watch. 'Don't come out with me. Do just as you like about going into the Hall and about meeting me afterwards. You needn't be the least bit anxious, I assure you; I'm not going to make myself ridiculous.'

They stood up.

'I shall be at the door with a cab,' said Harvey.

'Very well; I won't keep you waiting.'

She left him, and walked from the restaurant with a quick step. Harvey drank a little more wine, and made a pretence of tasting the dish before him, then paid his bill and departed. He had now no intention whatever of going to hear Alma play; but he wished to know whether certain persons were among her audience, and, as he could not stand to watch the people entering, he took the only other means of setting his mind at rest – this was to drive forthwith to Oxford and Cambridge Mansions.

On his knocking at the Carnabys' door, a servant informed him that neither her master nor her mistress was at home. Something unusual in the girl's manner at once arrested his attention; she was evidently disinclined to say anything beyond the formula of refusal, but with this Harvey would not be satisfied. He mentioned his name, and urged several inquiries, on the plea that he had urgent business with his friends. All he could gather was that Carnaby had left home early this morning, and that Mrs Carnaby was out of town; it grew more evident that the girl shrank from questions.

'Has anyone been here before me, anxious to see them?'

'I don't know, sir; I can't tell you anything else.'

'And you have no idea when either of them will be back?'

'I don't know at all; I don't know anything about it.'

He turned away, as if to descend the stairs; but, as there was no sound of a closing door, he glanced back, and caught a glimpse of the servant, who stood looking after him. No sooner did their eyes meet than the girl drew hastily in and the door was shut.

Beset by a grave uneasiness, he walked into Edgware Road, and followed the thoroughfare to its end at the Marble Arch. One thing seemed certain: neither Carnaby nor his wife could be at Prince's Hall. It was equally certain that only a serious cause could have prevented their attendance. The servant manifestly had something to conceal; under ordinary circumstances she would never have spoken and behaved in that strange way.

At the Marble Arch boys were crying newspapers. He bought two, and in each of them found the sensational headlines; but the reports added nothing to that he had already seen; all, it was clear, came from the same source.

He turned into the Park, and walked aimlessly by crosspaths hither and thither. Time had to be killed; he tried to read his papers, but every item of news or comment disgusted him, and he threw the sheets away. When he came out at Knightsbridge, there was still half an hour to be passed, so he turned eastward, and walked the length of Piccadilly. Now at length Alma's fate was decided; the concert drew to its close. In anxiety to learn how things had gone with her, he all but forgot Hugh Carnaby, until, just as he was about to hail a cab for the purpose of bringing Alma from the Hall, his eye fell on a fresh newspaper placard, which gave its largest type to the Wimbledon affair, and promised a 'Startling Revelation'. He bought the paper, and read. It had become known, said the reporter, that the gentleman who, on his own avowal, had caused Mr Redgrave's death, was Mr H. Carnaby, resident at Oxford and Cambridge Mansions. The rumour that Mr Carnaby had presented himself to the authorities was unfounded; as a matter of fact, the police had heard nothing from him, and could not discover his whereabouts. As to the mysterious disappearance of Mr Redgrave's housekeeper – Mrs Lant by name – nothing new could be learnt. Mrs Lant had left all her personal belongings, and no one seemed able to conjecture a reason for her conduct.

Harvey folded up the paper, and crushed it into his pocket. He felt no surprise; his brooding on possibilities had prepared him for this disclosure, and, from the moment that his fears were confirmed, he interpreted everything with a gloomy certainty. Hugh's fatal violence could have but one explanation, and that did not come upon Harvey with the shock of the incredible. Neither was he at any loss to understand why Hugh had failed to surrender himself. Ere-long the newspapers would rejoice in another 'startling revelation', which would make the tragedy complete.

In this state of mind he waited for Alma's coming forth. She was punctual as she had promised. At the first sight of her he knew that nothing disagreeable had befallen, and this was enough. As soon as the cab drove off with them he looked an inquiry.

'All well,' she answered, with subdued exultation. 'Wait till you see the notices.'

Her flushed face and dancing eyes told that she was fresh from congratulation and flattery. Harvey could not spoil her moment of triumph by telling what he had just learnt. She wished to talk of herself, and he gave her the opportunity.

'Many people?'

'A very good hall. They say such an audience at a first recital has hardly ever been known.'

'You weren't nervous?'

'I've often been far more when I played in a drawing-room; and I never played so well – not half so well!'

She entered upon a vivid description of her feelings. On first stepping forward, she could see nothing but a misty expanse of faces; she could not feel the boards she trod upon; yet no sooner had she raised her violin than a glorious sense of power made her forget everything but the music she was to play. She all but laughed with delight. Never had she felt so perfect a mastery of her instrument. She played without effort, and could have played for hours without weariness. Her fellow-musicians declared that she was 'wonderful'; and Harvey, as he listened to this flow of excited talk, asked himself whether he had not, after all, judged Alma amiss. Perhaps he had been the mere dull Philistine, unable to recognise the born artist, and doing his paltry best to obstruct her path. Perhaps so; but he would look for the opinion of serious critics – if any such had been present.

At Baker Street they had to wait for a train, and here it happened that Alma saw the evening placards. At once she changed; her countenance was darkened with anxiety.

'Hadn't you better get a paper?' she asked in a quick undertone.

'I have one. Do you wish to see it now?'

'Is there anything more?'

'Yes, there is. You don't know, I suppose, whether Carnaby and his wife were at the Hall?'

'I could hardly distinguish faces,' she replied, with tremor. 'What is it? Tell me.'

He took out his newspaper and pointed to the paragraph which mentioned Carnaby's name. Alma seemed overcome with painful emotion; she moved towards the nearest seat, and Harvey, alarmed by her sudden pallor, placed himself by her side.

'What does it mean?' she whispered.

'Who can say?'

'They must have quarrelled about business matters.'

'Perhap so.'

'Do you think he – Mr Carnaby – means to hide away – to escape?'

'He won't hide away,' Harvey answered. 'Yet he may escape.'

'What do you mean? Go by ship? – get out of the country?'

'I don't think so. He is far more likely to be found somewhere – in a way that would save trouble.'

Alma flashed a look of intelligence.

'You think so,' she panted. 'You really think he has done that?'

'I feel afraid of it.'

Alma recovered breath; and, but that her face was bent low over the newspaper, Harvey must have observed that the possibility of his friend's suicide seemed rather to calm her agitation than to afflict her with fresh dismay.

But she could speak no more of her musical triumph. With the colour of her cheeks she had lost all animation, all energy; she needed the support of Harvey's arm in stepping to the railway carriage; and on her arrival at home, yielding, as it seemed, to physical exhaustion, she lay pallid, mute, and nerveless.

## CHAPTER 15

At night she had recourse to the little bottle, but this time it was less efficacious. Again and again she woke from terrifying dreams, wearied utterly, unable to rest, and longing for the dawn. Soon after daybreak she arose and dressed; then, as there was yet no sound of movement in the house, she laid her aching head upon the pillow again, and once more fell into a troubled sleep. The usual call aroused her; she went to the door and bade the servant bring her some tea and the morning paper as soon as it was delivered.

In a few minutes the tea and the newspaper were both brought. First she glanced at the paragraphs relating to the Wimbledon tragedy; there was nothing added to yesterday's news except that the inquest would be held this morning. Then she looked eagerly for the report of her recital, and found it only after much searching, barely a dozen lines, which spoke of her as 'a lady of some artistic promise', said that much allowance must be made for her natural nervousness, and passed on to the other performers, who were unreservedly praised. Anger and despondency struggled within her as she read the lines over and over again. Nervous! Why, the one marvellous thing was her absolute conquest of nervousness. She saw the hand of an enemy. Felix Dymes had warned her of the envy she must look for in certain quarters, and here appeared the first instance of it. But the post would bring other papers.

It brought half a dozen and a number of letters. At the sound of the knock, Alma hurried downstairs, seized upon her budget,* and returned to the bedroom. Yes; as it happened, she had seen the least favourable notice first of all. The other papers devoted more space to her (though less than she had expected), and harmonised in their tone of compliment; one went so far as to congratulate those who were present on 'an occasion of undoubted importance'. Another found some fault with her choice of pieces, but hoped soon to hear her again, for her 'claims to more than ordinary attention' were 'indubitable'. There was a certain lack of 'breadth', opined one critic; but 'natural nervousness', &c. Promise, promise – all agreed that her 'promise' was quite exceptional.

Tremulous from these lines of print, she turned to the letters, and here was full-fed with flattery. 'Your most brilliant début' – 'How shall we thank you for such an artistic treat?' – 'Oh, your divine rendering of,' &c. – 'You have taken your place, at once and *sans phrase*,* in the very front rank of violinists.' She smiled once more, and lost a little of her cadaverous hue. Felix Dymes, scribbling late, repeated things that he had heard since the afternoon. He added: 'I'm afraid you'll be awfully upset about your friends the Carnabys. It's very unfortunate this should have happened just now. But cheer up, and let me see you as soon as possible. Great things to come!'

She went down to breakfast with shaking limbs, scarce able to hold up her head as she sat through the meal. Harvey ran his eye over the papers, but said nothing, and kept looking anxiously at her. She could not touch food; on rising from table she felt a giddiness which obliged her to hold the chair for support. At her husband's beckoning she followed him into the library.

'Hadn't you better go back to bed?'

'I shall lie down a little. But perhaps if I could get out – '

'No, that you won't. And if you feel no better by afternoon I shall send for the doctor.'

'You see what the papers say – ?'

'Yes.'

'Wouldn't it be graceful to own that you are surprised?'

'We'll talk about that when you look less like a corpse. Would you like me to send any message to Mrs Carnaby?'

Alma shook her head.

'I'll write – today or tomorrow – there's no hurry – '

'No hurry?' said Rolfe, surprised by something in her tone. 'What do you mean by that?'

'Are you going to see Mr Carnaby?' was her answer.

'I don't know where to find him, unless I go to the inquest.'

'I had rather you stayed here today,' said Alma; 'I feel far from well.'

'Yes, I shall stay. But I ought to let him hear from me. Best, perhaps, if I send a telegram to his place.'

The morning passed miserably enough. Alma went to her bedroom and lay there for an hour or two, then she strayed to the nursery and sat a while with Hugh and his governess. At luncheon she had no more appetite than at breakfast, though for very faintness her body could scarce support itself. After the meal Harvey went out to procure the earliest evening papers, and on his way he called at the doctor's house. Not till about five o'clock was a report of the Wimbledon inquest obtainable. Having read it, Harvey took the paper home, where he arrived just as the doctor drove up to the door.

Alma was again lying down; her eyes showed that she had shed tears. On Harvey's saying that the doctor was in the house, she answered briefly that she would see him. The result of the interview was made known to Rolfe. Nervous collapse; care and quiet; excitement of any kind to be avoided; the patient better in bed for a few days, to obtain complete rest. Avoidance of excitement was the most difficult of all things for Alma at present. Newspapers could not be kept from her; she waited eagerly for the report of the inquest.

'Carnaby tells an astonishing story,' said Rolfe, as he sat down by her when the doctor was gone.

'Let me read it for myself.'

She did so with every sign of agitation; but on laying the

paper aside she seemed to become quieter. After a short silence a word or two fell from her.

'So Sibyl was at Weymouth.'

Harvey communed with his thoughts, which were anything but pleasant. He did not doubt the truth of Hugh Carnaby's narrative, but he had a gloomy conviction that, whether Hugh knew it or not, an essential part of the drama lay unrevealed.

'Will they find that woman, do you think?' were Alma's next words.

'It doesn't seem very likely.'

'What is the punishment for manslaughter?'

'That depends. The case will go for trial, and – in the meantime—'

'What?' asked Alma, raising herself.

'The woman *may* be found.'

There was another silence. Then Alma asked –

'Do you think I ought to write to Sibyl?'

'No,' he answered decisively. 'You must write to no one. Put it all out of your mind as much as possible.'

'Shall you see Mr Carnaby?'

'Only if he sends for me.'

And this was just what happened. Admitted to bail by the magistrate, Hugh presently sent a note from Oxford and Cambridge Mansions, asking his friend to see him there. Harvey did not let Alma know of it. He found some difficulty in getting away from home for a couple of hours, so anxious had she become to keep him within call, and, when he of necessity went out, to be informed of his movements. He attributed this to her morbid condition; for, in truth, Alma was very ill. She could take only the lightest food, and in the smallest quantities; she fell repeatedly into fits of silent weeping; she had lost all strength, and her flesh had begun to waste. On this same day Harvey heard that Mrs Frothingham was making ready to come, and the news relieved him.

On reaching the Carnabys', he was admitted by the same servant whose behaviour had excited his suspicions a day or two ago. Without a word she conducted him to Hugh's room.

'Well, old man,' said the familiar voice, though in the tone of one who is afraid of being overheard, 'it has come to this, you see. You're not surprised? What else could be expected of a fellow like me, sooner or later?'

His face had the marks of sleeplessness; his hand was hot. He pressed Harvey into a chair, and stood before him, making an obvious effort to look and speak courageously.

'It never struck me before how devilish awkward it is for a man in his own home when he gets into a public scrape – I mean the servants. One has to sit under them, as usual, you know, and feel their eyes boring into one's back. Did you ever think of it?'

'How long have you to wait?' asked Rolfe.

'Only a fortnight. But there may be bother about that woman. I wish to God they could catch her!'

Harvey made no reply, and his eyes wandered. In a moment he became aware that Hugh was looking at him with peculiar intentness.

'I wish I could do anything for you, Carnaby.'

'You can,' replied the other, with emphasis, his face growing stern.

'What is it?'

'Get rid of that ugly thought I see you have in your mind.'

Hugh's voice, though still cautious, had risen a little; he spoke with severity that was almost harshness. Their eyes met.

'What ugly thought?'

'Don't be dishonest with me, Rolfe. It's a queer-sounding tale, and you're not the only man, I warrant, who thinks there's something behind it. But I tell you there isn't – or nothing that concerns *me*.' He paused for an instant. 'I shouldn't have dared to tell it, but for my wife. Yes, my wife,' he repeated vehemently. 'It was Sibyl forced me to tell the truth. Rather than have *her* mixed up in such a thing as this, I would have told any lie, at whatever cost to myself; but she wouldn't let me. And she was right; I see now that she was, though it a been hard enough, I tell you, to think of what people might be saying – damn them! Don't you be one, Rolfe. My wife is as pure and innocent as any woman living.\* I tell you that. I ask you to believe that; and it's the one thing, the only thing, you can do for me.'

His voice quivered, and he half-choked upon the passionate words. Moved, though not to conviction, Harvey made the only possible reply.

'I believe you; and if ever I have the chance I will repeat what you say.'

'Very well. But there's something else. I don't ask you to see anything of Sibyl, or to let your wife see her; it will be much better not. I don't know whether she will stay here, or in London at all; but she will see as few people as possible. Don't think it necessary to write to her; don't let your wife write. If we all live through it – and come out again on the other side – things may be all right again; but I don't look forward to anything. All I can think of now is that I've killed a man who was a good friend to me, and have darkened all the rest of Sibyl's life. And I only wish someone had knocked my brains out ten years ago, when nobody would have missed such a blackguard and ruffian.'

'Is it on your wife's account, or on ours that you want us to keep apart?' asked Rolfe gravely.

'Both, my dear fellow,' was the equally grave reply. 'I'm saying only what I mean; it's no time for humbug now. Think it over, and you'll see I'm right.'

'Alma won't see any one just yet awhile,' said Harvey. 'She has made herself ill, of course.'

'Ill? How?'

'The concert, and the frenzy that went before it.'

'The concert – .' Carnaby touched his forehead. 'I remember. If I were you, Rolfe—'

'Well?'

'I don't want to take advantage of my position and be impertinent but do you think that kind of thing will do her any good in the end?'

'It's going to stop,' replied Harvey, with a meaning nod.

'I'm glad to hear you say so – very glad. Just stick to that. You're more civilised than I am, and you'll know how to go about that kind of thing as a man should.'

'I mean to try.'

'She is not seriously ill, I hope?' Hugh inquired, after reflecting for a moment.

'Oh, the nerves – breakdown – nothing dangerous, I believe.'

'Life ought to be easy enough for you, Rolfe,' said the other. 'You're at home here.'

'It depends what you mean by "here". I'm at home in England, no doubt; but it's very uncertain whether I shall hold out in London. You know that we're going west to Gunnersbury. That's on the child's account; I want him to go to school with a friend of ours. If we can live there quietly and sanely, well and good; if the whirlpool begins to drag us in again – then I have another idea.'

'The whirlpool!' muttered Carnaby, with a broken laugh. 'It's got hold of *me*, and I'm going down, old man – and it looks black as hell.'

'We shall see the sunlight again together,' replied Rolfe, with forced cheerfulness.

'You think so? I wish I could believe it.'

In less than half an hour Harvey was back at the station, waiting for his train. He suffered pangs of self-rebuke; it seemed to him that he ought to have found some better way, in word or deed, for manifesting the sympathy of true friendship. He had betrayed a doubt which must for ever affect Hugh's feeling towards him. But this was his lot in life, to blunder amid trying circumstances, to prove unequal to every grave call upon him. He tried vainly to see what else he could have done, yet felt that another man would have faced the situation to better purpose. One resolve, at all events, he had brought out of it: Hugh Carnaby's reference to Alma declared the common-sense view of a difficulty which ought to be no difficulty at all, and put an end to vacillation. But in return for this friendly service he had rendered nothing, save a few half-hearted words of encouragement. Rolfe saw himself in a mean, dispiriting light.

On the next day Mrs Frothingham arrived at Pinner, and Harvey's anxieties were lightened. The good, capable woman never showed to such advantage as in a sick-room; scarcely had she entered the house when Alma's state began to improve. They remarked that Alma showed no great concern on Sibyl's account, but was seemingly preoccupied with thought of Carnaby himself. This being the case, it was with solicitude that Harvey and Mrs Frothingham awaited the result of Hugh's trial for manslaughter. Redgrave's housekeeper could not be found; the self-accused man stood or fell by his own testimony; nothing was submitted to the court beyond the fact of Redgrave's death, and Hugh Carnaby's explanation of how it came about. Nothing of direct evidence; indirect, in the shape of witness to character, was abundantly forthcoming, and from 'people of importance'. But the victim also was a person of importance, and justice no doubt felt that, under whatever provocation, such a man must not be slain with impunity. It sentenced the homicide to a term of two years' imprisonment, without hard labour.

Alma heard the sentence with little emotion. Soon after she fell into a deeper and more refreshing sleep than any she had known since her illness began.

'It is the end of suspense,' said Mrs Frothingham.

'No doubt,' Harvey assented.

A few days more and Mrs Frothingham took Alma away into Hampshire. Little Hugh went with them, his mother strongly desiring it. As for Rolfe, he escaped to Greystone, to spend a week with Basil Morton before facing the miseries of the removal from Pinner to Gunnersbury.

PART THE THIRD

# CHAPTER I

The house had stood for a century and a half, and for eighty years had been inhabited by Mortons. Of its neighbours in the elm-bordered road, one or two were yet older; all had reached the age of mellowness. 'Sicut umbra præterit dies'* – so ran the motto of the dial set between porch and eaves; to Harvey Rolfe the kindliest of all greetings, welcoming him to such tranquillity as he knew not how to find elsewhere.

It was in the town, yet nothing town-like. No sooty smother hung above the house-tops and smirched the garden leafage; no tramp of crowds, no clatter of hot-wheel traffic, sounded from the streets hard by. But at hours familiar, bidding to task or pleasure or repose, the music of the grey belfries floated over-head; a voice from the old time, an admonition of mortality in strains sweet to the ear of childhood. Harvey had but to listen, and the days of long ago came back to him. Above all, when at evening rang the curfew. Stealing apart to a bowered corner of the garden, he dreamed himself into the vanished years, when curfew-time was bed-time, and a hand with gentle touch led him from his play to that long sweet slumber which is the child's new birth.

Basil Morton was one of three brothers, the youngest. His father, a corn-factor, assenting readily to his early inclination for the Church, sent him from Greystone Grammar-School to Cambridge, where Basil passed creditably through the routine, but in no way distinguished himself. Having taken his degree, he felt less assured of a clerical vocation, and thought that the law might perhaps be more suitable to him. Whilst he thus wavered, his father died, and the young man found that he had to depend upon himself for anything more than the barest livelihood. He decided, after all, for business, and became a partner with his eldest brother, handling corn as his father and his grandfather had done before him. At eight and twenty he married, and a few years afterwards the elder Morton's death

left him to pursue commerce at his own discretion. Latterly the
business had not been very lucrative, nor was Basil the man to
make it so; but he went steadily on in the old tracks, satisfied
with an income which kept him free from care.

'I like my trade,' he said once to Harvey Rolfe; 'it's clean and
sweet and useful. The Socialist would revile me as a middleman;
but society can't do without me just yet, and I ask no more than
I fairly earn. I like turning over a sample of grain; I like the
touch of it, and the smell of it. It brings me near to the good old
Mother Earth, and makes me feel human.'

His house was spacious, well built, comfortable. The furniture, in great part, was the same his parents had used; solid
mahogany, not so beautiful as furniture may be made, but
serviceable, if need be, for another fifty years. He had a library
of several thousand volumes, slowly and prudently collected,
representing a liberal interest in all travail of the mind, and a
special taste for the things of classical antiquity. Basil Morton
was no scholar in the modern sense, but might well have been
described by the old phrase which links scholar with gentleman.
He lived by trade, but trade did not affect his life. The day's
work over, he turned, with no feeling of incongruity, to a page
of Thucydides, of Tacitus, or to those less familiar authors who
lighted his favourite wanderings through the ruins of the Roman
Empire. Better grounded for such studies than Harvey Rolfe, he
pursued them with a steadier devotion and with all the advantages of domestic peace. In his mental habits, in his turns of
speech, there appeared perhaps a leaning to pedantry; but it was
the most amiable of faults, and any danger that might have
lurked in it was most happily balanced and corrected by the
practical virtues of his life's companion.

Mrs Morton had the beauty of perfect health, of health
mental and physical. To describe her face as homely was to pay
it the highest compliment, for its smile was the true light of
home, that never failed. *Filia generosi*, daughter of a house that
bred gentlewomen, though its ability to dower them had
declined in these latter days, she conceived her duty as wife and
mother after the old fashion, and was so fortunate as to find no
obstacle in circumstance. She rose early; she slept early; and her
day was full of manifold activity. Four children she had borne –
the eldest a boy now in his twelfth year, the youngest a baby
girl; and it seemed to her no merit that in these little ones she

saw the end and reason of her being. Into her pure and healthy mind had never entered a thought at conflict with motherhood. Her breasts were the fountain of life; her babies clung to them, and grew large of limb. From her they learnt to speak; from her they learnt the names of trees and flowers and all things beautiful around them; learnt, too, less by precept than from fair example, the sweetness and sincerity wherewith such mothers, and such alone, can endow their offspring. Later she was their instructress in a more formal sense; for this also she held to be her duty, up to the point where other teaching became needful. By method and good-will she found time for everything, ruling her house and ordering her life so admirably, that to those who saw her only in hours of leisure she seemed to be at leisure always. She would have felt it an impossible thing to abandon her children to the care of servants; reluctantly she left them even for an hour or two when other claims which could not be neglected called her forth. In play-time they desired no better companion, for she was a child herself in gaiety of heart and lissom sportiveness. No prettier sight could be seen at Greystone than when, on a summer afternoon, they all drove in the pony carriage to call on friends, or out into the country. Nowadays it was often her eldest boy who held the reins, a bright-eyed, well-built lad, a pupil at the old Grammar-School, where he used the desk at which his father had sat before him. Whatever fault of boyhood showed itself in Harry Morton, he knew not the common temptation to be ashamed of his mother, or to flout her love.

For holiday they never crossed the sea. Morton himself had been but once abroad, and that in the year before his father's death, when he was trying to make up his mind what profession he should take up; he then saw something of France and of Italy. Talking with travelled friends, he was wont to praise himself in humorous vein for the sober fixity of his life, and to quote, in that mellow tone which gave such charm to his talk, the line from Claudian, 'Erret et extremos alter scrutetur Iberos'*; for he had several friends to whom a Latin or a Greek quotation was no stumbling-block. Certain of his college companions, men who had come to hold a place in the world's eye, were glad to turn aside from beaten tracks and smoke a pipe at Greystone with Basil Morton – the quaint fellow who at a casual glance might pass for a Philistine, but was indeed something quite other. His wife had never left her native island. 'I will go abroad,' she said, 'when my boys can take me.' And that might not be long hence; for Harry, who loved no book so much as the atlas, abounded in schemes of travel, and had already mapped the grand tour on which the whole family was to set forth when he stood headboy at the Grammar-School.

In this household Harvey Rolfe knew himself a welcome guest, and never had he been so glad as now to pass from the noisy world into the calm which always fell about him under his friend's roof. The miseries through which he had gone were troubling his health, and health disordered naturally retacted upon his mind, so that, owing to a gloomy excitement of the imagination, for several nights he had hardly slept. No sooner had he lain down in darkness than every form of mortal anguish beset his thoughts, passing before him as though some hand unfolded a pictured scroll of life's terrors. He seemed never before to have realised the infinitude of human suffering. Hour after hour, with brief intervals of semi-oblivion, from which his mind awoke in nameless horror, he travelled from land to land, from age to age; at one moment picturing some dread incident of a thousand years ago; the next, beholding with intolerable vividness some scene of agony reported in the day's newspaper. Doubtless it came of his constant brooding on Redgrave's death and Hugh Carnaby's punishment. For the first time, tragedy had been brought near to him, and he marvelled at the indifference with which men habitually live in a world where tragedy is every hour's occurrence.

He told himself that this was merely a morbid condition of the brain, but could not bring himself to believe it. On the contrary, what he now saw and felt was the simple truth of things, obscured by everyday conditions of active life. And that History which he loved to read – what was it but the lurid record of woes unutterable? How could he find pleasure in keeping his eyes fixed on century after century of ever-repeated torment – war, pestilence, tyranny; the stake, the dungeon; tortures of infinite device, cruelties inconceivable? He would close his books, and try to forget all they had taught him.

Tonight he spoke of it, as he sat with Morton after everyone else had gone to bed. They had talked of Hugh Carnaby (each divining in the other a suspicion they were careful not to avow), and their mood led naturally to interchange of thoughts on grave subjects.

'Everyone knows that state of mind, more or less,' said Morton, in his dreamy voice – a voice good for the nerves. 'It comes generally when one's stomach is out of order. You wake at half-past two in the morning, and suffer infernally from the blackest pessimism. It's morbid – yes; but for all that it may be a glimpse of the truth. Health and good spirits, just as likely as not, are the deceptive condition.'

'Exactly. But for the power of deceiving ourselves, we couldn't live at all. It's not a question of theory, but of fact.'

'I fought it out with myself,' said Basil, after a sip of whisky, 'at the time of my "exodus from Houndsditch".* There's a point in the life of every man who has brains, when it becomes a possibility that he may kill himself. Most of us have it early, but it depends on circumstances. I was like Johnson's friend:* be as philosophical as I might, cheerfulness kept breaking in. And at last I let cheerfulness have its way. As far as I know' – he gurgled a laugh – 'Schopenhauer* did the same.'

Harvey puffed at his pipe before answering.

'Yes; and I suppose we may call that intellectual maturity. It's bad for a man when he *can't* mature – which is my case. I seem to be as far from it as ever. Seriously, I should think few men ever had so slow a development. I don't stagnate: there's always movement; but – putting aside the religious question – my stage at present is yours of twenty years ago. Yet, not even that; for you started better than I did. You were never a selfish lout – a half-baked blackguard—'

'Nor you either, my dear fellow.'

'But I was! I've got along fairly well in self-knowledge; I can follow my course in the past clearly enough. If I had my rights, I should live to about a hundred and twenty, and go on ripening to the end. That would be a fair proportion. It's confoundedly hard to think that I'm a good deal past the middle of life, yet morally and intellectually am only beginning it.'

'It only means, Rolfe, that we others have a pretty solid conceit of ourselves. – Listen! "We have heard the chimes at midnight, Master Shallow."* I don't apply the name to you; but you'll be none the worse for a good night's sleep. Let us be off.'

Harvey slept much better than of late. There was an air of comfort in this guest-chamber which lulled the mind. Not that the appointments were more luxurious than in his own bed-room, for Morton had neither the means nor the desire to equip his house with perfections of modern upholstery; but every detail manifested a care and taste and delicacy found only in homes which are homes indeed, and not mere dwelling-places fitted up chiefly for display. Harvey thought of the happiness of children who are born, and live through all their childhood, in such an atmosphere as this. Then he thought of his own child, who had in truth no home at all. A house in Wales – a house at Pinner – a house at Gunnersbury – presently a house somewhere else. He had heard people defend this nomad life – why, he himself, before his marriage, had smiled at the old-fashioned stability represented by such families as the Mortons; had talked of 'getting into ruts', of 'mouldering', and so on. He saw it from another point of view now, and if the choice were between rut and whirlpool –

When he awoke, and lay looking at the sunlit blind, in the stillness of early morning he heard a sound always delightful, always soothing, that of scythe and whetstone; then the long steady sweep of the blade through garden grass. Morton, old stick-in-the-mud, would not let his gardener use a mowing machine, the scythe was good enough for him; and Harvey, recalled to the summer mornings of more than thirty years ago, blessed him for his pig-headedness.

But another sound he missed, one he would have heard even more gladly. Waking thus at Pinner (always about six o'clock), he had been wont to hear the voice of his little boy, singing. Possibly this was a doubtful pleasure to Miss Smith, in whose room Hughie slept; but, to her credit, she had never bidden the child keep quiet. And there he lay, singing to himself, a song without words; singing like a little bird at dawn; a voice of innocent happiness, greeting the new day. Hughie was far off; and in a strange room, with other children, he would not sing. But Harvey heard his voice – the odd little bursts of melody, the liquid rise and fall, which set to tune, no doubt, some childish fancy, some fairy tale, some glad anticipation. Hughie lived in the golden age. A year or two more, and the best of life would be over with him; for boyhood is but a leaden time compared with the borderland between it and infancy; and manhood – the curse of sex developed –

It was a merry breakfast-table. The children's sprightly talk, their mother's excellent spirits, and Morton's dry jokes with one and all, made Harvey feel ashamed of the rather glum habit which generally kept him mute at the first meal of the day. Alma, too, was seldom in the mood for breakfast conversation; so that, between them, they imposed silence upon Hughie and Miss Smith. One might have thought that the postman had brought some ill news, depressing the household. Yet things were not wont to be so bad in Wales; at that time, the day, as a rule, began cheerfully enough. Their life had darkened in the shadow of London; just when, for the child's sake, everything should have been made as bright as possible. And he saw little hope of change for the better. It did not depend upon him. The note of family life is struck by the house-mistress, and Alma seemed fallen so far from her better self that he could only look forward with anxiety to new developments of her character.

'School?' he exclaimed, when Harry, with satchel over shoulder, came to bid him good morning. 'I wish I could go in your place! It's just thirty-one years since I left the old Grammar-School.'

The boy did not marvel at this. He would not have done so if the years had been sixty-one; for Mr Rolfe seemed to him an old man, very much older than his own father.

As usual when at Greystone, Harvey took his first walk to the spots associated with his childhood. He walked alone, for Morton had gone to business until midday. On the outskirts of the town, in no very pleasant situation, stood the house where he was born; new buildings had risen round about it, and the present tenants seemed to be undesirable people, who neglected the garden and were careless about their window curtains. Here he had lived until he was ten years old – till the death of his father. His mother died long before that; he just, and only just, remembered her. He knew from others that she was a gentle, thoughtful woman, always in poor health; the birth of her second child, a girl, led to a lingering illness, and soon came the end. To her place as mistress of the house succeeded Harvey's aunt, his father's sister. No one could have been kinder to the children, but Harvey, for some reason yet obscure to him, always disliked her. Whom, indeed, did he not dislike, of those set over him? He recalled his perpetual rebellion against her authority from the first day to the last. What an unruly cub! And his father's anger when he chanced to overhear some boyish insolence – alas! alas!

For he saw so little of his father. Mr Rolfe's work as a railway engineer kept him chiefly abroad; he was sometimes absent for twelve months at a time. Only in the last half-year of his life did he remain constantly at home, and that because he was dying. Having contracted a fever in Spain, he came back to recruit; but his constitution had suffered from many hardships, and now gave way. To the last day (though he was ten years old) Harvey never dreamt of what was about to happen. Self-absorbed in a degree unusual even with boys, he feared his father, but had not learnt to love him. And now, looking back, he saw only too well why the anxious parent treated him with severity more often than with gentleness and good humour. A boy such as he must have given sore trouble to a father on his death-bed.

When it was too late, too late by many a year, he mourned the loss which had only startled him, which had seemed hardly a loss at all, rather an emancipation. As a man of thirty, he knew his father much better than when living with him day after day. Faults he could perceive, some of them inherited in his own character; but there remained the memory of a man whom he could admire and love – whom he did admire and love more sincerely and profoundly the older he grew. And he held it the supreme misfortune of his life that, in those early years which count so much towards the future, he had been so rarely under his father's influence.

Inevitable, it seemed. Yet only so, perhaps, because even a good and conscientious man may fail to understand the obligation under which he lies towards his offspring.

He and his sister Amy passed into the guardianship of Dr Harvey, Mr Rolfe's old friend, the boy's godfather, who had done his best to soothe the mind of the dying man with regard to his children's future. There were no pecuniary difficulties; the children's education was provided for, and on coming of age each would have about two thousand pounds. Dr Harvey, a large-hearted, bright-witted Irishman, with no youngsters of his own, speedily decided that the boy must be sent away to a boarding-school, to have some of the self-will knocked out of him. Amy continued to live with her aunt for two years more; then the good woman died, and the Doctor took Amy into his own house, which became Harvey's home during holidays.

The ivy-covered house, in the best residential street of Greystone. Harvey paused before it. On the railings hung a brass plate with another name; the good old Doctor had been in his grave for many a year.

What wonder that he never liked the boy? Harvey, so far as anyone could perceive, had no affection, no good feeling, no youthful freshness or simplicity of heart; moreover, he exhibited precocious arrogance, supported by an obstinacy which had not even the grace of quickening into fieriness; he was often a braggart, and could not be trusted to tell the truth where his self-esteem was ever so little concerned. How unutterably the Harvey Rolfe of today despised himself at the age of fifteen or so! Even at that amorphous age, a more loutish, ungainly boy could scarcely have been found. Bashfulness cost him horrid torments, of course exasperating his conceit. He hated girls; he scorned women. Among his school-fellows he made a bad choice of comrades. Though muscular and of tolerable health, he was physically, as well as morally, a coward. Games and sports had no attraction for him; he shut himself up in rooms, and read a great deal, yet even this, it seemed, not without an eye to winning admiration.

Brains he had – brains undeniably; but for a long time there was the greatest doubt as to what use he could make of them. Harvey remembered the day when it was settled that he should study medicine. He resolved upon it merely because he had chanced to hear the Doctor say that he was not cut out for *that*.

He saw himself at twenty, a lank, ungainly youth, with a disagreeable complexion and a struggling moustache. He was a student at Guy's; he had 'diggings'*; he tasted the joy of independence. As is the way with young men of turbid passions and indifferent breeding, he rapidly signalised his independence by plunging into sordid slavery. A miserable time to think of; a wilderness of riot, folly, and shame. Yet it seemed to him that he was enjoying life. Among the rowdy set of his fellow-students he shone with a certain superiority. His contempt of money, and his large way of talking about it, conveyed the impression that abundant means awaited him. He gave away coin as readily as he spent it on himself; not so much in a true spirit of generosity (though his character had gleams of it), as because he dreaded above all things the appearance of niggardliness and the sus-picion of a shallow purse.

Then came the memorable interview with his guardian on his twenty-first birthday. Harvey flinched and grew hot in thinking

of it. What an ungrateful cur! What a self-sufficient young idiot!
The Doctor had borne so kindly with his follies and vices, had
taken so much trouble for his good, was it not the man's right
and duty to speak grave words of counsel on such an occasion
as this? But to counsel Mr Harvey Rolfe was to be guilty of
gross impertinence. With lofty spirit the young gentleman proclaimed that he must no longer be treated as a school-boy!
Whereupon the Doctor lost his temper, and spoke with a
particularly strong Hibernian accent – spoke words which to
this moment stung the hearer's memory. He saw himself march-
ing from the room – that room yonder, on the ground-floor. It
was some small consolation to remember that he had been
drinking steadily for a week before that happened. Indeed, he
could recall no scene quite so discreditable throughout the
course of his insensate youth.

Well, he had something like two thousand pounds. Whether
he had looked for more or less he hardly knew, or whether he
had looked for anything at all. At one-and-twenty he was the
merest child in matters of the world. Surely something must
have arrested the natural development of his common-sense.
Even in another ten years he was scarcely on a level, as regards
practical intelligence, with the ordinary lad who is leaving
school.

He at once threw up his medical studies, which had grown
hateful to him. He took his first taste of foreign travel. He
extended his reading and his knowledge of languages. And
insensibly a couple of years went by.

The possession of money had done him good. It clarified his
passions, or tended that way. A self-respect, which differed
appreciably from what he had formerly understood by that
term, began to guard him against grossness; together with it
there developed in him a new social pride which made him
desire the acquaintance of well-bred people. Though he had no
longer any communication with the good old Doctor, Amy
frequently wrote to him, and in one of her letters she begged
him to call on a family in London, one of whose younger
members lived at Greystone and was Amy's friend. After much
delay, he overcame his bashfulness, and called upon the worthy
people – tailored as became a gentleman at large. The acquaintance led to others; in a short time he was on pleasant terms with
several well-to-do families. He might have suspected – but at the

time, of course, did not – that Dr Harvey's kindly influence had
something to do with his reception in these houses. Self-centred,
but painfully self-distrustful, he struggled to overcome his
natural defects of manner. Possibly with some success; for did
not Lily Burton, who at first so piqued him by her critical smile,
come to show him tolerance, friendliness, gracious interest?

Lily Burton! – how emptily, how foolishly the name tinkled
out of that empty and foolish past! Yet what a power it had
over him when he was three and twenty! Of all the savage
epithets which he afterwards attached to its owner, probably
she merited a few. She was a flirt, at all events. She drew him
on, played upon his emotions, found him, no doubt, excellent
fun; and at last, when he was imbecile enough to declare himself,
to talk of marriage, Lily, raising the drollest eyes, quietly wished
to know what his prospects were.

The intolerable shame of it, even now! But he laughed,
mocking at his dead self.

His mind's eye beheld the strange being a year later. Still in
good clothes, but unhealthy, and at his last half-crown; four and
twenty, travelled, and possessed of the elements of culture, he
had only just begun to realise the fact that men labour for their
daily bread. Was it the peculiar intensity of his egoism that so
long blinded him to common anxieties? Even as the last coins
slipped between his fingers, he knew only a vaguely irritable
apprehension. Did he imagine the world would beg for the
honour of feeding and clothing Mr Harvey Rolfe?

It came back to him, his first experience of hunger – so very
different a thing from appetite. He saw the miserable bedroom
where he sat on a rainy day. He smelt the pawnshop. His heart
sank again under the weight of awful solitude. Then, his illness;
the letter he wrote to Amy; her visit to him; the help she brought.
But she could not persuade him to go back with her to Greystone
to face the Doctor. Her money was a loan; he would bestir
himself and find occupation. For a wonder, it was found – the
place at the Emigration Agency; and so, for a good many years,
the notable Mr Harvey Rolfe sank into a life of obscure routine.

Again and again his sister Amy besought him to visit Greystone. Dr Harvey was breaking up; would he not see the kind
old man once more? Yes, he assured himself that he would; but
he took his time about it, and Dr Harvey, who at threescore
and ten could not be expected to wait upon a young man's

convenience, one day very quietly died. To Amy Rolfe, who had become as a daughter to him, he left the larger part of his possessions, an income of nine hundred a year. Not long after this, Harvey met his sister, and was astonished to find her looking thin, pale, spiritless. What did it mean? Why did she gaze at him so sadly? Come, come, he cried, she had been leading an unnatural life, cloistered, cheerless. Now that she was independent, she must enjoy herself, see the world! Brave words; and braver still those in which he replied to Amy's entreaty that he would share her wealth. Not he, indeed! If, as she said, the Doctor meant and hoped it, why did he not make that plain in his will? Not a penny would he take. He had all he wanted. And he seemed to himself the most magnanimous of men.

Amy lived on at Greystone; amid friends, to be sure, but silent, melancholy; and he, the brother whom she loved, could spare her only a day or two once a year, when he chattered his idle self-conceit. Anyone else would have taken trouble to inquire the cause of her pallor, her sadness. He, forsooth, had to learn with astonishment, at last, that she wished to see him – on her deathbed.

He had often thought of her, and kindly. But he knew her not at all, took no interest in her existence. She, on the other hand, had treasured every miserable little letter his idleness vouchsafed; she had hoped so for his future, ever believing in him. When Amy lay dead, he saw the sheet of paper on which she had written the few lines necessary to endow him with all she left – everything 'to my dear brother'. What words could have reproached him so keenly?

His steps turned to the churchyard, where on a plain upright stone he read the names of his mother, of his father. Amy's grave was hard by. He, too, if he had his wish, would some day rest here; and here his own son would stand, and read his name, and think of him. Ah, but with no such remorse and self-contempt! That was inconceivable. The tenderness which dimmed his eyes would have changed to misery had he dreamed it possible that his own boy could palter so ignobly with the opportunities of life.

Upon these deep emotions intruded the thought of Alma. Intruded; for he neither sought nor welcomed his wife's companionship at such a moment, and he was disturbed by a perception of the little claim she had to be present with him in spirit. He could no longer pretend to himself that he loved Alma; whatever the right name for his complex of feelings – interest, regard, admiration, sexual attachment – assuredly it must be another word than that sacred to the memory of his parents, to the desires and hopes centring in his child. For all that, he had no sense of a hopeless discord in his wedded life; he suffered from no disillusion, with its attendant bitterness. From this he was saved by the fact, easy at length to recognise, that in wooing Alma he had obeyed no dictate of the nobler passion; here, too, as at every other crisis of life, he had acted on motives which would not bear analysis, so large was the alloy of mere temperament, of weak concession to circumstance. Rather than complain that Alma fell short of the ideal in wifehood, should he not marvel, and be grateful that their marriage might still be called a happy one? Happiness in marriage is a term of such vague application: Basil Morton, one in ten thousand, might call himself happy; even so, all things considered, must the husband who finds it *just* possible to endure the contiguity of his wife. Midway between these extremes of the definition stood Harvey's measure of matrimonial bliss. He saw that he had no right to grumble.

He saw, moreover, and reflected constantly upon it in these days, how largely he was himself to blame for the peril of estrangement which threatened his life with Alma. Meaning well, and thinking himself a pattern of marital wisdom, he had behaved, as usual, with gross lack of discretion. The question now was, could he mend the harm that he had done? Love did not enter into the matter; his difficulty called for common-sense – for rational methods in behaviour towards a wife whom he could still respect, and who was closely bound to him by common interest in their child.

He looked up, and had pleasure once more in the sunny sky. After all, he, even he, had not committed the most woeful of all blunders; though it was a mystery how he had escaped it. The crown of his feeble, futile career should, in all fitness, have been marriage with a woman worse than himself. And not on his own account did he thank protecting fortune. One lesson, if one only, he had truly learnt from nature: it bade him forget all personal disquietude, in joy that he was not guilty of that crime of crimes, the begetting of children by a worthless mother.

Mrs Morton felt a lively interest in Mrs Rolfe's musical enterprise, and would have liked to talk about it, but she suspected
that the topic was not very agreeable to her guest. In writing to
Morton, Harvey had just mentioned the matter, and that was
all. On the second day of his visit, when he felt much better, and
saw things in a less troubled light, he wished to remove the
impression that he regarded Alma's proceedings with sullen
disapproval; so he took the opportunity of being alone with his
hostess, and talked to her of the great venture with all the good
humour he could command. Mrs Morton had seen two notices
of Alma's début; both were so favourable that she imagined
them the augury of a brilliant career.

'I doubt that,' said Harvey; 'and I'm not sure that it's
desirable. She has made herself miserably ill, you see. Excitement
is the worst possible thing for her. And then there's the whole
question of whether professional life is right and good for a
married woman. How do you think about it?'

The lady instanced cases that naturally presented themselves.
She seemed to have no prejudice. Mrs Rolfe appeared to her a
person of artistic temper; but health was of the first importance;
and then –

Harvey waited; but only a thoughtful smile completed the
remark.

'What other consideration had you in mind?'

'Only a commonplace – that a married woman would, of
course, be guided by her husband's wish.'

'You think that equivalent to reason and the will of God?'*
said Harvey jocosely.

'If we need appeal to solemn sanction.'

Rolfe was reminded, not unpleasantly, that he spoke with a
woman to whom 'the will of God' was something more than a
facetious phrase.

'I beg your pardon; let us say reason alone. But is it reasonable
for the artist to sacrifice herself because she happens to have
married an everyday man?'

Mrs Morton shook her head and laughed.

'If only one know what is meant by the everyday man! My
private view of him is rather flattering, perhaps. I'm inclined to

think him, on the whole, not inferior to the everyday woman; and *she* – she isn't a bad sort of creature, if fairly treated. I don't think the everyday man will go very far wrong, as a rule, in the treatment of his wife.'

'You really believe that?' asked Harvey, with a serious smile.

'Why, is it such a heresy?'

'I should rather have thought so. One is so accustomed to hear the other view – I mean, it's in the air. Don't think I'm asking your sympathy. I have always wished Alma to act on her own judgment; she has been left quite free to do so. But if the results seem worse than doubtful, then comes the difficulty.'

'To be settled, surely, like all other difficulties between sensible people.'

Mrs Morton's faith was of enviable simplicity. She knew, as a matter of fact, that husbands and wives often found their difficulties insuperable; but why this should be so, seemed to her one of the dark and mournful enigmas of life. It implied such a lack not only of good sense, but of right feeling. In her own experience she had met with no doubt, no worry, which did not yield to tact, or generous endeavour, or, at worst, to the creed by which she lived. One solicitude, and one only, continued to affect her as wife and mother; that it could not overcome her happy temper was due to the hope perpetually inspired by her husband's love – a hope inseparable from her profoundest convictions. She and Morton differed in religious views, and there had come a grave moment when she asked whether it would be possible to educate her children in her own belief without putting a distance between them and their father. The doubt had disappeared, thanks to Morton's breadth of view, or facility of conscience; there remained the trouble in which it had originated, but she solaced herself with the fond assurance that this also would vanish as time went on. In the same mood of kindly serenity she regarded the lives of her friends, always hoping for the best, and finding it hard to understand that anyone could deliberately act with unkindness, unreasonableness, or any other quality opposed to the common good.

Rolfe had no desire of talking further about his private affairs. He had made up his mind on the points at issue, and needed no counsel, but the spirit of Mrs Morton's conversation helped him to think tranquilly. The great danger was that he might make things worse by his way of regarding them. Most unluckily,

Alma's illness had become connected in his imagination with the tragedy of the Carnabys; he could not keep the things apart. Hugh Carnaby's miserable doom, and the dark surmises attaching to his wife, doubtless had their part in bringing about a nervous crisis; why could he not recognise this as perfectly natural, and dismiss the matter? In spite of all reasoning, Alma's image ever and again appeared to him shadowed by the gloom which involved her friend – or the woman who *was* her friend. He knew it (or believed it) to be the merest illusion of his perturbed mind; for no fact, how trivial soever, had suggested to him that Alma knew more of the circumstances of Redgrave's death than she seemed to know. On the one hand, he was glad that Alma and Sibyl no longer cared to meet; on the other, he could not understand what had caused this cessation of their friendship, and he puzzled over it. But these idle fancies would pass away; they were already less troublesome. A long country walk with Morton, during which they conversed only of things intellectual, did him much good. Not long ago Morton had had a visit from an old Cambridge friend, a man who had devoted himself to the study of a certain short period of English history, and hoped, some ten years hence, to produce an authoritative work on the subject.

'There's a man I envy!' cried Rolfe, when he had listened to Basil's humorous description of the enthusiast. 'It's exactly what I should like to do myself.'

'What prevents you?'

'Idleness – irresolution – the feeling that the best of my life is over. I have never been seriously a student, and it's too late to begin now. But if I were ten years younger, I would make myself master of something. What's the use of reading only to forget? In my time I have gone through no small library of historical books – and it's all a mist on the mind's horizon. That comes of reading without method, without a purpose. The time I have given to it would have made me a pundit, if I had gone to work reasonably.'

'Isn't my case the same?' exclaimed Morton. 'What do I care! I enjoyed my reading and my knowledge at the time, and that's all I ever expected.'

'Very well – though you misrepresent yourself. But for me it isn't enough. I want to know something as well as it can be known. Purely for my own satisfaction; the thought of "doing something" doesn't come in at all. I was looking at your county histories this morning, and I felt a huge longing to give the rest of my life to some little bit of England, a county, or even a town, and exhaust the possibilities of knowledge within those limits. Why, Greystone here – it has an interesting history, even in relation to England at large; and what a delight there would be in following it out, doggedly, invincibly – making it one's single subject – grubbing after it in muniment-rooms* and libraries – learning by heart every stone of the old town – dying at last with the consolation that nobody could teach one anything more about it!'

'I know the mood,' said Morton, laughing.

'I'm narrowing down,' pursued Harvey. 'Once I had tremendous visions – dreamt of holding half a dozen civilisations in the hollow of my hand. I came back from the East in a fury to learn the Oriental languages – made a start, you know, with Arabic. I dropped one nation after another, always drawing nearer home. The Latin races were to suffice me. Then early France, especially in its relations with England; – Normandy, Anjou. Then early England, especially in its relations with France. The end will be a county, or a town – nay, possibly a building. Why not devote one's self to the history of a market-cross? It would be respectable, I tell you. Thoroughness is all.'

When they were alone in the library at night, Morton spoke of his eldest boy, expressing some anxiety about him.

'The rascal will have to earn his living – and how? There's time, I suppose, but it begins to fidget me. He won't handle corn – I'm clear as to that. At his age, of course, all lads talk about voyages and so on, but Harry seems cut out for a larger sphere than Greystone. I shan't balk him. I'd rather he hadn't anything to do with fighting – still, that's a weakness.'

'We think of sending Wager's lad into the navy,' said Rolfe, when he had mused awhile. 'Of course, he'll have to make his own way.'

'Best thing you can do, no doubt. And what about his little sister?'

'That's more troublesome. It's awkward that she's a relative of Mrs Abbott. Otherwise, I should have proposed to train her for a cook.'

'Do you mean it?'

'Why not? She isn't a girl of any promise. What better thing for her, and for the community, than to make her a good cook? They're rare enough, Heaven knows. What's the use of letting her grow up with ideas of gentility, which in her case would mean nothing but uselessness? She must support herself, sooner or later, and it won't be with her brains. I've seriously thought of making that suggestion to Mrs Abbott. Ten years hence, a sensible woman cook will demand her own price, and be a good deal more respected than a dressmaker or a she-clerk. The stomach is very powerful in bringing people to common-sense. When all the bricklayers' daughters are giving piano lessons, and it's next to impossible to get any servant except a lady's-maid, we shall see women of leisure develop a surprising interest in the boiling of potatoes.'

Morton admitted the force of these arguments.

'What would you wish your own boy to be?' he asked presently.

'Anything old-fashioned, unadventurous, happily obscure; a country parson, perhaps, best of all.'

'I understand. I've had the same thoughts. But one has to get over that kind of thing. It won't do to be afraid of life – nor of death either.'

'And there's the difficulty of education,' said Rolfe. 'If I followed my instincts, I should make the boy unfit for anything but the quietest, obscurest life. I should make him hate a street, and love the fields. I should teach him to despise every form of ambition; to shrink from every kind of pleasure, but the simplest and purest; to think of life as a long day's ramble, and death as the quiet sleep that comes at the end of it. I should like him not to marry – never to feel the need of it; or if marry he must, to have no children. That's my real wish; and if I tried to carry it out, the chances are that I should do him an intolerable wrong. For fear of it, I must give him into the hands of other people; I must see him grow into habits and thoughts which will cause me perpetual uneasiness; I must watch him drift further and further away from my own ideal of life, till at length, perhaps, there is scarce a possibility of sympathy between us.'

'Morbid – all morbid,' remarked the listener.

'I don't know. It may only mean that one sees too clearly the root facts of existence. I have another mood (less frequent) in which I try to persuade myself that I don't care much about the child; that his future doesn't really concern me at all. Why should it? He's just one of the millions of human beings who come and go. A hundred years hence – what of him and of me? What can it matter how he lived and how he died? The best kind of education would be that which hardened his skin and blunted his sympathies. What right have I to make him sensitive? The thing is, to get through life with as little suffering as possible. What monstrous folly to teach him to wince and cry out at the sufferings of other people! Won't he have enough of his own before he has done? Yet that's what we shall aim at – to cultivate his sympathetic emotions, so that the death of a bird shall make him sad, and the sight of human distress wring his heart. Real kindness would try to make of him a healthy ruffian, with just enough conscience to keep him from crime.'

'Theory for theory, I prefer this,' said Morton. 'To a certain extent I try to act upon it.'

'You do?'

'Just because I know that my own tendency is to over-softness. I have sometimes surprised my wife by bidding Harry disregard things that appealed to his pity. You remember what old Hobbes says: "*Homo malus, puer robustus*"?* There was more truth in it in his day than in ours. It's natural for a boy to be a good deal of a savage, but our civilisation is doing its best to change that. Why, not long ago the lad asked me whether fishing wasn't cruel. He evidently felt that it was, and so do I; but I couldn't say so. I laughed it off, and told him that a fish diet was excellent for the brains!'

'I hope I may have as much courage,' said Harvey.

'Life is a compromise, my dear fellow. If the world at large would suddenly come round to a cultivation of the amiable virtues – well and good. But there's no hope of it. As it is, our little crabs must grow their hard shell,* or they've no chance.'

'What about progress? In educating children, we are making the new world.'

Morton assented.

'But there's no hurry. The growth must be gradual – will be, whether we intend it or not. The fact is, I try not to think overmuch about my children. It remains a doubt, you know, whether education has any influence worth speaking of.'

'To me,' said Harvey, 'the doubt seems absurd. In my own case, I know, a good system of training would have made an enormous difference. Practically, I was left to train myself, and a nice job I made of it. Do you remember how I used to talk about children before I had one? I have thought it was the talk of a fool; but, perhaps, after all, it had more sanity than my views nowadays.'

'*Medio tutissimus*,'* murmured Basil.

'And what about your girls?' asked the other, when they had smoked in silence. 'Is the difficulty greater or less?'

'From my point of view, less. For one thing, I can leave them entirely in the hands of their mother; if they resemble her, they won't do amiss. And there's no bother about work in life; they will have enough to live upon – just enough. Of course, they may want to go out into the world. I shall neither hinder nor encourage. I had rather they stayed at home.'

'Don't lose sight of the possibility that by when they are grown up there may be no such thing as "home". The word is dying out.'

Morton's pedantry led him again to murmur Latin –

'*Multa renascentur quæ jam cecidere.*'*

'You're the happiest man I know, or ever shall know,' said Rolfe, with more feeling than he cared to exhibit.

'Don't make me think about Crœsus,* King of Lydia. On the whole, happiness means health, and health comes of occupation. In one point I agree with you about yourself: it would have been better if someone had found the right kind of work for you, and made you stick to it. By-the-bye, how does your friend, the photographic man, get on?'

'Not at all badly. Did I tell you I had put money into it? I go there a good deal, and pretend to do something.'

'Why pretend? Couldn't you find a regular job there for a few hours every day?'

'I dare say I could. It'll be easier to get backwards and forwards from Gunnersbury. How would you like,' he added, with a laugh, 'to live at Gunnersbury?'

'What does it matter where one lives? I have something of a prejudice against Hoxton or Bermondsey; but I think I could get along in most other places. Gunnersbury is rather pleasant, I thought. Isn't it quite near to Kew and Richmond?'

'Do those names attract you?'

'They have a certain charm for the rustic ear.'

'It's all one to me. Hughie will go to school, and make friends with other children. You see, he's had no chance of it yet. We know a hundred people or so, but have no intimates. Is there such a thing as intimacy of families in London? I'm inclined to think not. Here, you go into each other's houses without fuss and sham; you know each other, and trust each other. In London there's no such comfort, at all events for educated people. If you have a friend, he lives miles away; before his children and yours can meet, they must travel for an hour and a half by 'bus and underground.'

'I suppose it *must* be London?' interrupted Morton.

'I'm afraid so,' Harvey replied absently, and his friend said no more.

He had meant this visit to be of three days at most; but time slipped by so pleasantly that a week was gone before he could resolve on departure. Most of the mornings he spent in rambles alone, rediscovering many a spot in the country round which had been familiar to him as a boy, but which he had never cared to seek in his revisitings of Greystone hitherto. One day, as he followed the windings of a sluggish stream, he saw flowers of arrowhead, white flowers with crimson centre, floating by the bank, and remembered that he had once plucked them here when on a walk with his father, who held him the while, lest he should stretch too far and fall in. To reach them now, he lay down upon the grassy brink; and in that moment there returned to him, with exquisite vividness, the mind, the senses, of childhood; once more he knew the child's pleasure in contact with earth, and his hand grasped hard at the sweet-smelling turf as though to keep hold upon the past thus fleetingly recovered. It was gone – no doubt, for ever; a last glimpse vouchsafed to him of life's beginning as he set his face towards the end. Then came a thought of joy. The keen sensations which he himself had lost were his child's inheritance. Somewhere in the fields, this summer morning, Hughie was delighting in the scent, the touch, of earth, young amid a world where all was new. The stereotyped phrase about parents living again in their children became a reality and a source of deep content. So does a man repeat the experience of the race, and with each step onward live into the meaning of some old word that he has but idly echoed.

On the day before he left, a letter reached him from Alma. He had felt surprise at not hearing sooner from her; but Alma's words explained the delay.

'I have been thinking a great deal,' she wrote, 'and I want to tell you of my thoughts. Don't imagine they are mere fancies, the result of ill-health. I feel all but well again, and have a perfectly clear head. And perhaps it is better that I should write what I have to say, instead of speaking it. In this way I oblige you to hear me out. I don't mean that you are in the habit of interrupting me, but perhaps you would if I began to talk as I am going to write.

'Why can't we stay at Pinner?

'There, that shall have a line to itself. Take breath, and now listen again. I dislike the thought of removing to Gunnersbury – really and seriously I dislike it. You know I haven't given you this kind of trouble before; when we left Wales I was quite willing to have stayed on if you had wished it – wasn't I? Forgive me, then, for springing this upon you after all your arrangements are made; I could not do it if I did not feel that our happiness (not mine only) is concerned. Would it be possible to cancel your agreement with the Gunnersbury man? If not, couldn't you sublet, with little or no loss? The Pinner house isn't let yet – is it? Do let us stay where we are. I think it is the first serious request I ever made of you, and I think you will see that I have some right to make it.

'I had rather, much rather, that Hughie did not go to Mrs Abbott's school. Don't get angry and call me foolish. What I mean is, that I would rather teach him myself. In your opinion I have neglected him, and I confess that you are right. There now! I shall give up my music; at all events, I shall not play again in public. I have shown what I could do, and that's enough. You don't like it – though you have never tried to show me *why* – and again I feel that you are right. A professional life for me would mean, I see it now, the loss of things more precious. I will give it up, and live quietly at home. I will have regular hours for teaching Hughie. If you prefer it, Pauline shall go, and I will take charge of him altogether. If I do this, what need for us to remove? The house is more comfortable than the new one at Gunnersbury; we are accustomed to it; and by being farther from London I shall have less temptation to gad about. I know exactly what I am promising, and I feel I *can* do it, now that my mind is made up.

'Need I fear a refusal? I can't think so. Give the matter your best thought, and see whether there are not several reasons on my side. But, please, answer as soon as you can, for I shall be in suspense till I hear from you.'

Alma signed herself 'Yours ever affectionately', but Harvey could find no trace of affection in the letter. It astonished and annoyed him. Of course, it could have but one explanation; Alma might as well have saved herself trouble by writing, in a line or two, that she disliked Mrs Abbott, and could not bear that the child should be taught by her. He read through the pages again, and grew angry. What right had she to make such a request as this, and in the tone of a demand? Twice in the letter she asserted that she *had* a right, asserted it as if with some mysterious reference. Had he sat down immediately to reply, Harvey would have written briefly forcibly; for, putting aside other grounds of irritation, there is nothing a man dislikes more than being called upon at last moment to upset elaborate and troublesome arrangements. But he was obliged to postpone his answer for a few hours, and in the meantime he grew more tolerant of Alma's feelings. Had her objection come earlier, accompanied by the same proposals, he would have been inclined to listen; but things had gone too far. He wrote, quite good-temperedly, but without shadow of wavering. There was nothing sudden, he pointed out, in the step he was about to take; Alma had known it for months, and had acquiesced in it. As for her music, he quite agreed with her that she would find it better in every way to abandon thoughts of a public career; and the fact of Hughie's going to school for two or three hours a day would in no wise interfere with her wish to see more of him. What her precise meaning was in saying that she had some 'right' to make this request, he declared himself unable to discover. Was it a reproach? If so, his conscience afforded him no light, and he hoped Alma would explain the words in a letter to him at Pinner.

This correspondence clouded his last evening at Greystone. He was glad that some acquaintances of Morton's came, and stayed late; sitting alone with his friend, he would have been tempted to talk of Alma, and he felt that silence was better just now.

By a train soon after breakfast next morning, he left the old town, dearer to him each time that he beheld it, and travelled slowly to the main-line junction, whence again he travelled slowly to Peterborough. There the express caught him up, and flung him into roaring London again. Before going to Pinner, he wished to see Cecil Morphew, for he had an idea to communicate – a suggestion for the extending of business by opening correspondence with out of the way towns, such as Greystone.

On reaching the shop in Westminster Bridge Road, he found that Morphew also had a communication to make, and of a more exciting nature.

## CHAPTER 3

Morphew was engaged upstairs with the secretary of an Amateur Photographic Society. Waiting for this person's departure, Rolfe talked with the shopman – a capable fellow, aged about thirty, whose heart was in the business; he looked at a new hand-camera, which seemed likely to have a good sale, and heard encouraging reports of things in general. Then Morphew came down, escorting his visitor. As soon as he was free, he grasped Harvey by the arm, and whispered eagerly that he had something to tell him. They went upstairs together, into a room furnished as an office, hung about with many framed photographs.

'He's dead!' exclaimed Cecil – 'he's dead!'

A name was needless. Only one man's death could be the cause of such excitement in Morphew, and it had been so long awaited that the event had no touch of solemnity. Yet Harvey perceived that his friend's exultation was not unmixed with disquietude.

'Yesterday morning, early. I heard it by chance. Of course, she hasn't written to me, but no doubt I shall hear in a few days. I walked about near the house for hours last night – like an idiot. The thing seemed impossible; I had to keep reminding myself, by looking at the windows, that it was true. Eight years – think of that! Eight years' misery, due to that fellow's snobbishness!'

In Harvey's mind the story had a somewhat different aspect. He knew nothing personally of this Mr Winter, who might indeed be an incarnation of snobbery; on the other hand, Cecil Morphew had his defects, and even to a liberal-minded parent might not recommend himself as a son-in-law. Then again, the young lady herself, now about six and twenty, must surely have been influenced by some other motive than respect for her parents' wishes, in thus protracting her engagement with a lover who had a secure, though modest, income. Was it not conceivable that she inherited something of the paternal spirit? or, at all events, that her feelings had not quite the warmth that Morphew imagined?

'I'm glad it's over,' he replied cordially. 'Now begins a new life for you.'

'But eight years – eight years of waiting – '

'Hang it, what is your age? Thirty! Why, you're only just old enough. No man ought to marry before thirty.'

Morphew interrupted vehemently.

'That's all rot! Excuse me; I can't help it. A man ought to marry when he's urged to it by his nature, and as soon as he finds the right woman. If I had married eight years ago—.' He broke off with an angry gesture, misery in his eyes. 'You don't believe that humbug, Rolfe; you repeat it just to console me. There's little consolation, I can assure you. I was two and twenty; she, nineteen. Mature man and woman; and we longed for each other. Nothing but harm could come of waiting year after year, wretched both of us.'

'I confess,' said Harvey, 'I don't quite see why she waited after twenty-one.'

'Because she is a good, gentle girl, and could not bear to make her father and mother unhappy. The blame is all theirs – mean, shallow, grovelling souls!'

'What about her mother now?'

'Oh, she was never so obstinate as the old jackass. She'll have little enough to live upon, and we shall soon arrange things with her somehow. Is it credible that human beings can be so senseless? For years now, their means have been growing less and less, just because the snobbish idiot *would* keep up appearances. If he had lived a little longer, the widow would have had practically no income at all. Of course, she shared in the folly, and I'm only sorry she won't suffer more for it. They didn't enjoy their lives – never have done. They lived in miserable slavery to the opinion of their fellow-snobs. You remember that story about the flowers at their silver wedding: two hundred pounds – just because Mrs Somebody spent as much – when they couldn't really afford two hundred shillings. And they

groaned over it – he and she – like people with the stomach-
ache. Why, the old fool died of nothing else; he was worn out
by the fear of having to go into a smaller house.'

Harvey would have liked to put a question: was it possible
that the daughter of such people could be endowed with virtues
such as become the wife of a comparatively poor man? But he
had to ask it merely in his own thoughts. Before long, no doubt,
he would meet the lady herself and appease his curiosity.

Whilst they were talking, there came a knock at the door; the
shopman announced two ladies, who wished to inquire about
some photographic printing.

'Will you see them, Rolfe?' asked Cecil. 'I don't feel like it –
indeed I don't. You'll be able to tell them all they want.'

Harvey found himself equal to the occasion, and was glad of
it; he needed occupation of some kind to keep his thoughts from
an unpleasant subject. After another talk with Morphew, in
which they stuck to business, he set off homeward.

Here news awaited him. On his arrival all seemed well; Ruth
opened the door, answered his greeting in her quiet, respectful
way, and at once brought tea to the study. When he rang to
have the things taken away, Ruth again appeared, and he saw
now that she had something unusual to say.

'I didn't like to trouble you the first thing, sir,' she began –
'but Sarah left yesterday without giving any notice; and I think
it's perhaps as well she did, sir. I've heard some things about her
not at all nice.'

'We must find someone else, then,' replied Harvey. 'It's lucky
she didn't go at a less convenient time. Was there some
unpleasantness between you?'

'I had warned her, for her own good, sir, that was all. And
there's something else I had perhaps better tell you now, sir.'
Her voice, with its pleasant Welsh accent, faltered ominously.
'I'm very sorry indeed to say it, sir, but I shall be obliged to
leave as soon as Mrs Rolfe can spare me.'

Harvey was overwhelmed. He looked upon Ruth as a permanent member of the household. She had made herself indispensable; to her was owing the freedom from domestic harassment
which Alma had always enjoyed – a most exceptional blessing,
yet regarded, after all this time, as a matter of course. The
departure of Ruth meant conflict with ordinary servants, in
which Alma would assuredly be worsted. At this critical moment

of their life, scarcely could anything more disastrous have happened. Seeing her master's consternation, Ruth was sore troubled, and hastened to explain herself.

'My brother's wife has just died, sir, and left him with three young children, and there's no one else can be of help to him but me. He wanted me to come at once, but, of course, I told him I couldn't do that. No one can be sorry for his wife's death; she was such a poor, silly, complaining, useless creature; he hasn't had a quiet day since he married her. She belonged to Liverpool, and there they were married, and when he brought her to Carnarvon I said to myself as soon as I saw her that *she* wouldn't be much use to a working-man. She began the very first day to complain and to grumble, and she's gone on with it ever since. When I was there in my last holiday I really wondered how he bore his life. There's many women of that kind, sir, but I never knew one as bad as her – never. Everything was too much trouble for her, and she didn't know how to do a thing in the house. I didn't mean to trouble you with such things, sir. I only told you just to show why I don't feel I can refuse to go and help him, and try to give him a little peace and quiet. He's a hard-working man, and the children aren't very healthy, and I'm sure I don't know how he'd manage – '

'You have no choice, Ruth, I see. Well, we must hope to find some one in your place – *but* – '

Just as he shook his head, the house-bell rang, and Ruth withdrew to answer it. In a minute or two the study door opened again. Harvey looked up and saw Alma.

'I was obliged to come,' she said, approaching him, as he rose in astonishment. 'I thought at first of asking you to come on to Basingstoke, but we can talk better here.'

No sign of pleasure in their meeting passed between them. On Harvey's face lingered something of the disturbance caused by Ruth's communication, and Alma understood it as due to her unexpected arrival; the smile with which she had entered died away, and she stood like a stranger doubtful of her reception.

'Was it necessary to talk?' asked Rolfe, pushing forward a chair, and doing his best to show good humour.

'Yes – after your reply to my letter this morning,' she answered coldly.

'Well, you must have some tea first. This is cold. Won't you go and take your things off, and I'll tell Ruth. By-the-bye, we're in confusion.'

He sketched the position of things; but Alma heard without interest.

'It can't be helped,' was her absent reply. 'There are plenty of servants.'

Fresh tea was brought, and after a brief absence Alma sat down to it. Her health had improved during the past week, but she looked tired from the journey, and was glad to lean back in her chair. For some minutes neither of them spoke. Harvey had never seen an expression on Alma's features which was so like hostility; it moved him to serious resentment. It is common enough for people who have been several years wedded to feel exasperation in each other's presence, but for Rolfe the experience was quite new, and so extremely disagreeable, that his pulses throbbed with violence, and his mouth grew dry. He determined to utter not a word until Alma began conversation. This she did at length, with painful effort.

'I think your answer to me was very unkind.'

'I didn't mean it so.'

'You simply said that you wouldn't do as I wished.'

'Not that I wouldn't, but that it was impossible. And I showed you the reasons – though I should have thought it superfluous.'

Alma waited a moment, then asked –

'Is this house let?'

'I don't know. I suppose not.'

'Then there is no reason whatever why we shouldn't stay here.'

'There is every reason why we shouldn't stay here. Every arrangement has been made for our leaving – everything fully talked over. What has made you change your mind?'

'I haven't really changed my mind. I always disliked the idea of going to Gunnersbury, and you must have seen that I did; but I was so much occupied with – with other things; and, as I have told you, I didn't feel quite the same about my position as I do now.'

She expressed herself awkwardly, growing very nervous. At the first sign of distress in her, Harvey was able to change his tone.

'Things are going horribly wrong somehow, Alma. There's

only one way out of it. Just say in honest words what you mean. Why do you dislike the thought of our moving?'

'I told you in my letter,' she answered, somewhat acridly.

'There was no explanation. You said something I couldn't understand, about having a *right* to ask me to stay here.'

She glanced at him with incredulous disdain.

'If you don't understand, I can't put it into plainer words.'

'Well now, let *me* put the whole matter into plainer words than I have liked to use.' Rolfe spoke deliberately, and not unkindly, though he was tempted to give way to wrath at what he imagined a display of ignoble and groundless jealousy. 'All along I have allowed you to take your own course. No, I mustn't say "allowed", the word is inapplicable; I never claimed the right to dictate to you. We agreed that this was the way for rational husband and wife. It seemed to us that I had no more right to rule over you than you to lay down the law for me. Using your freedom, you chose to live the life of an artist – that is to say, you troubled yourself as little as possible about home and family. I am not complaining – not a bit of it. The thing was an experiment, to be sure; but I have held to the conditions, watched their working. Latterly I began to see that they didn't work well, and it appears that you agree with me. This is how matters stand; or rather, this is how they stood until, for some mysterious reason, you seemed to grow unfriendly. The reason is altogether mysterious; I leave you to explain it. From my point of view, the failure of our experiment is simple and natural enough. Though I had only myself to blame, I have felt for a long time that you were in an utterly false position. Now you begin to see things in the same light. Well and good; why can't we start afresh? The only obstacle is your unfriendly feeling. Give me an opportunity of removing it. I hate to be on ill terms with you; it seems monstrous, unaccountable. It puts us on a level with married folk in a London lodging-house. Is it necessary to sink quite so low?'

Alma listened with trembling intensity, and seemed at first unable to reply. Her agitation provoked Harvey more than it appealed to his pity.

'If you can't do as I wish,' she said at length, with an endeavour to speak calmly, 'I see no use in making any change in my own life. There will be no need of me. I shall make arrangements to go on with my professional career.'

Harvey's features for a moment set themselves in combative-ness, but as quickly they relaxed, and showed an ambiguous smile.

'No need of you – and Ruth going to leave us?'

'There oughtn't to be any difficulty in finding someone just as good.'

'Perhaps there ought not to be; but we may thank our stars if we find anyone half as trustworthy. The chances are that a dozen will come and go before we settle down again. I don't enjoy that prospect, and I shall want a good deal of help from you in bearing the discomfort.'

'What kind of help? Of course, I shall see that the house goes on as usual.'

'Then it's quite certain you will have no time left for a "professional career".'

'If I understand you, you mean that you don't wish me to have any time for it.'

Harvey still smiled, though he could not conceal his nervousness.

'I'm afraid it comes to that.'

So little had Alma expected such a declaration, that she gazed at him in frank surprise.

'Then you are going to oppose me in everything?'

'I hope not. In that case we should do much better to say good-bye.'

The new tone perplexed her, and a puzzled interest mingled with the lofty displeasure of her look.

'Please let us understand each other.' She spoke with demon-strative calmness. 'Are we talking on equal terms, or is it master and servant?'

'Husband and wife, Alma, that's all.'

'With a new meaning in the words.'

'No; a very old one. I won't say the oldest, for I believe there was a time when primitive woman had the making of man in every sense, and somehow knocked a few ideas into his head; but that was very long ago.'

'If I could be sure of your real meaning – .' She made an irritated gesture. 'How are we going to live? You speak of married people in lodging-houses. I don't know much about them, happily, but I imagine the husband talks something like this – though in more intelligible language.'

'I dare say he does – poor man. He talks more plainly, because he has never put himself in a false position – has never played foolishly with the facts of life.'

Alma sat reflecting.

'Didn't I tell you in my letter,' she said at length, 'that I was quite willing to make a change, on one condition?'

'An impossible condition.'

'You treat me very harshly. How have I deserved it? When I wrote that, I really wished to please you. Of course, I knew you were dissatisfied with me, and it made me dissatisfied with myself. I wrote in a way that ought to have brought me a very different answer. Why do you behave as if I were guilty of something – as if I had put myself at your mercy? You never found fault with me – you even encouraged me to go on –'

Her choking voice made Harvey look at her in apprehension, and the look stopped her just as she was growing hysterical.

'You are right about my letter,' he said, very gravely and quietly. 'It ought to have been in a kinder tone. It would have been, but for those words you won't explain.'

'You think it needs any explanation that I dislike the thought of Hughie going to Mrs Abbott's?'

'Indeed I do. I can't imagine a valid ground for your objection.'

There was a word on Alma's tongue, but her lips would not utter it.* She turned very pale under the mental conflict. Physical weakness, instead of overcoming her spirit, excited it to a fresh effort of resistance.

'Then,' she said, rising from the chair, 'you are not only unkind to me, but dishonest.'

Harvey flushed.

'You are making yourself ill again. We had far better not talk at all.'

'I came up for no other purpose. We have to settle everything.'

'As far as I am concerned, everything *is* settled.'

'Then I have no choice,' said Alma, with subdued passion. 'We shall live as we have done. I shall accept any engagement that offers, in London or the country, and regard music as my chief concern. You wished it, and so it shall be.'

Rolfe hesitated. Believing that her illness was the real cause of this commotion, he felt it his duty to use all possible forbearance; yet he knew too well the danger of once more yielding, and at such a crisis. The contest had declared itself – it was will against will; to decide it by the exertion of his sane strength against Alma's hysteria might be best even for the moment. He had wrought himself to the point of unwonted energy, a state of body and mind difficult to recover if now he suffered defeat. Alma, turning from him, seemed about to leave the room.

'One moment – '

She looked round, carelessly attentive.

'That wouldn't be living as we have done. It would be an intolerable state of things after this.'

'It's your own decision.'

'Far from it. I wouldn't put up with it for a day.'

'Then there's only one thing left: I must go and live by myself.'

'I couldn't stand that either, and wouldn't try.'

'I am no slave! I shall live where and how I choose.'

'When you have thought about it more calmly, your choice will be the same as mine.'

Trembling violently, she backed away from him. Harvey thought she would fall; he tried to hold her by the arm, but Alma shook him off, and in the same moment regained her strength. She faced him with a new defiance, which enabled her at last to speak the words hitherto unutterable.

'How do you think I can bear to see Hughie with *those* children?'

Rolfe stood in amaze. The suddenness of this reversion to another stage of their argument enhanced his natural difficulty in understanding her.

'What children?'

'Those two – whatever their name may be.'

'Wager's boy and girl?'

'You call them so.'

'Are you going crazy? I *call* them so? – what do you mean?'

A sudden misgiving appeared in Alma's eyes; she stared at him so strangely that Harvey began to fear for her reason.

'What is it, dear? What have you been thinking? Tell me – speak like yourself – '

'Why do you take so much interest in them?' she asked faintly.

'Heavens! You have suspected – ? What *have* you suspected?'

'They are your own. I have known it for a long time.'

Alarm notwithstanding, Rolfe was so struck by the absurdity

of this charge that he burst into stentorian laughter. Whilst he laughed, Alma sank into a chair, powerless, tearful.

'I should much like to know,' exclaimed Harvey, laying a hand upon her, 'how you made that astounding discovery. Do you think they are like me?'

'The girl is – or I thought so.'

'After you had decided that she must be, no doubt.' Again he exploded in laughter. 'And this is the meaning of it all? This is what you have been fretting over? For how long?'

Alma brushed away her tears, but gave no answer.

'And if I am their father,' he pursued, with resolute mirthfulness, 'pray, who do you suppose their mother to be?'

Still Alma kept silence, her head bent.

'I'll warrant I can give you evidence against myself which you hadn't discovered,' Rolfe went on – 'awful and unanswerable evidence. It is I who support those children, and pay for their education! – it is I, and no other. See your darkest suspicion confirmed. If only you had known this for certain!'

'Why, then, do you do it?' asked Alma, without raising her eyes.

'For a very foolish reason: there was no one else who could or would.'

'And why did you keep it a secret from me?'

'This is the blackest part of the whole gloomy affair,' he answered, with burlesque gravity. 'It's in the depraved nature of men to keep secrets from their wives, especially about money. To tell the truth, I'm hanged if I know why I didn't tell you before our marriage. The infamous step was taken not very long before, and I might as well have made a clean breast of it. Has Mrs Abbott never spoken to you about her cousin, Wager's wife?'

'A word or two.'

'Which you took for artful fiction? You imagined she had plotted with me to deceive you? What, in the name of common-sense, is your estimate of Mrs Abbott's character?'

Alma drew a deep breath, and looked up into her husband's face. 'Still – she knew you were keeping it from me, about the money.'

'She had no suspicion of it. She always wrote to me openly, acknowledging the cheques. Would it gratify you to look through her letters?'

'I believe you.'

'Not quite, I fancy. Look at me again and say it.'

He raised her head gently.

'Yes, I believe you – it was very silly.'

'It was. The only piece of downright feminine foolishness I ever knew you guilty of. But when did it begin?'

Alma had become strangely quiet. She spoke in a low, tired voice, and sat with head turned aside, resting against the back of the chair; her face was expressionless, her eyelids drooped. Rolfe had to repeat his question.

'I hardly know,' she replied. 'It must have been when my illness was coming on.'

'So I should think. It was sheer frenzy. And now that it's over, have you still any prejudice against Mrs Abbott?'

'No.'

The syllable fell idly from her lips.

'You are tired, dear. All this sound and fury has been too much for you. Lie down on the sofa till dinner-time.'

She allowed him to lead her across the room, and lay down as he wished. To his kiss upon her forehead she made no response, but closed her eyes and was very still. Harvey seated himself at his desk, and opened two or three unimportant letters which had arrived this morning. To one of them he wrote an answer. Turning presently to glance at Alma, he saw that she had not stirred, and when he leaned towards her, the sound of her breathing told him that she was asleep.

He meditated on Woman.

A quarter of an hour before dinner-time he left the room; on his return, when the meal was ready, he found Alma still sleeping, and so soundly that it seemed wrong to wake her. As rays of sunset had begun to fall into the room, he drew the blind, then quietly went out, and had dinner by himself.

At ten o'clock Alma still slept. Using a closely-shaded lamp, Harvey sat in the room with her and read – or seemed to read; for ever and again his eyes strayed to the still figure, and his thoughts wandered over all he knew of Alma's life. He wished he knew more, that he might better understand her. Of her childhood, her early maidenhood, what conception had he? Yet he and she were *one* – so said the creeds. And Harvey laughed to himself, a laugh more of melancholy than of derision.

The clock ticked on; it was near to eleven. Then Alma stirred, raised herself, and looked towards the light.

'Harvey – ? Have I been asleep so long?'

'Nearly five hours.'

'Oh! That was last night – '

'You mean, you had no sleep?'

'Didn't close my eyes.'

'And you feel better now?'

'Rather hungry.'

Rolfe laughed. He had seated himself on the couch by her and held her in his arms.

'Why, then we'll have some supper – a cold fowl and a bottle of Burgundy – a profligate supper, fit for such abandoned characters; and over it you shall tell me how the world looked to you when you were ten years old.'

## CHAPTER 4

Alma returned to Basingstoke, and remained there until the new house was ready for her reception. With the help of her country friends she engaged two domestics, cook and housemaid, who were despatched to Gunnersbury in advance; they had good 'characters', and might possibly co-operate with their new mistress in her resolve to create an admirable household. Into this ambition Alma had thrown herself with no less fervour than that which carried her off to wild Wales* five years ago; but her aim was now strictly 'practical', she would have nothing more to do with 'ideals'. She took lessons in domestic economy from the good people at Basingstoke. Yes, she had found her way at last! Alma saw it in the glow of a discovery, this calm, secure, and graceful middle-way. She talked of it with an animation that surprised and pleased her little circle down in Hampshire; those ladies had never been able to illumine their everyday discharge of duty with such high imaginative glory. In return for their humble lessons, Alma taught them to admire themselves, to see in their place and functions a nobility they had never suspected.

For a day or two after her arrival at Gunnersbury, Harvey

thought that he had never seen her look so well; certainly she had never shown the possibilities of her character to such advantage. It seemed out of the question that any trouble could ever again come between them. Only when the excitement of novelty had subsided did he perceive that Alma was far from having recovered her physical strength. A walk of a mile or two exhausted her; she came home from an hour's exercise with Hughie pale and tremulous; and of a morning it was often to be noticed that she had not slept well. Without talking of it, Harvey planned the holiday which Alma had declared would be quite needless this year; he took a house in Norfolk for September. Before the day of departure, Alma had something to tell him, which, by suggesting natural explanation of her weakness, made him less uneasy. Remembering the incident which had brought to a close their life in Wales, he saw with pleasure that Alma no longer revolted against the common lot of woman. Perhaps, indeed, the announcement she made to him was the cause of more anxiety in his mind than in hers.

They took their servants with them, and left the house to a caretaker. Pauline Smith, though somewhat against Harvey's judgment, had been called upon to resign; Alma wished to have Hughie to herself, save during his school hours; he slept in her room, and she tended him most conscientiously. Harvey had asked whether she would like to invite any one, but she preferred to be alone.

This month by the northern sea improved her health, but she had little enjoyment. After a few days, she wearied of the shore and the moorland, and wished herself back at Gunnersbury. Nature had never made much appeal to her; when she spoke of its beauties with admiration, she echoed the approved phrases, little more; all her instincts drew towards the life of a great town. Sitting upon the sand, between cliff and breakers, she lost herself in a dream of thronged streets and brilliant rooms; the voice of the waves became the roar of traffic, a far sweeter music. With every year this tendency had grown stronger; she could only marvel, now, at the illusion which enabled her to live so long, all but contentedly, in that wilderness where Hughie was born. Rather than return to it, she would die – rather, a thousand times. Happily, there was no such danger. Harvey would never ask her to leave London. All he desired was that she should hold apart from certain currents of town life; and this she was resolved to do, knowing how nearly they had swept her to destruction.

'Wouldn't you like to take up your sketching again?' said Harvey one day, when he saw that she felt dull.

'Sketching? Oh, I had forgotten all about it. It seems ages ago. I should have to begin and learn all over again. No, no; it isn't worth while. I shall have no time.'

She did not speak discontentedly, but Rolfe saw already the justification of his misgivings. She had begun to feel the constant presence of the child a restraint and a burden.

Happily, on their return home, Hughie would go to school for a couple of hours each morning. Alma could have wished it any other school than Mary Abbott's, but the thought was no longer so insupportable as when she suffered under her delusion concerning the two children. Now that she had frequently seen Minnie Wager, she wondered at the self-deception which allowed her to detect in the child's face a distinct resemblance to Harvey. Of course, there was nothing of the kind. She had been the victim of a morbid jealousy – a symptom, no doubt, of the disorder of the nerves which was growing upon her. Yet she could not overcome her antipathy to Mary Abbott. Harvey, she felt sure, would never have made himself responsible for those children, but that in doing so he benefited their teacher; and it was not without motive of conscience that he kept the matter secret. By no effort could Alma banish this suspicion. She resolved that it should never appear; she commanded her face and her utterance; but it was impossible for her ever to regard Mrs Abbott with liking, or even with respect.

In a darker corner of her mind lay hidden another shape of jealousy – jealousy unavowed, often disguised as fear, but for the most part betraying itself through the mask of hatred.

Times innumerable, in nights that brought no rest, and through long hours of weary day, Alma had put her heart to the proof, and acquitted it of any feeling save a natural compassion for the man Hugh Carnaby had killed. She had never loved Redgrave, had never even thought of him with that curiosity which piques the flesh; yet so inseparably was he associated with her life at its points of utmost tension and ardour, that she could not bear to yield to any other woman a closer intimacy, a prior claim. At her peril she had tempted him, and up to the fatal moment she was still holding her own in the game which had become to her a passion. It ended – because a rival came between. Of Sibyl's guilt she never admitted a doubt; it was manifest in the story made public by Hugh Carnaby, the story which he, great simple fellow, told in all good faith, relying absolutely on his wife's assertion of innocence. Saving her husband, who believed Sibyl innocent?

She flattered herself with the persuasion that it was right to hate Sibyl – a woman who had sold herself for money, whose dishonour differed in no respect from that of the woman of the pavement. And all the more she hated her because she feared her. What security could there be that Redgrave's murderer (thus she thought of him) had kept the secret which he promised to keep? That he allowed no hint of it to escape him in public did not prove that he had been equally scrupulous with Sibyl; for Hugh was a mere plaything in the hands of his wife, and it seemed more than likely that he had put his stupid conscience at rest by telling her everything. Were it so, what motive would weigh with Sibyl to keep her silent? One, and one only, could be divined: a fear lest Alma, through intimacy with Redgrave, might have discovered things which put her in a position to dare the enmity of her former friend. This, no doubt, would hold Sibyl to discretion. Yet it could not relieve Alma from the fear of her, and of Hugh Carnaby himself – fear which must last a lifetime; which at any moment, perhaps long years hence, might find its bitter fulfilment, and work her ruin. For Harvey Rolfe was not a man of the stamp of Hugh Carnaby: he would not be hoodwinked in the face of damning evidence, or lend easy ear to specious explanations. The very fact that she *could* explain her ambiguous behaviour was to Alma an enhancement of the dread with which she thought of such a scene between herself and Harvey; for to be innocent, and yet unable to force conviction of it upon his inmost mind, would cause her a deeper anguish than to fall before him with confession of guilt. And to convince him would be impossible, for ever impossible. Say what she might, and however generous the response of his love, there must still remain the doubt which attaches to a woman's self-defence when at the same time she is a self-accuser

In the semi-delirium of her illness, whilst waiting in torment for the assurance that Carnaby had kept her secret, she more than once prayed for Sibyl's death. In her normal state of mind Alma prayed for nothing; she could not hope that Sibyl's life would come to a convenient end; but as often as she thought of her, it was with a vehemence of malignity which fired her imagination to all manner of ruthless extremes. It revolted her to look back upon the time when she sat at that woman's feet, a disciple, an affectionate admirer, allowing herself to be graciously patronised, counselled, encouraged. The repose of manner which so impressed her, the habitual serenity of mood, the unvarying self-confidence – oh, these were excellent qualities when it came to playing the high part of cold and subtle hypocrisy! She knew Sibyl, and could follow the workings of her mind: a woman incapable of love, or of the passion which simulates it; worshipping herself, offering luxuries to her cold flesh as to an idol; scornful of the possibility that she might ever come to lack what she desired; and, at the critical moment, prompt to secure herself against such danger by the smiling, cynical acceptance of whatsoever shame. Alma had no small gift of intuition; proved by the facility and fervour with which she could adapt her mind to widely different conceptions of life. This characteristic, aided by the perspicacity which is bestowed upon every jealous woman, perchance enabled her to read the mysterious Sibyl with some approach to exactness. Were it so, prudence should have warned her against a struggle for mere hatred's sake with so formidable an antagonist. But the voice of caution had never long audience with Alma, and was not likely, at any given moment, to prevail against a transport of her impetuous soul.

Harvey, meanwhile, fearing her inclination to brood over the dark event, tried to behave as though he had utterly dismissed it from his thoughts. He kept a cheerful countenance, talked much more than usual, and seemed full of health and hope. As usual between married people, this resolute cheerfulness had, more often than not, an irritating effect upon Alma. Rolfe erred once more in preferring to keep silence about difficulties rather than face the unpleasantness of frankly discussing them. One good, long, intimate conversation about Mrs Carnaby, with unrestricted exchange of views, the masculine and the feminine, with liberal acceptance of life as it is lived, and honest contempt of leering hypocrisies, would have done more, at this juncture, to put healthy tone into Alma's being than any change of scene and of atmosphere, any medicament or well-meant summons to forgetfulness. Like the majority of good and thoughtful men, he could not weigh his female companion in the balance he found good enough for mortals of his own sex. With a little obtuseness to the 'finer' feelings, a little native coarseness in his habits towards women, he would have succeeded vastly better amid the complications of his married life.

Troubles of a grosser kind, such as heretofore they had been wonderfully spared, began to assail them during their month in Norfolk. One morning, about midway in the holiday, Harvey, as he came down for a bathe before breakfast, heard loud and angry voices from the kitchen. On his return after bathing, he found the breakfast-table very carelessly laid, with knives unpolished, and other such neglects of seemliness. Alma, appearing with Hughie, spoke at once of the strange noises she had heard, and Harvey gave his account of the uproar.

'I thought something was wrong,' said Alma. 'The cook has seemed in a bad temper for several days. I don't like either of them. I think I shall give them both notice, and advertise at once. They say that advertising is the best way.'

The housemaid (in her secondary function of parlour-maid) waited at table with a scowl. The fish was ill fried, the eggs were hard, the toast was soot-smeared. For the moment Alma made no remark; but half an hour later, when Harvey and the child had rambled off to the sea-shore, she summoned both domestics, and demanded an explanation of their behaviour. Her tone was not conciliatory; she had neither the experience nor the tact which are necessary in the mistress of a household, and it needed only an occasion such as this to bring out the contemptuousness with which she regarded her social inferiors. Too well-bred to indulge in scolding or wrangling, the delight of a large class of housewives, Alma had a quiet way of exhibiting displeasure and scorn, which told smartly on the nerves of those she rebuked. No one could better have illustrated the crucial difficulty of the servant-question, which lies in the fact that women seldom can rule, and all but invariably dislike to be ruled by, their own sex; a difficulty which increases with the breaking-up of social distinctions.

She went out into the sunshine, and found Harvey and Hughie building a great castle of sand. Her mood was lightsome, for she felt that she had acted with decision and in a way worthy of her dignity.

'They will both go about their business. I only hope we may get meals for the rest of the time here.'

Harvey nodded, with closed lips.

'It's a pity Pauline went,' he remarked presently.

'I'm afraid it is. I hadn't quite realised what it would mean.'

'I rather think I ventured to say something of that kind, didn't I? She *may* not have taken another place. Suppose you write to her?'

Alma seemed to waver.

'What I am thinking,' she said in a lower tone, 'is that – before long – we shall need – I suppose – someone of a rather different kind – an ordinary nurse-girl. But you wouldn't like Hughie to be with anyone of that sort?'

'It wouldn't matter now.'

'Here's the philosophy of the matter in a nut-shell,' said Harvey afterwards. 'Living nowadays means keeping up appearances, and you must do it just as carefully before your own servants as before your friends. The alternatives are, one general servant, with frank confession of poverty, or a numerous household and everything *comme il faut*. There's no middle way, with peace. I think your determination to take care of Hughie yourself was admirable; but it won't work. These two women think you do it because you can't afford a nurse, and at once they despise us. It's the nature of the beasts – it's the tone of the time. Nothing will keep them and their like in subordination but a jingling of the purse. One must say to them all day long, "I am your superior; I can buy you by the dozen, if need be; I never need soil my finger with any sort of work, and you know it." Ruth was a good creature, but I seriously doubt whether she would have been quite so good if she hadn't seen us keeping our horse and our gardener and our groom down yonder – everything handsome about us. For the sake of quietness we must exalt ourselves.'

'You're quite right about Ruth,' replied Alma, laughing. 'Several times she has let me see how she admired my life of idleness; but it's just that I don't want to go back to.'

'No need. Ruth was practically a housekeeper. You can manage your own house, but you must have a servant for everything. Get a nurse, by all means.'

Alma drew a breath of contentment.

'You are not dissatisfied with *me*, Harvey?'

'Of course not.'

'But tell me – how does Mrs Morton manage? Why isn't she despised by her servants when she's always so busy?'

Harvey had to close his lips against the first answer which occurred to him.

'For one thing,' he replied, 'there's a more natural state of things in those little towns; something of the old spirit still lives. Then the Mortons have the immense advantage of being an old family, settled there for generations, known and respected by everyone. That's a kind of superiority one can't buy, and goes for a great deal in comfortable living. Morton's servants are the daughters of people who served his parents. From their child-hood they have thought it would be a privilege to get into that house.'

'Impossible in London.'

'Unless you are a duchess.'

'What a pleasant thing it must be,' said Alma musingly, 'to have ancestors.'

Harvey chuckled.

'The next best thing is to have descendants.'

'Why, then,' exclaimed Alma, 'we become ancestors ourselves. But one ought to have an interesting house to live in. Nobody's ancestors ever lived in a semi-detached villa. What I should like would be one of those picturesque old places down in Surrey – quite in the country, yet within easy reach of town; a house with a real garden, and perhaps an orchard. I believe you can get them very cheap sometimes. Not rent the house, but buy it. Then we would have our portraits painted, and – '

Harvey asked himself how long Alma would find satisfaction in such a home; but it pleased him to hear her talking thus of the things which were his own hopeless dream.

'That reminds me, Alma, you have never sat yet for your picture, as I said you should.'

'We must wait – now.'

'It shall be done next year.'

They were content with each other this evening, and looked forward to pleasures they might have in common. For Harvey had learnt to nourish only the humblest hopes, and Alma thought she had subdued herself to an undistinguished destiny.

Determined to have done once for all with a task she loathed, Alma wrote out her advertisements for cook, house-parlour-maid, and nurse, and sent them to half a dozen newspapers. After three weeks of correspondence with servants and mistresses – a correspondence which, as Rolfe said, would have made a printed volume of higher sociological interest than anything yet published, or likely to be – the end of her patience and her strength compelled her to decide half desperately, and engage the three young women who appeared least insolent. At the same time she had to find a new boy for boots, windows, knives, and coals, the youngster hitherto employed having been so successful with his 'book' on Kempton Park and Hurst Park* September meetings that he relinquished menial duties and devoted himself wholly to the turf; but this was such a simple matter, compared with the engaging of indoor domestics, that she felt it almost a delight. When a strong, merry-looking lad presented himself, eager for the job, and speaking not a word that was beside the point, Alma could have patted his head.

She amused Harvey that evening by exclaiming with the very accent of sincerity –

'How I like men, and how I detest women!'

Her nerves were so upset again that, when all was over, she had to keep her bed for a day or two. At the sea-side she had generally slept pretty well, but now her insomnia returned, and once more she had recourse to the fashionable specific.* Harvey knew nothing of this; she was careful to hide it from him; and each time she measured out her dose she assured herself that it should be the last.

Oh, but to lie through those terrible small hours, her brain feverishly active, compelling her to live again in the scenes and the emotions she most desired to forget! She was haunted by the voice of Cyrus Redgrave, which at times grew so distinct to her hearing that it became an hallucination. Her memory reproduced his talk with astonishing fidelity; it was as though she had learnt it by heart, instead of merely listening to it at the time. This only in the silence of night; during the day she could not possibly have recalled a tenth of what her brain thus treacherously preserved.

In sleep she sometimes dreamt of him, and that was perhaps worse; for whilst the waking illusion only reproduced what he had actually said, with all his tricks of tone, his suavities of expression, sleep brought before her another Redgrave. He looked at her with a smile, indeed, but a smile of such unutterable malignity that she froze with terror. It was always the same. Redgrave stood before her smiling, silent; stood and gazed until in a paroxysm of anguish she cried out and broke the dream. Once, whilst the agony was upon her, she sprang from bed, meaning to go to her husband and tell him everything, and so, it might be, put an end to her sufferings. But with her hand upon the door she lost courage. Impossible! She could not hope to be believed. She could never convince her husband that she had told him all.

Upon *her* lay the guilt of Redgrave's death. This had entered slowly into her consciousness; at first rejected, but ever returning until the last argument of self-solace gave way. But for her visit to the bungalow that evening, Hugh Carnaby would not have been maddened to the point of fatal violence. In the obscurity he had mistaken her figure for that of Sibyl; and when Redgrave guarded her retreat, he paid for the impulse with his life.

On the Sunday before her concert, she had thought of going to see Redgrave, but the risk seemed too great, and there was no certainty of finding him at home. She wished above all things to see him, for there was a suspicion in her mind that Mrs Strangeways had a plot against her, though of its nature she could form no idea. It might be true that Redgrave was purposely holding aloof, whether out of real jealousy, or simply as a stratagem, a new move in the game. She would not write to him; she knew the danger of letters, and had been careful never to write him even the simplest note. If she must remain in uncertainty about his attitude towards her, the approaching ordeal would be intensified with a new agitation: was he coming to her recital, or was he not? She had counted upon triumphing before him. If he could stay away, her power over him was incomplete, and at the moment when she had meant it to be irresistible.

The chance encounter on Monday with Hugh Carnaby made her think of Sibyl, and she could not rest until she had endeavoured to learn something of Sibyl's movements. As Carnaby was leaving town, his wife would be free; and how did

Sibyl use her freedom? On that subject Mrs Strangeways had a decided opinion, and her knowledge of the world made it more than probable that she was right. Without any scheme of espionage, obeying her instinct of jealous enmity, Alma hastened to Oxford and Cambridge Mansions. But Sibyl had left home, and – was not expected to return that night.

How she spent the next few hours Alma could but dimly remember. It was a vortex of wretchedness. As dark fell she found herself at the gate leading to the bungalow, lurking, listening, waiting for courage to go farther. She stole at length over the grass behind the bushes, until she could see the lighted window of Redgrave's study. The window was open. She crept nearer and nearer, till she was actually in the veranda and looking into the room. Redgrave sat within, smoking and reading a newspaper. She purposely made a movement which drew his attention.

How would it have ended but for Hugh Carnaby?

Beyond ascertaining that Sibyl was not there, she had of course discovered nothing of what she wished to know. As likely as not she had come too early. Redgrave's behaviour when she drew his attention suggested that such a sound at the open window did not greatly surprise him; the surprise appeared when he saw who stood there – surprise and momentary embarrassment, which would be natural enough if he expected a different visitor. And he was so anxious that she should come in at once. Had she done so, Redgrave's life would have been saved; but –

Its having been publicly proved that Mrs Carnaby was then far away from Wimbledon did not tend to shake Alma's conviction. The summons to her mother's deathbed had disturbed Sibyl's arrangements, that was all. Most luckily for her, as it turned out. But women of that kind (said Alma bitterly) are favoured by fortune.

Locked in a drawer of her writing-table lay a bundle of letters and papers which had come to her immediately after the concert. To none of the letters had she replied; it was time for her to go through them, and answer, with due apologies, those which deserved an answer. Several did not; they were from people whom she hoped never to see again – people who wrote in fulsome terms, because they fancied she would become a celebrity. The news of her breakdown had appeared in a few newspapers, and brought her letters of sympathy; these also lay unanswered. On a day of late autumn she brought herself to the task of looking through this correspondence, and in the end she burnt it all. Among the half-dozen people to whom she decided to write was Felix Dymes; not out of gratitude, or any feeling of friendliness, but because she could not overcome a certain fear of the man. He was capable of any meanness, perhaps of villainy; and perhaps he harboured malice against her, seeing that she had foiled him to the last. She penned a few lines asking him to let her have a complete statement of the financial results of her recital, which it seemed strange that he had not sent already.

'My health,' she added, 'is far from re-established, and I am unable either to go to town or to ask you to come and see me. It is rather doubtful whether I shall ever again play in public.'

In her own mind there lingered no doubt at all, but she thought it better not to be too abrupt with Dymes.

After burning all the letters, she read once more through the press notices of her performance. It was significant that the musical critics whose opinion had any weight gave her only a word or two of cautious commendation; her eulogists were writers who probably knew much less about music than she, and who reported concerts from the social point of view. Popular journalism represented her début as a striking success. Had she been able to use her opportunity to the utmost, doubtless something of a 'boom'* – the word then coming into fashion – might have resulted for her; she could have given two or three more recitals before the end of the season, have been much photographed and paragraphed, and then have gone into the country 'to spread her conquests farther'. This was Felix Dymes's hope. Writing with all propriety, he had yet allowed it to be seen how greatly he was vexed and disappointed at her failure to take the flood. Alma, too, had regretful moments; but she fought against the feeling with all her strength. Today she all but found courage to throw these newspapers into the fire; it would be a final sacrifice, a grave symbolic act, and might bring her peace. Yet she could not. Long years hence, would it not be a legitimate pride to show these things to her children? A misgiving mingled with the thought, but her reluctance pre-vailed. She made up a parcel, wrote upon it, 'My Recital, May 1891', and locked it up with other most private memorials.

She had not long to wait for her answer from Dymes. He apologised for his delay in the matter of business, and promised that a detailed statement should be sent to her in a very few days. The unfortunate state of her health – there Alma smiled – moved him to sympathy and profound regret; her abandonment of a professional career *could* not, *must* not, be a final decision!

Something prompted her to hand this letter to Harvey.

'I took it for granted,' he said humorously, 'that the man had sent you a substantial cheque long ago.'

'I believe the balance will be on my side.'

'Would you like me to see to the rest of the business for you?'

'I don't think that's necessary, is it?'

To her relief, Harvey said no more. She waited for the promised balance-sheet, but weeks passed by and it did not arrive. An explanation of this readily occurred to her: Dymes calculated upon bringing her to an interview. She thought of Harvey's proposal, and wished she could dare to accept it; but the obscure risks were too great. So, months elapsed, till the affair seemed forgotten.

They never spoke to each other of Hugh Carnaby or of Sibyl.

Meanwhile, Alma did not lack society. Mrs Abbott, whom, without change of feeling, she grew accustomed to see frequently, introduced her to the Langland family, and in Mrs Langland she found a not uncongenial acquaintance. This lady had known many griefs, and seemed destined to suffer many more; she had wrinkles on her face which should not have been there at forty-five; but no one ever heard her complain or saw her look downhearted.

In her zeal for housewifery, Alma saw much to admire and to imitate in Mrs Langland. She liked the good-humoured modesty with which the elder lady always spoke of herself, and was not displeased at observing an air of deference when the conversation turned on such high matters as literature and art. Mrs Langland knew all about the recital at Prince's Hall; she knew, moreover, as appeared from a casual remark one day, that Mrs Rolfe had skill in 'landscape painting'.

'Who told you that?' asked Alma, with surprise.

'I hope it wasn't a secret. Mrs Abbott spoke of your water-colours once. She was delighted with them.'

Praise even from Mary Abbott gratified Alma; it surprised her, and she doubted its sincerity, but there was satisfaction in knowing that her fame went abroad among the people at Gunnersbury. Without admiration she could not live, and nothing so severely tested her resolution to be content with the duties of home as Harvey's habit of taking all for granted, never remarking upon her life of self-conquest, never soothing her with the flatteries for which she hungered.

She hailed with delight the first visit after several months from her friends Dora and Gerda Leach. During the summer their father's health had suffered so severely that the overwrought man found himself compelled to choose between a long holiday abroad and the certainty of complete collapse if he tried to pursue his ordinary life. The family went away, and returned in November, when it seemed probable that the money-making machine known as Mr Leach had been put into tolerable working order for another year or so. Not having seen Alma since her recital, the girls overflowed with talk about it, repeating all the eulogies they had heard, and adding such rapturous laudation of their own that Alma could have hung upon their necks in gratitude. They found it impossible to believe that she would no more play in public.

'Oh, but when you are *quite* well!' they exclaimed. 'It would be a shame – a sin!'

In writing to them, Alma had put her decision solely on the ground of health. Now, assuming a countenance of gentle gravity, she made known her higher reasons.

'I have felt it to be my duty. Remember that I can't consider myself alone. I found that I must either devote myself wholly to music or give it up altogether. You girls can't very well understand. When one is a wife and a mother – I thought it all over during my illness. I had been neglecting my husband and Hughie, and it was too bad – downright selfishness. Art and housekeeping won't go together; I thought they might, but found my mistake. Of course, it cost me a struggle, but that's over. I have learnt to *renounce*.'

'It's very noble of you!' murmured Dora Leach.

'I never heard anything so noble!' said her sister.

Alma flushed with pleasure.

'And yet you know,' Dora pursued, 'artists have a duty to the world.'

'I can't help questioning,' said Gerda, 'whether you had a *right* to sacrifice yourself.'

Alma smiled thoughtfully.

'You can't quite see it as I do. When one has children – '

'It must make a great difference' – 'Oh, a great difference!' – responded the sisters. And again they exclaimed at the spectacle of such noble devotedness.

By natural transition the talk turned to Mrs Carnaby. The girls spoke of her compassionately, but Alma soon perceived that they did not utter all their thoughts.

'I'm afraid,' she said, 'that some people take another view. I have heard – but one doesn't care to repeat such things.'

Dora and Gerda betrayed a lively interest. Yes, they too had heard disagreeable gossip; what a shame it was!

'Of course, you see her?' said Dora.

Alma shook her head, and seemed a trifle embarrassed.

'I don't even know whether she still lives there.'

'Oh yes, she does,' replied Miss Leach eagerly. 'But I've been told that very few people go. I wondered – we rather wished to know whether *you* did.'

Again Alma gently shook her head.

'I haven't even heard from her. I suppose she has her reasons. To tell you the truth, I'm not quite sure that my husband would like me to call. It isn't a pleasant subject, is it? Let us talk of something else.'

So, when Dora and Gerda went away, they carried with them the conviction that Mrs Carnaby was an 'impossible' person and of course lost no opportunity of imparting it to their friends.

About a week before Christmas, when the new servants seemed to have settled to their work, and the house routine needed less supervision, Alma and her husband dined at the Langlands', to meet a few quiet people. Among the guests was Mrs Langland's brother, of whom Alma had already heard, and whom, before the end of the evening, she came to regard with singular interest. Mr Thistlewood had no advantages of physique, and little charm of manner; his long, meagre body never seemed able to put itself at ease; sitting or standing, he displayed the awkwardness of a naturally shy man who has not studied the habits of society. But his features, in spite of irregularity, and a complexion resembling the tone of 'foxed' paper, attracted observation, and rewarded it; his eye had a pleasant twinkle, oddly in contrast with the lines of painful thought upon his forehead, and the severity of strained muscles in the lower part

of his face. He was head-master of a small school of art in a
northern county; a post which he had held only for a twelvemonth. Like his sister's husband, Thistlewood suffered from
disappointed ambition, for he had aimed at great things as a
painter; but he accepted his defeat, and at thirty-five was seeking
content in a 'sphere of usefulness' which promised, after all, to
give scope to his best faculties. Not long ago he would have
scorned the thought of becoming a 'teacher'; yet for a teacher
he was born, and the truth, in dawning upon his mind, had
brought with it a measure of consolation.

A finger missing from his left hand told a story of student life
in Paris. It was a quarrel with a young Frenchman, about a girl.
He and his rival happening to sit opposite to each other at a
restaurant table, high words arose between them, and the
Frenchman eventually made a stab at Thistlewood's hand with
his dinner-fork. That ended the dispute, but the finger had to
come off. Not long afterwards Thistlewood accepted an engagement to go as artist with a party of English explorers into
Siberia. On his return he lingered for a week or two in St
Petersburg, and there chanced to meet the girl who had cost him
one of his digits. She, like himself, had been in pursuit of
adventures; but, whereas the artist came back with a well-filled
purse, the wandering damsel was at her last sou. They journeyed
together to London, and for the next year or two Thistlewood
had the honour of working himself almost to death to support a
very expensive young woman, who cared no more for him than
for her cast-off shoes. Happily, some richer man was at length
found who envied him his privilege, and therewith ended
Thistlewood's devotion to the joys of a bohemian life. Ever
since, his habits had been excessively sober – perhaps a little
morose. But Mrs Langland, who now saw him once a year,
thought him in every respect improved. Moreover, she had a
project for his happiness, and on that account frequently glanced
at him during dinner, as he conversed, much more fluently than
of wont, with his neighbour, Mrs Abbott.

Alma sat on the other side of the table, and was no less
observant than the hostess of a peculiar animation on Mr
Thistlewood's dark visage. To be sure, she knew nothing of him,
and it might be his habit to wear that look when he talked with
ladies; but Alma thought it unlikely. And it seemed to her that
Mary Abbott, though much as usual in manner, had a just

perceptible gleam of countenance beyond what one was accustomed to remark in her moments of friendly conversation. This, too, might be merely the result of a little natural excitement, seeing that the school-mistress so seldom dined from home. But, in any case, the proximity of these two persons was curiously interesting and suggestive.

In the drawing-room, presently, Alma had a pleasant little talk with Mr Thistlewood. By discreet experiment, she satisfied herself that Mrs Abbott's name certainly quickened his interest; and, having learnt so much, it was easy, by representing herself as that lady's old and intimate friend, to win from the man a significant look of pleasure and confidence. They talked of art, of landscape, and it appeared that Thistlewood was acquainted with the part of Carnarvonshire where Alma had lived. What was more, he had heard of her charming water-colours, and he would so much like to see them.

'Some enemy has done this,' replied Alma, laughing gaily. 'Was it Mrs Abbott?'

'No, it was not,' he answered, with corresponding vivacity.

'Why, then, it must have been Mrs Langland, and I have a good mind to put her to open shame by asking you to come and see my wretched daubs.'

Nothing would please him better, declared Thistlewood; and thereupon he accepted an invitation to tea for the following afternoon.

Alma asked no one else. She understood that this man was only to be observed under favourable conditions by isolating him. She wished, moreover, to bring him into fireside conversation with Harvey, and to remark her husband's demeanour. By way of preparation for this conjuncture, she let fall, in private chat with Harvey, a word or two which pointed humorously at her suspicions concerning Thistlewood and Mary Abbott. The hearer exhibited an incredulous surprise.

'It was only a fancy,' said Alma, smiling rather coldly; and she felt more desirous than ever of watching her husband in Thistlewood's presence.

Unexpectedly, from her point of view, the two men got along together very well indeed. Harvey, thoroughly cordial, induced their guest to speak of his work at the School of Art, and grew so interested in it that the conversation went on for a couple of hours. Thistlewood had pronounced and enthusiastic ideas on the subject.

'My difficulty is,' he exclaimed, 'that I can't get hold of the children young enough. People send their boys and girls to be taught drawing as an "accomplishment" – the feeble old notion. I want to teach it as a most important part of elementary education – in fact, to take youngsters straight on from the kindergarten stage.'

'Did I tell you,' put in Alma, 'that our little boy goes to Mrs Abbott's?' and her eyes were on both men at once.

'I should say you couldn't have done better than send him there,' replied Thistlewood, shuffling his feet and fidgeting with his hands. 'Mrs Abbott is an admirable teacher. She quite agrees with me – I should say that I quite agree with her. But I am forgetting, Mrs Rolfe, that you know her better than I do.'

Hughie was allowed to come into the room for a little while, and to give an account of what he learnt at school. When at length Thistlewood took his leave, it was with a promise that he would come again and dine a few days hence. His visit at Mrs Langland's would extend over another fortnight. Before the day of his departure northwards, Alma met him several times, and succeeded in establishing almost an intimate friendship with him. He came to bid her goodbye on a black and bitter January afternoon, when it happened that Harvey was away. As soon as he entered, she saw upon his face a look of ill augury, a heavy-eyed dejection very unlike the twinkling hopefulness with which he had hitherto regarded her.

'What's the matter?' she asked, holding his hand for a moment. 'Don't you like going back to work?'

'I enjoy my work, Mrs Rolfe, as you know.'

'But you are not like yourself.'

'My friends here have made the time very pleasant. Naturally, I don't like leaving them.'

He was a little abrupt, and decidedly showed the less genial phase of his disposition.

'Have some tea,' said Alma, 'and warm yourself at the fire. You will thaw presently, Mr Thistlewood. I suppose, like other unregenerate men, you live in rooms? Has that kind of life an irresistible charm for you?'

He looked at her with a frown which, to say the least, was

discouraging; it changed, however, to a more amiable expression as she handed him his tea.

'What do you imagine my income is, Mrs Rolfe?' came growlingly from him.

'I have no idea. You mean, I'm afraid' – Alma's voice fell upon its gentlest note – 'that it doesn't allow you to think of – of any change?'

'It *ought* not to allow me,' replied the other. 'I have about two hundred pounds a year, and can't hope much more for a long time.'

'And that,' exclaimed Alma, 'seems to you insufficient? I should have thought in a little town – so far away – Oh! you want to surround yourself with luxuries – '

'I don't! – I beg your pardon, Mrs Rolfe, I meant to say that you surely know me better.' His hand trembled and spilt the tea, which he had not yet touched. 'But how can you suppose that – that anyone – ?'

He turned his face to the fire, the light of which made his eyes glare fiercely. Forthwith, Alma launched upon a spirited remonstrance. Never, even in the days just before her marriage, had she been so fervid and eloquent on behalf of the 'simple life'. Two hundred pounds! Why, it was wealth for rational people! She inveighed against display and extravagance.

'You are looking round the room. – Oh, don't apologise; it was quite natural. I confess, and I'm ashamed of myself. But ask Mrs Abbott to tell you about our little house in Wales; she came once to see us there. We lived – oh so simply and cheaply; and it was our happiest time. If only we could go back to it! But the world has been too much for us. People call it comfort; it means, I assure you, ceaseless trouble and worry. Who knows? some day we may come to our senses, and shake off the burden.'

Thistlewood smiled.

'If we could all have cottages among the mountains,' he said. 'But a little provincial town – '

'Set an example! Who would have a better right to defy foolish prejudice? A teacher of the beautiful – you might do infinite good by showing how beautifully one can live without obeying mere fashion in a single point.'

'I heartily agree with you,' replied Thistlewood, setting down his empty cup. 'You express my own thoughts much better than

I could myself. And your talk has done me good, Mrs Rolfe. Thank you for treating me with such friendly kindness.'

Therewith he rose and said goodbye to her, with a hope that they might meet again. Alma was vexed that he would not stay longer and take her more completely into his confidence; but she echoed the hope, and smiled upon him with much sweetness.

His behaviour could have only one interpretation: he had proposed to Mary Abbott, and she had refused him. The longer Alma thought, the more certain she was – and the more irritated. It would be very difficult to continue her civility to Mrs Abbott after this.

## CHAPTER 6

In these days Rolfe had abandoned even the pretence of study. He could not feel at home among his books; they were ranked about him on the old shelves, but looked as uncomfortable as he himself; it seemed a temporary arrangement; he might as well have been in lodgings. At Pinner, after a twelvemonth, he was beginning to overcome the sense of strangeness; but a foreboding that he could not long remain there had always disturbed him. Here, though every probability pointed to a residence of at least two or three years, he scarcely made an effort to familiarise himself with the new surroundings; his house was a shelter, a camp; granted a water-tight roof, and drains not immediately poisonous, what need to take thought for artificial comforts? Thousands of men, who sleep on the circumference of London, and go each day to business, are practically strangers to the district nominally their home; ever ready to strike tent, as convenience bids, they can feel no interest in a vicinage which merely happens to house them for the time being, and as often as not they remain ignorant of the names of streets or roads through which they pass in going to the railway station. Harvey was now very much in this case. That he might not utterly waste his time, he had undertaken regular duties under Cecil Morphew's direction, and spent some hours daily in Westminster Bridge Road. Thence he went to his club, to see the papers; and in returning to Gunnersbury he felt hardly more sense of vital

connection with this suburb than with the murky and r̶
street in which he sat at business. By force of habit he contin̶
to read, but only books from the circulating library, thrown̶
upon his table pell-mell – novels, popular science, travels,
biographies; each as it came to hand. The intellectual disease of
the time took hold upon him: he lost the power of mental
concentration, yielded to the indolent pleasure of desultory
page-skimming. There remained in him but one sign of grace:
the qualms that followed on every evening's debauch of mind,
the headachey impression that he was going through a morbid
experience which somehow would work its own cure.

Alma seemed quite unaware of any change in him. To his
physical comfort she gave all due attention, anxious lest he
should catch cold in this hideous weather, and doing her best to
rule the house as he desired; but his intellectual life was no
concern to her. Herein, of course, Harvey did but share the
common lot of men married; he recognised the fact, and was
too wise to complain of it, even in his own mind. Yet it puzzled
him a little, now and then, that a woman so intelligent as Alma
should in this respect be simply on a level with the brainless
multitude of her sex. One evening, when they were together in
his room, he took down a volume, and blew the dust off it,
saying as he did so –

'They're not often disturbed nowadays, these solid old
fellows.'

'But I suppose you like to have them about you?' Alma replied
carelessly, as she glanced at the shelves.

'Why, yes, they're good furniture; help to warm the room.'

'No doubt they do,' Alma replied. 'It's always more comfortable here than in the drawing-room.'

Daily he asked himself whether she was reconciled to the loss
of her ambitions, and he could not feel any certainty. In the
present state of her health it might be natural for her to acquiesce
in a humdrum life; but when the next few months were over,
and she found herself once more able to move about as she
pleased, would her mind remain the same? Happy she was not,
and probably nothing in his power to do could make her so.
Marriage rarely means happiness, either for man or woman; if
it be not too grievous to be borne, one must thank the fates and
take courage. But Harvey had a troublesome conscience. In
acting with masculine decision, with the old-fashioned authority

had made himself doubly responsible for any
⟩t come to Alma through the conditions of her
⟩ that, on the higher plane of reasoning, he was
⟩stified; there might have been found a middle
⟩hilst guarding Alma from obvious dangers, still
⟩enjoy and to aspire. What he had done was very
⟩clipping of wings. Practically it might be needful,
and of safe result; but there is a world beyond the barnyard, for
all that; and how should he know, with full assurance, whether
Alma had not suffered a grave wrong! He durst not reopen the
discussion with her. He had taken his stand, and must hold it,
or lose all self-respect.

Marriage is like life itself, easiest to those who think least
about it. Rolfe knew that well enough, and would gladly have
acted upon the knowledge; he came nearest to doing so at the
times when Hughie was his companion. Relieved by the nursemaid from duties she had only borne by the exertion of
something like heroism, Alma once more drew a broad line of
demarcation between nursery and drawing-room; it was seldom
she felt in a mood for playing with the child, and she had no
taste for 'going walks'. But Harvey could not see too much of
the little boy, indoors or out, and it rejoiced him to know that
his love was returned in full measure; for Hughie would at any
time abandon other amusements to be with his father. In these
winter months, when by rare chance there came a fine Saturday
or Sunday, they went off together to Kew or Richmond, and
found endless matter for talk, delightful to both of them.
Hughie, now four years old, was well grown, and could walk
two or three miles without weariness. He had no colour in his
cheeks, and showed the nervous tendencies which were to be
expected in a child of such parentage, but on the whole his
health gave no cause for uneasiness. If anything chanced to ail
him, Harvey suffered an excessive disquiet; for the young life
seemed to him so delicate a thing that any touch of pain might
wither it away. Because of the unutterable anguish in the
thought, he had often forced himself to front the possibility of
Hughie's death, and had even brought himself to feel that in
truth it would be no reason for sorrow; how much better to fall
asleep in playtime, and wake no more, than to outlive the
happiness and innocence which pass for ever with childhood.
And when the fear of life lay heaviest upon him, he found solace

in remembering that after no great lapse of time he and those he loved would have vanished from the earth, would be as though they had not been at all; every pang and woe awaiting them suffered and forgotten; the best and the worst gone by for ever; the brief flicker of troubled light quenched in eternal oblivion. It was Harvey Rolfe's best substitute for the faith and hope of the old world.

He liked to feel the soft little hand clasping his own fingers, so big and coarse in comparison, and happily so strong. For in the child's weakness he felt an infinite pathos; a being so entirely helpless, so utterly dependent upon others' love, standing there amid a world of cruelties, smiling and trustful. All his heart went forth in the desire to protect and cherish. Nothing else seemed of moment beside this one duty, which was also the purest joy. The word 'father' however sweet to his ear, had at times given him a thrill of awe; spoken by childish lips, did it mean less than 'God'? He was the giver of life,* and for that dread gift must hold himself responsible. A man in his agony may call upon some unseen power, but the heavens are mute; can a father turn away in heedlessness if the eyes of his child reproach him? All pleasures, aims, hopes that concerned himself alone, shrank to the idlest trifling when he realised the immense debt due from him to his son; no possible sacrifice could discharge it. He marvelled how people could insist upon the duty of children to parents. But did not the habit of thought ally itself naturally enough with that strange religion which, under direst penalties, exacts from groaning and travailing humanity a tribute of fear and love to the imagined Author of its being?

With delight he followed every step in the growth of under-standing; and yet it was not all pleasure to watch the mind outgrowing its simplicity. Intelligence that has learnt the mean-ing of a doubt compares but sadly with the charm of untouched ingenuousness – that exquisite moment (a moment, and no more) when simplest thought and simplest word seek each other unconsciously, and blend in sweetest music. At four years old Hughie had forgotten his primitive language. The father regret-ted many a pretty turn of tentative speech, which he was wont to hear with love's merriment. If a toy were lost, a little voice might be heard saying, 'Where has that gone now to?' And when it was found again – 'There is it!' After a tumble one day, Hughie was cautious in running. 'I shall fall down and break myself.' Then came distinction between days of the week. 'On Sunday I do' so and so; 'on Monday days I do' something else. He said, 'Do you remember?' and what a pity it seemed when at last the dull grown-up word was substituted. Never again, when rain was falling, would Hughie turn and plead, 'Father, tell the sun to come out!' Nor, when he saw the crescent moon in daytime, would he ever grow troubled and exclaim, 'Someone has broken it!'

It was the rule now that before his bedtime, seven o'clock, Hughie spent an hour in the library, alone with his father. A golden hour, sacred to memories of the world's own childhood. He brought with him the book that was his evening's choice – Grimm, or Andersen, or Æsop. Already he knew by heart a score of little poems, or passages of verse, which Rolfe, disregarding the inept volumes known as children's anthologies, chose with utmost care from his favourite singers, and repeated till they were learnt. Stories from the Odyssey had come in of late; but Polyphemus was a doubtful experiment – Hughie dreamt of him. Great caution, too, was needful in the matter of pathos. On hearing for the first time Andersen's tale of the Little Tin Soldier, Hughie burst into tears, and could scarce be comforted. Grimm was safer; it seemed doubtful whether Andersen was really a child's book at all, every page touched with the tears of things, every line melodious with sadness.

And all this fostering of the imagination – was it right? was it wise? Harvey worried himself with doubts insoluble. He had merely obeyed his own instincts. But perhaps he would be doing far better if he never allowed the child to hear a fairy-tale or a line of poetry. Why not amuse his mind with facts, train him to the habit of scientific thought? For all he knew, he might be giving the child a bias which would result in a life's unhappiness; by teaching him to see only the hard actual face of things, would he not fit him far more surely for citizenship of the world?

He would have liked to talk about the child with Mary Abbott, but there never came an opportunity. Though it shamed and angered him to be under such constraint, he felt obliged to avoid any private meeting with her. Alma, he well understood, still nursed the preposterous jealousy which had been in her mind so long; and in the present state of things, dubious, transitional, it behoved him to give no needless occasion of disquiet. As the months went on, he saw her spirits fail; with the utmost difficulty she was persuaded to leave the house, and for hours at a time she sat as if in melancholy brooding, unwilling to talk or to read. Harvey tried reading to her, but in the daytime she could not keep her thoughts from wandering, and after dinner it merely sent her to sleep. Yet she declared that there was nothing to trouble about; she would be herself again before long.

But one day the doctor who was attending her had a few words in private with Rolfe, and told him that he had made an unpleasant discovery – Mrs Rolfe was in the habit of taking a narcotic. At first, when the doctor asked if this was the case, she had denied it, but in the end he had elicited a confession, and a promise that the dangerous habit should be relinquished.

'I was on no account to mention this to you, and you mustn't let it be seen that I have done so. If it goes on, and I'm rather afraid it will for a short time, I shall tell her that you must be informed of it.'

Harvey, to whom such a suspicion had never occurred, waited anxiously for the doctor's further reports. As was anticipated, Alma's promise held good only for a day or two, and when again she confessed, her husband was called into counsel. The trio went through a grave and disagreeable scene. On the doctor's departure, Alma sat for a long time stubbornly and dolorously mute; then came tears and passionate penitence.

'You mustn't think I'm a slave to it,' she said. 'It isn't so at all. I can break myself off it at once, and I will.'

'Then why did you go on after the doctor's first warning?'

'Out of perversity, nothing else. I suffer much from bad nights, but it wasn't that; I could bear it. I said to myself that I should do as I liked.' She gave a tearful laugh.

'That's the whole truth. I felt just like a child when it's determined to be naughty.'

'But this is far too serious a matter—'

'I know, I know. There shall be an end of it. I had my own way, and I'm satisfied. Now I shall be reasonable.'

Judging from results, this seemed to be a true explanation. From that day the doctor saw no reason for doubt. But Harvey had a most uncomfortable sense of strangeness in his wife's behaviour; it seemed to him that the longer he lived with Alma, the less able he was to read her mind or comprehend her motives. It did not reassure him to reflect that a majority of husbands are probably in the same case.

Meanwhile trouble was once more brewing in the back regions of the house. The cook made an excuse for 'giving notice'. Rolfe, in his fury, talked about abandoning the house and going with wife and child to some village in the heart of France; yet this was hardly practicable. Again were advertisements sent forth; again came the ordeal of correspondence – this time undertaken by Harvey himself, for Alma was unequal to it. The cook whom they at length engaged declared with fervour that the one thing she panted for was downright hard work; she couldn't abide easy places, and in fact had left her last because too little was expected of her.

'She will stay for two months,' said Harvey, 'and then it will be time for the others to think of moving. Oh, we shall get used to it.'

At the end of March, Alma's second child was born – a girl. Remembering what she had endured at Hughie's birth, Rolfe feared that her trial would be even worse this time; but it did not prove so. In a few days Alma was well on the way to recovery. But the child, a lamentable little mortal with a voice scarce louder than a kitten's, held its life on the frailest tenure; there was doubt at first whether it could draw breath at all, and the nurse never expected it to live till the second day. At the end of a week, however, it still survived; and Alma turned to the poor weakling with a loving tenderness such as she had never shown for her first-born. To Harvey's surprise she gladly took it to her breast, but for some reason this had presently to be forbidden, and the mother shed many tears. After a fortnight things looked more hopeful. Nurse and doctor informed Harvey that for the present he need have no uneasiness.

It was a Saturday morning, and so cheerful overhead that Rolfe used his liberty to have a long stretch towards the fields. Hughie, who had no school today, would gladly have gone with him, but after such long restraint Harvey felt the need of four miles an hour, and stole away. He made for Twickenham and Hampton Court, then by a long circuit came round into Richmond Park. The Star and Garter gave him a late luncheon, after which he lit his cigar and went idly along the terrace. There, whom should he meet but Mary Abbott.

She was seated, gazing at the view. Not till he came quite near did Harvey recognise her, and until he stopped she did not glance in his direction. Thus he was able to observe her for a moment, and noticed that she looked anything but well; one would have thought her overworked, or oppressed by some trouble. She did not see what her eyes were fixed upon, and her features had a dreaming tenderness of expression which made them more interesting, more nearly beautiful, than when they were controlled by her striving will. When Harvey paused beside her she gave him a startled smile, but was at once herself again.

'Do you care for that?' he asked, indicating the landscape.

'I can't be enthusiastic about it.'

'Nor I. A bit of ploughed field in the midlands gives me more pleasure.'

'It was beautiful once.'

'Yes; before London breathed upon it. – Do you remember the view from Carn Bodvean?'

'Oh, indeed I do! The larches are coming out now.'

'And the gorse shines, and the sea is blue, and the mountains rise one behind the other! – Did you talk about it with Mr Thistlewood? I found that he knew all that country.'

'We spoke of it,' replied Mrs Abbott, taking a step forward.

'An interesting man, don't you think?'

Harvey glanced at her, remembering the odd suggestion he had heard from Alma; and in truth it seemed that his inquiry caused her some embarrassment.

'Yes, very interesting,' answered his companion quietly, as she walked on.

'You had met him before – ?'

'He always comes to the Langlands' at Christmas.' She added in another voice, 'I was glad to hear from Hughie yesterday that all was well at home.'

They sauntered along the path. Harvey described the walk he had had this morning. Mrs Abbott said that the bright day had tempted her to an unusual distance; she had come, of course, by train, and must now think of turning back towards the station.

'Let me go so far with you,' said Harvey. 'What is your report of the boy? He gives you no trouble, I hope?'

She replied in detail, with the conscientiousness which always appeared in her when speaking of her work. It was not the tone of one who delights in teaching; there was no spontaneity, no enthusiasm; but every word gave proof of how seriously she regarded the duties she had undertaken. And she was not without pride in her success. The little school had grown, so that it now became a question whether she should decline pupils or engage an assistant teacher.

'You are resolved to go on with the infantry?' said Rolfe, smiling.

'The little ones – yes. I begin to feel some confidence with *them*; I don't think I'm in danger of going far wrong. But I shouldn't have the least faith in myself, now, with older children. – Of course I have Minnie Wager. She'll soon be eleven, you know. I do my best with her.'

'Mrs Langland says you have done wonders.'

'Minnie will never learn much from books; I feel pretty sure of that. But' – she laughed – 'everyone has a strong point, if it can be discovered, and I really think I have found Minnie's at last. It was quite by chance. The other day I was teaching my maid to make pastry, and Minnie happened to stand by. Afterwards, she begged me to let *her* try her hand at it, and I did, and the result was surprising. For the very first time she had found something that she enjoyed doing. She went to it with zeal, and learnt in no time. Since then she has made tarts, and puddings, and cakes – '

Harvey broke into laughter. It was an odd thing that the employment he had suggested for this girl, in his talk at Greystone, should prove to be her genuine vocation.

'Don't you think it's as well to encourage her?' said Mrs Abbott.

'By all manner of means! I think it's a magnificent discovery. I should give her the utmost encouragement. Let her learn cookery in all its branches, steadily and seriously.'

'It may solve the problem of her future. She might get employment in one of the schools of cookery.'

'Never again be uneasy about her,' cried Rolfe delightedly. 'She is provided for. She will grow old with honour, love, obedience, troops of friends!* – A culinary genius! Why, it's the one thing the world is groaning and clamouring for. Let her burn her school-books. Sacrifice everything to her Art. – You have rejoiced me with this news.'

Slenderly endowed on the side of humour, Mary Abbott could not feel sure whether he was really pleased or not; he had to repeat to her, with all gravity, that he no longer felt anxious on the girl's account.

'For my own part,' said Mary, 'I would rather see her a good cook in a lady's kitchen, if it came to that, than leading a foolish life at some so-called genteel occupation.'

'So would any one who has common-sense. – And her brother; I don't think we can go wrong about him. The reports from school are satisfactory; they show that he loathes everything but games and fighting. At fifteen they'll take him on a training ship. – I wonder whether their father's alive or dead?'

'It is to be hoped they'll never see him again.'

Harvey was smiling – at a thought which he did not communicate.

'You say you wouldn't trust yourself to teach older children. You mean, of course, that you feel so much the difficulty of the whole thing – of all systems of education.'

'Yes. And I dare say it's nothing but foolish presumption when I fancy I can teach babies.'

'You have at all events a method,' said Harvey, 'and it seems to be a very good one. For the teaching of children after they can read and write, there seems to be no method at all. The old classical education was fairly consistent, but it exists no longer. Nothing has taken its place. Muddle, experiment, and waste of lives – too awful to think about. We're savages yet in the matter of education. Somebody said to me once: "Well, but look at the results; they're not so bad." Great heavens! not so bad – when the supreme concern of mankind is to perfect their instruments of slaughter! Not so bad – when the gaol and the gallows are taken as a matter of course! Not so bad – when huge filthy cities are packed with multitudes who have no escape from toil and hunger but in a wretched death! Not so bad – when all but every man's life is one long blunder, the result of ignorance and unruled passions!'

Mrs Abbott showed a warm assent.

'People don't think or care anything about education. Seriously, I suppose it has less place in the thoughts of most men and women than any other business of life?'

'Undoubtedly,' said Rolfe. 'And one is thought a pedant and a bore if one ever speaks of it. It's as much against good manners as to begin talking about religion. But a pedant must relieve his mind sometimes. I'm so glad I met you today; I wanted to hear what you thought about the boy.'

For the rest of the way, they talked of lighter things; or rather, Rolfe talked and his companion listened. Nothing more difficult than easy chat between a well-to-do person of abundant leisure and one whose days are absorbed in the earning of a bare livelihood. Mary Abbott had very little matter for conversation beyond the circle of her pursuits; there was an extraordinary change in her since the days of her married life, when she had prided herself on talking well, or even brilliantly. Harvey could not help a feeling of compassion as she walked at his side. For all his admiration of her self-conquest, and of the tasks to which she had devoted herself, he would have liked to free her from the daily mill. She was young yet, and should taste of joy before the years began to darken about her. But these are the thoughts that must not be uttered. To show pity is to insult. A merry nod to the friend who staggers on beneath his burden; and, even at his last gasp, the friend shall try to nod merrily back again.

He took leave of her at the station, saying that he meant to walk by the river homeward. A foolish scruple, which would never have occurred to him but for Alma's jealousy.

When he reached his house at about four o'clock, he felt very tired; it was a long time since he had walked so far. Using his latch-key to enter, he crossed the hall to the study without seeing anyone or hearing a sound. There was a letter on his table. As he opened it, and began to read, the door – which he had left ajar – was pushed softly open; there entered Hughie, unusually silent, and with a strange look in his bright eyes.

'Father – Louie says that baby is dead.'

Harvey's hand fell. He stared, stricken mute.

'Father – I don't want baby to be dead! Don't let baby be dead!'

The child's voice shook, and tears came into his eyes. Without a word, Rolfe hastened from the room and up the stairs. As he reached the landing, a wail of grief sounded from somewhere near; could that be Alma's voice? In a moment he had knocked at her door. He durst not turn the handle; the beating of his heart shook him in every limb. The door opened, and the nurse showed her face. A hurried whisper; the baby had died two hours ago, in convulsions.

Alma's voice sounded again.

'Who is that? – Harvey – oh, come, come to me! My little baby is dead!'

He sat alone with her for an hour. He scarcely knew her for his wife, so unlike herself had she become under the stress of passionate woe; her face drawn in anguish, yet illumined as he had never seen it; her voice moving on a range of notes which it had never sounded. The little body lay pressed against her bosom; she would not let it be taken from her. Consolation was idle. Harvey tried to speak the thought which was his first and last as he looked at the still, waxen face; the thought of thankfulness, that this poor feeble little being was saved from life; but he feared to seem unfeeling. Alma could not yet be comforted. The sight of the last pitiful struggles had pierced her to the heart; she told of it over and over again, in words and tones profoundly touching.

The doctor had been here, and would return in the evening. It was Alma now who had to be cared for; her state might easily become dangerous.

When Harvey went downstairs again, he met Hughie and his nurse in the hall. The little boy ran to him.

'Mayn't I come to you, Father? Louie says I mustn't come.'

'Yes, yes; come, dear.'

In the library he sat down, and took Hughie upon his knee, and pressed the soft little cheek against his own. Without mention of baby, the child asked at once if his father would not read to him as usual.

'I don't think I can tonight, Hughie.'

'Why not, Father? Because baby is dead?'

'Yes. And Mother is very poorly. I must go upstairs again soon.'

'Is Mother going to be dead?' asked the child, with curiosity rather than fear.

'No! No!'

'But – but if mother went there, she could fetch baby back again.'

'Went where?'

Hughie made a vague upward gesture.

'Louie says baby is gone up into the sky.'

Perhaps it was best so. What else can one say to a little child of four years old? Harvey Rolfe had no choice but to repeat what seemed good to Louie the nursemaid. But he could refrain from saying more.

Alma was in a fever by night-time. There followed days and days of misery; any one hour of which, as Rolfe told himself, outbalanced all the good and joy that can at best be hoped for in threescore years and ten. But Alma clung to life. Harvey had thought she would ask for her little son, and expend upon him the love called forth by her dead baby; she seemed, however, to care even less for Hughie than before. And, after all, the bitter experience had made little change in her.

## CHAPTER 7

Since the removal from Pinner, Rolfe had forgotten his anxieties with regard to money. Expenses were reduced; not very greatly, but to a point which made all the difference between just exceeding his income and living just within it. He had not tried to economise, and would scarcely have known how to begin; it was the change in Alma's mode of life that brought about this fortunate result. With infinite satisfaction he dismissed from his mind the most hateful of all worries.

It looked, too, as if the business in Westminster Bridge Road might eventually give a substantial return for the money he had invested in it. Through the winter, naturally, little trade was done; but with springtime things began to look brisk and hopeful. Harvey had applied himself seriously to learning the details of the business; he was no longer a mere looker-on, but could hold practical counsel with his partner, make useful suggestions, and help in carrying them out.

In the sixth month after her father's decease, Rolfe enjoyed the privilege of becoming acquainted with Miss Winter. Morphew took him one afternoon to the house at Earl's Court, where the widow and her daughter were still living, the prospect of Henrietta's marriage having made it not worth while for them to change their abode in the interim. With much curiosity, with not a little mistrust, Harvey entered the presence of these ladies, whose names and circumstances had been so familiar to him for years. Henrietta proved to be very unlike the image he had formed of her. Anticipating weakness, conventionality, and some affectation, he was surprised to meet a lady of simple, grave manners; nervous at first, but soon perfectly self-possessed; by no means talkative, but manifesting in every word a well-informed mind and a habit of reflection. It astonished him that such a man as Cecil Morphew should have discovered his ideal in Henrietta Winter; it perplexed him yet more that Cecil's attachment should have been reciprocated.

Mrs Winter was a very ordinary person; rather pretentious, rather too fluent of speech, inclined to fretfulness, and probably of trying temper. Having for many years lived much beyond his means (in the manner so often described by Morphew), Mr Winter had left his family as good as unprovided for. There was money to be divided between mother and daughter, but so small a sum that it could not be regarded as a source of income. To the widow was bequeathed furniture; to Henrietta, a library of two thousand volumes; *finally*, the testator directed that the sum of five hundred pounds should be spent on a window of stained glass (concerning which full particulars were given), to be set up, in memory of himself, in the church he had been wont to honour with his pious attendance. This item of her husband's will had so embittered Mrs Winter, that she hardly ever spoke of him; if obliged to do so, it was with cold severity that she uttered his name. Immediately, she withdrew all opposition to Henrietta's marriage with the man she had considered so objectionable; she would not have been sorry had her daughter chosen to be married with the least possible delay. As for the future, of course she must live in her daughter's house; together, they must make what they could of their small capital, and hope that Cecil's business would prosper.

Harvey had been acquainted with these facts since Mr Winter's death. Bearing them in mind as he talked with Henrietta, and exerting his powers of observation to the utmost, he still found himself as far as ever from a definite opinion as to the wisdom of the coming marriage. That Mrs Winter would be a great obstacle to happiness admitted of no doubt; but Henrietta herself might or might not prove equal to the change of circumstances. Evidently one of her characteristics was an extreme conscientiousness; it explained, perhaps, her long inability to decide between the claims of parents and lover. Her tastes in literature threw some light upon the troubles which had beset her; she was a student of George Eliot, and spoke of the ethical problems with which that author is mainly concerned, in a way suggestive of self-revelation. Conversing for the first time with Morphew's friend, and finding him sufficiently intelligent, she might desire to offer some indirect explanation of the course she had followed. Harvey could not question her sincerity, but she seemed to him a trifle morbid. It might be natural reaction, in a temper such as hers, against the monstrous egotism by which her life had been subdued and shadowed. She inclined to mystical views; mentioned Christina Rossetti as one of her favourites; cared little or nothing for the louder interests of the time. Impossible to detect the colour of her thoughts with regard to Cecil; she spoke of him gravely and gently, but without the least perceptible emotion. Harvey noticed her when Morphew was saying goodbye; her smile was sweet, and perhaps tender, but even then she seemed to be debating with herself some point of conscience. Perhaps Cecil had pressed her hand rather too fervently?

The friends walked away in silence along the dim-lighted street, between monotonous rows of high sombre houses, each with its pillared portico which looked like the entrance to a tomb. Glancing about him with a sense of depression, Harvey wondered that any mortal could fix his pride on the fact of residence in such a hard, cold, ugly wilderness.

'Has she altered much since you first knew her?' he asked at length.

'A good deal,' answered the other. 'Yes, a good deal. She used to laugh sometimes; now she never does. She was always quiet – always looked at things seriously – but it was different. You think her gloomy?'

'No, no; not gloomy. It's all natural enough. Her life wants a little sunlight, that's all.'

For the rest, he could speak with sincere admiration, and Cecil heard him delightedly.

The choice of a dwelling was a most difficult matter. As it must be quite a small house, the remoter suburbs could alone supply what was wanted; Morphew spent every Saturday and Sunday in wearisome exploration. Mrs Winter, though in theory she accepted the necessity of cheapness, shrank from every practical suggestion, declaring it impossible to live in such places as Cecil requested her to look at. She had an ideal of the 'nice little house', and was as likely to discover it in London's suburbs as to become possessed once more of the considerable fortune which she and her husband had squandered in mean extravagance. Morphew had already come to the conclusion, and Henrietta agreed with him, that their future home must be chosen without regard to Mrs Winter's impracticable ideas. And the sooner the better, in her own interests; for it was plain that so long as she continued in the old house she would thoughtlessly waste her means. The end of the twelvemonth, at latest, must see them all in their new home.

But meanwhile fate was preparing a new trial for Henrietta's much-disciplined conscience.

On a Saturday afternoon, when the crisis of Alma's illness was over, Harvey received a telegram summoning him to Westminster Bridge Road. 'Come if you possibly can. Or I must come to you.' Only yesterday he had been with Morphew for a couple of hours, and all seemed well; Cecil thought he had found the house that would suit him; he was in jubilant spirits, laughing, singing, more boylike than ever. Suspecting new obstructiveness on the part of Mrs Winter, Harvey went to town in an impatient mood. He found the shop closed, as usual at this hour on Saturday, and rang the house-door bell. Morphew himself replied, with a countenance which made known forthwith that something extraordinary had happened; eyes red and swollen, cheeks puffy, colourless, smeared.

'Well?'

Cecil clutched at his hand, and drew him in. They went upstairs to the office, where all was quiet.

'Rolfe, if I hadn't had you to send for, I should have been dead by now. There's poison enough in this place. It has tempted me fearfully.'

'What is it?' asked the other, in a not very sympathetic voice. His own troubles of the past month made mere love-miseries seem artificial.

'I shall have to tell you what I wanted to tell you long ago. If I had, most likely this would never have happened. – It's all over with me, Rolfe. I wish to God you had let me die in that hotel at Brussels. – She has been told something about me, and there's an end of everything. She sent for me this morning. I never thought she could be so pitiless. – The kind of thing that a man thinks nothing of. And herself the cause of it, if only I had dared to tell her so!'

'The old story, I suppose,' said Harvey. 'Some other woman?'

'I was very near telling you, that day you came to my beastly garret in Chelsea; do you remember? It was the worst time with me then – except when you found me in Brussels. I'd been gambling again; you knew that. I wanted money for something I felt ashamed to speak of. – You know the awful misery I used to suffer about Henrietta. I was often enough nearly mad with – what is one to call it? Why isn't there a decent name for the agony men go through at that age? I simply couldn't live alone any longer – I couldn't; and only a fool and a hypocrite would pretend to blame me. A man, that is; women seem to be made different. – Oh, there's nothing to tell. The same thing happens a hundred times every day in London. A girl wandering about in the Park – quarrel at home – all the rest of it. A good many lies on her side; a good deal of selfishness on mine. I happened to have money just then. And just when I had *no* money – about the time you met me – a child was born. She *said* it was mine; anyway, I had to be responsible. Of course I had long ago repented of behaving so badly to Henrietta. But no woman can understand, and it's impossible to explain to them. You're a beast and a villain, and there's an end of it.'

'And how has this become known to Miss Winter?' Harvey inquired, seeing that Morphew lost himself in gloom.

'You might almost guess it; these things always happen in the same way. You've heard me speak of a fellow called Driffel – no? I thought I might have mentioned him. He got to know the girl. He and I were at a music-hall one night, and she met us; and I heard, soon after, that she was living with him. It didn't last long. She got ill, and wrote to me from Westminster Hospital; and I was foolish enough to give her money again, off and on, up to only a few months ago. She talked about living a respectable life, and so on, and I couldn't refuse to help her. But I found out it was all humbug, and of course I stopped. Then she began to hunt me, out of spite. And she heard from someone – Driffel, as likely as not – all about Henrietta; and yesterday Henrietta had a letter from her. This morning I was sent for, to explain myself.'

'At one time, then, you had lost sight of her altogether?'

'She has always had money from me, more or less regularly,

except at the time that Driffel kept her. But there has been nothing else between us, since that first year. I kept up payments on account of the child, and she was cheating me in that too. Of course she put out the baby to nurse, and I understood it lived on; but the truth was it died after a month or two – starved to death, no doubt. I only learnt that, by taking a good deal of trouble, when she was with Driffel.'

'Starved to death at a month or two old,' murmured Rolfe. 'The best thing for it, no doubt.'

'It's worse than anything *I* have done,' said Morphew, miserably. 'I think more of it now than I did at the time. A cruel, vile thing!'

'And you told Miss Winter everything?'

'Everything that can be spoken about. The plain truth of the story. The letter was a lie from beginning to end, of course. It made me out a heartless scoundrel. I had been the ruin of the girl – a helpless innocent; and now, after all these years, wanted to cut her adrift, not caring what became of her. My defence seemed to Henrietta no defence at all. The fact that there had been such an episode in my life was quite sufficient. Everything must be at an end between us, at once and for ever. She *could* not live with me, knowing this. No one should learn the cause; not even her mother; but I must never see her again. And so I came away, meaning to end my life. It wasn't cowardice that prevented me; only the thought that *she* would be mixed up in it, and suffer more than I had made her already.'

Voice and look constrained Harvey to believe this. He spoke more sympathetically.

'It's better that it happened before than after.'

'I've tried to think that, but I can't. Afterwards, I could have made her believe me and forgive me.'

'That seems to me more than doubtful.'

'But why should it have happened at all?' cried Cecil, in the tone of despairing bitterness. 'Did I deserve it? Haven't I behaved better, more kindly, than most men would have done? Isn't it just because I was too good-natured that this has come on me?'

'I myself readily take that view,' answered Rolfe. 'But I can perfectly understand why Miss Winter doesn't.'

'So can I – so can I,' groaned Cecil. 'It's in her nature. And do you suppose I haven't cursed myself for deceiving her? The

thought has made me miserable, often enough. I never dreamt
she would get to know of it; but it weighed upon me all the
same. Yet who was the cause of it, really and truly? I'm glad I
could keep myself from saying all I thought. She wouldn't have
understood; I should only have looked more brutal in her eyes.
But if she had married me when she might have done! *There*
was the wrong that led to everything else.'

Harvey nodded and muttered.

'At one and twenty she might have taken her own way. I
wasn't a penniless adventurer. My name is as good as hers. We
could have lived well enough on my income, until I found a way
of increasing it, as I should have done. Girls don't know what
they are doing when they make men wait year after year. No
one can tell them. But I begged – I prayed to her – I said all I
dared. It was her cursed father and mother! If I had had three
thousand, instead of three hundred, a year, they would have
rushed her into marriage. No! we must have a big house, like
their own, and a troop of thieving servants, or we were eternally
disgraced. *How* I got the money didn't matter, so long as I got
it. And she hadn't courage – she thought it wrong to defy them.
As if the wrong wasn't in giving way to such a base superstition!
I believe she has seen that since her father's death. And now – '

He broke down, shaking and choking in an agony of sobs.
Harvey could only lay a kind hand upon him; there was no
verbal comfort to offer. Presently Cecil talked on again, and so
they sat together as twilight passed into darkness. Rolfe would
gladly have taken the poor fellow home with him, out of solitude
with its miseries and dangers, but Cecil refused. Eventually they
walked westward for a few miles; then Morphew, with a
promise to see his friend next day, turned back into the crowd.

## CHAPTER 8

Alma was walking on the sea-road at Penzance,* glad to be
quite alone, yet at a loss how to spend the time. Rolfe had sailed
for Scilly,* and would be absent for two or three days; Mrs
Frothingham, with Hughie for companion, was driving to
Marazion. Why – Alma asked herself – had she wished to be left

alone this morning? Some thought had glimmered vaguely in her restless mind; she could not recover it.

The little shop window, set out with objects carved in serpentine, held her for a moment; but remembering how often she had paused here lately, she felt ashamed, and walked on. Presently there moved towards her a lady in a Bath-chair; a lady who had once been beautiful, but now, though scarcely middle-aged, looked gaunt and haggard from some long illness. The invalid held open a newspaper, and Alma, in passing, saw that it was *The World*. At once her step quickened, for she had remembered the desire which touched her an hour ago.

She walked to the railway station, surveyed the papers on the bookstall, and bought three – papers which would tell her what was going on in society. With these in hand she found a quiet spot, sheltered from the August sun, where she could sit and read. She read eagerly, enviously. And before long her eye fell upon a paragraph in which was a name she knew. Lady Isobel Barker, in her lovely retreat at Boscombe,* was entertaining a large house-party; in the list appeared – Mrs Hugh Carnaby. Unmistakable: Mrs Hugh Carnaby. Who Lady Isobel might be, Alma had no idea; nor were any of the other guests known to her, but the names of all seemed to roll upon the tongue of the announcing footman. She had a vision of Sibyl in that august company; Sibyl, coldly beautiful, admirably sage, with – perhaps – ever so little of the air of a martyr, to heighten her impressiveness.

When she could command herself, she glanced hurriedly through column after column of all the papers, seeking for that name again. In one, an illustrated publication, she came upon a couple of small portraits, side by side. Surely she recognised that face – the bold, coarse-featured man, with his pretentious smile? But the girl, no; a young and very pretty girl, smirking a little, with feathery hair which faded off into an aureole. The text was illuminating.

'I am able to announce,' wrote Ego, 'and I think I shall be one of the first to do so, that the brilliant composer, Mr Felix Dymes, will shortly vanish from the gay (if naughty) world of bachelor-hood. I learn on excellent authority that Mr Dymes has quite recently become engaged to Miss Lettice Almond, a very charming young lady, whose many gifts (especially musical) have as yet been known only to a comparatively small circle, and for the delightful reason that she is still only eighteen. Miss Almond is the daughter of Mr Haliburton Almond, senior partner in the old and well-known firm of Almond Brothers, the manufacturers of fireworks. She is an only daughter, and, though she has two brothers, I may add (I trust without indiscretion) that the title of heiress may be fittingly applied to her. The marriage may take place in November, and will doubtless be a brilliant as well as a most interesting affair. By-the-bye, Mr Dymes's new opera is not likely to be ready till next year, but some who have been privileged to hear the parts already composed declare that it will surpass even "Blue Roses" in the charm of sweet yet vivacious melody.'

When she had read and mused for more than an hour, Alma tore out the two passages that had a personal interest for her, and put them in her purse. The papers she left lying for anyone who chose to pick them up.

A fortnight later she was back at Gunnersbury; where, indeed, she would have been content to stay all through the summer, had not Harvey and the doctor insisted on her leaving home. All sorts of holidays had been proposed, but nothing of the kind attracted her. She declared that she was quite well, and that she preferred home to anywhere else; she had got used to it, and did not wish to be unsettled. Six weeks at Penzance simply wearied her; she brightened wonderfully on the day of return. Harvey, always anxious, tried to believe that the great sorrow through which she had passed was effecting only a natural change, subduing her troublesome mutability of temper, and leading her to find solace in domestic quietude.

On the third day after her return, she had lunched alone, and was sitting in the library. Her dress, more elaborate than usual, and the frequent glances which she cast at the clock, denoted expectation of some arrival. Hearing a knock at the front door, she rose and waited nervously.

'Mr Dymes is in the drawing-room, mum.'

She joined him. Dymes, with wonted frankness, not to say impudence, inspected her from head to foot, and did not try to conceal surprise.

'I was awfully glad to get your note. As I told you, I called here about a month ago, and I should have called again. I didn't care to write until I heard from you. You've been ill, I can see. I heard about it. Awfully sorry.'

Alma saw that he intended respectful behaviour. The fact of being in her own house was, of course, a protection, but Dymes, she quite understood, had altered in mind towards her. She treated him distantly, yet without a hint of unfriendliness.

'I began to wonder whether I had missed a letter of yours. It's some time since you promised to write – on business.'

'The fact is,' he replied, 'I kept putting it off, hoping to see you, and it's wonderful how time slips by. I can hardly believe that it's more than a year since your recital. How splendidly it came off! If only you could have followed it up – but we won't talk about that.'

He paused for any remark she might wish to make. Alma, dreamy for a moment, recovered herself, and asked, in a disinterested tone –

'We paid all expenses, I suppose?'

'Well – not quite.'

'Not quite? I understood from you that there was no doubt about it.'

'I thought,' said Dymes, as he bent forward familiarly, 'that my silence would let you know how matters stood. If there had been anything due to you, of course I should have sent a cheque. We did very well indeed, remarkably well, but the advertising expenses were very heavy.' He took a paper from his pocket. 'Here is the detailed account. I shouldn't have spent so much if I hadn't regarded it as an investment. You had to be boomed, you know – floated, and I flatter myself I did it pretty well. But, of course, as things turned out – '

Alma glanced over the paper. The items astonished her.

'You mean to say, then, that I am in your debt for a hundred and thirty pounds?'

'Debt be hanged!' cried Dymes magnanimously. 'That's all done with, long ago. I only wanted to explain how things were.'

Alma reddened. She was trying to remember the state of her banking account, and felt sure that, at this moment, considerably less than a hundred pounds stood to her credit. But she rose promptly.

'Of course, I shall give you a cheque.'

'Nonsense! Don't treat me like a regular agent, Mrs Rolfe. Surely you know me better than that? I undertook it for the pleasure of the thing – '

'But you don't suppose I can accept a present of money from you, Mr Dymes?'

'Hang it! Just as you like, of course. But don't make me take it now, as if I'd looked in with my little bill. Send the cheque, if you must. But what I really came for, when I called a few weeks ago, was something else – quite a different thing, and a good deal more important. Just sit down again, if you can spare me a few minutes.'

With face averted, Alma sank back into her chair. Harvey would give her the money without a word, but she dreaded the necessity of asking him for it. So disturbed were her thoughts that she did not notice how oddly Dymes was regarding her, and his next words sounded meaningless.

'By-the-bye, can we talk here?'

'Talk – ?'

'I mean' – he lowered his voice – 'are we safe from interruption? It's all right; don't look frightened. The fact is, I want to speak of something rather awkward – but it's something you ought to know about, if you don't already.'

'I am quite at leisure,' she replied; adding, with a nervous movement of the head, 'there will be no interruption.'

'I want to ask you, then, have you seen Mrs Strangeways lately?'

'No.'

'Nor Mrs Carnaby?'

'No.'

'I understand you've broken with them altogether? You don't want anything more to do with that lot?'

'I have nothing whatever to do with them,' Alma replied, steadying her voice to a cold dignity.

'And I think you're quite right. Now, look here – you've heard, I dare say, that I'm going to be married? Well, I'm not the kind of fellow to talk sentiment, as you know. But I've had fair luck in life, and I feel pretty pleased with myself, and if I can do anybody a friendly turn – anybody that deserves it – I'm all there. I want you just to think of me as a friend, and nothing else. You're rather set against me, I know; but try and forget all about that. Things are changed. After all, you know, I'm one of the men that people talk about; my name has got into the "directories of talent", as somebody calls them; and I have a good deal at stake. It won't do for me to go fooling about any more. All I mean is, that you can trust me, down to the ground. And there's nobody I would be better pleased to help in a friendly way than you, Mrs Rolfe.'

Alma was gazing at him in surprise, mingled with apprehension.

'Please say what you mean. I don't see how you can possibly do me any service. I have given up all thought of a professional career.'

'I know you have. I'm sorry for it, but it isn't that I want to talk about. You don't see Mrs Carnaby, but I suppose you hear of her now and then?'

'Very rarely.'

'You know that she has been taken up by Lady Isobel Barker?'

'Who is Lady Isobel Barker?'

'Why, she's a daughter of the Earl of Bournemouth, and she married a fellow on the Stock Exchange. There are all sorts of amusing stories about her. I don't mean anything shady – just the opposite. She did a good deal of slumming at the time when it was fashionable, and started a home for women of a certain kind – all that sort of thing. Barker is by way of being a millionaire, and they live in great style; have Royalties down at Boscombe, and so on. Well, Mrs Carnaby has got hold of her. I don't know how she managed it. Just after that affair it looked as if she would have a bad time. People cut her – you know all about that?'

'No, I don't. You mean that they thought – '

'Just so; they did think.' He nodded and smiled. 'She was all the talk at the clubs, and, no doubt, in the boudoirs. I wasn't a friend of hers, you know – I met her now and then, that was all; so I didn't quite know what to think. But it looked – *didn't* it?'

Alma avoided his glance, and said nothing.

'I shouldn't wonder,' pursued Dymes, 'if she went to Lady Isobel and talked about her hard case, and just asked for help. At all events, last May we began to hear of Mrs Carnaby again. Women who wanted to be thought smart had quite altered their tone about her. Men laughed, but some of them began to admit that the case was doubtful. At all events, Lady Isobel was on her side, and that meant a good deal.'

'And she went about in society just as if nothing had happened?'

'No, no. That would have been bad taste, considering where

her husband was. She wasn't seen much, only talked about. She's a clever woman, and by the time Carnaby's let loose she'll have played the game so well that things will be made pretty soft for him. I'm told he's a bit of a globe-trotter, sportsman, and so on. All he has to do is to knock up a book of travels, and it'll go like wildfire.'

Alma had pulled to pieces a tassel on her chair.

'What has all this to do with me?' she asked abruptly.

'I'm coming to that. You don't know anything about Mrs Strangeways either? Well, there *may* be a doubt about Mrs Carnaby, but there's none about Mrs S. She's just about as bad as they make 'em. I could tell you things – but I won't. What I want to know is, did you quarrel with her?'

'Quarrel! Why should we have quarrelled? What had I to do with her?'

'Nothing about Redgrave?' asked Dymes, pushing his head forward and speaking confidentially.

'What do you mean?'

'No harm, I assure you – all the other way. I *know* Mrs Strangeways, and I've had a good deal of talk with her lately, and I couldn't help suspecting you had a reason of your own for getting clear of her. Let me tell you, first of all, that she's left her house in Porchester Terrace. My belief is that she and her husband haven't a five-pound note between them. And the queer thing is, that this has come about since Redgrave's death.'

He paused to give his words their full significance. Alma, no longer disguising her interest, faced him with searching eyes.

'She's a bad un,' pursued the musician, 'and I shouldn't care to tell all I think about her life for the last few years. I've seen a good deal of life myself, you know, and I don't pretend to be squeamish; but I draw a line for women. Mrs Strangeways goes a good bit beyond it, as I know for certain.'

'What is it to *me*?' said Alma, with tremulous impatience.

'Why, this much. She is doing her best to harm you, and in a devilish artful way. She tries to make *me* believe – and it's certain she says the same to others – that what happened at Wimbledon was *the result of a plot between you and Redgrave's housekeeper!*'

Alma stared at him, her parted lips quivering with an abortive laugh.

'Do you understand? She says that you were furiously jealous of Mrs Carnaby, and didn't care what you did to ruin her; that you put Redgrave's housekeeper up to telling Carnaby lies about his wife.'

'How long has she been saying this?'

'I heard it for the first time about two months ago. But let me go on. The interesting thing is that, at the time of the trial and after it, she was all the other way. She as good as told me that she had proof against Mrs Carnaby; I fancy she told lots of people the same. She talked as if she hated the woman. But now that Mrs Carnaby is looking up – you see? – she's going to play Mrs Carnaby's game at your expense. What I should like to know is whether they've done it together?'

'There can't be much doubt of that,' said Alma, between her teeth.

'I don't know,' rejoined the other cautiously. 'Have you reason to think that Mrs Carnaby would like to injure you?'

'I'm quite sure she would do so if it benefited herself.'

'And yet you were fast friends not long ago, weren't you?' asked Dymes, with a look of genuine curiosity.

'We don't always know people as well as we think. Where is that woman living now? – I mean, Mrs Strangeways.'

'That's more than I can tell you. She is – or is supposed to be – out of town. I saw her last just before she left her house.'

'Is the other in town?'

'Mrs Carnaby? I don't know. I was going to say,' Dymes pursued, 'that the story Mrs S. has been telling seems to me very clumsy, and that's why I don't think the other has any hand in it. She seemed to have forgotten that Redgrave's housekeeper, who was wanted by the police, wasn't likely to put herself in Carnaby's way – the man she had robbed. I pointed that out, but she only laughed. "We're not bound to believe," she said, "all that Carnaby said on his trial."'

'We are not,' Alma remarked, with a hard smile.

'You think he dressed things up a bit?'

'I think,' answered Alma, 'that he may have known more than he told.'

'That's my idea, too. But never mind; whatever the truth may be, that woman is doing you a serious injury. I felt you ought to know about it. People have talked about you a good deal, wondering why on earth you dropped out of sight so suddenly after that splendid start; and it was only natural they should connect your name with the Carnaby affair, knowing, as so many did, that you were a friend of theirs, and of Redgrave too.'

'I knew Mr Redgrave,' said Alma, 'but I was no friend of his.'

Dymes peered at her.

'Didn't he interest himself a good deal in your business?'

'Not more than many other people.'

'Well, I'm very glad to hear that,' said Dymes, looking about the room. 'I tell you, honestly, that whenever I have a chance of speaking up for you, I shall do it.'

'I am very much obliged, but I really don't think it matters what is said of me. I am not likely ever to meet the people who talk about such things.'

She said it in so convincing a tone that Dymes looked at her gravely.

'I never know any one change so much,' he observed. 'Is it really your health? No other reason for giving up such magnificent chances?'

'Of course, I have my reasons. They concern nobody but myself.'

'I might give a guess, I dare say. Well, you're the best judge, and we won't say any more about that. But look here – about Mrs S. and her scandal. I feel sure, as I said, that she's toadying to Mrs Carnaby, and expects to make her gain out of it somehow. Her husband's a loafing, gambling fellow, and I shouldn't wonder if he gave her the skip. Most likely she'll have to live by her wits, and we know what that means in a woman of her kind. She'll be more or less dangerous to everybody that's worth blackmailing.'

'You think she had – she was dependent in some way upon Mr Redgrave?' asked Alma, in an undertone.

'I've heard so. Shall I tell you what a woman said who is very likely to know? Long ago, in the time of her first marriage, she got hold of something about him that would have made a furious scandal, and he had to pay for her silence. All gossip; but there's generally a foundation for that kind of thing. If it's true, no doubt she has been at his relatives since his death. It doesn't look as if they were disposed to be bled. Perhaps they turned the tables on her. She has looked sour and disappointed enough for a long time.'

'I was just thinking,' said Alma, with an air of serious

deliberation, 'whether it would be worth while for *me* to turn
the tables on her, and prosecute her for slander.'

'If you take my advice, you'll keep out of that,' replied the
other, with emphasis. 'But another thing has occurred to me. I
see your opinion of Mrs Carnaby, and no doubt you have good
reason for it. Now, would it be possible to frighten her? Have
you' – he peered more keenly – 'any evidence that would make
things awkward for Mrs Carnaby?'

Alma kept close lips, breathing rapidly.

'If you *have*,' pursued the other, 'just give her a hint that Mrs
Strangeways had better stop talking. You'll find it effectual, no
doubt.'

He watched her, and tried to interpret the passion in her eyes.

'If I think it necessary,' said Alma, and seemed to check
herself.

'No need to say any more. I wished to put you on your guard,
that's all. We've known each other for a longish time, and I've
often enough felt sorry that something didn't come off – you
remember when. No good talking about that; but I shall always
be glad if I can be a friend to you. And, I say, don't think any
more about that cheque, there's a good girl.'

The note of familiar patronage was more than distasteful to
Alma.

'I shall, of course, send it,' she replied curtly.

'As you please. Would you like to hear a bit from my new
opera? It isn't every one gets the chance, you know.'

Quite in his old way, he seated himself at the piano, and ran
lightly through a few choice *morceaux*, exacting praise, and
showing himself vexed because it was not fervent. In spite of her
wandering thoughts, Alma felt the seductiveness of these melodies – their originality, their grace – and once more she wondered at their coming from the mind of such a man.

'Very pretty.'

'Pretty!' exclaimed the composer scornfully. 'It's a good deal
more than that, and you know it. I don't care – there's somebody
else feels deuced proud of me, and good reason too. Well, ta-ta!'

There are disadvantages in associating with people whose
every word, as likely as not, may be an insidious falsehood.
Thinking over what she had heard from Dymes, Alma was
inclined to believe him; on the other hand, she knew it to be
quite possible that he sought her with some interested motive.

The wise thing, she knew, would be to disregard his reports, and hold aloof from the world in which they originated. But she had a strong desire to see Mrs Strangeways. There might be someone at the house in Porchester Terrace who could help her to discover its late tenant. However dangerous the woman's wiles and slanders, an interview with her could do no harm, and might set at rest a curiosity long lurking, now feverishly stimulated. With regard to Sibyl, there could be little doubt that Dymes had heard, or conjectured, the truth. Sibyl was clever enough to make her perilous reverse a starting-point for new social conquests. Were there but a hope of confronting her with some fatal disclosure, and dragging her down, down!

That cheque must be sent. She would show Harvey the account this evening, and have done with the unpleasantness of it. Probably he remembered from time to time that she had never told him how her business with Dymes was settled. No more duplicity. The money would be paid, and therewith finish to that dragging chapter of her life.

Harvey came home at five o'clock, and, as usual, had tea with her. Of late he had been uneasy about Cecil Morphew, whose story Alma knew; today he spoke more hopefully.

'Shall I bring him here tomorrow, and make him stay over Sunday? Sunday is his bad day, and no wonder. If there were a licensed poison-shop in London, they'd do a very fair trade on Sundays.'

'There are the public-houses,' said Alma.

'Yes; but Morphew doesn't incline that way. The fellow has delicate instincts, and suffers all the more; so the world is made. I can't help hoping it may come right for him yet. I have a suspicion that Mrs Winter may be on his side; if so, it's only a question of time. I keep at him like a slave-driver; he *has* to work whilst I'm there; and he takes it very good-humouredly. But you mustn't give him music, Alma; he says he can't stand it.'

'I'm much obliged to him,' she answered, laughing.

'You understand well enough.'

After dinner Alma found her courage and the fitting moment.

'I have something disagreeable to talk about. Mr Dymes called this afternoon, and handed in his *bill*.'

'His bill? Yes, yes, I remember. – What's all this? Surely you haven't obliged him to come looking after his money?'

'It's the first account I have received.'

Rolfe puckered his face a little as he perused the document, but ended, as he began, with a smile. In silence he turned to the writing-table, took out his cheque-book, and wrote.

'You don't mind its being in my name?'

'Not at all. Indeed, I prefer it. But I am sorry and ashamed,' she added in a murmur.

'Let it be taken to the post at once,' said Rolfe quietly.

When this was done, Alma made known what Dymes had told her about Sibyl, speaking in an unconcerned voice, and refraining from any hint of suspicion or censure.

'I had heard of it,' said Harvey, with troubled brow, and evidently wished to say no more.

'What do you suppose Mr Carnaby will do?' Alma inquired.

'Impossible to say. I'm told that the business at Coventry is flourishing, and no doubt his interest in it remains. I hear, too, that those Queensland mines are profitable at last. So there'll be no money troubles. But what he will do – '

The subject was dropped.

Harvey had succeeded in hiding his annoyance at the large debt to Dymes, a sum he could ill afford; but he was glad to have paid it, and pleased with Alma's way of dismissing it to oblivion. The talk that followed had turned his mind upon a graver trouble: he sat thinking of Hugh Carnaby. Dear old Hugh! Not long ago the report ran that his health was in a bad state. To one who knew him the wonder was that he kept alive. But the second year drew on.

## CHAPTER 9

On Monday morning, when Harvey and his friend had started for town, and Hughie was at school, Alma made ready to go out. In many months she had been to London only two or three times. Thus alone could she subdue herself. She tried to forget all that lay eastward from Gunnersbury, rejecting every kind of town amusement, and finding society in a very small circle of acquaintances who lived almost as quietly as herself. But this morning she yielded to the impulse made irresistible by Dymes's visit. In leaving the house, she seemed to escape from an atmosphere so still and heavy that it threatened her blood with stagnation; she breathed deeply of the free air, and hastened towards the railway as if she had some great pleasure before her.

But this mood had passed long before the end of her journey. Alighting at Queen's Road, she walked hurriedly to Porchester Terrace, and from the opposite side of the way had a view of Mrs Strangeways' house. It was empty, to let. She crossed, and rang the bell, on the chance that some caretaker might be within; but no one answered. Her heart throbbing painfully, she went on a little distance, then stood irresolute. A cab crawled by; she raised her hand, and gave the direction, 'Oxford and Cambridge Mansions'. Once here, she had no difficulty in carrying out her purpose. Passion came to her aid; and when Sibyl's door opened she could hardly wait for an invitation before stepping in.

The drawing-room was changed; it had been refurnished, and looked even more luxurious than formerly. For nearly ten minutes she had to stand waiting; seat herself she could not. Then entered Sibyl.

'Good morning, Mrs Rolfe. I am glad to see you.'

The latter sentence was spoken not as a mere phrase of courtesy, but with intention, with quiet yet unmistakable significance. Sibyl did not offer her hand; she moved a chair so that its back was to the light, and sat down very much as she might have done if receiving an applicant for a 'situation'.

'You had some reason for coming so early?'

Alma, who had felt uncertain how this interview would begin, was glad that she had to meet no pretences of friendship. Her heart burned within her; she was pallid, and her eyes shone fiercely.

'I came to ask if you could tell me where Mrs Strangeways is to be found?'

'Mrs Strangeways?' Sibyl repeated, with cold surprise. 'I know nothing about her.'

Feeling in every way at a disadvantage – contrast of costume told in Sibyl's favour, and it was enhanced by the perfection of her self-command – Alma could not maintain the mockery of politeness.

'Of course, you say that,' she rejoined haughtily; 'and, of course, I don't believe it.'

'That is nothing to me, Mrs Rolfe,' remarked the other, smiling. 'Doubtless you have your own reasons for declining to believe me; just as you have your own reasons for – other things. Your next inquiry?'

'Hasn't it been rather unwise of you, keeping away from me all this time?'

'Unwise? I hardly see your meaning.'

'It looked rather as if you felt afraid to meet me.'

'I see; that is your point of view.' Sibyl seemed to reflect upon it calmly. 'To me, on the other hand, it appeared rather strange that I neither saw nor heard from you at a time when other friends were showing their sympathy. I heard that you were ill for a short time, and felt sorry I was unable to call. Later, you still kept silence. I didn't know the reason, and could hardly be expected to ask for it. As for being afraid to meet you – that, I suppose, is a suspicion natural to your mind. We won't discuss it. Is there any other question you would like to ask?'

Humiliated by her inability to reply with anything but a charge she could not support, and fearing the violence of her emotions if she were longer subjected to this frigid insult, Alma rose.

'One moment, if you please,' continued Mrs Carnaby. 'I was glad that you had come, as I had half wished for an opportunity of speaking a few words to you. It isn't a matter of much importance, but I may as well say, perhaps, that you are indiscreet in your way of talking about me to your friends. Of course, we haven't many acquaintances in common, but I happen to have heard the opinion of me which you expressed to – let me see, some ladies named Leach, whom I once knew slightly. It seems hardly worth while to take serious steps in the matter – though I might find it necessary. I only wish, in your own interest, to say a word of warning. You have behaved, all things considered' – she dwelt on the phrase – 'rather indiscreetly.'

'I said what I knew to be the truth,' replied Alma, meeting her look with the satisfaction of defiance.

Sibyl approached one step.

'You knew it?' she asked, very softly and deliberately, searching the passionate face with eyes as piercing as they were beautiful.

'With certainty.'

'I used to think you intelligent,' said Sibyl, 'but I fancy you don't perceive what this "certainty" of yours suggests.' She paused, with a curling lip. 'Let me put you on your guard. You have very little command of your primitive feelings, and they bring you into danger. I should be sorry to think that an unpleasant story I have heard whispered was anything more than ill-natured scandal, but it's as well to warn you that *other* people have a taste for that kind of gossip.'

'I'm well aware of it,' flashed the listener. 'And that was the very reason why I came to ask you where Mrs Strangeways is hiding.'

'Mrs Rolfe, you are aware of too many things. In your position I should be uneasy.'

'I will leave you to enjoy your *own* uneasiness,' returned Alma, with a contemptuous laugh. 'You must have enough of it, without imagining that of others.'

She half turned. Sibyl again took one step forward, and spoke with ever so little tremor in the even voice.

'You have understood me, I hope?'

'Oh, quite. You have shown plainly how – afraid you are. Good morning, Mrs Carnaby.'

Baker Street station being so near, Alma was tempted to go straightway and demand from the Leach sisters an explanation of what she had heard; they, too, seemed to be behaving treacherously. But she was unwilling to miss the luncheon hour at home, for Hughie would speak of it to his father, and so oblige her to make false excuses. Besides, she had suffered more than enough indignity (though not unavenged!), and it was better to summon the sisters to her presence.

On reaching home, she at once sent them an ordinary invitation, but of the briefest. In the evening she received Dymes's acknowledgment of the cheque. Next day she wrote to him, a few formal lines, requesting that he would let her know Mrs Strangeways' address as soon as he had discovered it.

Dora Leach came to Gunnersbury alone. She was in distress and worry, for her father had fallen ill again, and the doctors doubted whether he would ever be fit to resume work; it had just dawned upon Dora that the breadwinner of the family deserved rather more consideration than he had been wont to receive, and that his death might involve unpleasant conse-quences for those dependent upon him. To Alma's questioning she replied frankly and with self-reproach. It was true that she had whispered her friend's suspicions of Mrs Carnaby, but only to one person, and in strictest confidence. Neither she nor Gerda had met Mrs Carnaby, and how the whisper could have reached Sibyl's ears was inconceivable to her.

'It doesn't matter in the least,' said Alma, finally. 'To tell you the truth, I'm not sorry.'

'Why, that's just what I thought!' exclaimed Dora, with sudden clearing of her countenance.

In a fortnight or so there came a note from Dymes, written at Brussels. He had ascertained that Mrs Strangeways was somewhere on the Continent, but as yet he could not succeed in 'running her down'. Let Mrs Rolfe depend upon his zeal in this search, as in any other matter in which he could be of use to her. Unfortunately, this envelope came under Harvey's eyes, and Alma, knowing he had seen it, felt obliged to speak.

'Mr Dymes refuses to believe that I shall never play again in public,' she remarked, putting down his letter, as carelessly as possible, by her plate at breakfast.

'Does he pester you? If so, it might be better for me to—'

'Oh dear, no! I can manage my own correspondence, Harvey, thank you.'

Her tone of slight petulance was due to fear that he might ask to see the letter, and it had its effect. But Alma's heart sank at the deception, and her skill in practising it. Was it impossible to become what she desired to be, an honest woman! Only yesterday Harvey had spoken to her with vexation of a piece of untruthfulness in Hughie, and had begged her to keep a watch upon the child's habit in this respect. And she had promised, with much earnestness, much concern.

There are women who can breathe only in the air of lies and of treachery. Alma rebelled against the fate which made her life dishonourable. Fate – she declared – not the depravity of her own heart. From the dark day that saw her father's ruin, she had been condemned to a struggle with circumstances. She meant honestly; she asked no more than the free exercise of instincts nature had given her; but destiny was adverse, and step by step had brought her into a position so false, so hopeless, that she wondered at her strength in living on.

Hughie had begun to learn the maps of countries, and prided himself on naming them as he turned over an atlas. One day, about this time, she looked over his shoulder and saw the map of Italy.

'Those are lakes,' said the child, pointing north. 'Tell me their names, Mother.'

But she was silent. Her eye had fallen upon Garda, and at the head of the lake was a name which thrilled her memory. What if she had gone to Riva? Suddenly, and for the first time, she saw it as a thing that might have happened; not as a mere dark suggestion abhorrent to her thought. Had she known the world a little better, it might have been. Then, how different her life! Pleasure, luxury, triumph; for she had proved herself capable of triumphing. He, the man of money and influence, would have made it his pride to smooth the way for her. And perhaps never a word against her reputation; or, if whispers, did she not know by this time how indulgent society can be to its brilliant favourites?

As it was: a small house at Gunnersbury, a baffled ambition, a life of envy, hatred, fear, suffered in secret, hidden by base or paltry subterfuge. A husband whom she respected, whose love she had never ceased to desire, though, strange to say, she knew not whether she loved him. Only death could part them; but how much better for him and for her if they had never met! Their thoughts and purposes so unlike; he, with his heart and mind set on grave, quiet, restful things, hating the world's tumult, ever hoping to retire beyond its echo; she, her senses crying for the delight of an existence that loses itself in whirl and glare.

In a crowded drawing-room she had heard someone draw attention to her – 'the daughter of Bennet Frothingham'. That was how people thought of her, and would it not have been wiser if she had so thought of herself? Daughter of a man who had set all on a great hazard; who had played for the world's reward, and, losing, flung away his life. What had *she* to do with domestic virtues, and the pleasures of a dull, decorous circle? Could it but come over again, she would accept the challenge of circumstance, which she had failed to understand; accept the scandal and the hereditary shame; welcome the lot cast for her, and, like her father, play boldly for the great stakes. His widow might continue to hold her pious faith in him, and refuse to believe that his name merited obloquy; his child knew better. She had mistaken her path, lost the promise of her beauty and her talent, led astray by the feeble prejudice of those who have neither one nor the other. Too late, and worse than idle now, to recognise it. She would be a good woman, rule her little house, bring up her child, and have no will but her husband's.

House-ruling was no easy matter. Things did not go as she wished; the servants were inefficient, sometimes refractory, and she loathed the task of keeping them up to their duties. Insomnia began to trouble her again, and presently she had recourse to the forbidden sleeping-draught. Not regularly, but once a week or so, when the long night harried her beyond endurance. Rolfe did not suspect it, for she never complained to him. Winter was her bad time. In the spring her health would improve, as usual, and then she would give up the habit.

At Christmas the Langlands had the customary visit from their relative, Mr Thistlewood, who renewed his acquaintance with Alma. At their first meeting she was struck by his buoyant air, his animated talk. A week later, he called in the afternoon. Two ladies happened to be with Alma, and they stayed a long time; but Thistlewood, who comported himself rather oddly, saying little and sometimes neglecting a remark addressed to him, stayed yet longer. When he was alone with his hostess, he took a chair near to her, bent forward, and said, smiling –

'You remember our talk about marriage on a minute income?'

'I do, very well.'

'I have found someone who isn't afraid of it.'

'You have? The same person who formerly *was*?'

'No; she was not afraid of the income, but of me. I couldn't be surprised, though it hit me hard. Time has spoken for me.'

Harvey was dining in town. He came back with vexatious news about Cecil Morphew, who neglected business, looked ill, and altogether seemed in a bad way. As he talked, he began to notice that Alma regarded him with brighter and happier eyes than for many a day.

'Why does it amuse you?' he asked, stopping in his narrative.

'It doesn't; I'm as sorry as you are. But I have a surprise for you.'

'A pleasant one, this time, I see.'

'Mrs Abbott is going to marry Mr Thistlewood.'

She watched the effect of her words, and for an instant felt the old pang, the old bitterness. But Harvey's confusion of feeling soon passed, giving way to a satisfaction that could not be mistaken.

'Who has told you?'

'The happy man himself.'

'I am glad – heartily glad! But I didn't think it would interest you so much.

'Oh, women – marriages – !'

She threw a pretty scorn upon herself.

'Yes, that's good news. They will suit each other. But she'll give up her school, and that's a nuisance.'

'There are others as good.'

'But not here. Another removal, I suppose. – When is it to be?'

'Not till the Easter holidays.'

They were in the library. Harvey began to fill his pipe, and nothing more was said until he had drawn a few meditative puffs.

'Another removal,' then escaped him, with half a groan.

'Why should you care?' asked Alma thoughtfully. 'You don't like this place.'

'As well as any other. It's convenient for town.'

'Do you really think of going on in that business, which you detest?'

'It has brought in a little money, and may – ought to – bring more. But if Morphew goes down – '

Alma glanced at him, and said timidly –

'You are going to Greystone at Easter.'

'We shall all go. What of that?'

'Haven't you' – she spoke with an effort – 'sometimes thought you would like to live there?'

'Great heavens – Alma!'

He stared at her in humorous astonishment, then slowly shook his head. How could *she* live in such a place as Greystone? And what on earth did she mean by disturbing him with such a suggestion? But Alma, gravely and repeatedly, assured him that she could live there very well; that in all likelihood she would be much more contented there than here.

'I should bring out my violin again, and the Greystone people would admire me. There's a confession – to prove that I am in earnest. I can't conquer the world; I don't wish it; that's all over.

But I should find it pleasant to have a reputation in Greystone – I should indeed.'

Harvey sighed, and could not look at her.

'And Hughie,' she continued, 'would go to the Grammar-School. You know how you would like that. And living there is cheap; we might keep our horse again. – Don't say anything now, but think about it.'

He raised his eyes, and fixed them upon her with a look of infinite tenderness and gratitude. It was Alma now who sighed, but not audibly.

Before Thistlewood went north again, Harvey enjoyed long talks with him. Mary Abbott he saw only in the presence of other people. But on an evening in February, when Alma was at the Langlands' and he had promised to call for her at ten o'clock, he left home an hour earlier and walked past Mrs Abbott's house. A light in the window of her sitting-room showed that Mary was at home. After a turn or two backwards and forwards, he went up to the door and knocked. A very young servant took his name to her mistress, and then admitted him.

'Will you let me answer your letter personally?' he said, as Mrs Abbott welcomed him in the room where she sat alone.

She had written about Minnie Wager, begging that he would in future cease to contribute to the girl's support, and be responsible only for the boy. In her new home there would be no need of a servant; she and Minnie would do the housework together. Impossible, she wrote, to speak of his kindness both to her and the children. For Minnie, who might henceforth be looked upon as self-supporting, he must no longer be taxed. The child owed him every hope in her life; let him be satisfied with what he had done so generously.

Of these things they talked for a few minutes. It was easy to see how great a change had befallen Mary Abbott's outlook upon life. She was younger by several years, yet not like herself of that earlier time; much gentler, much sweeter in face and word. Harvey observed her with keen pleasure, and, becoming aware of his gaze, his smile, she blushed like a girl.

'Mr Rolfe – I am sure you feel that I am deserting my post.'

'To be sure you are. I shall always owe you a grudge for it.'

'I thought of it all – of Hughie and the others. I didn't know how I should ever face you.'

"'Twas a shameless thing. And yet I can find it in my heart to forgive you. You are so ingenuous about it.'

Mary looked up again.

'What shall you do – about Hughie?'

'Oh, there's a great scheme on foot. Alma suggests that we shall go and live at Greystone. It tempts me.'

'That it must, indeed! I know how you would like it.'

'We shouldn't be so very far apart then – an hour's journey or so. You would come to us, and we to you.'

'Delightful!'

They had not much more to say, but each was conscious of thought in the other's mind that supplemented their insufficient phrases. As they shook hands, Mary seemed trying to speak. The lamplight made a glimmer in her eyes, and their lids drooped as she said at length –

'I am so glad that you like each other.'

'He's a splendid fellow,' replied Rolfe joyously. 'I think no end of him.'

'And he of you – for I have told him everything.'

Then Harvey quitted the house, and walked about under the starry sky until it was time to call for Alma.

## CHAPTER 10

Yet once again did Alma hypnotise her imagination with a new ideal of life. Her talk was constantly of Greystone. She began a correspondence with Mrs Morton, who did her best to encourage all pleasant anticipations – careful the while, at her husband's bidding and Harvey's too, not to exaggerate the resources of Greystone for a mind and temper such as Alma's. Of course the little town had its musical circle, in which Mrs Rolfe's talent would find an appreciative reception. Touching on this point to her correspondent, Alma remarked, with emphasised modesty, that she must *not* be regarded as a professional violinist; it would be better, perhaps, if nothing were said about her 'rather audacious experiment' in London. Meanwhile, a suitable house was being looked for. There need be no hurry; Midsummer was the earliest possible date for removal, and a few months later might prove more convenient.

At Easter came Mary Abbott's wedding, which was celebrated as quietly as might be. Alma had done her utmost to atone for bygone slights and coldness; she and Mary did not love each other, nor ever could, and for that reason they were all the more affectionate at this agitating time. When all was over, the Rolfes set forth on their visit to Greystone. Harvey could not look forward to complete enjoyment of the holiday, for by this time Cecil Morphew had succumbed to his old habits of tossing indolence, and only pretended to look after his business. If Harvey withdrew, the shop must either be closed or pass into other hands. Pecuniary loss was the least vexatious part of the affair. Morphew, reckless in the ruin of his dearest hope, would seek excitement, try once more to enrich himself by gambling, and so go down to the depths whence there is no rescue. As a last hope, Harvey had written to Henrietta Winter a long letter of all but passionate appeal; for answer he received a few lines, infinitely sorrowful, but of inflexible resolve. 'In the sight of God, Mr Morphew already has a wife. I should be guilty of a crime if I married him.' With a desperate ejaculation, Rolfe crushed up the sheet of paper, and turned to other things.

Whilst she was at Greystone, Alma heard again from Felix Dymes, his letter having been forwarded. He wrote that Mrs Strangeways was about to return to England, and that before long she might be heard of at a certain hotel in London. As this letter had escaped Harvey's notice, Alma was spared the necessity of shaping a fiction about it. Glad of this, and all but decided to put Mrs Strangeways utterly out of her life and mind, she sent no answer.

But when she had been back again for some weeks at Gunnersbury; when a house at Greystone was taken (though it would not be ready for them till Michaelmas); when she was endeavouring, day after day, to teach Hughie, and to manage her servants, and to support a wavering hope, there arrived one morning a letter from Mrs Strangeways. It was dated from the hotel which Dymes had mentioned, and it asked Alma to call there. A simple, friendly invitation, suggestive of tea and chat. Alma did not speak of it, and for an hour or two thought she could disregard it altogether. But that evening she talked to

Harvey of shopping she had to do in town, and the following afternoon she called upon Mrs Strangeways.

A lift carried her to the topmost, or all but topmost, storey of the vast hotel, swarming, murmurous. She entered a small sitting-room, pretentiously comfortless, and from a chair by the open window – for it was a day of hot sunshine – Mrs Strangeways rose to greet her; quite in the old way, smiling with head aside, cooing rapidly an effusive welcome. Alma looked round to see that the door was shut; then, declining the offered hand, she said coldly –

'You are mistaken if you think I have come as a friend.'

'Oh! I am so sorry to hear you say that. Do sit down, and let me hear all about it. I have so looked forward to seeing you.'

'I am only here to ask what good it can do you to talk ill of me.'

'I really don't understand. I am quite at a loss.'

'But I know for certain that you have tried to injure me by telling extraordinary falsehoods.'

Mrs Strangeways regarded her with an air of gently troubled deprecation.

'Oh, you have been grievously misled. Who can have told you this?'

'The name doesn't matter. I have no doubt of the fact.'

'But at least you will tell me what I am supposed to have said.'

Alma hesitated, and only after several interchanges of question and answer did the full extent of her accusation appear. Thereupon Mrs Strangeways smiled, as if with forbearance.

'Now I understand. But I have been cruelly misrepresented. I heard such a rumour, and I did my best to contradict it. I heard it, unfortunately, more than once.'

Again Alma found herself in conflict with an adroitness, a self-possession, so much beyond her own, that the sense of being maliciously played with goaded her into rage.

'No one but yourself could ever have started such a story!'

'You mean,' sounded the other voice, still soft, though not quite so amiable, 'that I was the only person who knew –'

And there Mrs Strangeways paused, as if discreetly.

'Knew? Knew what?'

'Only that you had reason for a little spite against your dear friend.'

'Suppose it was so,' exclaimed Alma, remembering too well her last conversation with this woman. 'Whatever you knew, or thought you knew, about me – and it was little enough – you have been making use of it disgracefully.'

'You say I knew very little,' put in the other, turning a ring upon her hand; 'but you will admit that it was enough to excite my curiosity. May I not have taken trouble to learn more?'

'Any amount of trouble would have taught you nothing; there was nothing to discover. And that you know as well as I do.'

Mrs Strangeways moved her head, as if in good-natured acquiescence.

'Don't let us be harsh with each other, my dear. We have both had our worries and trials in consequence of that unfortunate affair. You, I can see, have gone through a good deal; I assure you, so have I. But oughtn't you to remember that our misfortunes were caused by the same person? If I—'

'Your misfortunes are nothing to me. And I shouldn't think you would care to talk about them.'

'Surely I might say the same to you, my dear Alma? Is there very much to choose between us?'

Alma flushed with resentment, but had no word ready on her parched tongue. The other went on in an unbroken flow of mocking good humour.

'We ought to be the best of friends. I haven't the least wish to do you harm, and nothing would please me better than to gratify your little feeling against a certain person. I may be able to manage that. Let me tell you something – of course in the strictest confidence.' Her voice was playful for a moment. 'I have been trying to find someone – you know who I mean – who mysteriously disappeared. That interests you, I see. It's very difficult; such people don't let themselves be dropped upon by chance a second time. But, do you know, I have something very like a clue, at last. Yes' – she nodded familiarly – 'I have.'

In vain Alma tried to lock her lips.

'What if you find her?'

'Do you forget that someone will very soon be at large again, and that someone's wife, a very clever woman, counts on deceiving the world as she deceived *him*?'

'You are sure she *did* deceive him?'

Mrs Strangeways laughed.

'You are acute, my dear. You see the puzzle from all sides.

But I won't go into that just now. What I want to show you is, that our interests are the same. We should both dearly like to see a certain person shown up. I begin to see my way to do it very thoroughly. It would delight you if I were at liberty to tell what I actually *have* got hold of, but you must wait a little. My worst difficulty, now, is want of money. People have to be bought, you know, and I am not rich – . Don't you think you could help a little?'

The question came out with smooth abruptness, accompanied by a look which startled the hearer.

'I? I have no money.'

'What an idea!'

'I tell you I haven't a penny of my own!'

'My dear Alma, you have obliging bankers. One of them is doing very well indeed. You didn't go to his wedding?'

Alma felt a chill of fear. The woman's eyes seemed to cast a net about her, and to watch her struggle as it tightened.

'I don't understand you. I have nothing to do with your plots.'

She strung her muscles and stood up; but Mrs Strangeways, scarcely moving, still looked at her with baleful directness.

'It would be a shame to lose our sport for want of a little money. I must ask you to help, really.'

'I can't – and won't.'

'I feel sure you will – rather than have anything happen. You are leading, I hear, a most exemplary life; I should be so sorry to disturb it. But really, you *must* help in our undertaking.'

There was a very short silence.

'A week, even a fortnight hence, will do. No great sum; two or three hundred pounds. We won't say any more about it; I depend upon you. In a fortnight's time will do.'

'Do you imagine,' exclaimed Alma, on a high, quivering note, 'that I am in your power?'

'Hush! It is very dangerous to talk like that in a hotel. – Think over what I have said. You will find me here. Think, and remember. You will be quite satisfied with the results, but your help is indispensable.'

Therewith Mrs Strangeways turned to the open window. Looking at her elaborately plaited yellow hair, her thin neck, her delicate fingers just touching the long throat, Alma felt instinct of savagery; in a flash of the primitive mind, she saw herself spring upon her enemy, tear, bite, destroy. The desire still shook her as she stood outside in the corridor, waiting to descend. And in the street she walked like a somnambulist, with wide eyes, straight on. Curious glances at length recalled her to herself; she turned hurriedly from the crowded highway.

Before reaching home, she had surveyed her position, searched her memory. 'The wretch is counting on my weakness. Knowing she can do nothing, she thinks I shall be frightened by the threat. Money? And perhaps all she said only a lie to tempt me! Let her do her worst – and that will be nothing.'

And by this she held, letting the days go by. The fortnight passed. She was ill with apprehension, with suspense; but nothing happened. Three weeks, and nothing happened. Then Alma laughed, and went about the house singing her deliverance.

On that day, Mrs Strangeways sat talking with Mrs Carnaby, in the latter's drawing-room. Her manner was deferential, but that of a friend. Sibyl, queening it at some distance, had the air of conferring a favour as she listened.

'I haven't the least doubt that I shall soon lay my hand upon her. I have had an answer to my last advertisement.'

'Then let me see it,' replied Sibyl coldly.

'Impossible. I put myself in a position of much danger. I dare not trust even you, Mrs Carnaby.'

'Very well. You know my promise. Get her into the hands of the police, and your reward is waiting.'

'But I may lose my opportunity, for want of money. If you would trust me with only – say a hundred pounds.'

'Not a farthing. I didn't ask you to undertake this. If you do it, well and good, I will pay you. But nothing till then.'

Mrs Strangeways perused the carpet.

'Anyone else,' she murmured, 'might be tempted to think that you didn't really care to have her caught.'

'You may be tempted to think exactly what you like,' answered Sibyl, with fine scorn.

The other scrutinised her, with an eye of anxious uncertainty.

'Have you thought, again, of taking any steps in the other matter?'

'Have you anything to show?'

'No. But it can be obtained. A charge of slander could be brought against her at any moment. If you prefer libel, it is merely taking a little trouble.'

Sibyl reflected.

'There is no hurry. I will pay you, as I said, for any trustworthy evidence – of any kind. You bring me none. – Does she come to see you?'

'Occasionally.'

'And – have you succeeded in making *her* pay?' asked Sibyl, with a curl of the lips.

Mrs Strangeways merely smiled. After a brief pause, Sibyl looked at her watch, and rose.

'I have an engagement. And – pray don't trouble to come again unless you have really something to come for. I can't pretend to have any taste for this kind of conversation. It really matters very little; we know that woman will be caught some day, and I shall have the pleasure of prosecuting her for stealing my jewellery and things. The other person – perhaps she is a little beneath my notice.'

She rang the bell, and Mrs Strangeways, having no alternative, slightly bent her head and withdrew.

Mrs Carnaby had no engagement; she was quite at leisure, and, as usual nowadays, spent her leisure in thought. She did not read much, and not at all in the solid books which were to be seen lying about her rooms; but Lady Isobel Barker, and a few other people, admired her devotion to study. Certainly one or two lines had begun to reveal themselves on Sibyl's forehead, which might possibly have come of late reading and memory overstrained; they might also be the record of other experiences. Her beauty was more than ever of the austere type; in regarding her, one could have murmured –

> Chaste as the icicle
> That's curded by the frost from purest snow,
> And hangs on Dian's temple.*

But in privacy Sibyl did not look her best. Assuredly not after the withdrawal of Mrs Strangeways, when her lips, sneering away their fine contour, grew to an ugly hardness, and her eyes smalled themselves in a vicious intensity of mental vision.

Major Carnaby, Hugh's brother, was now in England. A stranger to the society in which Mrs Carnaby had lived, he knew nothing of the gossip at one time threatening her with banishment from polite circles. An honest man, and taking for granted the honesty of his kinsfolk, he put entire faith in Hugh's story, despatched to him by letter a few days after the calamitous event at Wimbledon. On arriving in London, the good Major was pleased, touched, flattered by the very warm welcome with which his sister-in-law received him. Hitherto they had seen hardly anything of each other; but since the disaster their correspondence had been frequent, and Sibyl's letters were so brave, yet so pathetic, that Major Carnaby formed the highest opinion of her. She did not pose as an injured woman; she never so much as hinted at the activity of slanderous tongues; she spoke only of Hugh, the dear, kind, noble fellow, whom fate had so cruelly visited. The favourable impression was confirmed as soon as they met. The Major found that this beautiful, high-hearted creature had, among her many virtues, a sound capacity for business; no one could have looked after her husband's worldly interests with more assiduity and circumspection. He saw that Hugh had been quite right in assuring him (at Sibyl's instance) that there was no need whatever for him to neglect his military duties and come home at an inconvenient time. Hugh's affairs were in perfect order; all he would have to think about was the recovery of health and mental tranquillity.

To this end, they must decide upon some retreat in which he might pass a quiet month or two. That dear and invaluable friend, to whom Sibyl owed 'more than she could tell' (much more than she could tell to Major Carnaby), was ready with a delightful suggestion. Lady Isobel (that is to say, her auriferous husband, plain Mr Barker) had a little house in the north, cosy amid moor and mountain, and she freely offered it. There Hugh and his wife might abide in solitude until the sacred Twelfth, when religious observance would call thither a small company of select pilgrims. The offer was gratefully accepted. Major Carnaby saw no reason for hesitating, and agreed with Sibyl that the plan should be withheld from Hugh until the last moment, as a gratifying surprise. By some means, however, on the day before Hugh's release, there appeared in certain news-papers a little paragraph making known to the public this proof of Lady Isabel's friendship for Sibyl and her husband.

'It's just as well,' said Mrs Carnaby, after appearing vexed for a moment. 'People will be saved the trouble of calling here. But it really is mysterious how the papers get hold of things.'

She was not quite sure that Hugh would approve her arrange-ment, and the event justified this misgiving. Major Carnaby was to bring his brother to Oxford and Cambridge Mansions, and, if possible, all were to travel northward that same day. But Hugh, on hearing what was proposed, made strong objection: he refused to accept the hospitality of people quite unknown to him; why, with abundant resources of their own, should they become indebted to strangers? So vehement was his resistance, and so pitiful the state of body and mind which showed itself in his all but hysterical excitement, that Sibyl pretended to abandon the scheme. Today they would remain here, talking quietly; by tomorrow they might have decided what to do.

At ten o'clock next morning, when Sibyl had been up for an hour, Hugh still lay asleep. She went softly into the room, lighted by the sun's yellow glimmer through blind and lace curtains, and stood looking at him, her husband. To him she had given all the love of which she was capable; she had admired him for his strength and his spirit, had liked him as a companion, had prized the flattery of his ardent devotion, his staunch fidelity. To have married him was, of course, a mistake, not easy of explanation in her present mind; she regretted it, but with no bitterness, with no cruel or even unkind thought. His haggard features, branded with the long rage of captivity; his great limbs, wasted to mere bone and muscle, moved her indignant pity. Poor dear old boy!

He believed her; he still believed her. She saw that these two years of misery had made his faith in her something like a religion; he found it his one refuge from despair. 'But for that, Sibyl, I shouldn't be alive now!' She had known self-reproach; now again it touched her slightly, passingly – poor old boy! But unfaithful to him? To call *that* unfaithfulness? The idea was too foolish.

Her fears were all outlived. She had dared the worst, and daring was grown an easy habit. But in the life that lay before them, *her* judgment, *her* ambitions, must prevail and direct.

Yesterday she had no course save yielding; today her rule must begin.

Hugh was stirring. He groaned, and threw out one of his arms; muttered, as if angrily. She touched him, and on the instant he awoke.

'Sibyl? Good God! that's a queer thing – I dreamt that yesterday was a dream, and that I had woke up to find myself – Did you ever do that – dream you were dreaming?'

She stroked his head, laughing playfully.

'You've had a good long night. Don't you feel better? Shall I bring you some breakfast here?'

'No; I must get up. What's the time? Miles will be coming.'

Sibyl knew that the Major would not be here until two o'clock; but she said nothing, and left him to dress.

On the breakfast-table were delicacies to tempt his palate, but Hugh turned from them. He ate for a few minutes only, without appetite, and, as on the day before, Sibyl was annoyed by the strange rudeness with which he fed himself; he seemed to have forgotten the habits of refinement at table. Afterwards he lighted a cigar, but soon threw it aside; tobacco made him sick. In the drawing-room he moved aimlessly about, blundering now and then against a piece of furniture, and muttering a curse. The clothes he wore, out of his old wardrobe, hung loose about him; he had a stoop in the shoulders.

'Sibyl, what are we going to do?'

For this she had waited. She sat looking at him with a compassionate smile. It was an odd thing if this poor broken-down man could not be made subservient to her will.

'I still think, dear boy, that we ought to accept Lady Isobel's invitation.'

A nervous paroxysm shook him.

'Damn Lady Isobel! I thought that was done with.'

'I don't think you would speak of her like that, Hugh, if you knew all her kindness to me. I couldn't tell you all yesterday. May I now? Or shall I only irritate you?'

'What is it? Of course, I don't want you to offend her. But I suppose she has common-sense?'

'More than most women. There's no fear of offending her. I have another reason. Come and sit quietly by me, and let us talk as we used to do. Do you know, dear, it's a good thing for me that I had powerful friends; I needed all their help against my enemies.'

'What enemies?'

'Have you forgotten what you yourself said, and felt so strongly, at that time – what a dauger I was exposed to when we determined to tell the whole truth? You knew what some people would say.'

'They've said it, no doubt; and what harm has it done you? Tell me a name, and if it's a man—'

'Don't! I can't bear to see that look on your face, Hugh. You could do nothing but endless harm, trying to defend me that way. I have lived it down, thinking of you even more than of myself. There was a time when I almost despaired; people are so glad to think evil. If I had been a weak woman, I should have run away and hidden myself; and then everybody would have said, "I told you so." But I had to think of you, and that gave me strength. What could I do? Truth alone is no good against the world; but truth with a handle to its name and with a million of money – that's a different thing. It was life or death, dear boy, and I had to fight for it. So I went to Lady Isobel Barker. I only knew her by name. She, of course, knew *me* by name, and cold enough she was when I got admitted to her. But half an hour's talk – and I had won! She was my friend; she would stand by me, and all the world should know it. Stay! The worst is over, but there's still a good deal to be done. It has to be known that my friends are your friends also. There was a paragraph in the papers yesterday, saying that you and your wife were going as Lady Isobel's guests to that house of hers. She did that for me. And now, do you think we ought to seem – even seem – to slight her kindness?' Hugh was turning about, chafing impotently.

'Then you mean to go on here?' he asked, with half-appealing, half-resentful eyes.

Sibyl made a gesture of entreaty.

'What other life is there for me? What would you have me do?'

His arms fell; for a minute he sat with head hanging, his eyes fixed and blank like those of a drunken man. Then, as if goaded suddenly –

'Who are these enemies you talk about?'

Sibyl's look wandered; her lips moved in hesitancy.

'Name one of them.'

'Isn't it better to try to forget them?'

'Women, I suppose? – You say you haven't seen Rolfe. Has *he* heard this talk about you, do you think?'

'No doubt,' she answered distantly. 'Isn't he coming to see you?'

'If he saw that in the papers, he won't think I am here. But I should like to see him. I've a good mind to telegraph – but I don't know his address. Yes – I forgot – there's a letter from him somewhere.'

'I know the address,' said Sibyl, in the same tone of reserve.

'I should like to see old Rolfe – poor old Rolfe.'

'Why do you pity him?'

'Oh – only a way of speaking. You know the address, you say? Has he written? Has *she* written?'

'Oh no!'

'You haven't seen her?'

Sibyl evaded the question.

'Doesn't it seem to you rather strange,' she said, 'that the Rolfes should keep away from me – never call or write?'

Hugh's lips were set. When she repeated her inquiry more urgently, he gave a peevish answer.

'You cared very little about her at the last. And Rolfe – when a man marries – No, I won't see him just yet. I'll write to him when we're away.'

'It wouldn't astonish you' – Sibyl spoke in a thin voice, not quite under her control – 'if you heard that Mrs Rolfe had done her best and her worst against me?'

'She? Against you?'

'I don't know that it matters. You said "poor Rolfe". I should fancy he is poor, in every sense. As I have said so much, it's better to let you know all; it will show you that I am not exaggerating what I have gone through. People knew, of course, that she had called herself a friend of mine; and just then she came into notice – just enough to give her opportunities of being dangerous. Well, I heard before long that she was slandering me to all her acquaintances. Oh, *she* knew all about me! It was lucky for me I had a credulous husband. And it still goes on. She came here not long ago; yes, she came. She told me that she knew I was afraid of her, and she threatened me.'

Hugh sat staring like a paralytic.

'*She*? Rolfe's wife did this?'

'Her motive, I don't know. Pure hatred, it seemed. But I've had a strange fancy. She talked about a woman I used to know very slightly, a Mrs Strangeways, and seemed to be in fear of her; she said that woman and I were circulating stories about her. And I have wondered – Why are you looking like that?'

'She must be mad. – I'll tell you. I only wish I had told you before. She was *there* that night – at Redgrave's. But for *her* it would never have happened. I saw him standing with her, by the window of his room – that is, I saw a woman, but it wasn't light enough to know her; and all at once she ran back, through the open French windows into the house; and then I rushed in and found her there – it was Rolfe's wife.'

'Why did you keep this from me?'

'She implored me – vowed there was nothing wrong – cried and begged. And I thought of Rolfe. I see now that I ought to have told him. The woman must be crazy to have behaved like this to you.'

Sibyl's face shone.

'Now I understand. This explains her. Oh, my dear, foolish husband! After all, you did *not* tell the whole truth. To spare your friend's feelings, you risked your wife's reputation. And I have been at the mercy of that woman's malice! Don't you think, Hugh, that I have had to bear a little more than I deserved? Your distrust and what came of it – I have long forgiven you all that. But this – wasn't it rather too hard upon me?'

He flinched under her soft reproach.

'I couldn't be sure, Sibyl. Perhaps it was true – perhaps she was only there – '

A flash of scorn from her eyes struck him into silence.

'Perhaps? And perhaps she meant no harm in lying about me! You will send at once for Rolfe and tell him.'

Hugh moved from her, and stood with his face averted.

'Can you hesitate for a moment?' she asked severely

'Why need I tell Rolfe? Send for *her*, and say what you like. Won't that be enough? It's awful to think of telling Rolfe. Don't ask me do to that, Sibyl.'

He approached her, voice and attitude broken to humility. Sibyl grew only more resolute.

'You must tell him. Don't you owe it me?'

'By God, I can't do that! – I can't do that! Have her here, before us both. Shame her and threaten her as much as you like; but don't tell Rolfe. It's like you and me, Sibyl. Suppose she has really done no wrong, and we put that thought into his mind?'

'Have you lost all your senses?' she exclaimed passionately. 'Must I keep reminding you what she has done to *me*? Is a woman that will behave in that way likely to be innocent? Is her husband to be kept in the dark about her, deceived, cheated? I can't understand you. If you are too cowardly to do your plain duty – Hugh, how am I talking? You make me forget myself. But you know that it's impossible to spare your friend. It wouldn't be just to him. Here's a form; write the telegram at once.'

'Write it yourself,' he answered, in a low, nerveless voice, moving away again.

It was quickly done, though Sibyl paused to reflect after the first word or two. The message ran thus –

'I want to see you and Mrs Rolfe before going away. Please both come this evening if possible. If you cannot, reply when.'

Without showing what she had written, she left the room, and despatched a servant to the post-office.

## CHAPTER 12

As a last resource against Cecil Morphew's degeneration, Harvey had given up his daily work in Westminster Bridge Road. 'I shall go no more,' he wrote. 'I am quite unable to manage the business alone, and if you won't attend to it, it must smash. But please to remember that I took a share on certain conditions.' For a week he had stayed at home. Morphew did not reply, but the fact that no appeals arrived from the trusty shopman seemed to prove that this last step had been effectual. This morning Rolfe was half-minded to go up to town, but decided that he had better not. Thus the telegram from Oxford and Cambridge Mansions came into his hands at about twelve o'clock.

Alma, after giving Hughie his morning's lesson, had gone out

with him for an hour. As soon as she returned, Harvey showed
her the message.

'Why does he want both of us to go?' he asked uneasily.

Alma merely shook her head, as if the matter interested her
very little, and turned to leave the room again.

'I think I had better go alone,' said Harvey, his eyes on the
telegram.

'Just as you like,' answered Alma, and withdrew.

She spent the afternoon much as usual. Rolfe had said at
lunch that he would go to Carnaby's immediately after dinner.
Mrs Langland and one of her daughters called; they thought
Mrs Rolfe rather absent-minded, but noticed nothing else. At
dinner-time she said carelessly to her husband –

'I think I had better go with you, as I was asked.'

'No, no; I think not.'

'I had rather, Harvey, if you don't mind. I am quite ready;
shall only have to put my hat on.'

He made no further objection, but looked a little displeased,
and was silent through the meal.

They travelled by rail to Edgware Road, exchanging scarce a
word on the way. On the stairs of the Mansions, Alma found
the ascent too much for her; she stopped, and put out a hand to
support herself. Rolfe looked round.

'Nothing. You have made me walk rather quickly.'

'I'm sorry. Rest a moment.'

But Alma hastened upwards.

They were shown at once into the drawing-room, where Mrs
Carnaby, who was sitting alone, rose at the announcement of
their names. Alma stepped forwards, and seemed about to offer
her hand, but she was disregarded. Their hostess stood with her
eyes on Rolfe, who, observing the strangeness of this reception,
bowed and said nothing.

'It was I who sent the telegram, Mr Rolfe.' Sibyl's voice had
its wonted refinement, and hardly disturbed the silence. 'My
husband would have postponed the pleasure of seeing you, but
I thought it better you should meet him at once.' Her finger
touched an electric bell. 'And I particularly wished Mrs Rolfe to
be with you; I am so glad she was able to come. Pray sit down.'

Harvey, with no thought of accepting this invitation, cast
stern glances at the speaker and at his wife.

'What does all this mean, Mrs Carnaby?'

'Your old friend will tell you.'

The door had opened, and Hugh Carnaby slouched in. At the sight of Alma he stood still. Then meeting Harvey's eyes, he exclaimed, with hoarse indistinctness, 'Rolfe!' Each advanced, and their hands clasped.

'Rolfe!' – old fellow! – I'm the most miserable devil on earth.'

Tears were in his eyes and in his voice. He held Harvey's hand tight prisoned in both his own, and stood tottering like a feeble old man. 'Old friend, I can't help myself – don't feel hard against me – I have to tell you something.'

He looked towards Alma, who was motionless. Sibyl had sat down, and watched as at a play, but with no smile.

'Come into the next room with me,' added the choking voice.

'No. Here, if you please, Hugh,' sounded with gentle firmness.

'Sibyl – then tell it. I can't.'

'It's a simple story, Mr Rolfe,' began Sibyl. 'I am sure you are not aware that Mrs Rolfe, ever since our great misfortune, has lost no opportunity of slandering me. She has told people, in plain words, that she knew me to be guilty of what my husband was for a moment trapped into suspecting. Among others, she told it to her friend Miss Leach. Not long ago, she went so far as to call upon me here and accuse me to my face, telling me I was afraid of what she knew against me. I have thought of taking legal measures to protect myself; perhaps I shall still do so. Today something has come to my knowledge which possibly explains Mrs Rolfe's singular malice. My husband tells me – and it's a sad pity he kept it a secret so long – that there was a third person present that evening when he came upon Mr Redgrave. I dare say you remember the details of the story told in court. All was perfectly true; but my husband should have added that a woman was with Mr Redgrave, talking alone with him in the dark; and when the blow had been struck, this woman, who had quickly disappeared from the veranda into the house, was found to be Mrs Rolfe.'

Hugh's hand had fallen on to his friend's shoulder. He spoke as soon as Sibyl ceased.

'She said she had done no wrong. I had no proof of any – no proof whatever.'

Rolfe was looking at Alma. She, through the unimpassioned arraignment, stood with eyes fixed upon her enemy, rather as if lost in thought than listening; her mouth was tortured into a

smile, her forehead had the lines of age and misery. At the sound
of Hugh's voice, she turned to him, and spoke like one recovering consciousness.

'You have told the truth.'

'Why did you compel me to make this known, Mrs Rolfe?'

'Oh, that's quite a mistake. It was she who made you tell it –
as she will make you do anything, and believe anything, she
likes. I can imagine how delighted she was. But it doesn't matter.
If you care to know it, either of you' – she included Carnaby
and her husband in one glance, as equally remote from her – 'I
haven't gone about seeking to injure her. Perhaps I let one or
two people know what I thought; but they had heard the truth
already. It wasn't prudent; and it wasn't a right return for the
kindness you had shown me, Mr Carnaby. But I'm not sure that
I should have done better in helping to deceive you. Has she
anything more to say? If not, I will leave you to talk about it.'

The tone of this speech, so indifferent that it seemed light-
headed, struck the hearers mute. Rolfe, speaking for the first
time since Hugh's entrance, said at length, with troubled stern-
ness –

'Alma, you have repeated your charge against Mrs Carnaby;
what grounds have you for it?'

She looked at him with a vague smile, but did not answer.

'Surely you don't make an accusation of this kind without
some proof?'

'Harvey!' The cry quivered on a laugh. 'O Harvey! who
would know you with that face?'

Sibyl rose. The men exchanged a quick glance. Rolfe moved
to his wife's side, and touched her.

'Yes, yes, I *know*,' she went on, drawing away – 'I know what
you asked me. Keep quiet, just a little. There are three of you,
and it's hard for me alone. It isn't so easy to make *you* believe
things, Harvey. Of course, I knew how it would be if this came
out. I can tell you, but not now; some other time, when we are
alone. You won't believe me; I always knew *I* shouldn't be
believed. I ought to have been cautious, and have kept friends
with her. But it wasn't as if I had anything to hide – anything
that mattered. Let me go, and leave you three to talk. And when
you come home – '

Turning, looking for the door, she fell softly on to her knees.
In a moment Harvey had raised her, and seated her in the chair

which Hugh pushed forward. Sibyl, motionless, looked on. Seeing that Alma had not lost consciousness, she awaited her next word.

'We will go away,' said Hugh, under his breath; and he beckoned to Sibyl. Reluctantly she took a step towards him, but was stopped by Alma's voice.

'Don't go on my account. Haven't *you* any question to ask me? When I go, I shan't be anxious to see you again. Don't look frightened; I know what I am talking about. My head went round for a moment – and no wonder. Stand there, face to face. – Leave me alone, Harvey; I can stand very well. I want her to ask me anything she has to ask. It's her only chance, now. I won't see her again – never after this.'

'Mrs Carnaby,' said Rolfe, 'there must be an end of it. You had better ask Alma what she has against you.'

Sibyl, summoning all her cold dignity, stood before the half-distraught woman, and looked her in the eyes.

'What harm or wrong have I done you, Mrs Rolfe, that you hate me so?'

'None that I know of, until you brought me here today.'

'But you have said that you think me no better than a guilty hypocrite, and isn't it natural that I should defend myself?'

'Quite natural. You have done it very cleverly till now, and perhaps you will to the end. I feel sure there is no evidence against you, except the word of the woman who told your husband; and even if she comes forward, you have only to deny, and keep on denying.'

'Then why do you believe that woman rather than me?'

Alma answered only with a frivolous laugh. Sibyl, turning her head, looked an appeal to the listeners.

'Mrs Rolfe,' said Hugh, in a rough, imploring voice, 'have you no other answer? You can't ruin people's lives like this, as if it were sport to you.'

Alma gazed at him, as if she had but just observed his face.

'You have gone through dreadful things,' she said earnestly. 'I'm sorry to cause you more trouble, but the fault is hers. She got that secret from you, and it delighted her. Go on believing what she says; it's the best way when all's over and done with. You can never know as *I* do.'

She laughed again, a little spurt of joyless merriment. Upon that, in the same moment, followed a loud hysterical cry; then sobs and wailing, with movements as if to tear open the clothing that choked her. Sibyl hastened away, and returned with her vinaigrette, which she handed to Rolfe. But already the crisis was over. Alma lay back in a chair, sobbing quietly, with head bent aside.

Carnaby and his wife, after an exchange of signals, silently left the room. Rolfe paced backwards and forwards for a minute or two, until he heard his name spoken; then he drew near, and Alma looked at him with her own eyes once more.

'I won't go back home unless you wish, Harvey.'

'Do you feel able to go?'

'If you wish me. If not, I'll go somewhere else.'

He sat down by her.

'Are you yourself, Alma? Do you know what you are saying?'

'Yes – indeed I do. I know I lost myself; my head went round; but I am well again now.'

'Then tell me in a word – is there any reason why you should *not* go home with me?'

'What's the use? You won't believe me. You can't believe me!'

He grasped her hand, and spoke imperatively, but not unkindly.

'Stop that! Answer me, and I will believe what you say.'

'There is no reason. I have done no wrong.'

'Then come, if you feel able to.'

She rose without help, and walked to a mirror, at which she arranged her dress. Harvey opened the door, and found all quiet. He led her through the passage, out into the common staircase, and down into the street. Here she whispered to him that a faintness was upon her; it would pass if she could have some restorative. They found a four-wheeled cab, and drove to a public-house, where Rolfe obtained brandy and brought it out to her. Then, wishing to avoid the railway station until Alma had recovered her strength, he bade the cabman drive on to Notting Hill Gate.

'May I sit at your side?' she asked, bending towards him in the darkness, when they had been silent for a few minutes.

Harvey replied by changing his own place.

'I want to tell you,' she resumed, her face near to his. 'I can't wait, and know you are thinking about me. There isn't much to tell. Are you sure you can believe me?'

'I have promised that I will.'

'I don't ask you to be kind or to love me. You will never love me again. Only believe that I tell the truth, that's all. I am not like that woman.'

'Tell me,' he urged impatiently.

'I wanted to make use of Mr Redgrave to use his influence with people in society, so that I could have a great success. I knew he wasn't to be trusted, but I had no fear; I could trust myself. I never said or did anything – it was only meeting him at people's houses and at concerts, and telling him what I hoped for. You couldn't take any interest in my music, and you had no faith in my power to make a success. I wanted to show you that you were wrong.'

'I was wrong in more ways than one,' said Harvey.

'You couldn't help it. If you had tried to make me go another way, it would only have led to unhappiness. At that time I was mad to make my name known, and, though I loved you, I believe I could have left you rather than give up my ambition. Mr Redgrave used to invite people to his house in the summer to afternoon tea, and I went there once with a lady. Other people as well – a lot of other people. That's how I knew the house. I was never there alone until that last evening. – Don't shrink away from me!'

'I didn't. Go on, and be quick.'

'I suspected Sibyl from the moment you told me about her husband and Mr Redgrave. You did, too, Harvey.'

'Leave her aside.'

'But it was because of her. I saw she was getting to dislike me, and I thought she knew Mr Redgrave was doing his best for me, and that she was jealous, and would prevent him – do you understand? He was my friend, nothing else; but *she* would never believe that. And a few days before my recital he seemed to lose interest, and I thought it was her doing. Can you understand how I felt? Not jealousy, for I never even liked him. I was living only for the hope of a success. Do you believe me, Harvey?'

'Easily enough.'

Thereupon she related truly, without omission, the train of circumstances that brought her to Wimbledon on the fatal night, and all that happened until she fled away into the darkness.

'It would be silly to say I oughtn't to have gone there. Of

course, I knew all I was risking; but I felt I could give my life to detect that woman and have her in my power.'

'It's just that I don't understand. If it had been ordinary jealousy – why, of course – '

'Men never can understand why women hate each other. She thought herself so superior to me, and showed it in every look and word; and all the time I knew she was a wicked hypocrite.'

'*How* did you know that?' Rolfe broke in vehemently, staring into her white face as a ray from the street illumined it.

'Oh, I can't tell you!' she replied, in a moaning, quivering voice. 'I knew it – I knew it – something told me. But I don't ask you to believe that. Only about myself – can you believe about myself?'

He replied mechanically, 'Yes.' Alma, with a sigh as much of hopelessness as of relief, lay back and said no more.

At Notting Hill Gate they waited for a train. Alma wandered about the platform, her head bent, silent and heeding nothing. In the railway carriage she closed her eyes, and Harvey had to draw her attention when it was time to alight. On entering the house she went at once upstairs. Harvey loitered about below, and presently sat down in the study, leaving the door ajar.

He was trying to persuade himself that nothing of much moment had come to pass. A doubt troubled him; most likely it would trouble him for the rest of his life; but he must heed it as little as possible. What other course was open to a sensible man? To rave and swear in the high tragic style would avail nothing, one way or the other; and the fact was – whatever its explanation – that he felt no prompting to such violence. Two years had passed; the man was dead; Alma had changed greatly, and was looking to new life in new conditions. His worst uneasiness arose from the hysteria which had so alarmingly declared itself this evening. He thought of Bennet Frothingham, and at length rose from his chair, meaning to go upstairs. But just then a step sounded in the hall; his door was pushed open, and Alma showed herself.

'May I come?' she asked, looking at him steadily

He beckoned with his head. She closed the door, and came slowly forward, stopping at a few paces from him.

'Harvey – '

'Well?'

'I want you to decide tonight. If you think it would be better for both of us, let me go. I shouldn't part from you unkindly; I don't mean that. I should ask you to let me have money as long as I needed it. But you know that I could support myself very soon. If you think it better, do say so, and we'll talk about it as friends.'

'I don't think anything of the kind. I shouldn't let you go, say what you might.'

'You wouldn't? But if you find that you *can't* believe me – '

'It would make no difference, even that. But I do believe you.'

She drew nearer, looking wistfully into his face.

'But *she* has made her husband believe her. You will always think of that – always.'

'You must remember, Alma, that I have no serious reason for doubting her word.'

She uttered a cry of distress.

'Then you doubt mine! – you doubt mine!'

'Nonsense, dear. Do try to think and talk more reasonably. What is it to you and me whether she was guilty or not? I may doubt your judgment about her, and yet believe perfectly all you tell me about yourself.'

'Then you think I have slandered her?'

'There's no earthly use in talking about it. You can give no reasons; you *have* no reasons. Your suspicion may be right or wrong; I don't care the toss of a button. All I know is, that we mustn't talk of it. Sit down and be quiet for a little. Oughtn't you to eat something before you go up?'

Alma put her hands upon his shoulders, bending her face so as to hide it from him.

'Dear – if you could just say that you believe me; not about myself – I know you do – but about *her*. Could you say that?'

He hesitated, all a man's common-sense in revolt against the entreaty; but he saw her quiver with a sob, and yielded.

'Very well, I will believe that too.'

Her touch became an embrace, gentle and timid; she threw her head back, gazing at him in rapture.

'You will never again doubt it?'

'Never again.'

'Oh, you are good! – you are kind to me, dear! And will you love me a little? Do you think you can, just a little?'

His answer satisfied her, and she lay in his arms, shedding tears of contentment. Then, for a long time, she talked of the new life before them. She would be everything he wished; no moment's trouble should ever again come between him and her. Nothing now had any charm for her but the still, happy life of home; her ambitions were all dead and buried. And Harvey answered her with tenderness; forgetting the doubt, refusing to look forward, knowing only that Alma had a place for ever in his heart.

Tonight she must sleep. Whilst undressing she measured the familiar draught of oblivion, and said to herself: 'The last time.' She lay down in darkness, closed her eyes, and tried to think only of happy things. But sleep would not come, and quiet thoughts would not linger with her. More than an hour must have passed, when she heard Harvey come upstairs. His step paused near her door, and she raised herself, listening. He went on, and his own door closed.

Then, for a short time, she lost herself, but in no placid slumber. Startled to wakefulness, she found that she had left her bed and was sitting on the chair beside it. She felt for the matches, and lit a candle. A great anguish of mind came upon her, but she could not shed tears; she wished to escape from her room to Harvey's, but durst not look out into the dark passage.

When her heart grew quieter, she went again to the drawer in which she kept her remedy for insomnia. Saying to herself, 'The last time – I shall be well again after tomorrow,' she measured another dose, a larger, and drank it off. Trembling now with cold, she crept into bed again, and lay watching the candle-flame.

Half an hour after this – it was about two o'clock – the handle of her door was turned, and Rolfe quietly looked in. He had awoke with an anxious feeling; it seemed to him that he heard Alma's voice, on the borderland of dream, calling his name. But Alma lay asleep, breathing steadily, her face turned from the light. As the candle had nearly burnt down, he blew it out, and went back to his bed.

At breakfast time Alma did not appear. The housemaid said that, half an hour ago, she was still sleeping. When he had had his meal with Hughie, Rolfe went up and entered his wife's room. Alma lay just as he had seen her in the night. He looked close – laid his hand upon her –

A violent ringing of the bedroom bell brought up the servant.

Harvey met her at the door, and bade her run instantly to the doctor's house, which was quite near.

The doctor could only say, 'We warned her.'

## CHAPTER 13

*Sicut umbra præterit dies.*

The dial on the front of the old house was just shadowing four o'clock. Harvey Rolfe and his friend Morton sat on the lawn, Harvey reading aloud from a small volume which he had slipped into his pocket before walking over this afternoon. From another part of the garden sounded young voices, musical in their merriment.

It was a little book called 'Barrack-Room Ballads'.* Harvey read in it here and there, with no stinted expression of delight, occasionally shouting his appreciation. Morton, pipe in mouth, listened with a smile, and joined more moderately in the reader's bursts of enthusiasm.

'Here's the strong man made articulate,' cried Rolfe at length. 'It's no use; he stamps down one's prejudice – what? It's the voice of the reaction. Millions of men, natural men, revolting against the softness and sweetness of civilisation; men all over the world; hardly knowing what they want and what they don't want; and here comes one who speaks for them – speaks with a vengeance.'

'Undeniable.'

'*But –*'

'I was waiting for the *but*,' said Morton, with a smile and a nod.

'The brute savagery of it! The very lingo – how appropriate it is! The tongue of Whitechapel blaring lust of life in the track of English guns! – He knows it; the man is a great artist; he smiles at the voice of his genius. – It's a long time since the end of the Napoleonic wars. Since then Europe has seen only sputterings of temper. Mankind won't stand it much longer, this encroachment of the humane spirit. See the spread of athletics. We must look to our physique, and make ourselves ready. Those

Lancashire operatives, laming and killing each other at football, turning a game into a battle. For the milder of us there's golf – an epidemic. Women turn to cricket – tennis is too soft – and tomorrow they'll be bicycling by the thousand; – they must breed a stouter race. We may reasonably hope, old man, to see our boys blown into small bits by the explosive that hasn't got its name yet.'

'Perhaps,' replied Morton meditatively. 'And yet there are considerable forces on the other side.'

'Pooh! The philosopher sitting on the safety-valve. He has breadth of beam, good sedentary man, but when the moment comes – The Empire; that's beginning to mean something. The average Englander has never grasped the fact that there was such a thing as a British Empire. He's beginning to learn it, and itches to kick somebody, to prove his Imperialism. The bully of the music-hall shouting "Jingo" had his special audience. Now comes a man of genius, and decent folk don't feel ashamed to listen this time. We begin to feel our position. We can't make money quite so easily as we used to; scoundrels in Germany and elsewhere have dared to learn the trick of commerce. We feel sore, and it's a great relief to have our advantages pointed out to us. By God! we are the British Empire, and we'll just show 'em what *that* means!'

'I'm reading the campaigns of Belisarius,'* said Morton, after a pause.

'What has that to do with it?'

'Thank Heaven, nothing whatever.'

'I bore you,' said Harvey, laughing. 'Well, I read little or nothing, except what I can use for Hughie. We're doing the geography of Asia, and I try to give him a few clear notions. Do you remember the idiotic way in which they used to teach us geography? I loathed the lesson. – That reminds me; Henrietta Winter is dead.'

'Is she? How did it remind you?'

'Why, because Morphew is going to New Zealand. I had a letter from him this morning. Here it is. "I heard yesterday that H. W. is dead. She died a fortnight ago, and a letter from her mother has only just reached me in a roundabout way. She had been ailing for some time. They suspected drains, and had workmen in, with assurance that all had been put right. Since H.'s death the drains have again been examined, and it was found that the men who came before so bungled and scamped their work that an abominable state of things was made much worse." – Those fellows will shout nobly for the Empire one of these days! – "I never saw her, but she spoke of me just before the end; spoke very kindly, says her mother. Damnation! I can write no more about it. I know you don't care to hear from me, but I'll just say that I'm going out to New Zealand. I don't know what I shall do there, but a fellow has asked me to go with him, and it's better than rotting here. It may help me to escape the devil yet; if so, you shall hear. Goodbye!"'

He thrust the letter back into his pocket.

'I rather thought the end would be pyrogallic acid.'

'He has the good sense to prefer ozone,' said Morton.

'For a time, at all events. – Look behind you. The young rascal is creeping this way. He'd rather sit and listen to our talk than be with the other youngsters. That's wrong, you know.'

Morton look round, and saw Hugh Rolfe. Seven years old now; slight, and with little or no colour in his cheeks; a wistful, timid smile on the too intelligent face. He was gazing towards his father, and evidently wished to draw near, yet feared that his presence might not be welcome. Morton beckoned him, and at once he ran and threw himself upon the grass by his father's side.

'Tired of playing?' asked Harvey, with voice and look which betrayed a tenderness he was always trying to conceal.

'A little tired. We are going to have tea soon. – May I look at this book, Father?'

'No pictures.'

'I don't mind. – Yes, there's a picture; a soldier!'

Interest quickened in the boy's eyes, and he turned eagerly from title-page to text. But just then there came a loud calling of his name from the other end of the garden.

'They want you,' said Harvey. 'Off you go. You can have the book another time.'

Hughie obeyed without hesitation, but his face had a weary look as he walked away to join the other children.

'I must send him to the Grammar-School next year,' said Rolfe. 'It won't do; he must be among boys, and learn to be noisy. Perhaps I have been altogether wrong in teaching him myself. What right has a man to teach, who can't make up his mind on any subject of thought? Of course I don't talk to *him* about my waverings and doubtings, but probably they affect him.'

'Don't bother your head so much about it,' replied Morton. 'He'll be all right as he grows stronger.'

A servant had brought out two little tables; tea was going to be served in the garden. When it was ready, Mrs Morton appeared; the men rose as she came towards them, a newspaper in her hand.

'Have you noticed this?' she asked of Rolfe, with a smile, pointing out a paragraph to him.

He read it; first to himself, then aloud.

'Yesterday, at Lady Isobel Barker's house in Pont Street, a meeting was held of ladies interested in a project for the benefit of working-class women in the West End. It is proposed to arrange for a series of lectures, specially adapted to such an audience, on subjects of literary and artistic interest. Unfortunately, Lady Isobel herself was unable to take part in the proceedings, owing to sudden indisposition; but her views were most suggestively set forth by Mrs Hugh Carnaby, who dwelt on the monotony of the lives of decent working-class women, and showed how much they would be benefited by being brought into touch with the intellectual movements of the day. Practical details of the scheme will shortly be made public.'

Morton chuckled quietly.

'Splendid idea,' said Rolfe. 'Anyone who knows anything of the West End working-class woman will be sure to give it warm support.'

The tea-bell rang; the children came running. Morton's eldest boy, who had been busy in his workshop, exhibited a fine model schooner, just finished. Presently, the hostess asked Rolfe whether he had heard of late from Mr Carnaby.

'A week ago; the first time for a year. The demand for shares in their company was tremendous, and they are turning out the new bicycle at the rate of hundreds a week.'

'Has he quite got over that illness?'

'Says he suffers much from dyspepsia; otherwise, fairly well. The prospect of money-making on a great scale seems pleasant to him.'

'To Mrs Carnaby, also, I dare say.'

'No doubt,' replied Rolfe absently.

After tea, a trio of little singers, one of whom was Hughie, gave the songs they had newly learnt with Mrs Morton, she accompanying them on the piano. Rolfe sat in a corner of the room and listened, as always, with keen pleasure.

'One more,' he asked, when they were about to cease.

They sang that which he liked best –

Fear no more the heat o' the sun*

After it there came a minute's silence; then Harvey rose.

'Say goodbye, Hughie; we must be going home.'

Hand in hand, each thinking his own thoughts, they walked homeward through the evening sunshine.

THE END

# NOTES

Abbreviations used:

*CL*: Paul F. Mattheisen, Arthur C. Young and Pierre Coustillas (eds), *The Collected Letters of George Gissing*, 9 vols, Ohio University Press, (1990–7).

Diary: Pierre Coustillas (ed.), *London and the Life of Literature in Late Victorian England: The Diary of George Gissing, Novelist*, Harvester Press, 1978.

GG: George Gissing.

Kropholler: P. F. Kropholler, 'Additional Notes to *The Whirlpool*', *Gissing Newsletter*, 21 (2) (April 1985): 16–21.

Parrinder: Patrick Parrinder (ed.), George Gissing, *The Whirlpool*, Harvester Press, 1977.

p. 6 **The suit of ceremony**: full evening dress.

p. 8 **blackleg**: here, a swindler. The implication is that financial speculators are just as corrupt as the crooked gamblers of Brussels.

p. 8 **Bennet Frothingham**: banker, and father of Alma, fashioned out of a notorious financier, the Liberal MP Jabez Balfour (1843–1916). He was sentenced in 1895 to fourteen years' imprisonment for fraud in the case of the Liberator Permanent Building and Investment Society which, by 1892, had defaulted to its small investors to the tune of £27 million. If Balfour had 'died (suicide or otherwise) at the moment of the Liberator crash', Gissing enquired of his brother Algernon, 'what would have been done with his estate? ... I want the information for my book' (GG to Algernon Gissing, 20 May 1896, *CL*, VI, 127, and note 2, 127, and David Kynaston, *The City of London Vol. 2: The Golden Years 1890–1914*, London: Chatto and Windus, 1995, pp. 65–6). Frothingham is the name of a servant in Henry

James's story 'A London Life' (1889), which Gissing almost certainly read.

**p. 9 Hamilton Terrace:** St John's Wood, north-west London.

**p. 9 the vast subject of domestic management:** 'I am convinced that the *tendency* of things,' Gissing wrote in 1896, 'is towards impatience with domestic cares ... the world is moving towards hotel-life ...' (GG to Clara Collet, 3 July 1896, *CL*, VI, 149–50).

**p. 9 Colebrook smash:** Gissing was certainly alive to some of the wider cultural meanings of the City of London. In his novel *Born in Exile* (1892) the City 'represents the triumphant forces of our time ... the power which centres in the world's money-markets – plutocracy' (*Born in Exile*, 3, 5). 'The "City" is so oppressive to the spirit because it represents the *triumph* of the vulgar man,' he wrote in his *Commonplace Book* (ed. J. Korg, (1962), p. 44); see also *The Crown of Life* (1899), ch.20. According to David Kynaston, '*The Whirlpool* persuasively [places] the City at the heart of a much larger argument about what later generations would call the state of the nation' (Kynaston, *The City of London Vol. 2*, pp. 160–1).

**p. 11 Guy's:** Guy's Hospital, London.

**p. 12 Colonel Bosworth:** Colonel W. J. Bosworth (1858–1923), a noted big-game hunter.

**p. 13 bustard-stalking in Spain:** Parrinder points out that Gissing used Abel Chapman and Walter J. Buck's *Wild Spain* (1893) as a source for this passage.

**p. 14 francolin:** a species of partridge.

**p. 14 beccaficoes:** small birds fattened on grapes or figs.

**p. 14 'Empress' and 'Paradox' etc.:** references to sporting-rifles and ammunition of the period.

**p. 15 Cabala:** esoteric interpretation of the Jewish scriptures.

**p. 16 They're a burden ... survival of the fittest:** this passage was quoted by H. G. Wells in his controversial review of *The Whirlpool* in support of his view that Harvey was a through and through social Darwinist. However, Gissing replied that this passage 'is meant to contrast strongly with his way of thinking & speaking in the latter part of the book' (GG to H. G. Wells, *CL*, 6, 320, and fn. 2 (p. 321)). Social

Darwinism, which reductively applied popular Darwinian ideas from evolutionary biology to the social and political realm of human activity, had gained considerable authority by the turn of the century. See also note to p. 415.

**p. 16 Davos:** a fashionable winter resort in Switzerland.

**p. 16 England's just beginning her big fight:** the irrationality at the heart of the rhetoric of late nineteenth-century nationalism and imperialism was memorably analysed by the economist Joseph Schumpeter: 'Driven out everywhere else,' he wrote, 'the irrational seeks refuge in nationalism – the irrational which consists of belligerence, the need to hate, a goodly quota of inchoate idealism . . .' (J. A. Schumpeter, *Imperialism and Social Classes*, tr. H. Nordon, Oxford: Basil Blackwell, 1951, p. 14). The period after 1870 saw the 'new imperialism', dominated by the 'scramble for Africa' and expansion in the Near and Far East. J. R. Seeley's *The Expansion of England* (1883), which Gissing read in March 1895 (*Diary*, p. 365) envisaged the unification of English blood across the world. *The Whirlpool* opens in 1886, the year of the London Colonial and Indian Exhibition and the year of J. A. Froude's *Oceana* in which he argued that the colonies would provide an arena 'where the race might for ages renew its mighty youth' (*Oceana*, p. 9).

**p. 17 buccaneering shopkeeper etc.:** compare Gissing's comments in a letter of 23 February 1896, when he was about to start *The Whirlpool*: 'The late troubles in S. Africa are of course due entirely to capitalist greed. I cannot see any hope for peace, so long as these men of the money-market are permitted to control public life – as they now practically do' (*CL*, VI, pp. 100–1).

**p. 17 pyrites:** a sulphide of iron.

**p. 18 Stanford's:** London's best-known map-shop, then in Cockspur Street, Pall Mall; now in Long Acre, Covent Garden.

**p. 19 War is England's Banting:** William Banting (1797–1878) was the author of *Corpulence* (1864), a work on how to reduce weight.

**p. 20 within a few minutes' walk of Royal Oak Station:** between Paddington and Bayswater, west London.

**p. 20 Pall Mall:** a fashionable street in central London.

**p. 21 Beethoven's F minor:** Beethoven's F minor String Quartet (Op. 95).

**p. 21 Greystone:** an invention of Gissing's.

**p. 21 Alexandreia Eschate:** 'Alexandrea the Farthest', a fortress built by Alexander the Great (329 BC), in Central Asia.

**p. 21 Byzantine Historians:** late Greek historians, *c.* AD 600–1400. A collected edition *Corpus scriptorum historiae Byzantinae* was published 1828–78.

**p. 22 *Solvetur vivendo*:** the matter is settled by living.

**p. 22 London Library:** the leading British subscription library, St James's Square, founded 1841.

**p. 23 'He threw physic to the dogs':** an allusion to Shakespeare, *Macbeth*, V.i. 37. The manuscript of the novel has 'medicine' (f. 10).

**p. 24 emigration agent:** in the years 1871–90 more than four million people emigrated from British ports.

**p. 28 Kilburn:** an inner suburb of north-west London.

**p. 29 Ribot's *L'Hérédité Psychologique*:** Théodule Armand Ribot (1839–1916) was a pioneer of experimental psychology in France and the most influential figure in the field. His *L'Hérédité psychologique* (1873) was published in England as *Heredity*, (1875). A Lamarkian, Ribot showed how individual faculties which reflected the experience of the environment could be passed on to later generations. Gissing recorded substantial extracts from this work in his *Commonplace Book* in 1889 (pp. 59–62).

**p. 30 Tussaud's:** the famous waxwork museum founded in 1835 by Marie Tussaud (1761–1850). It moved to its present site in the Marylebone Road, central London, in 1884.

**p. 30 Fitzjohn Avenue:** this probably refers to Fitzjohn's Avenue, Hampstead, London.

**p. 31 palingenesis:** metamorphosis or change of form. Not to be confused with the biologist Ernst Haeckel's use of the term in the sense of continuity of inheritance.

**p. 31 Gewandhaus:** Leipzig's concert hall, built 1880–4.

p. 31 **Thomaskirche:** the famous church in Leipzig where J. S. Bach was organist.

p. 35 *Klaviermäszig:* delicate enough for the piano.

p. 35 *Sehnsucht:* a sense of longing or desire.

p. 39 **calenture:** fever (figurative).

p. 39 **'Wie bist du, meine Königinn':** Where are you, oh my queen. A song by Brahms (Op. 32), 1864.

p. 39 **the Melody in F:** a popular piano piece by Anton Rubinstein (1829–94).

p. 40 **Life at high pressure:** for the explosive consequences of 'high pressure' activity on the financial markets, see p. 45 of the novel. Gissing adopted the title 'At High Pressure' for a short story he wrote in September 1895 (see *Diary*, p. 389), published in February 1896 (collected in *Human Odds and Ends* (1898)).

p. 44 **no theological or scientific dogma . . . the laws of life:** this ostentatiously callous, but modish, redrawing of Victorian high-mindedness in ethical matters was explained by the young Somerset Maugham: 'The ethical standard is as ephemeral as all else in the world,' he noted in 1901. 'Failure or success in the struggle for existence is the sole moral standard. Good is what survives' (*A Writer's Notebook*, Harmondsworth: Penguin, 1967, p. 66); see also John Goode, *George Gissing: Ideology and Fiction* (1978), pp. 185–6.

p. 46 **Gregorovius:** a German historian (1821–91) whom Gissing was reading in preparation for his unfinished novel *Veranilda*. His most notable work was *Geschichte der Stadt Rom im Mittelalter* (*8 vols, 1859–72*), translated into English from 1895 as *A History of Rome in the Middle Ages* (see GG to Eduard Bertz, 16 April 1897, *CL*, VI, 272).

p. 47 **a ghastly whirlpool which roars over the bottomless pit:** the first reference to the title-word; see also pp. 147, 175, 201, 232, 297, 306. The 'pit' is Hell: see *Revelation*, IX.i: 'the key of the bottomless pit' (Kropholler).

p. 51 **Gunnersbury:** a west London suburb.

p. 52 *felo de se:* suicide.

p. 52 **'Where's that from? I remember it somehow':** the source is Thomas Hood's poem 'Faithless Nelly Gray' (Kropholler).

p. 60 Mrs Grundy: the archetypal puritanical and censorious zealot, frequently called upon by critics of Victorian prudery. She is first invoked in Thomas Morton's play *Speed the Plough* (1798).

p. 63 Jingoism: a term for narrow patriotic fervour, first sounded in G. H. Macdermott's music-hall song – 'We don't want to fight, but, by jingo if we do' – which appeared shortly after the outbreak of hostilities between Turkey and Russia in 1878.

p. 65 *'Ein Englander ... verbricht!'*: idiomatic German for 'An English gentleman, who speaks very funny German'. Gissing had asked Bertz for the 'idiomatic German' as spoken by 'a boy' (GG to Bertz, 20 May 1896, *CL*, VI, 127). Bertz later was unhappy with the result, not realising that Gissing had intended a 'little boy': 'in the mouth of such a little fellow the word "verbricht" is not childlike enough' (Eduard Bertz to GG, 19 April 1897, *CL* VI, 266).

p. 66 St James's Hall: built 1857, in Piccadilly, London, demolished 1905. 'The most popular locale for orchestral concerts', wrote the music critic Eduard Hanslick in 1886. 'It is also used by such virtuosos (Rubinstein and Sarasate) as can count on a numerous audience' (it could accommodate about 2500). 'This hall is anything but elegant, but is commodious' (Eduard Hanslick, 'Letter From London' (1886) in H. Pleasants (ed.) *Music Criticism 1846–99*, Harmondsworth: Peregrine, 1963, pp. 246–74 (p. 262)). See also notes to p. 172 and p. 238.

p. 70 Bregenz: Austrian town on the shores of Lake Constance (Bodensee) and the site of the Roman settlement whose ruins Alma and Fräulein Steinfeld explore in ch. 8.

p. 79 Antioch: ancient capital of Syria, founded 300 BC on River Orontes; now modern Antakya, Turkey.

p. 80 guarded by the divinity which doth hedge a member of the upper-middle class: an echo of Shakespeare: 'There's such divinity doth hedge a king,/That treason can but peep to what it would' *Hamlet*, IV.iv. 123–4.

p. 81 An insult such as this: Redgrave proposes that Alma become his mistress.

p. 84 La Roche Chalais: situated between Angoulême and Bordeaux.

p. 84 *grabat:* a bed of straw.

p. 85 pyrogallic acid: developing agent used in early photography.

p. 85 **mephitis:** exceptionally noxious air pollution.

p. 87 **Swiss Cottage:** a district in West Hampstead, London.

p. 99 **this still little town:** Nefyn in Caernarvonshire on the Lleyn Peninsula. Gissing stayed at Nefyn 15–17 April 1896 (see Gwyn Neale, *All the Days Were Glorious: George Gissing in North Wales*: Llanrwst, Carreg Gwalch, 1994). See notes to p. 141 and p. 142.

p. 100 **people are taking to flats:** Mrs Frothingham's comments were topical since flat-dwelling did not become common in London until the late Victorian period. 'Flat' was not in general use before the mid-1880s.

p. 119 **the six folios of Muratori:** Ludovico Muratori (1672–1750) published *Antiquitates italicae medii aevi* (6 vols, 1738–42).

p. 127 **plain living and high thinking:** an echo of a line from Wordsworth's sonnet beginning 'O Friend! I know not' – 'Plain living and high thinking are no more.'

p. 128 **questions of heredity:** see note to p. 29.

p. 129 *date-boil*: a type of tropical sore which was endemic in nineteenth-century Baghdad.

p. 129 **a bicycle factory:** Gissing rightly locates this business interest of Hugh Carnaby's in Coventry (see p. 164) which, since the late 1860s, was associated with the commercial development of the bicycle principally through James Starley (1831–81). J. K. Starley later developed the first safety bicycle, in 1885 (see Robert L. Selig, *George Gissing* (1983), pp. 83–4, 152). The massive demand for bicycles in this period (prompted by the development of the pneumatic tyre by J. B. Dunlop in 1888) encouraged speculative investment on a large scale. The entrepreneur, Ernest Hooley, who masterminded several highly profitable flotations in the 1890s, overreached himself and became bankrupt in 1898, amid well-founded allegations of fraud (Kynaston, *The City of London Vol. 2*, 161, 179–81). Gissing was composing *The Whirlpool* at the height of the cycling boom.

p. 133 *Nihil quod tetigit non ornavit*: She touched nothing which she did not adorn. The Latin is from Samuel Johnson's Epitaph on Goldsmith (1776); see James Boswell, *Life of Johnson*, Oxford, 1933, ii, 59.

p. 139 **Tre'r Caeri ... Nant Gwrtheyrn:** famous landmarks on the

Lleyn Peninsula, north-east of Nefyn. Tre'r Caeri (the town of the giants) is an ancient Welsh fortification, while Nant Gwrtheyrn is a chasm running down to the sea below the mountains of Yr Eifl.

**p. 139 Vortigern:** a legendary fifth-century British king. These details are to be found in Black's *Guide to Wales* which Gissing bought prior to his journey to North Wales (see *Diary*, p. 406).

**p. 140 a Tarantelle of Schubert:** a tarantella is a fast and increasingly furious dance in 6/8 time.

**p. 141 Carn Bodvean:** 'Very hard work' was how Gissing recorded the business of writing this episode (*Diary*, p. 411) – a month after his own encounter with the mountain overlooking the Lleyn Peninsula outside Nefyn. The labour involved is understandable given that Gissing both needed to recall the episode in the particularities of his own experience of place, and, crucially, to shape that experience into symbolic form out of the initial imaginative encounter. Climbing Carn Bodvean was, in any case, a deeply pleasurable personal experience for the author – the culmination of three days of welcome freedom from the domestic pressures of the moment. Of his final full day (17 April) he recorded: 'Unbroken sunshine, till half-past four, then cloudy. In morning climbed Carn Bodvean and lay on top in the glorious air for two hours. Too misty to see the Snowdon mountains. Made some notes for my book . . . On the whole, one of the days of my life to be looked back upon with joy' (*Diary*, p. 408). As Gwyn Neale suggests, 'it is in this idyllic place that we begin to realize the significance of the title of the novel' (see Neale, *All the Days Were Glorious*, p. 41, and, generally, pp. 36–42).

**p. 142 An old, old language . . . not yet begun to shape itself:** Gissing draws on his reflections made while writing from the Nanhoran Arms, Nefyn, where he was staying. 'I hear the talk of a lot of men drinking in the next room. They are all Welsh, & it is a strange thing to hear this (to me) unintelligible tongue in my native island. The Welsh language has immense vitality . . . Strange to think that these people have a better right in England than I have, & that my language is a modern, new-fangled thing, compared with theirs' (GG to Bertz, 16 April 1896, *CL*, VI, 113–14).

**p. 150 a lucid diagnosis:** this implies a miscarriage, later confirmed by the authorial comment that Alma's illness produced a result 'which some women would have wept over' (p. 152).

**p. 158 wise and noble disinterestedness:** at this point in the manuscript there appears a passage, subsequently deleted, which is explicitly critical of Harvey: 'Singular instance of a man, two and a half years after marriage, still subject to the illusions that prefaced it; a striking example of the futility of the philosophic spirit in things matrimonial' (f. 70). This is a rare instance of Gissing's misjudgement in allowing such a passage to be deleted.

**p. 159 Basingstoke:** a town in Hampshire.

**p. 160 Plymouth:** a major port in Devon.

**p. 162 Lord's:** Lord's cricket Ground, St John's Wood, north-west London. The headquarters of English cricket.

**p. 166 in durance vile:** in prison.

**p. 167 Porchester Terrace:** Bayswater, west-central London.

**p. 168 paradise regained:** Gissing's allusion to Milton has the satiric intention of belittling Alma's worldly aspirations.

**p. 169 *causeuse*:** a two-seater settee.

**p. 171 though by your smiling you seem to say so:** an allusion to Hamlet's aside to Rosencrantz and Guildenstern, *Hamlet*, II.i. 314–15. The manuscript version had this phrase in quotation marks.

**p. 171 the Metropolitan Railway:** this was extended to Harrow in 1880 and to Pinner in 1885.

**p. 172 a Richter concert:** the German musician Hans Richter (1843–1916), achieved great popularity in Britain as a conductor. 'Richter Concerts', inaugurated in 1879, were a regular and notable feature of the London musical scene at St James's Hall until 1896 (see note to p. 66).

**p. 176 'Vuillaume':** a violin of nineteenth-century French manufacture.

**p. 176 in the summer of 1890:** the text should read '1891'. This is the first example of mistaken chronology by Gissing, which from a reference ten pages earlier (p. 168), is one year out. For a few pages he was misled by a mistake in his timing of events, but not with any serious consequences for the reader. The narrative opens in 1886 (p. 22) with the failure of Bennet Frothingham's bank and his suicide (p. 43). It ends with Alma's death in 1894. A coda, in the last chapter, has Harvey, now a widower, settled in his native town in 1896: his son is 'seven years old now'. Harvey and Alma were married 'the twentieth of December' (p. 119) in 1887. The correct time-scheme emerges from indications such as 'more than three years . . . since the fatal evening' (p. 168), but above all from references at various points to the age of the child Hughie. From this chronology it can be established that Alma's recital at Prince's Hall took place in May 1892, although she writes on the parcel she keeps of her press notices, 'My Recital, May 1891' (p. 346). Curiously, this mistake by one year does not prevent Gissing from getting back on track by the end. Harvey and Alma's married life can thus be dated as follows: they live in North Wales from December 1887 to the summer of 1890; in Pinner from the autumn of 1890 to the summer of 1892; and at Gunnersbury until Alma's death in summer 1894.

p. 177 the *demi-monde*: Gissing's point is that the expression has come to be used of the permissive rich and fashionable. Mrs Strangeways' friends were merely permissive – the true *demi-monde*, in Gissing's view.

p. 182 Prince's Hall: unaccountably omitted from Grove's *Dictionary of Music and Musicians*, and from other standard accounts of London musical life, it is mentioned by Baedeker (*London and Its Environs*, 1889 edition) as situated on the south side of Piccadilly, just west of St James's Church, opposite Sackville Street. Used for chamber and solo work, it makes fleeting appearances in the music criticism of G. B. Shaw, e.g. *Music in London 1890–94* (3 vols, 1932), i, p. 253, ii, p. 53. A notice of April 1890 in the *Musical Times* (consulted by Gissing whilst composing the novel – see *Diary*, p. 412) refers to 'Miss Synge's Afternoon Concert, Princes' Hall 1 May at 3' (*Musical Times*, 31 (1 April 1890), p. 242).

p. 182 Rhapsodie Hongroise: composed by the Hungarian violinist Miska Hauser (1822–87).

p. 182 the C minor: Dymes presumably refers to Beethoven's Symphony no. 5 in C minor (Op. 67).

p. 182 Chopin's A flat major Polonaise: first published 1843; this difficult work (Op. 53) is Dymes's mischievous choice of a 'nice piece'.

p. 184 fall: veil.

p. 189 Crystal Palace: moved after the Great Exhibition (1851) to Sydenham, south London, where it became a notable concert hall.

**p. 189 Sterndale Bennett's new concerto:** Sir William Sterndale Bennett (1816–75) was a popular composer and conductor. Gissing has overlooked the fact that at this point in the novel he had been dead for seventeen years, a point picked out by some reviewers.

**p. 194 debenture stock:** an investment with a limited term.

**p. 194 in this present year, 1891:** both references to the year 1891, in this paragraph, need to be advanced to 1892.

**p. 195 When he returned to England, in the summer of 1889:** each of the three dates alluded to in this paragraph should be advanced by a year.

**p. 199 Newgate:** an ancient London prison, demolished 1902.

**p. 201 a volume of Crowe and Cavalcaselle . . . in the original:** Sibyl is reading J. A. Crow and G. B. Cavalcaselle's *A New History of Painting in Italy* (2 vols, 1864) and John Addington Symonds's *History of the Renaissance in Italy* (1875–86). Benvenuto Cellini (1500–71) was a Florentine sculptor whose *Autobiography* was published in 1730. Symonds had translated it in 1887, but Sibyl is ostentatiously reading Cellini in the original. As Parrinder notes it is left to the reader 'to decide what are the causes of this sudden display of erudition'.

**p. 201 not only forgive, but sympathise:** at this point in the manuscript there is a deleted passage in which Sibyl's lack of maternal feeling is an evident sign for her selfishness: 'A cold and indolent woman he conceived her; fastidious in her tastes, not at all likely to hurt her self-respect by contact with baser society, but no doubt radically selfish and perhaps unfeeling. That she was childless seemed merely natural; it would have been difficult to think of Mrs Carnaby as a mother' (f. 88).

**p. 203 photography is going ahead so:** an instance of Gissing's eye for a 'boom', as an index of the modern. Fuelled by Eastman's invention of the Kodak box-camera in 1888, photography is now becoming rapidly accessible to the mass market.

**p. 204 bucket-shop:** an office run by an unrecognised stockbroker (American slang).

**p. 205 let me off the cover:** Tripcony's charge to guard against loss.

**p. 215 *grande tenue*:** evening dress.

**p. 229 civilisation in its subtlest phase . . . sympathy with infinite forms**

of life: Redgrave's choice of terms in this paragraph is intended to show his facile command of the phraseology of aestheticism as deployed by its leading British theorist, Walter Pater (particularly in his *Studies in the History of the Renaissance* [1873]).

p. 237 Sarasate ... Joachim: Pablo Sarasate, virtuoso Spanish violinist (1844–1908), Joseph Joachim, Hungarian violinist and conductor (1831–1907). They both frequently performed in England. Parrinder notes that the *cadenza* in Beethoven's violin concerto occurs in the third and not in the first movement.

p. 239 Steinway Hall: a concert-hall in Wigmore Street, London. Opened 1878, used mainly by younger musicians beginning their careers. Closed finally in 1938, damaged in the Second World War and demolished.

p. 240 *facile princeps*: easily the first.

p. 241 Millais: Sir John Millais (1829–96) was one of the original members of the Pre-Raphaelite Brotherhood, but became a successful and fashionable portrait painter and President of the Royal Academy.

p. 249 Weymouth: a resort in Dorset.

p. 283 a little bottle ... disorder of the nerves: a narcotic, probably morphia; cf. of Edgar Abbott, 'he has been taking morphia' (p. 48).

p. 292 budget: bundle.

p. 292 *sans phrase*: without mincing words.

p. 295 My wife is as pure and innocent as any woman living: Hugh Carnaby corresponds to the male type identified by George Egerton in her 1893 story, 'A Cross Line': 'his chivalrous, conservative devotion to the female idea he has created, blinds him, perhaps happily, to the problems of her complex nature' (*Keynotes*, Elkin Matthews & John Lane, 1893; Virago, 1983, p. 21).

p. 301 'Sicut umbra præterit dies': the day passes like a shadow.

p. 303 *Erret et extremos alter scrutetur Iberos*: Let he who will wander and explore furthest Spain. From Claudian, *Carmina Minora* XX, 'The Old Man of Verona'.

p. 305 exodus from Houndsditch: Houndsditch is an area between Aldgate and Bishopsgate in the City of London. In the nineteenth century it was still an old clothes market, mainly run by Jewish dealers.

As Parrinder states, Carlyle used the phrase 'Exodus from Houndsditch' with regard to the possible 'exodus' of Christian theology from the Old Testament.

p. 305 I was like Johnson's friend: Samuel Johnson's friend, Mr Edwards: 'you are a philosopher Dr Johnson. I have tried too in my time to be a philosopher; but, I don't know how, cheerfulness was always breaking in' (James Boswell, *Life of Johnson*, Oxford, 1933, ii, 230).

p. 305 Schopenhauer: Basil Morton's little joke: to the average reader the philosophy of Schopenhauer (1788–1860) (with which Gissing was well acquainted) is not usually associated with cheerfulness.

p. 305 'We have heard the chimes at midnight, Master Shallow': Shakespeare, *Henry IV, Part Two*, III.ii. 231. Gissing also uses this quotation in *The Private Papers of Henry Ryecroft* (Summer, XIX) (Oxford University Press, 1987), p. 83.

p. 309 diggings: digs or lodgings.

p. 314 reason and the will of God: a phrase from *Maxims of Piety and Christianity* (1789) by Bishop Wilson; Matthew Arnold's quotation of the phrase in *Culture and Anarchy* (1869) gave it general currency.

p. 317 muniment-rooms: rooms furnished with family documents and title-deeds.

pp. 318–19 'What would you wish your own boy to be ... our little crabs must grow their hard shell': Harvey and Basil's discussion echoes an important scientific debate of the late 1880s and early 1890s involving, principally, the biologist T. H. Huxley and the social Darwinist philosopher Herbert Spencer, about the place of ethics in a society conceptualised as progressing through biological struggle. In 'The Struggle for Existence in Human Society' (*Nineteenth Century*, 23 (February 1888): 161–80) (amplified in his famous Romanes lecture of 1893, 'Evolution and Ethics') Huxley challenged the simplistic view that man in society could derive an ethics from the unfettered 'struggle for existence'. Society, for Huxley, differed from 'nature' in having a 'definite moral object'. Whereas 'non-ethical man – the primitive savage, or man as a mere member of the animal kingdom – fights out the struggle for existence to the bitter end', ethical man 'devotes his best energies to the object of setting limits to the struggle for existence to the bitter end'. ('The Struggle For Existence', 165). This fallacy,

Huxley argued, arises out of 'the unfortunate ambiguity of the phrase "survival of the fittest"' (a phrase first coined by Spencer before it was adopted by Darwin). '"Fittest" has a connotation of "best"; and about "best" there hangs a moral flavour. In cosmic nature, however, what is "fittest" depends upon the conditions' ('Evolution and Ethics', p. 81). Such an argument, Huxley claims, puts a premium on self-preservation, which is the justification for the reductive brutalism of contemporary ideology implicit in Morton's belief that 'our little crabs must grow their hard shell'. Somerset Maugham's notebook entries for 1896 contain numerous comments questioning the extent to which man should have ethical obligations to others or to society, and can be taken as evidence that these debates were still very much in the air during the period in which Gissing was composing the novel (see Maugham, *A Writer's Notebook*, pp. 33, 35, 38–9).

p. 319 '*Homo malus, puer robustus*': Gissing's adaption of Hobbes's Latin: 'Ita ut vir malus idem fere sit quod puer robustus'. *De Cive* (1642) (Praefatio ad Lectores [13]), ed. H. Warrender, 2 vols (Oxford, 1983); Latin Version, p. 81, English Version, p. 33: 'a wicked man is almost the same thing with a childe growne strong and sturdy.' (I am grateful to Professor Franck Lessay of the University of Paris III, for supplying this reference.)

p. 320 '*Medio tutissimus*': *Medio tutissimus ibis*: you will go most safely by the middle way (Ovid, *Metamorphoses*, ii, 137).

p. 320 '*Multa renascentur quæ jam cecidere*': many words which have now fallen out of use will be born again (Horace, *Ars Poetica*, 70).

p. 320 '**Don't make me think about Crœsus**': Basil Morton alludes here to the story of Croesus, richest of men, expecting to be thought the happiest of men, but being told by the Athenian law-giver Solon: 'call no man happy till he dies'.

p. 331 **There was a word on Alma's tongue, but her lips would not utter it**: presumably, 'liar'.

p. 335 **wild Wales**: recalling George Borrow's *Wild Wales* which Gissing read, some weeks after his return from North Wales, in June 1896 (*Diary*, p. 414).

p. 343 **Kempton Park and Hurst Park**: racecourses on the outskirts of London.

p. 343 **fashionable specific**: see note to p. 283.

**p. 346 boom:** a first outburst of commercial activity, often associated with a rapid advance in share price. In American usage from the 1870s, by the 1890s it had firmly entered the British vernacular.

**p. 357 he was the giver of life:** an echo of Holy Communion: The Creed (in the *Book of Common Prayer*): 'The Lord and giver of life'.

**p. 362 'She will grow old with honour, love, obedience, troops of friends':** a jocular reference by Harvey to *Macbeth*, V.iii.25.

**p. 372 Penzance:** the most westerly port and resort in Cornwall, England.

**p. 372 Scilly:** isles off the Cornish coast.

**p. 373 Boscombe:** near Bournemouth, Hampshire.

**p. 398 'Chaste as the icicle/That's curded by the frost from purest snow,/ And hangs on Dian's temple':** from Shakespeare, *Coriolanus*, V.iii.65.

**p. 415 'Barrack-Room Ballads':** the decade's most widely read volume of poetry by Rudyard Kipling (1892), dedicated to the type it celebrates – the ordinary English soldier, 'Tommy Atkins'. Gissing's attitude to Kipling shifted during these years. When he first read *Barrack-Room Ballads* in May 1892 he called it a 'most remarkable work' (GG to Bertz, 20 May 1892, *CL*, V, 38). But after the publication of *The Whirlpool* Gissing was anxious to counter Wells's published view that Harvey endorsed the militant jingoism as represented by Kipling – and what Wells called the 'new and growing sense of the eternity and universality of conflict' (see the extract from H. G. Wells, 'The Novels of Mr George Gissing', and from Gissing's letter to Wells in the Gissing and his Critics section of this volume, p. 440 and p. 442).

**p. 416 the campaigns of Belisarius:** the Roman military commander (d. 565) under Justinian. His campaigns were narrated in Procopius's *History of the Wars of Justinian*.

**p. 419 'Fear no more the heat o' the sun':** this dirge in Shakespeare's *Cymbeline*, IV.ii. 259, is sung over the supposed-dead Fidele, the soon-to-be-revived Imogen.

# GISSING AND HIS CRITICS

Arnold Bennett reviewed *The Whirlpool* shortly after its publication, under his pseudonym 'Barbara' (*Woman*, 21 April 1897, pp. 8–9). His assessment of Alma reveals a fascinating blend of the enlightened and the blinkered in his appraisal of Alma's representativeness. His recognition of the visibility of the modern woman outside the private sphere of the home is notable, but in seeing her as the creature of impulse, he disparages her intentionality. While much of the review is lukewarm about the novel, in this passage Bennett, the apprentice-realist novelist, acknowledges Gissing's success in conveying the force of Alma's typicality.

> The character of Alma is possibly the best thing that Mr Gissing has done. I have seen Alma many times at St James Hall, at vegetarian restaurants, at schools of art, and adrift in Continental cities. There are hundreds of her in London – ineffectual women; women whose very birthright is an impulsive futility; fitful, feverish women. Mr Gissing exposes and expounds her with rare courage and lucidity.

Edmund Gosse was one of the leading men of letters of the period. His sympathetic and generous review ('Mr George Gissing's New Novel', *St James's Gazette*, 23 April 1897: 3–4) must have given Gissing considerable satisfaction. In this extract, Gosse carefully registers the subtlety of Gissing's treatment of Alma's deterioration, and is moved by its tragic effect. Given his serious analysis of another 'modern egotistical woman', Sue Bridehead, in his review (March 1896) of Hardy's *Jude the Obscure*, it is not surprising that Gosse gives due attention to Alma as a woman symptomatic of her age. He observes that 'Gissing has reserved his highest efforts' for his portrayal of Alma.

[Alma] . . . is an admirably careful study of the modern egotistical woman, anxious to be independent, to be famous, to be talked about, and incurably indifferent to her natural human interests. The curious effect of personal vanity on the spirits of such a woman, the phenomena produced by its disappointments and even its vulgarest indulgences, have rarely been described with so much skill. And yet Alma, with all her faults of character and temperament, is radically so human, and is so singularly unfortunate, that the reader ends by liking her and by grieving over her inevitable death.

One of the best general surveys of the novel's themes came from the anonymous reviewer in the *Academy* (*Academy*, 51 (15 May 1897): 516–17 (*Gissing: The Critical Heritage*, pp. 282–40)) whose robust, yet thoughtful, explication of the novel's realism registered the powerful effect (felt by many contemporary reviewers) of Gissing's 'dreadful and admirable story'. This reviewer was not alone in spotting that as a novelist Gissing is 'in love with ideas' (Virginia Woolf was later to remark that 'his men and women think') but also that 'his work lives'. It is a considerable tribute to Gissing that this reviewer sees no tension between these attributes of the novel.

The story turns upon money, and upon money in main connexion with marriage and its problems. Harvey Rolfe and his wife Alma, Hugh Carnaby and his wife Sibyl, with all the minor characters, their relatives and acquaintances, illustrate the action of the 'whirlpool', in which society, the middle classes, the rank and file of the professions and arts, the people of comparative leisure, the men of business, are engulfed. There is definite, straightforward tragedy in the book; suicide and homicide are among its important incidents. But the dominant tragic note is not struck in scenes of passionate action; it is heard in the obscurer colloquies and debates of the will, in the timorous hesitations of decision and choice, in the sense of life as the thing tangled, involved, perplexed. It seems dangerous to take any step in any direction; there is nowhere any simplicity; it is as though a rational human existence were no longer possible. Or, if possible it be, it is away from the whirl and clash of city life and interests: in some peaceful, ancient town, the home of your forefathers, where you have lived from childhood, where you pursue a life of decent business, keep your mind open and alert, and have wife and children as rational as yourself. That was the happy lot of Basil Morton, corn dealer and old-fashioned scholar; and, grimly enough, he and his are the only successful and contented folk in Mr Gissing's book. It had been more satisfactory had he planted them in Bloomsbury or West Kensington, and shown that, to alter a word of Arnold's sonnet, 'even in London life may be led well.' We cannot all, in Turgeneff's favourite phrase, 'simplify' ourselves by electing to live and prosper in Arcadia. But Mr Gissing has no relenting mercies: his other folk, with scarce an exception, succumb to the miasmatic influences of London and its ideals: most of them are well-meaning, but the fatality is heavy upon them all, and they drift or drive into unhappiness or dishonour. And the worst of it is, that Mr Gissing's method is terribly and disastrously strong unto conviction: subtly, quietly, imperceptibly he persuades us that these ghastly, marred, soiled broken lives are nothing uncommon. We have met so many of them: the futile weaklings, the just tolerable cads, the maddening toadies and artistic pretenders, the riff-raff of gentility and culture, the people of sinister success, and the people of pitiable failure, with the crowds of the entirely uninteresting, who do not enjoy the lives they lead, yet persist in living them. No one is to blame, nothing can be done: 'the whirlpool' or, in Aristophanes' phrase, 'whirligig is king.' Harvey Rolfe and Hugh Carnaby, each after his kind, were excellent fellows; but they and theirs are caught in the bewilderments of modern life, as it were by some pathetic necessity, some inevitable taint and infection in the air. One may seek peace and simpleness in Welsh valleys, the other chase adventure and prosperity at the Antipodes; but fatality, *plus* their wives, bring them back to malarious London, its rottenness and stifling ways. We are left with the consolation, of doubtful efficacy, that perhaps the robustious and shouting genius of Mr Kipling heralds an age of blood and iron, with the British Empire on the warpath – or the raid. The soliloquist of *Maud* spoke in that spirit; and he was mad.

This may not be Mr Gissing's masterpiece; but certainly no other of his books can show more brilliant characterisation. His creatures are marvellously living; here is realism of a real kind. Those men and women grip the memory; we have a perfect faith in every one of them. Yet the story, the plot, is not of itself arresting; it would lose all its excellence in a summary. But the play of forces, the collision of motives, the inner spring of action and passion, the spiritual pathology, these are felt and realised with rare strength and sureness. Mr Gissing is in love with ideas, and can illustrate them through flesh and blood: his work lives.

In his review ('London July 1, 1897', *Harper's Weekly*, 31 July 1897, 754 (Gissing: Critical Heritage, pp. 290–3)), Henry James, essayist and critic, as well as leading novelist, reviewed *The Whirlpool* (together with a novel by Pierre Loti). Characteristically, he focuses on Gissing's 'art of presentation', to the exclusion of much else which did interest most of Gissing's other critics. While his reservations about the novel's disregard of structure are eminently debatable, James shows that he has no equal as a critic in being able to convey the almost palpable sense of how the novel can work on the reader.

The Whirlpool, I crudely confess, was in a manner of grief to me, but the book has much substance, and there is no light privilege in an emotion so sustained. This emotion perhaps it is that most makes me, to the end, stick to Mr Gissing – makes me with an almost nervous clutch quite cling to him. I shall not know how to deal with him, however, if I withhold the last outrage of calling him an interesting case. He seems to me above all a case of saturation, and it is mainly his saturation that makes him interesting – I mean especially in the sense of making him singular. The interest would be greater were his art more complete; but we must take what we can get, and Mr Gissing has a way of his own. The great thing is that his saturation is with elements that, presented to us in contemporary English fiction, affect us as a product of extraordinary oddity and rarity: he reeks with the savour, he is bowed beneath the fruits, of contact with the lower, with the lowest middle-class, and that is sufficient to make him an authority – *the* authority in fact – on a region vast and unexplored . . .

So he *is* serious – almost imperturbably – about them, and, as it turns out, even quite manfully and admirably sad. He has the great thing: his saturation (with the visible and audible common) can project itself, let him get outside of it and walk round it. I scarcely think he stays, as it were, outside quite as much as he might; and on the question of form he certainly strikes me as staying far too little. It is form above all that is talent, and if Mr Gissing's were proportionate to his knowledge, to what may be

called his possession, we should have a larger force to reckon
with. That – not to speak of the lack of intensity in his imagination
– is the direction in which one would wish him to go further. Our
Anglo-Saxon tradition of these matters remains surely in some
respects the strangest. After the perusal of such a book as *The
Whirlpool* I feel as if I had almost to explain that by 'these matters'
I mean the whole question of composition, of foreshortening, of
the proportion and relation of parts. Mr Gissing, to wind up my
reserves, overdoes the ostensible report of spoken words: though I
hasten to add that this abuse is so general a sign, in these days, of
the English and the American novel as to deprive a challenge of
every hope of credit. It is attended visibly – that is visibly to those
who can see – with two or three woeful results. If it had none
other it would still deserve arraignment on the simple ground of
what it crowds out – the golden blocks themselves of the structure,
the whole divine exercise and mystery of the exquisite art of
presentation.

H. G. Wells first met Gissing in November 1896. A friendship
quickly developed which lasted until Gissing's death in 1903. In
a wide-ranging review of Gissing's fiction ('The Novels of Mr
George Gissing', *Contemporary Review*, 72, August 1897:
192–201 (*George Gissing: Critical Heritage*, pp. 295–305)),
Wells fastened onto the 'fighting' talk in *The Whirlpool* to
champion his own bio-social ethic of civilised militancy (which
he had been evolving through the decade) in which the 'securities
of civilisation' could be guaranteed only by 'struggle' – as a
'matter of morality'. Given his views, and his need to promote
them, it is not so surprising that Wells failed to register the irony
of Harvey's fighting talk in the final chapter, and that he saw in
Harvey an endorsement of Gissing's authorial position. Despite
his later admission to Gissing of his mistake over Harvey Rolfe,
Wells's misreading, here, is not so much wrong as intentionally
misconceived.

So far, children have played but a little part in Mr Gissing's
novels.
    In *The Whirlpool*, on the other hand, the implication is always
of the children, children being neglected, children dying untimely,
children that are never born. *The Whirlpool* is full of the suggestion of a view greatly widened, and to many readers it will

certainly convey the final condemnation of a 'noble' way of life which, as things are, must necessarily be built on ignoble expedients. Mrs Abbott's room, 'A very cosy room, where, amid books and pictures, and by a large fire, the lady of the house sat reading Ribot,' would surely have been the room of one of the most exemplary characters in the days before *New Grub Street*. But the new factor comes in with, 'She had had one child; it struggled through a few months of sickly life, and died of convulsions during its mother's absence at a garden party.' In the opening chapter, moreover, Rolfe speaks of children, putting the older teaching into brutal phrases:

> 'They're a burden, a hindrance, a perpetual source of worry and misery. Most wives are sacrificed to the next generation – an outrageous absurdity. People snivel over the death of babies; I see nothing to grieve about. If a child dies, why the probabilities are it *ought* to die; if it lives, it lives, and you get the survival of the fittest.'

The fashionable, delightful, childless Sibyl 'hates housekeeping'. And Alma, pursuing the phantom of a career as a musical genius, leaves for the future one little lad, 'slight, and with little or no colour in his cheeks, a wistful, timid smile on his too-intelligent face'. In the early novels it would seem that the worst evil Mr Gissing could conceive was crudity, passion, sordidness and pain. But *The Whirlpool* is a novel of the civilised, and a countervailing evil is discovered – sterility. This brilliant refinement spins down to extinction, it is the way of death. London is a great dying-place, and the old stupidities of the homely family are, after all, the right way. That is *The Whirlpool*'s implication, amounting very nearly to a flat contradiction of the ideals of the immature *The Emancipated*. The widowed Mrs Abbott, desolate and penitent, gets to work at the teaching of children. And finally we come on this remarkable passage: ... [Here Wells quotes with some foreshortening from Book 3 Chapter 13 (pp. 415–17)]

Of course Rolfe here is not Mr Gissing, but quite evidently his speeches are not a genuinely objective study of opinions expressed. The passage is essentially a lapse into 'exposition'. The two speakers, Morton and Rolfe, become the vehicles of a personal doubt, taking sides between the old idea of refined withdrawal from the tumult and struggle for existence, and the new and growing sense of the eternity and universality of conflict; it is a discussion, in fact, between a conception of spacious culture and a conception of struggle and survival. In his previous books Mr Gissing has found nothing but tragedy and the condemnation of life in the incompatibility between the refined way of life and life as it is. But here, in the mouth of a largely sympathetic character, is a vigorous exposition of the acceptance, the vivid appreciation of things as they are.

Enough has been written to show that *The Whirlpool* is a very remarkable novel, not only in its artistic quality, but in its presentation of a personal attitude. The clear change in the way of thinking that Mr Gissing's Rolfe is formulating (while the Whirlpool should be devouring him) is no incidental change of one man's opinion, it is a change that is sweeping over the minds of thousands of educated men. It is the discovery of the insufficiency of the cultivated life and its necessary insincerities; it is a return to the essential, to honourable struggle as the epic factor in life, to children as the matter of morality and the sanction of the securities of civilisation.

Gissing's reply to Wells's review (Letter to Wells, 7 August 1897, in P. Mattheisen, A. Young and P. Coustillas (eds) *The Collected Letters of George Gissing* VI, 319–21 (p. 320)), patiently, but emphatically, corrects Wells's interpretation of Harvey as espousing the 'Barrack-room' view of life.

In Rolfe I wished to present a man whose character develops with unusual slowness, & who would probably never have developed at all, after a certain stage, but for the change wrought in his views & sentiments by the fact of his becoming a father. The early passage of his talk which you quote (about children) is meant to contrast strongly with his way of thinking & speaking in the latter part of the book. As a bachelor, he was largely an egoist, & took the egoistic tone of a certain world. Later he is ripe in that experience which kills the cruder egoism. That he *does* nothing is natural in the man – 'Whirlpool' influences embarass any efficiency there might have been in him. Tho' the most likely man in my circle of characters (excluding Morton) to be a profitable citizen, that hope is spoilt by his surroundings. 'The Whirlpool,' you say, 'should be devouring him.' It *has* devoured only too much of him, as of many another such fellow.

In that last talk with Morton, I never meant to suggest that

Rolfe tended to the 'Barrack-room' view of life. In all he says, he is simply expressing his hopeless recognition of facts which fill him with disgust. Thus & thus – says he – is the world going; no refusing to see it; it stares us in the eyes; but *what* a course for things to take! – He talks with a little throwing-up of the arm, & in a voice of quiet sarcasm. Go ahead! I sit by & watch, & wonder what'll be the end of it all.

Now this, I rather think, is my own habit of mind of late years. I have come to recognize a course of things which formerly I could not – or would not – perceive; & I do it with just that tossing of arm & head – involuntary, of course. I have a conviction that all I love & believe in is going to the devil; at the same time, I try to watch with interest this process of destruction, admiring any bit of sapper-work that is well done.

*The Whirlpool* began to attract serious critical attention in the 1970s by, among others, Colin Partridge ('The Humane Centre: George Gissing's *The Whirlpool*', *Gissing Newsletter*, 9 (3) 1973: 1–10), Adrian Poole (*Gissing in Context* (Basingstoke: Macmillan, 1975)), Patrick Parrinder (his 1977 edition of the novel for Harvester Press), and the late John Goode. In his wide-ranging discussion of the novel (taken from *George Gissing: Ideology and Fiction* (London: Vision Press, 1978), pp. 182–85), Goode's principal concern is to argue that modernity is 'the novel's dominant motif'. He shows how Gissing engages with the 'modern cultural situation' by reproducing the conditions of 'mass urban mobility'. In this passage, for example, he cites Gissing's attention to the bicycling industry and photography – 'innovations' which, he says, are 'culturally decisive'.

*The Whirlpool* is a new kind of title for Gissing. It immediately draws attention to a condition of life: 'Was he himself to become a victim of this social disease? Was he, resistless, to be drawn into the muddy whirlpool, to spin round and round among gibbering phantoms, abandoning himself with a grin of inane conceit, or clutching in desperation at futile hopes?' (II, vii). 'Social disease' gives this title-word the same status as 'The Waste Land': it is a mythic image denoting a modern cultural situation, at the same time as being a specific landscape. Earlier in the novel, a discussion between the hero and his friend Mrs Abbott (herself widowed by the whirlpool of speculation) makes the nature of the social disease clear. Rolfe has said that there is no time for the proper upbringing of children, 'especially so if you live in a whirlpool', and his interlocutor replies:

> 'Yes, I know it too well, the whirlpool way of life,' said Mrs Abbott, her eyes on the far-off mountains. 'I know how easily one is drawn into it. It isn't only idle people.'
>   'Of course not. There's the Whirlpool of the furiously busy. Round and round they go; brains humming till they melt or explode.'

(II, ii)

The image is carefully worked out. The whirlpool way of life is defined against the 'far-off mountains' – the social illusion against the intractable silence of the natural world. But if it is phantasmal, it is also irresistible because it is a condition of social living – the way we live now. This condition is juxtaposed, however, not only against nature, but also against a lost world of human values: 'when there's no leisure, no meditation, no peace and no quiet-ness . . .' And that is why it is important that the theme should be introduced in the context of children – it concerns the breakdown of family life, the destruction of domesticity. *The Whirlpool* is about many things, but what is central is the disruption of the home by the social roundabout.

The image congeals the many levels of this disruption. The novel is set in motion by a financial crash which makes widows of wives and émigrés of fallen rentiers. Financial speculation and its precariousness recurs through the novel like a persistent itch, and it is both what domesticity depends on and is threatened by. The whirlpool of high capitalism then, but equally the whirlpool of metropolitan culture – the round of concerts, hit shows, agents and soirées, touching the demi-monde. Beyond this it is the whirlpool of modernity, of a new ethic, emancipated, tolerant, subjective, which throws all assumptions into the melting-pot. And above all, the image conjures up the place itself, the metrop-olis, the bustling outside, crowded and confused, within which or against which one has to contrive a privacy. The novel is an updated version of *The Way We Live Now*, but the constant reference back to the question of the children should remind us that it is strictly contemporary with James's most searching portrayal of the rentier world of London in the 'nineties, *The*

*Awkward Age.* The image of the Whirlpool itself with its accreted references, and its effect on the private life, is very much an image for its time.

The sense of an age, of 'now', is not incidental or even merely supportive – it is the *raison d'être* of the novel. Modernity is the novel's dominant motif. Rolf and Carnaby are introduced as both 'impressively modern' – in everything a contrast with one another, but drawn together by precisely their modernity. Alma castigates her stepmother for talking in 'that early Victorian way' (a phrase which echoes her mentor's comment on her husband's concern with simpler morality). There are persistent reminders that we are in a late Victorian world. Thus 'boom' for example is mentioned as a new word. At the end of the novel Rolfe is enjoying *Barrack Room Ballads* which first appeared in 1892. Both Rolfe and Carnaby are involved in commerce which is new and in which new advances were at that time made, Rolfe in photography (Eastman produced the Kodak box camera in 1888, and Rolfe is concerned with marketing a new hand camera), Carnaby in cycles (Dunlop had invented pneumatic tyres in 1889). This is not merely a matter of local detail. Photography and cycling are significant features of the development of communications.The cycle is to create mass urban mobility – the photograph to be the source of total revolution in the media. Curiously, Gissing seems to offer these as positive forms of commitment for his otherwise *desoeuvré* heroes. And against them the pseudo-Bohemian world of Alma, Rolfe's wife, is limited and static. But I think that this is part of the inevitability of the Whirlpool: you can find interesting things to do in it but it is still not the world at one with the far-off mountains. On the contrary, it is, in effect, a further extension of the Whirlpool. The cycle, for example, is instrumental in the urbanisation of the countryside – making it more accessible, and therefore more geared to urban leisure needs. What is most obviously important, however, about these historical details is that Gissing is concerned to locate his story in a specific time by images which indicate its new and forward pointing forces. 'Boom' is a word that belongs to a new intensification of *marketing process for the arts*. Kipling's work (especially *Barrack Room Ballads*) is the high point of middlebrow literature. The innovations are culturally decisive. *The Whirlpool* is a historical novel in the sense that it reproduces a phase in English life, but its history is inscribed as the history of the coming race. Hence the

emphasis on children and education, on how to prepare for the
future.

The modernity of the novel is reflected in the pervasive represen-
tation of an ideological formation responsive to this newness. At
the root of it is a way of seeing which is best identified as social
Darwinism. This in turn is reproduced as specific ideologies –
Imperialism on the one hand as a potential ethical response, and
on the other, a 'counter' ideology which we may identify as
Decadence. However sharply opposed the characters in the novel
are, they are all contained within this formation. Nobody poses
values which can countervail it. The 'real' Whirlpool is that
created by the boundaries of vision in which the novel is contained.

Even as late as 1982 it was thought that Gissing's reputation
would 'continue to depend on four books: *Demos*, *New Grub
Street*, *Born in Exile* and *The Odd Women*' (A. C. Ward,
'George Gissing' in I. Scott-Kilvert (ed.) *British Writers* (Charles
Scribner's: NY, 1982), pp. 423–38 (p. 433)). The 1984 Hogarth
Press edition (with an introduction by Gillian Tindall) soon
went out of print. But under the influence of post-structuralist
and feminist criticism further significant critical writing on the
novel emerged in the 1980s. Among the most interesting assess-
ments was a review article by Rachel Bowlby (*Gissing Newsletter*, 21 (2) 1985: 22–29). Bowlby finds Gissing's presentation of
women to be ambivalent. She traces this to the problematic of
the position of gender in modernity, so that vulnerability to
commercial values and superficial cultural standards is associated with the women (by this test inauthentic) rather than with
the men of the novel.

On the face of it, Rolfe and his wife are parallel seekers of self-
fulfilment within marriage. But Harvey's is clearly presented as
the more authentic quest, even though its object is never more
specific than a vague possibility of writing. Alma's pursuits have a
series of definite aims – musical expertise, the simple life, perform-
ing celebrity, being a good mother – and all appear under the sign
of artificiality, as emanating principally from a feminine wish for
flattery. On music, for instance:

Alma had no profound love of the art. Nothing more natural
than her laying it completely aside when, at home in Wales, she

missed her sufficient audience. To her, music was not an end in itself. Like numberless girls, she had, to begin with, a certain mechanical aptitude, which encouraged her through the early stages, until vanity stepped in and urged her to considerable attainments. (p. 228)

Alma's musical interests are merely on the surface. There exists a genuine 'art' of which she could but does not have a 'profound love', and this presumably would not need the approval of an outside 'audience' on which Alma depends. Superficiality and vanity go together as 'natural' to Alma who is 'like numberless girls'. She wishes to be taken for more than what she is, and her appearance of artistic dedication is actually a simulacrum of precisely what she is not.

Sibyl Carnaby's activities are represented in an equally questionable form:

She did not read much, and not at all in the solid books which were to be seen lying about her rooms; but Lady Isobel Barker, and a few other people, admired her devotion to study. Certainly one or two lines had begun to reveal themselves on Sibyl's forehead, which might possibly have come of late reading and memory overstrained; they might also be the record of other experiences. (p. 398)

The narrative voice here has all the insinuating snideness of the dubious Mrs Strangeways, centre of the melodramatic plot whose telling relies on the premise that things are not what they seem. The suggestion is not only that Sibyl's literary interests are inauthentic, but that she deliberately constructs an image of herself as the serious reader she is not, through the 'solid books . . . to be seen' in her home, and that the appearance of studious zeal is a cover for 'other experiences'. More than a misleading image, as in Alma's case, it is a sign open to a quite different and sinister interpretation.

In the case of Harvey, reading is not a pose but a real love ('He gets more and more booky' says his friend) (p. 63) – a love which is thwarted, however, by external circumstances. He succumbs to a literary whirlpool of 'books from the circulating library, thrown upon his table pell-mell . . . The intellectual disease of the time took hold upon him: he lost the power of mental concentration' (p. 355). Instead of the reasons for his failure being individual or related to gender, as with Alma, they are social. The implication is that it would be difficult for any man to resist the overwhelming forces of distraction and corruption which are outside himself not innate, and which infect a previously wholesome and serious love of literature.

Taking the novel as a whole, it seems that success in a cultural sphere already defined as degraded must be incompatible with genuine artistic values and is more likely to appeal to women's wish to appear, without being, artistically gifted. Femininity and commercialisation go hand in hand, and Rolfe's castigation of a 'draggle-tailed, novelette-reading feminine democracy' (p. 18) shows the extent to which the two could be assimilated. At one point Rolfe and Carnaby dream of a world without women, free from the problems of sexual mores, childrearing, domestic management and cultural degeneracy, which are all related to the whirlpool way of life in which women, for reasons said to be in their 'nature', rebel against their 'natural' place. And so the Rolfes' son is named after Hugh Carnaby, as if ideally he would be the child of the two men.

John Sloan shows (*George Gissing: The Cultural Challenge*, (Basingstoke: Macmillan, 1989) pp. 143–4) that, unlike much nineteenth-century realist fiction (including James's *Portrait of a Lady*), *The Whirlpool* dispenses with any resolution, formal and/or moral, of the complications produced by the 'vanishing moral centre' at the heart of the novel. As readers, we have to face the fact that neither 'new knowledge' nor prospect of 'transformation' is available to Gissing's protagonists.

Yet though Rolfe is not to be identified with the chauvinism of Empire, his ironic retreat behind its rhetoric, taken together with his confessed state of 'perpetual scepticism' and 'profound ignorance of everything', indicates his lack of access to an alternative ideology capable of counteracting the universal sense of decline. His correction is seen to be neutralised by his fatalism. 'Circumstance,' we are told, 'was Harvey's god' (I.iii). In marrying Alma, Rolfe may desire to redeem her from the 'vulgarism' of fashionable society; but paradoxically it is Alma who is the true Utopian, 'whether yearning for public triumphs, or eager to lead a revolution in domestic life' (I.xii). In *The Whirlpool* there is nothing of that exasperating withdrawal of ironic perspective from the hero that one finds in *In the Year of Jubilee*. It is not only that the heroine is here more articulate and incisive in challenging male assumptions: 'You think that you know the world, whilst I am ignorant of it, and that it's a sort of duty to offer warnings' (I.x). Rather, the ironic force lies in the novel's own exposure of the insufficiency of the offered alternatives – rural simplicity in Wales; suburban freedom in Pinner; the commitment to technological progress – as a means of escaping the debasements of metropolitan life.

In the face of this vanishing moral centre, Alma's death has more than a merely illustrative force. Her 'progress' does in fact expose important features of contemporary moral and cultural failure – notably the idolatrous delusions of a pseudo-Bohemian life-style, and the manoeuvring of the creative artist into a new role as either pander to public taste or idol of the coterie – but it does so in a way that avoids the suggestion of schematic and melodramatic convenience such as mars Gissing's earlier novel, *Denzil Quarrier*, in which the heroine's suicide supports a conservative resolution. There is in effect no support for Rolfe's condemnation of professional life 'for a married woman', nor for Alma's own painful resolve to 'be a good woman, rule her little house, bring up her child, and have no will but her husband's' (III.ix). Indeed Alma's acceptance of 'circumstance' and 'hereditary shame' is represented not as an ascent to wisdom, but as a repressive purgatorial resolve which is attended by a symptomatic recurrence of insomnia and drug dependence. In her final days of exile, nursing her 'baffled ambition' in 'a small house in Gunnersbury', Alma remains tragically divided between the desire for self-validation in a world she knows to be merely 'whirl and glare', and a life of 'house-ruling' which submits to the intolerable conditions of feminine sacrifice and restraint. The work stands in the end not as a register of a new knowledge and transformation, but rather of the scepticism and impotence of the bewildered spectator. Yet though Gissing's position within ideology may prevent him from revising his fictional method in a way that might satisfy the demand for moral and epistemological certainty, it is this very incapacity to reassure the reader which constitutes the effectiveness of his work. Indeed it is in this context that *The Whirlpool* stands as Gissing's last major novel. For here in the conflicts of female ambition and conjugal oppression, the moral imperatives of traditional institutions and personal validation clash in a way that resists the gratifications of ironic knowing, or traditional moral resolves. It was with prophetic satisfaction as well as regret that Gissing wrote of the novel: 'It is doubtful if I shall do anything better, or anything again so good.'

In her exploration of the presentation by Gissing of masculine identity (*Masculine Identity in Hardy and Gissing* (Rutherford: Farleigh Dickinson Press, 1991) pp. 25–5), Annette Federico subjects Harvey to close scrutiny, finding in his diffidence and passivity evidence of 'deep feeling of male anxiety' and uncertainty about his 'sexual identity'.

'The days are past when a man watched over his wife's coming and going as a matter of course,' Rolfe tells Carnaby. 'We should only make fools of ourselves if we tried it on. It's the new world, my boy; we live in it, and must make the best of it' (215). Apparently progressive, even optimistic, statements like this – only a sampling of Rolfe's modern-minded rhetoric – conceal a deep feeling of male anxiety and distrustfulness of change; the protagonist has persuaded himself that he is both disinterested, or unbiased, as well as uninterested, indifferent to the new order of sexual relationships. Yet he cannot remain psychologically secure in his self-imposed emotional and intellectual isolation. Even more than poor Jude Fawley, 'poor old Rolfe' (Carnaby's tender epithet) is fraught with insecurity; his rational pose is a shield against anything that could threaten his patient stoicism. Indeed, the almost constant refrain of this 'rational man' is one of self-reproach for being either too rational, or not rational enough. Clearly, he feels uncertain about his sexual identity and about masculine strength. For example, Rolfe repeatedly chastises his 'moral cowardice' (p. 26) yet does not assert himself in even the most trivial situations. He is always embarrassed by his 'incorrigible want of tact' (p. 144), a foible that seems only the result of a cultivated insensitivity. Certainly on one occasion, after he hears of Bennett Frothingham's suicide, Rolfe feels slightly abashed at his own coldness:

It occurred to him that it might be a refreshing and salutary change if for once he found himself involved in the anxieties to which other men were subject; this long exemption and security fostered a too exclusive regard of self, an inaptitude for sympathetic emotion, which he recognized as the defect of his character. (p. 44)

It seems that here we have one of Gissing's egoists on the edge of self-awareness; and yet, Rolfe is always and proudly self-possessed, a quality that 'differed little from unconcern', according to the narrator, and that eventually traps him in a manly pose of unruffled practicality that alienates him from the emotional – i.e., 'feminine' – side of his personality.

Despite his passivity, Rolfe's essential masculinity is never challenged in the novel. He is clearly 'manly' in everyone's eyes, and certainly he cannot be called, as Jude is, 'a tender-hearted fool'. But if Jude is sensitive to the sufferings of others, craving to give and receive love, he is also passionate and sensual. Rolfe, on the other hand, is neither tender-hearted nor sexually vibrant. He is virtually an ascetic, both emotionally and sexually, and he advertises himself as such ('circumstance' is his god and 'common sense' his creed), even though he perceives the falseness in the role he plays. It is as though the mask he purposefully wears to protect himself controls or limits his capacity for self-realization.

# SUGGESTIONS FOR FURTHER READING

## *Gissing and* The Whirlpool

Bowlby, Rachel, review article on edition of *The Whirlpool* (ed. P. Parrinder), *Gissing Newsletter* 21 (2) (April 1985): 22–9.

Federico, Annette, *Masculine Identity in Hardy and Gissing*, Rutherford: Farleigh Dickinson Press, 1991.

Goode, John, *George Gissing: Ideology and Fiction*, London: Vision Press, 1978.

Greenslade, William, *Degeneration, Culture and the Novel 1880–1940*, Cambridge: Cambridge University Press, 1994, ch. 7.

Grylls, David, *The Paradox of Gissing*, London: Allen and Unwin, 1986.

Korg, Jacob, *George Gissing: A Critical Biography*, Seattle: University of Washington Press, 1963.

Mattheisen P., Young A., and Coustillas, P. (eds), *The Collected Letters of George Gissing*, Ohio: Ohio University Press, 1990–7, vol. 6.

Neale, Gwyn, *All the Days Were Glorious: George Gissing in North Wales*, Llanrwst: Gwasg, Carreg Gwalch, 1994.

Parrinder, Patrick, Introduction to *The Whirlpool*, Brighton: Harvester Press, 1977.

Partridge, Colin, 'The Humane Centre: George Gissing's *The Whirlpool*', *Gissing Newsletter*, 9 (3) (July 1973): 1–10.

Poole, Adrian, *Gissing in Context*, Basingstoke: Macmillan Press, 1975.

Selig, Robert L., *George Gissing*, Boston: Twayne, 1983.

Sjoholm, Christine, *'The Vice of Wedlock': The Theme of Marriage in George Gissing's Novels*, Uppsala: Uppsala University Press, 1994.

Sloan, John, *George Gissing: The Cultural Challenge*, Basingstoke: Macmillan Press, 1989.

## *General*

Felski, Rita, 'The Gender of Modernity' in S. Ledger, J. McDonagh and J. Spencer (eds.), *Political Gender: Texts and Contexts*, Hemel Hempstead: Harvester Wheatsheaf, 1994, pp. 144–55.

Hobsbawn, E. J., *The Age of Empire 1875–1914*, London: Weidenfeld and Nicolson, 1987.

Huyssen, Andreas, 'Mass Culture as Woman: Modernism's Other', in *After The Great Divide: Modernism, Mass Culture and Postmodernism*, Basingstoke: Macmillan Press, 1986.

Keating, Peter, *The Haunted Study: A Social History of the English Novel*, London: Secker and Warburg, 1989.

Oppenheim, Janet, *'Shattered Nerves': Doctors, Patients and Depression in Victorian England*, Oxford: Oxford University Press, 1991.

Stokes, John, *Fin de Siècle/Fin du Globe*, Basingstoke: Macmillan Press, 1992.

# TEXT SUMMARY

## Part the First

### Chapter 1
London, 1886. Harvey Rolfe, a thirty-seven-year-old bachelor, hears rumours about the money market. His friend Abbott tells him of two abandoned children whom he and his wife must care for.

### Chapter 2
Harvey's friend Hugh Carnaby, burgled by his housekeeper, contemplates emigration.

### Chapter 3
Harvey's way of life in Bayswater. He talks with Mrs Abbott about the two Wager children.

### Chapter 4
Harvey attends a musical evening at the home of Bennet Frothingham, a banker. His daughter Alma plays the violin: Harvey listens and observes.

### Chapter 5
When Frothingham's bank fails he commits suicide. The Carnabys and the Abbotts lose investments. Abbott dies of an overdose.

### Chapter 6
Hugh and Sibyl Carnaby decide to travel abroad. Sibyl encourages Alma to leave home to pursue her music in Germany.

### Chapter 7
1887. Alma settles in Germany but neglects her music. She receives a semi-serious proposal of marriage from the composer Felix Dymes.

### Chapter 8
The rich dilettante, Cyrus Redgrave, follows Alma from Munich to Bregenz. She rejects his suggestion of a liaison.

*Chapter 9*
Harvey's friend Morphew takes up photography. Harvey renews his friendship with Mrs Frothingham and with Alma, on her return from Germany.

*Chapter 10*
Harvey, now a regular visitor to the Frothinghams, reveals his love for Alma.

*Chapter 11*
Alma keeps Harvey waiting, but after talk of marriage and the simple life, away from London, she finally accepts him.

*Chapter 12*
Mrs Frothingham confides in Harvey about compensating some of those who lost in the bank failure. After a quiet wedding Harvey and Alma settle in North Wales.

## Part the Second

*Chapter 1*
Two years later in 1890, the Rolfes are in North Wales with their son Hughie, born December 1888. Mrs Frothingham's visits. Invitation to Mary Abbott who has now set up a school.

*Chapter 2*
Visit of Mary Abbott. She and Harvey climb Carn Bodvean together and talk of education.

*Chapter 3*
Alma manages to avoid a serious driving accident. She subsequently has a miscarriage. Plans for meeting the Carnabys on their return from Australia.

*Chapter 4*
The Rolfes accompany the Carnabys to London and stay on. Hugh Carnaby at Coventry. Alma meets Cyrus Redgrave again at Mrs Strangeways's house. The Rolfes find a house in Pinner.

*Chapter 5*
The Rolfes settle in Pinner. Alma renews friendship with the Leach sisters and meets Dymes again in musical circles. Mrs Strangeways persuades Alma to accompany her to Redgrave's Wimbledon bungalow.

### Chapter 6
Alma and Mrs Strangeways are taken by surprise at Redgrave's unexpected return home. Alma tells Harvey that she is being encouraged to go professional.

### Chapter 7
Harvey needs to consider his finances. Carnaby reveals Redgrave's investment in his Coventry cycle firm, while Morphew hopes to purchase a photography business.

### Chapter 8
Harvey will not oppose Alma's plans to turn professional. Alma, resentful at her exclusion from good society, and Harvey's failure to obtain it for her, resolves to win fame as a violinist by exploiting Redgrave's interest in her. Encouragement comes from the Leaches, Sibyl and Dymes, now her agent.

### Chapter 9
Alma is concerned at her lack of funds. Alma and Harvey have a misunderstanding over Hughie's education and Mary Abbott. Alma meets Redgrave at a Crystal Palace concert.

### Chapter 10
Harvey invests in Morphew's photography business. Alma is convinced that Harvey is the Wager children's father. She impresses the company at musical gatherings. A mysterious, flattering notice of Alma appears in a society journal. Dymes is angry at being upstaged.

### Chapter 11
Mrs Strangeways increases her power over Alma. She uses Alma's fear of losing Redgrave's support and her jealousy of Sibyl's connection with Redgrave as her bait. Sibyl registers Alma's hostility to her.

### Chapter 12
Carnaby's former housekeeper, a thief, resists his attempt to arrest her by threatening to expose Sibyl as Redgrave's mistress. Maddened by suspicion Carnaby rushes back to Wimbledon and fells Redgrave with a blow.

### Chapter 13
Carnaby, finding Alma – not Sibyl – in the bungalow, sends her home. Redgrave is dead. Learning that Sibyl has been at Weymouth, Carnaby hastens there and tells her that because of his unworthy suspicion he has killed Redgrave. Sibyl will stand by her husband and go with him to the police.

*Chapter 14*
Alma returns home exhausted and takes a sleeping-draught. Next day brings news of Redgrave's death. Alma exults in her release from his power over her. Her recital is a triumph.

*Chapter 15*
Alma dreads that the inquest and trial will implicate her and suffers nervous collapse. Carnaby requests that the Rolfes will not contact Sibyl in his absence. News of his two-year sentence brings Alma some relief.

## Part the Third

*Chapter 1*
Harvey returns to his roots at Greystone and to the soothing atmosphere of the Morton household. He appraises himself from childhood onwards and holds himself responsible for past and present ills. Hope lies in his child.

*Chapter 2*
With Mrs Morton Harvey discusses marriage, and with Basil Morton, the future of their children. Alma writes to Harvey objecting to their imminent move to Gunnersbury where Mrs Abbott lives.

*Chapter 3*
Harvey, in effect, now forbids Alma to pursue her career. Alma reveals that the source of her hostility to Mrs Abbott is her belief that Harvey is father to the Wager children. Harvey explains all and Alma is reconciled.

*Chapter 4*
Alma sets up their new household at Gunnersbury with enthusiasm. She is pregnant. They spend a month by the sea. But Alma has a secret fear and obsessive hatred of Sibyl, while Harvey avoids talking of the Carnabys.

*Chapter 5*
Haunted by her sense of guilt over Redgrave's death, Alma suffers nightmares and insomnia. She makes innuendoes about Sibyl's character to the Leaches. Alma and Harvey join Mary Abbott's circle of friends.

*Chapter 6*
Harvey reflects on marriage, the consolations of fatherhood and Hughie's development. Alma cannot break her morphia habit, despite

doctor's orders. When her baby lives for only two weeks she is inconsolable and nearly dies herself.

*Chapter 7*
Cecil Morphew's long engagement is broken off by the revelation that he is father of a child.

*Chapter 8*
Visited by Dymes on her return from holiday, Alma hears that Mrs Strangeways had a hold over Redgrave and that she is responsible for the rumours about Redgrave's relations both with Sibyl and with Alma.

*Chapter 9*
In a bitter confrontation Alma and Sibyl each accuse the other of spreading malicious scandal.

*Chapter 10*
Harvey and Alma look forward to living quietly at Greystone but Mrs Strangeways threatens Alma with blackmail and fails to extract money from Sibyl.

*Chapter 11*
Carnaby is released from prison. When Sibyl tells him of Alma's slandering he at last admits that Alma had been at Redgrave's bungalow on the fatal night. Sibyl demands a meeting with the Rolfes.

*Chapter 12*
At the Carnabys, in Harvey's presence, Alma persists in her charge that Sibyl had been unfaithful to Hugh with Redgrave, but can offer no proof. Hysterically, she insists that Harvey must believe her. Alarmed and baffled he at last assents. At night, Alma sleeps after two draughts of morphia, but by morning she is dead.

*Chapter 13*
Two years have passed. With Hughie, seven years old, Harvey is settled at Greystone. He talks with Morton about the future of 'our boys'. Carnaby, he hears, is getting prosperous from his bicycle business.

# ACKNOWLEDGEMENTS

I should like to acknowledge the encouragement and assistance of Professor Pierre Coustillas, particularly in making available to me his copy of the manuscript of *The Whirlpool*, and to thank the Huntington Library, California for allowing me to quote from it. I should also like to acknowledge the help of the library at Senate House, University of London; the Music Library of the British Library and the Library of the Wellcome Institute, London.

The editor and publishers wish to thank the following for permission to use copyright material:

Associated University Presses for material from Annette Federico, *Masculine Identity in Hardy and Gissing* (1991), Farleigh Dickinson Press, pp. 24–5;

Rachel Bowlby for material from her article, 'Boom and Gloom', *Gissing Newsletter*, 21:2 (1985);

Macmillan Press Ltd and St Martin's Press for material from John Sloan, *George Gissing: The Cultural Challenge* (1989), pp. 143–4. Copyright © John Sloan;

A. P. Watt Ltd on behalf of the Literary Executors of the Estate of H. G. Wells for material from H. G. Wells, 'The Novels of Mr George Gissing', *Contemporary Review*, 72 (1897).

Every effort has been made to trace the copyright holders but if any have been inadvertently overlooked the publishers will be pleased to make the necessary arrangement at the first opportunity.

# CLASSIC NOVELS
## IN EVERYMAN

### The Time Machine
H. G. WELLS

*One of the books which defined 'science fiction' – a compelling and tragic story of a brilliant and driven scientist*
£3.99

### Oliver Twist
CHARLES DICKENS

*Arguably the best-loved of Dickens's novels. With all the original illustrations*
£4.99

### Barchester Towers
ANTHONY TROLLOPE

*The second of Trollope's Chronicles of Barsetshire, and one of the funniest of all Victorian novels*
£4.99

### The Heart of Darkness
JOSEPH CONRAD

*Conrad's most intense, subtle, compressed, profound and proleptic work*
£3.99

### Tess of the d'Urbervilles
THOMAS HARDY

*The powerful, poetic classic of wronged innocence*
£3.99

### Wuthering Heights and Poems
EMILY BRONTË

*A powerful work of genius – one of the great masterpieces of literature*
£3.99

### Pride and Prejudice
JANE AUSTEN

*Proposals, rejections, infidelities, elopements, happy marriages – Jane Austen's most popular novel*
£2.99

### North and South
ELIZABETH GASKELL

*A novel of hardship, passion and hard-won wisdom amidst the conflicts of the industrial revolution*
£4.99

### The Newcomes
W. M. THACKERAY

*An exposé of Victorian polite society by one of the nineteenth-century's finest novelists*
£6.99

### Adam Bede
GEORGE ELIOT

*A passionate rural drama enacted at the turn of the eighteenth century*
£5.99

---

All books are available from your local bookshop or direct from:
Littlehampton Book Services Cash Sales, 14 Eldon Way, Lineside Estate,
Littlehampton, West Sussex BN17 7HE (*prices are subject to change*)

To order any of the books, please enclose a cheque (in sterling) made payable to
*Littlehampton Book Services*, or phone your order through with credit card details (Access,
Visa or Mastercard) on 01903 721596 (24 hour answering service) stating card number
and expiry date. (*Please add £1.25 for package and postage to the total of your order.*)

In the USA, for further information and a complete catalogue call 1-800-526-2778

# AMERICAN LITERATURE
## IN EVERYMAN

**The Marble Faun**
NATHANIEL HAWTHORNE
*The product of Hawthorne's two
years in Italy, the thrilling story
of young Americans in Europe*
£5.99

**The Portrait of a Lady**
HENRY JAMES
*A masterpiece of psychological
and social examination, which
established James as a major
novelist*
£5.99

**Billy Budd and Other Stories**
HERMAN MELVILLE
*The compelling parable of
innocence destroyed by a fallen
world*
£4.99

**The Red Badge of Courage**
STEPHEN CRANE
*A vivid portrayal of a young
soldier's experience of the
American Civil War*
£3.99

**Leaves of Grass and
Selected Prose**
WALT WHITMAN
*The best of Whitman in
one volume*
£6.99

**The Age of Innocence**
EDITH WHARTON
*A tale of the conflict between love
and tradition by one of America's
finest women novelists*
£4.99

**Nineteenth-Century American
Short Stories**
*edited by* Christopher Bigsby
*A selection of the works of
Henry James, Edith Wharton,
Mark Twain and many other
great American writers*
£6.99

**Selected Poems**
HENRY LONGFELLOW
*A selection spanning the whole
of Longfellow's literary career*
£7.99

**The Last of the Mohicans**
JAMES FENIMORE COOPER
*The tale that shaped American
frontier myth*
£5.99

**The Great Gatsby**
F. SCOTT FITZGERALD
*Much loved story of passion
and betrayal, glamour and
the powerful allure of the
American dream*
£4.99

---

All books are available from your local bookshop or direct from:
Littlehampton Book Services Cash Sales, 14 Eldon Way, Lineside Estate,
Littlehampton, West Sussex BN17 7HE (*prices are subject to change*)

To order any of the books, please enclose a cheque (in sterling) made payable to
*Littlehampton Book Services*, or phone your order through with credit card details (Access,
Visa or Mastercard) on 01903 721596 (24 hour answering service) stating card number
and expiry date. (*Please add £1.25 for package and postage to the total of your order.*)

In the USA, for further information and a complete catalogue call 1-800-526-2778

# SHORT STORY COLLECTIONS
## IN EVERYMAN

**The Strange Case of Dr Jekyll and Mr Hyde and Other Stories**
R. L. STEVENSON
*An exciting selection of gripping tales from a master of suspense*
£1.99

**Nineteenth-Century American Short Stories**
*edited by* Christopher Bigsby
*A selection of the works of Henry James, Edith Wharton, Mark Twain and many other great American writers*
£6.99

**The Best of Saki**
*edited by* MARTIN STEPHEN
*Includes* Tobermory, Gabriel Ernest, Svedni Vashtar, The Interlopers, Birds on the Western Front
£4.99

**Souls Belated and Other Stories**
EDITH WHARTON
*Brief, neatly crafted tales exploring a range of themes from big taboo subjects to the subtlest little ironies of social life*
£6.99

**The Night of the Iguana and Other Stories**
TENNESSEE WILLIAMS
*Twelve remarkable short stories, each a compelling drama in miniature*
£4.99

**Selected Short Stories and Poems**
THOMAS HARDY
*Hardy's most memorable stories and poetry in one volume*
£4.99

**Selected Tales**
HENRY JAMES
*Stories portraying the tensions between private life and the outside world*
£5.99

**The Best of Sherlock Homes**
ARTHUR CONAN DOYLE
*All the favourite adventures in one volume*
£4.99

**The Secret Self 1: *Short Stories by Women***
*edited by* Hermione Lee
'A superb collection' The Guardian
£4.99

---

All books are available from your local bookshop or direct from:
Littlehampton Book Services Cash Sales, 14 Eldon Way, Lineside Estate,
Littlehampton, West Sussex BN17 7HE (*prices are subject to change*)

To order any of the books, please enclose a cheque (in sterling) made payable to
*Littlehampton Book Services*, or phone your order through with credit card details (Access,
Visa or Mastercard) on 01903 721596 (24 hour answering service) stating card number
and expiry date. (*Please add £1.25 for package and postage to the total of your order.*)

In the USA, for further information and a complete catalogue call 1-800-526-2778

# ESSAYS, CRITICISM AND HISTORY
## IN EVERYMAN

**Essays and Poems**
R. L. STEVENSON
*Stevenson's hidden treasures*
£4.99

**The Rights of Man**
THOMAS PAINE
*One of the great masterpieces
of English radicalism*
£4.99

**Speeches and Letters**
ABRAHAM LINCOLN
*A key document of the American
Civil War*
£5.99

**Essays**
FRANCIS BACON
*An excellent introduction to
Bacon's incisive wit and moral
outlook*
£4.99

**Biographia Literaria**
SAMUEL TAYLOR COLERIDGE
*A masterpiece of criticism,
marrying the study of literature
with philosophy*
£4.99

**Selected Writings**
JOHN RUSKIN
*'An excellent selection'*
The Guardian
£7.99

**Chesterton on Dickens:
Criticisms and Appreciations**
G. K. CHESTERTON
*A landmark in Dickens criticism,
rarely surpassed*
£4.99

**History of His Own Time**
BISHOP GILBERT BURNET
*A highly readable contemporary
account of the Glorious Revolution
of 1688*
£7.99

**Memoirs of the Life of Colonel
Hutchinson**
LUCY HUTCHINSON
*Biography by his wife of a man who
signed Charles I's death warrant*
£6.99

**Puritanism and Liberty: Being
the Army Debates (1647-49)
from the Clarke Manuscripts**
*edited by* A. S. P. Woodhouse
*A fascinating revelation of Puritan
minds in action*
£7.99

**The Embassy to Constantinople
and Other Writings**
LIUDPRAND OF CREMONA
*An insider's view of political
machinations in medieval Europe*
£5.99

---

All books are available from your local bookshop or direct from:
Littlehampton Book Services Cash Sales, 14 Eldon Way, Lineside Estate,
Littlehampton, West Sussex BN17 7HE *(prices are subject to change)*

To order any of the books, please enclose a cheque (in sterling) made payable to
*Littlehampton Book Services,* or phone your order through with credit card details (Access,
Visa or Mastercard) on 01903 721596 (24 hour answering service) stating card number
and expiry date. *(Please add £1.25 for package and postage to the total of your order.)*

In the USA, for further information and a complete catalogue call 1-800-526-2778